CW01507251

Word-Formation in the World's Languages

A pioneering book establishing the foundations for research into word-formation typology and tendencies. It fills a gap in cross-linguistic research by being the first systematic survey of the word-formation of the world's languages. Drawing on over 1,500 examples from fifty-five languages, it provides a wider global representation than any other volume. These data, from twenty-eight language families and forty-five language genera, reveal associations between word-formation processes in genetically and geographically distinct languages. Data presentation from two complementary perspectives, semasiological and onomasiological, shows both the basic functions of individual word-formation processes and the ways of expressing selected cognitive categories. Language data were gathered by way of detailed questionnaires completed by over eighty leading experts on the languages discussed. The book is aimed at academic researchers and graduate students in language typology, linguistic fieldwork and morphology.

PAVOL ŠTEKAUER is Professor of English Linguistics at Šafárik University, Košice, Slovakia.

SALVADOR VALERA is Associate Professor of English Morphology and Syntax at the University of Granada, Spain.

LÍVIA KÖRTVÉLYESSY is a lecturer in English Linguistics at Šafárik University, Košice, Slovakia.

Word-Formation in the World's Languages

A Typological Survey

PAVOL ŠTEKAUER, SALVADOR VALERA, LÍVIA KÖRTVÉLYESSY

CAMBRIDGE
UNIVERSITY PRESS

University Printing House, Cambridge CB2 8BS, United Kingdom

Cambridge University Press is part of the University of Cambridge.

It furthers the University's mission by disseminating knowledge in the pursuit of education, learning and research at the highest international levels of excellence.

www.cambridge.org
Information on this title: www.cambridge.org/9781107533646

© Pavol Štekauer, Salvador Valera and Lívia Körtvélyessy 2012

First published 2012
First paperback edition 2015

A catalogue record for this publication is available from the British Library

ISBN 978-0-521-76534-3 Hardback
ISBN 978-1-107-53364-6 Paperback

Cambridge University Press has no responsibility for the persistence or accuracy of URLs for external or third-party internet websites referred to in this publication, and does not guarantee that any content on such websites is, or will remain, accurate or appropriate.

Contents

Figures

Tables

Acknowledgements

The authors wish to express their gratitude to all the informants who were so kind as to supply the necessary data for this research. Without their invaluable help, this book would have been unthinkable. Unless otherwise specified, the contents of this book on each of the following languages were provided as personal communications and/or in the form of questionnaires by the informants. The source of examples is cited in the text only in languages for which two informants supplied data. Where the same data were provided by the two informants, the source is not explicit in the text. The informants are, in alphabetical order by language:

Afrikaans	Suléne Pilon and Gerhard B. van Huyssteen
Amele	John R. Roberts
Amharic	Grover Hudson
Anejom	John Lynch
Bardi	Claire Bowern
Belorussian	Svetlana Rudaja and Alena Rudenka
Breton	Greg T. Stump
Catalan	Max Wheeler
Cirecire	Andy Chebanne
Clallam	Timothy Montler
Dangaléat	Erin Shay
Datooga	Roland Kießling
Diola-Fogny	Kirsten Fudeman
Dutch	Jan Don
English	Andrew Carstairs-McCarthy
Estonian	Annika Kilgi
Finnish	Vesa Koivisto and Johana Laakso
French	Dany Amiot
Gã	M.E. Kropp Dakubu
Georgian	Nino Amiridze
German	Christiane Dalton-Puffer
Greek	Angela Ralli

Hausa	Paul Newman
Hebrew	Ora Schwarzwald
Hungarian	Ferenc Kiefer
Ilocano	Carl Rubino
Indonesian	Franz Müller
Italian	Livio Gaeta
Japanese	Mark Volpe
Kalkatungu	Barry Blake
Karao	Sherri Brainard
Ket	Edward Vajda
Konni	Michael Cahill
Lakhota	Regina Pustet
Luganda	Xavier Luffin
Luo	Joost Zwarts
Maipure	Raoul Zamponi
Malayalam	K.-P. Mohanan
Mandarin Chinese	Karen Steffen Chung
Māori	Ray Harlow
Marathi	Veena Dixit
Nelemwa	Isabelle Bril
Portuguese	Rui Marques
Romanian	Niculina Iacob and Gina Măciucă
Russian	Peter Arkadiev
Serbian-Croatian	Gordana Štasni
Slavey	Keren Rice
Slovak	Ján Horecký and Martin Ološtiak
Spanish	Laura Malena Kornfeld
Swahili	Ellen Contini-Morava
Swedish	Arne Olofsson
Tamil	Harold F. Schiffman
Tatar	Uli Schamiloglu and Susan Wertheim
Telugu	Sailaja Pingali
Tibetan	Nathan W. Hill
Totonac	David Beck
Trinidadean Creole	Donald Winford
Ukrainian	Peter Lizanec
Vietnamese	Mark Alves and Nguyên Thái Ân

West Greenlandic	Michael Fortescue
Wichí	Verónica Nercesian
Yoruba	Oye Taiwo
Zulu	Andrew van der Spuy

This publication was supported by the the Slovak Academic Grant Agency (VEGA), grant No. 1/2236/05, and Spanish Junta de Andalucía (Incentivos de Carácter Científico y Técnico de la Junta de Andalucía, 3/2008). We also owe a great deal to the linguists who generously shared their expertise with us and gave such insightful advice, recommendations and comments. They are, in alphabetical order:

Laurie Bauer
Winifred Bauer
Ruth A. Berman
Shmuel Bolozky
Geert Booij
Klára Buzássyová
Adelia Carstens
Taro Kageyama
Viktor Krupa
Rochelle Lieber
Lubor Mojdl
Jonathan Owens
Sergio Scalise
Dana Slančová
Chad Thompson
Ghil'ad Zuckermann

Special thanks are owed to four anonymous referees and to Leanne V. Bartley, Fraser T. Bayles, Miguel Ángel Benítez Castro, Karen Steffen Chung, Ana Díaz-Negrillo, Jesús Fernández-Domínguez, Encarnación Hidalgo Tenorio, Arne Olofsson, Sailaja Pingali, Franz Rainer, Francisco Valera Hernández and Mark Volpe for reading and commenting on the manuscript and to all those who were so kind as to provide us with the examples in their original script: Mark Alves (Vietnamese), Nino Amiridze (Georgian), Karen Steffen Chung (Mandarin Chinese), Niladri Dash (Hindi), Veena Dixit (Marathi), Taro Kageyama (Japanese), Harold Schiffman (Tamil), Ghil'ad Zuckermann and Ruth Berman (Hebrew) and Joost Zwarts (Luo).

Notes on language-specific symbols

Cirecire

This language has two clicks:

(1)   dental   [|]
(2)   lateral   [||]

Clicks can appear with:

(3)   aspiration   [||h], [|h]
(4)   voicing   [|g], [||g]
(5)   rarely, uvularization   [||x], [|x]

Other symbols used are:

[c]   for non-voiced affricated palatal stop
[dj]   for voiced affricated palatal stop
[q]   for affricated uvular stop

Jaqaru

"   aspiration

Kwakw'ala

!   glottalization
= before suffix   sonantized sound
= before suffix   sonantized sound

Telugu

T, D, N, L	=	retroflex sounds
t, d	=	dentals
ph, th, etc.	=	aspirated sounds
c, j	=	post-alveolar affricates

Totonac

Orthography:

x	=	/ʃ/
h	=	/ʔ/
j	=	/x/
lh	=	/ɬ/
tz	=	/ts/
ch	=	/tʃ/
'	=	laryngealization of preceding vowel
'	=	glottalization of preceding consonant

Zulu

C1, C2, C3, ... Zulu nouns are divided into classes, each with its own agreement pattern. Many of the classes are marked with an identifying prefix. These prefixes are glossed here as C1, C2, C3, etc. Odd-numbered classes from 1 to 11 are singular classes. Classes 2, 4, 6 and 10 are plural classes. Other classes (14 and 15) are used exclusively for non-count nouns. There are no classes 8, 12 or 13 in Zulu.

Abbreviations

A	Active personal pronominal affix (followed by 1, 2, 3, 0 – referring to the 1st, 2nd, 3rd person and zero)
ABL	Ablative
ABN	Abstract noun
ABS	Absolutive
ACC	Accusative
ACN	Action noun
ACT	Active
ADE	Adessive
ADJ	Adjective
ADR	Adverb
ADV	Adverse
AFF	Affective
AG	Agent
ALL	Allative
AMB	Ambulative
ANP	Anaphoric
ANX	Action nominal affix
APP	Applicative
APS	Antipassive
ATTR	Attribute
AUG	Augmentative
AV	Agent/Actor voice
+ ATR	Advanced (retracted) tongue root
− ATR	Non-advanced (retracted) tongue root
BEN	Benefactive
BFR	Back-formation
BLN	Blending
CAL	Consonant alternation
CAU	Causative
CFX	Confix
CHN	Change
CLA	Classifier

CLS	Classifying particle
CMP	Comparative
CMT	Comitative
CNV	Conversion
COL	Collective
COM	Companionate
CON	Continuous
COO	Coordination
COU	Countable
CPL	Completion
CPN	Compound
CRX	Circumfix
CV	Consonant-vowel (indicates reduplication)
DEF	Definite marker
DET	Determinative
DIM	Diminutive
DIR	Directional
DIS	Discontinuity
DIV	Diversative
DNL	Denominal
DST	Distal
DTB	Distributive
DUA	Dual
DUR	Durative
EMP	Empty particle
ERG	Ergative
ESS	Essive
EVN	Event
EXC	Excessive
EXP	Experiential
F	Feminine
FCT	Factitive
FEA	Feature
FRE	Frequentative
FUT	Future
GEN	Genitive
GND	Gender
GRC	Generic
GRN	Gerund
ICL	Inclusive
ICP	Inceptive

IDF	Indefinite
IFL	Inflection
IFX	Infix
IMP	Imperative
INC	Inchoative
IND	Indicative
INF	Infinitive
INS	Instrumental
INT	Intensive
INTR	Intransitive
IO	Indirect object
IPF	Imperfective
IPS	Impersonal
IRR	Irrealis
ITE	Iterative
ITX	Interfix
LNK	Linking element
LOC	Locative
M	Masculine
MOM	Punctual, momentaneous or single-event verb
MRK	Marker
MS	Morphotactic separator (connector in finite verb forms)
MUT	Mutual
N	Noun
NEG	Negative, negation
NIN	Noun incorporation
NMR	Nominalizer
NOM	Nominative
NTR	Neuter gender
O	Direct object pronoun
OBJ	Object
OBL	Oblique
PAS	Passive
PAT	Patient
PEF	Personifier
PER	Personal article
PFV	Perfective
PK	Personal knowledge
PL	Plural
PLC	Place

POS	Possessive
PRG	Progressive
PRI	Privative
PRS	Present
PRX	Prefix
PST	Past
PTC	Participle
QNT	Quantity
QUO	Quotation
QSN	Question
RAP	Root-and-pattern
RCP	Reciprocal
RDP	Reduplication
REA	Realis
REL	Relational
REV	Reversative
RFL	Reflexive
S	Stative personal pronominal affix (followed by 1, 2, 3, 0 – referring to the 1st, 2nd, 3rd person and zero)
SBJ	Subject
SFX	Suffix
SG	Singular
SGT	Singulative
SIM	Simultaneity
SOC	Sociative
SPE	Specific
SS	Sentence suffix
ST	First part of stem, probably part of a compound of unclear meaning, preceding pronominal prefixes
STA	Stative
STM	Stem
STR	Stress
STT	State
SUP	Supine morpheme
TAM	Tense/Aspect/Mood marker
TH	Thematic prefix/suffix
THM	Theme
TI	Time
TOP	Tone/pitch
TOT	Totality

TR	Transitive
TRN	Translative
V	Verb
VAL	Vowel alternation
VL	Verbal
VR	Verbalizer
1	1st person
1>2	Verbal grammatical first to second person 'I>you'
2	2nd person
3	3rd person
3o	3rd person direct object
3>3	Verbal grammatical 3rd to 3rd person 'she>him'
₍c₎ + Suffix	the preceding morpheme drops its vowel
₍v₎ + Suffix	the preceding morpheme retains its vowel

Introduction

> Derivation has not attracted sustained interest in typologically oriented research. At most, information on derivation in hand-books of typology concerns specific phenomena in comparatively few languages.
>
> (Laca 2001: 1214)

The aim of this book is to identify typological differences in the word-formation of a number of languages of the world, as well as any associations which may exist between them. The purpose is to provide an overview of how word-formation is organized in different languages. From the point of view of languages, its focus is on the use of common resources in languages which belong to different genetic groups, insofar as this may be indicative of the import of those resources. From the point of view of word-formation processes and categories, its focus is on their relation as co-existing devices for the formation of new vocabulary.

The book is intended to provide a preliminary survey of what is usually called *derivational morphology*.[1] This is because the most significant achievements in the study of morphological typology and morphological universals tend to rely on cross-linguistic research into inflectional categories and properties and on their description, but not on derivation. Inflection has also been the subject of various typological classifications of languages since the times of Friedrich Schlegel (1808). Interestingly, while Edward Sapir (1921), the author of one of the most widespread morphological classifications of languages, meant to apply his typological categories to both inflection and derivation, the use of his classification and terminology, like *isolating, agglutinative, fusional, symbolic, analytic, synthetic* or *polysynthetic*, has been mostly biased towards inflection.

While the field of word-formation universals and word-formation typology is not an untilled area, the motto of this 'Introduction' and more recent assessments of the present state of knowledge in word-formation typology suggest that 'the result is rather miserable: no homogeneous picture either regarding the derivational categories investigated or the morphological techniques involved seems to emerge' (Gaeta 2005: 168).

One of the main causes of this state of affairs is that representative word-formation data of a substantial number and variety of languages are

---

[1] The terms *word-formation, derivation* and *derivational morphology* are used as synonyms in this book.

extremely difficult to gather. This is largely because of the lack of relevant descriptions of this kind. In turn, this is due to the almost total absence of attention paid in typological and morphological research to inflectional characteristics of languages outside the best-known European languages and perhaps some others. This is a frequent limitation of the field which has consequences of some importance. Thus, in a paradigmatic study on this issue (L. Bauer 2000), the choice of the languages examined was determined by the very low availability of detailed descriptions of derivation in the limited grammars of languages that were accessible. Bauer argues that this is due to the little attention that some grammarians pay to derivational morphology. This is meaningful and illustrative of the state of affairs in itself, but the consequences are even more telling: 'it is frequently unclear to the reader of a description ... what is inflection and what is derivation; writers of descriptions (particularly descriptions of lesser-known languages) may not have all information to answer questions which can be answered for other languages – accordingly descriptions are not strictly comparable' (L. Bauer 2000: 38–9).

This gap in typological research is not new nor has it been filled by renewed interest in typological studies over the past decade. While Plank and Filimonova's (2000) ongoing data bank of linguistic universals (*The Universals Archive*, University of Konstanz) also covers morphological universals, the proportion between the total number of universals (about 2,000) and the number of inflectional morphology-related universals in the *Archive* on the one hand (about 170) and those pertaining to word-formation on the other (about sixty) speaks for itself. Significantly, in a 300-page volume published in 2007 on the occasion of the tenth anniversary of the existence of the journal *Linguistic Typology*, one can hardly find any specific reference to word-formation. It is therefore small wonder that Baerman and Corbett (2007) argue in favour of the typologists' increased attention to morphological questions.

Antecedents

While the overall picture of the field in question is not very encouraging, the realm of derivationally relevant typology is not *terra incognita*. The general interest in word-formation over the past forty years and the growing awareness of the importance of this kind of study have set the appropriate conditions for a step forward in research into word-formation universals and typology.

Of the works of the past three decades, specifically since 1978, Volume 3 of Greenberg's *Universals of Human Language* (1978) deals primarily with 'word structure'. Reference should also be made to some general handbooks in the field, particularly since some of them have (usually brief) chapters/sections of morphological/derivational relevance (e.g. Whaley 1997 and Croft

2003). Two editions of *Language Typology and Syntactic Description* (1985, 2007) by Shopen start with a chapter entitled 'Typological Distinctions in Word Formation' written by Anderson (1985) and Aikhenvald (2007) respectively for each edition. The two chapters cover the same topic and clearly reflect the immense progress in the theory of word-formation over the twenty-two years which separate them. In the same volume, Comrie and Thompson (1985) discuss lexical nominalization processes in the languages of the world and Comrie (1985) maps the formation of causative verbs. Malkiel's (1978) 'Derivational Categories' and Moravcsik's (1978) 'Reduplicative Constructions' go significantly deeper into word-formation. Some of these works, like Malkiel's, had no pretence to be representative of the world languages. In Malkiel's case, this is because it limited itself to a selection of Indo-European and Semitic languages. Moravcsik, like Wiltshire and Marantz (2000), also shows a bias, this time towards one derivational process (reduplication, apparently because it is indispensable for the description of inflectional categories, especially for plural formation).

A number of authors have also focused on specific word-formation processes: Ultan (1975) undertook an important cross-linguistic analysis of infixation, Mithun (1984) studied noun incorporation, a frequent topic probably due to the controversy between the syntactic and lexicalist conceptions of noun incorporation, and L. Bauer (1996 and 1997) wrote a cross-linguistic analysis of evaluative morphology. Other similar works, like Anderson (1985) and Bybee (1985), stand out for their cross-linguistic approach to word-formation. The latter used a sample of fifty languages to examine the relation between inflectional and derivational morphology. More recently, Wälchli (2005) contributed to cross-linguistic research into co-compounds. All these are highly valuable and seminal for their scope of languages and their import, but most of them study individual word-formation processes without regard to other processes and/or categories in the languages covered.

A different type of antecedent is the research on the description of individual languages or families of languages, some of them endangered ones, as in specific series by publishers like Mouton de Gruyter and Lincom. Many of these monographs include sections about the description of word-formation processes and are an important source of data for research into word-formation universals and typology. Thus, Lüdtke (1996) wrote on word-formation tendencies in Romance languages and Werner on word-formation in the Yeniseian languages (1998). The scope of languages was wider in Kroeber (1910), who wrote on noun incorporation in American languages, Harrison (1973) on reduplication in Micronesian languages and Bril (2005) on special types of prefixes in New Caledonian and other Austronesian languages.

Typological research may focus on a specific fine-grained variable, as advocated for by Bickel (2007), or it may examine what is common and what is not between languages at a more complex level, e.g. at the level of compounding or at the level of affixation. Regarding the latter, it may admittedly be difficult to find associations between broadly defined linguistic structures (like agglutinative or incorporating languages) and/or whole languages. Bakker (2004) provides evidence of this: his analysis of *The World Atlas of Language Structures* (Haspelmath, Dryer, Gil and Comrie 2005) concludes that less than 1 per cent of its logically possible associations are statistically relevant, and only a part of them is linguistically relevant.[2] However, this does not necessarily mean that there is no point in searching for associations. Typological research at all levels of language structure complexity is important and the results of each such research are complementary and contribute to a better understanding of languages of the world.

Research in the field of word-formation universals and typology also benefits from general theoretical frameworks, like Dressler's theory of word-formation within Natural Morphology (1981, 1982, 1985, 1987, 1988, 1997, 2005; and Dressler, Mayerthaler, Panagl and Wurzel 1987). Its focus on semiotic principles and extra-linguistic conditioning of word-formation processes establishes crucial theoretical foundations for cross-linguistic research and identifies a number of universal tendencies and implicational universals in the field of word-formation.

As can be seen, typological research may take different directions and may pursue a variety of objectives: from Greenbergian large-scale research data from various languages to Chomskyan research within the tradition of Universal Grammar aiming at the generalization of a theoretical analysis of a single language. The following sections describe the approach taken in this book.

Word-Formation in the World's Languages: purpose, method and scope

Purpose

Croft (2003: 1) maintains that typology is the study of patterns that occur systematically across languages and that 'the characteristic feature of linguistic typology is cross-linguistic comparison' (Croft 2003: 13). This is also a point of departure for our research.

Nichols (2007: 261) lays emphasis on the fact that a small-sample approach (labelled *Basic Principles*) and a large-sample approach (*Phenomena Survey*) to typological research are not opposing or competing approaches: what is needed, Nichols argues, is that one methodology be able to use the results of the other. Moravcsik (2007) also highlights important parallelisms between cross-linguistic and single-language research approaches.

---

[2] Bakker, D. 2004. 'LINFER and the WALS database', paper presented at the Workshop on Interpreting Typological Distributions, December 2004, Leipzig.

For obvious reasons, all the targets set by the two approaches cannot be encompassed within a book like this. This book makes use of the *Phenomena Survey* in view of the absence of any similar typological research in the field of word-formation, but it also uses the available achievements in the area of *Basic Principles*, e.g. in the discussion of the interrelation between inflectional morphology and derivational morphology, word-formation and compounding, noun incorporation, reduplication, compounding, conversion and other topics. While the description presented here is intended to be as theory-neutral as possible, as recommended by many typologists, we show that typological research necessarily depends on how various linguistic phenomena are viewed. Plurality, incorporation, exocentric compounding and conversion are cases in point, to name just some of them.

Even such a brief review as this of the antecedents shows that this field is in no way a *tabula rasa*. What we find to be missing is comprehensive cross-linguistic research on various word-formation processes and categories (semasiological aspect) as well as the major cognitive categories (onomasiological aspect) in their interrelation by means of a representative sample of languages. Therefore, this book focuses on the identification of possible associations as a contribution to a typological classification in this area. At the same time, picking up on L. Bauer's (2000: 38–9) remark above, the book reviews wider distinctions, like the separation between inflectional and derivational morphology. This traditional separation seems to us to be justified in respect of the situation in the field of word-formation and, at a more general level, of the effort of a number of morphologists to understand and explain the relation between inflectional and derivational morphology. The traditional morphological classification has been called into question by a number of typologists, but it still has relevance, especially because no better large-scale morphological classification of languages has been accepted yet. In any case, there is no reason to exclude large-scale classifications of languages from the scope of typological research. Therefore, one of the goals of this book has also been to contribute towards the degree of similarities/ differences between languages in terms of the classical morphological classification. The similarities would give support to the idea of a single morphology, while the differences would be an argument for the split morphology view.

For the purposes cited above, we rely on questionnaire-based research as well as drawing on grammars of individual languages. This method has limitations, like the availability of experts willing to fill out questionnaires for their languages and the very design of the questionnaire, which must be extensive and rigorous but still not exceed certain limits. Despite these and other limitations, questionnaires dispose of the most serious problem connected with relying on grammars of languages, i.e. 'the great diversity in individual coverage, focus of interest, and analytic approach [which] do not make for the descriptive homogeneity which would be ideally suited to a study of this kind' (Ultan 1978: 529).

Overall, this book deals with the following areas of linguistic typology:

(a)   associations or patterns, aiming to identify cross-linguistic interrelatedness between:

   (i)   various word-formation processes and/or categories,

   (ii)   word-formation processes/categories, on the one hand, and the genetic classification of languages present in the sample (language family) on the other,

   (iii)   word-formation processes/categories, on the one hand, and the morphological classification of languages present in the sample (inflectional type) on the other, and

   (iv)   word-formation processes/categories, on the one hand, and the prototypical word order of languages present in the sample on the other.

(b)   variation in a number of word-formation processes and categories, aiming to show the existing cross-linguistic and language-specific diversity of phenomena falling within one broadly defined category. This diversity is best describable in terms of a scale ranging from prototypical to peripheral manifestations of a particular word-formation process, category or feature. Fuzziness appears as a natural consequence of the scalar nature of linguistic facts, frequently reflected in vague boundaries between word-formation processes and categories on the one hand, and between word-formation *per se* and other levels of language on the other (e.g. inflection, syntax, phonology). What is thus characteristic for word-formation is not discrete variables, but continuous variables, as in Wälchli's (2005: 24) terminology.

(c)   descriptive complementarity, by evaluation of the above mentioned issues from the semasiological (traditional form-oriented) and the onomasiological (cognitively grounded) perspective.

Method

This book uses the terminology common to research on word-formation even if it admittedly is English-centred. Unfortunately, linguistics in general is a long way from using unified terminology. The interpretation of various terms may depend on a particular theoretical framework, on the specific conception of a linguist/informant covering the field of derivational morphology/word-formation in a particular language and also on the nature of languages covered.

Certain linguistic phenomena may also manifest themselves differently from the perspective of different languages or language types. This has given rise to different interpretations of certain points covered by our question-naire and, consequently, to further consultations with the informants.[3]

Using as a reference Song's (2007: 9) five steps of typological research (identification of a phenomenon to be investigated, generation of a language sample, creation of a typological classification, formulation of a typological generalization and explanation of the typological generalization), the method used here relies on the following foundations.

Regarding the first of these steps, the identification of the subject of study, typological studies of the Greenbergian tradition, which is also applied in this study, range from the examination of specific linguistic phenomena up to broadly outlined research into the typology and universals of a particular (sub)discipline. The focus of this book, word-formation, is defined broadly, largely because no comprehensive research where various word-formation processes and word-formation categories are interrelated has been implemented yet, but also for a number of other reasons. Word-formation established itself as an independent linguistic discipline with its own field of research and its own specific methods in the 1960s as the result of the publication of three major works: Lees (1960), Marchand (1960) and Dokulil (1962). Each developed the foundations of word-formation theory in a different paradigm pre-determined by the author's theoretical frameworks: the transformationalist account on Chomsky's transformational-generative grammar, the structuralist tradition of de Saussure and Coseriu, and the onomasiological approach in the tradition of the Prague School of Linguistics, respectively. The influence of these backgrounds favoured the rapid dissemination of theories developed in these frameworks and guaranteed the diversity and complementarity of theoretical approaches. Still, as an independent discipline, derivational morphology faced a number of theoretical issues to be dealt with, ranging from the description of word-formation almost exclusively in the most widespread Indo-European languages through a range of theoretical problems of diverse complexity (e.g. productivity, the nature of word-formation rules, different types of affixes, various word-formation processes, lexicalization, etc.). Not surprisingly, word-formation typology has been ignored for a long time. It must also be taken into consideration that a sound typological study is pre-conditioned by the availability of data. Therefore, some fifty years after the above landmarks in word-formation, the description of non-Indo-European languages

---

[3] Cf. Haspelmath's view that there are no pre-established universal categories. Rather, 'the categories of language structure are language-particular' (2007: 121). This position rests on a fairly long tradition of the negation of the existence of universal grammatical relations and categories (e.g. Boas 1911; Lazard 1992; Dryer 1997; Croft 2001). Consequently, Haspelmath argues that linguistic typology must be 'substance-based, because substance (unlike categories) is universal' (2007: 126), and this implies for morphology that it must rest on semantics. For an opposite view, cf. Newmeyer (2007). This requirement is reflected in the onomasiological section of this book (cf. chapter 6).

is rather limited and the discussion in morphological typology has confined itself mainly to inflectional categories and processes, which were considered more or less representative for the whole of morphology. With this in mind, for a better knowledge of the intricacies of the study of word-formation and of its features, it is necessary to draw the reader's attention to those works which attempt to identify the scope of word-formation in relation to the other subfield of morphology, i.e. inflectional morphology (especially, Anderson 1982, 1992; Scalise 1988; Dressler 1989; Booij 1994, 1995, 2006; Plank 1994; van Marle 1995). The discussion about the scope of word-formation in chapter 1 is embedded in this framework.

As to the second of Song's steps, the generation of a language sample, comprehensive descriptions of the word-formation systems of the languages of the world are just not available. Sampling for typological research is here, perhaps more than in any other respect, a compromise that tries to reconcile the minimum standards of quality and quantity of sampling for objective results, with the very limited availability of descriptive sources, of experts capable of providing relevant and reliable data and of speakers of some of the endangered languages to consult the issues not described by grammars, to name only some of the limitations. As mentioned above, the method used here is based on questionnaires.

Third, regarding the creation of a typological classification, various sorts of typological classifications can be inferred from the data presented here. They are primarily determined by the specific method of analysis, semasiological or onomasiological. In particular, the typological classification pertains to the preferences for formal ways of expression of cognitive categories and for the semantic scope of the individual formal means of expression of genetically, morphologically and/or geographically related languages.

Concerning the fourth step, the formulation of a typological generalization, these generalizations may be of various natures and degrees of validity, ranging from existential typologies through statistical and implicational universals up to absolute universals (Moravcsik 2007: 28ff.). While statistical universals, extrapolated from samples, show what is possible in languages, absolute universals identify what is necessary. What is, however, important in this context and what any reader of a typological work like this should realize is that 'both probabilistic and absolute generalizations ... always remain hypothetical due to the unavoidable gap between the language sample that they are based on and the set of all human languages that they make a claim about' (Moravcsik 2007: 36). In fact, it has been pointed out that 'large databases almost invariably reveal exceptions to universals, and this, together with a substantial increase of newly described languages ... has practically done away with notions of absolute universals and impossibilities' (Bickel 2007: 245). Our analysis of results is therefore conservative to be on the safe side. In chapters 3 to 5 we identify cross-linguistic data for various word-formation categories, processes and relations. These data are used in chapter 7 for the identification of associations by means of statistical methods (cf. 7.2).

Finally, explanations in word-formation can be sought at various levels. In our view, the universal principles of Natural Morphology and its three sub-theories (universal preferences, typological adequacy and system-dependent naturalness), are at the heart of typological explanations. The remarks contained here usually combine various explanations, e.g. about the non-existence of noun incorporation in Slavic languages and its high productivity in certain Amerindian languages, which can hardly be explained by any universal functional principle and is probably due to genetic and geographic factors. Each individual observation seems to result from the interplay of a number of functional, structural, genetic, geographic and language-specific factors.

Scope

It has already been mentioned that data of word-formation characteristics of languages are not easy to obtain in view of the lack of relevant descriptions due to almost exclusive attention of typological research to inflectional characteristics of languages outside the best-known European (and not many other) languages. Therefore, this book relies for the most part on questionnaire-based data, supported by specific bibliographical references whenever necessary to meet Nichols' (2007) requirement for a large sample survey type of typological investigation.[4]

Questionnaires have advantages and disadvantages. Their success as data collection tools depends on the availability of qualified informants, but this in turn imposes limits on the design of a well-structured cross-linguistic sample of languages. To paraphrase L. Bauer's (1997: 534) characterization of his sample on evaluative morphology, the sample used here is partly a sample of convenience, even if it is intended to comply with requirements like a certain representativeness and balance. Also, the range of the parameters within the questionnaire must be reduced to a psychological optimum to ensure the continuous cooperation of informants throughout the process of data collection and consultation.

Even so, questionnaires ensure the coherence and comparability of the data obtained, the use of common criteria for their collection and the possibility to ask morphologists and/or field researchers for further evidence or clarification. In fact, useful clarification-oriented consultations with some of our informants were frequent. These, we believe, are factors that, with a set of high-quality informants, compensate for many drawbacks. Specifically,

---

[4] Data on seven languages rely exclusively on publications for want of an informant. In these cases, the decision to accept exclusively other-than-questionnaire data was based on the availability of a comprehensive description of word-formation. These languages are Diola-Fogny, Hindi, Jaqaru, Kwakw'ala, Movima, Pipil and Tzotzil.

and since 'the representativeness of samples is defined genealogically and/or areally' (Plank 2007: 48), we use a sample of fifty-five languages representative of twenty-eight language families and forty-five language genera distributed over all continents and examined for almost seventy word-formation parameters.

Two language samples have been used: the basic sample and the study sample. The basic sample encompasses seventy languages and is used only as an illustration of the diverse manifestations of individual word-formation phenomena. The structure of the basic sample and its areal distribution are presented in Table 0.1 and Figure 0.1.

Table 0.1. *The basic sample by genetic criterion and by geographic distribution*

Genetic criterion[5]	
Language families	28
Language genera	45

Geographic distribution	
Africa	15
America	13
Eurasia	30
South East Asia and Oceania	12

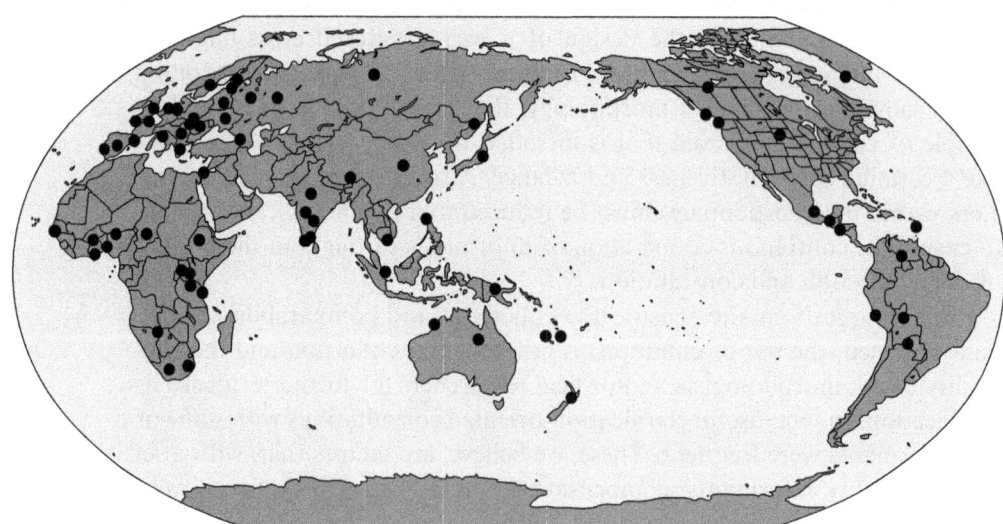

Figure 0.1. *Geographic distribution of the basic sample languages (seventy languages) as in Haspelmath, Dryer, Gil and Comrie (2005)*

---

[5] Classified primarily according to Haspelmath, Dryer, Gil and Comrie (2005), and then by consultation with informants.

As this sample is biased towards Indo-European languages (twenty-one languages), a study sample of fifty-five languages was extracted for a better balance excluding fifteen languages.[6] Language family representation was therefore reduced to the second highest number of languages of one and the same language family (seven, as in the Niger-Congo language family). The study sample is intended to represent the diverse genetic and morphological types that it contains as well as the geographic distribution of languages to an extent that enables us to draw relevant generalizations and to point out at least some cross-linguistic associations in word-formation. To minimize the loss of data inherent in such a sample reduction and allow for as much variety as possible within the sample, the reduction was carried out selecting languages which belong to different genera. When several languages complied with this requirement, selection was made at random. The resulting genus diversity within language families has the effect of disallowing any statistical claim regarding genera within families for the low number of the former within the latter.

The languages sampled differ substantially from each other in terms of the number of speakers, ranging from hundreds of millions of English, Hindi, Mandarin Chinese or Russian to about one hundred speakers of Udihe, twenty of Bardi and the extinct Australian Aboriginal language Kalkatungu, the Salishan language Clallam without any 'known living speakers' (Montler 1989: 92) or the Arawakan language Maipure that became extinct at the end of the eighteenth century (Zamponi 2009: 584).

The final sample may not be the ideal one and, like other samples used in typological research, it is not beyond reproach.[7] The structure of the study sample and its areal distribution are presented in Table 0.2 and Figure 0.2.

Table 0.2. *The study sample by genetic criterion and by geographic distribution*

Genetic criterion	
Language families	28
Language genera	45

Morphological (Sapirean) classification	
Agglutinative languages (of various types)	30
Fusional (of various types)	12
Isolating (of various types)	7
Polysynthetic (of various types)	6

[6] Afrikaans, Belorussian, Catalan, Dutch, French, German, Hindi, Italian, Portuguese, Romanian, Russian, Serbian-Croatian, Swedish, Trinidadian Creole and Ukrainian.
[7] For the issue of problems with sampling, cf., among others, Stassen (1985); Rijkhoff and Bakker (1998); Maslova (2000), Maslova, E. and Nikitina T. 2006. 'Stochastic universals and dynamics of cross-linguistic distributions: the case of alignment types'. Cf. also Daniel (2007) and Song (2007).

Geographic distribution	
Africa	14
America	12
Eurasia	17
South East Asia and Oceania	12

The languages of the study sample are listed in Table 0.3. This table includes their genetic information, their morphological type and the geographic area in which individual languages are spoken. The classification is primarily based on Haspelmath, Dryer, Gil and Comrie (2005) and, where necessary, completed by informants. Where different denominations are possible for one and the same language, this book uses the one given in Haspelmath, Dryer, Gil and Comrie (2005). Language family and location of languages not sampled here but mentioned in the book is by macro area as in Haspelmath, Dryer, Gil and Comrie (2005).

Table 0.3. *Sample languages (fifty-five languages)*

Language	Family	Morphological type	Area
Amele	Trans-New Guinea	Polysynthetic/synthetic	Australia-New Guinea/ Madang
Amharic	Afro-Asiatic	Inflectional	Africa/Ethiopia
Anejom	Austronesian	Agglutinative	SE Asia and Oceania/Vanuatu

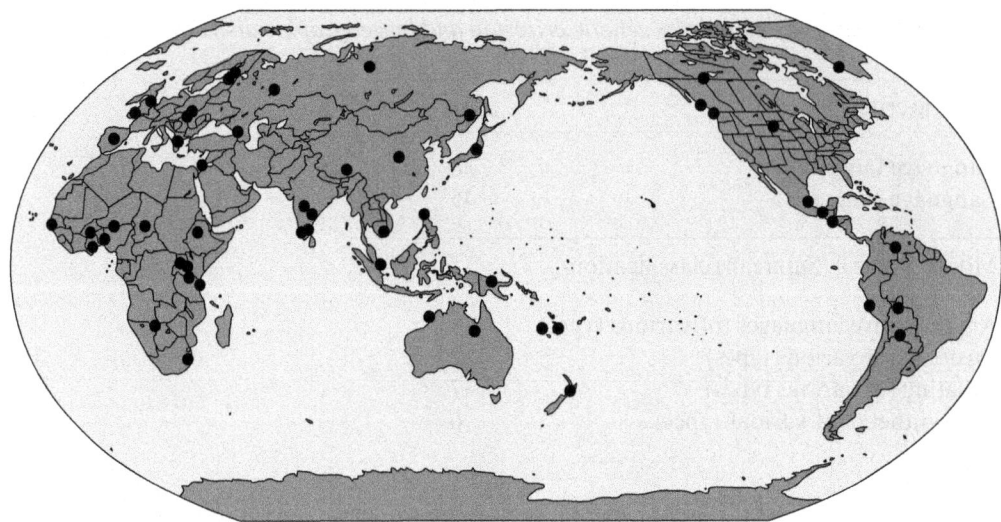

Figure 0.2. *Geographic distribution of the study sample languages (fifty-five languages) as in Haspelmath, Dryer, Gil and Comrie (2005)*

Language	Family	Morphological type	Area
Bardi	Australian	Fusional	Australia-New Guinea/ Australia
Breton	Indo-European	Fusional	Eurasia/France
Cirecire	Khoisan	Isolating	Africa/Botswana
Clallam	Salishan	Polysynthetic	North America/USA
Dangaléat	Afro-Asiatic	Agglutinative	Africa/Chad
Datooga	Nilo-Saharan	Agglutinative/ fusional	Africa/Tanzania
Diola-Fogny	Niger-Congo	Agglutinative	Africa/Gambia, Senegal
English	Indo-European	Isolating	Eurasia/Ireland and UK
Estonian	Uralic	Agglutinative/fusional	Eurasia/Estonia
Finnish	Uralic	Agglutinative	Eurasia/Finland
Gã	Niger-Congo	Agglutinative	Africa/Ghana
Georgian	Kartvelian	Inflectional/agglutinative	Eurasia/Georgia
Greek	Indo-European	Fusional	Eurasia/Greece
Hausa	Afro-Asiatic	Fusional	Africa/Niger, Nigeria
Hebrew	Afro-Asiatic	Inflectional	Africa/Israel
Hungarian	Uralic	Agglutinative	Eurasia/Hungary
Ilocano	Austronesian	Agglutinative	SE Asia and Oceania/ Philippines
Indonesian	Austronesian	Agglutinative	SE Asia and Oceania/ Indonesia
Japanese	Japanese	Agglutinative	Eurasia/Japan
Jaqaru	Aymaran	Agglutinative	South America/Peru
Kalkatungu	Australian- Aboriginal	Agglutinative	Australia-New Guinea/ Australia
Karao	Austronesian	Inflectional/ polysynthetic	SE Asia and Oceania/ Philippines
Ket	Yeniseian	Agglutinative	Eurasia/Russia
Konni	Niger-Congo	Agglutinative	Africa/Ghana
Kwakw'ala	Wakashan	Polysynthetic	North America/Canada
Lakhota	Siouan	Synthetic/ polysynthetic	North America/USA
Luganda	Niger-Congo	Agglutinative	Africa/Uganda
Luo	Nilo-Saharan	Agglutinative	Africa/Kenya, Tanzania
Maipure	Arawakan	Agglutinative	South America/Venezuela
Malayalam	Dravidian	Agglutinative	Eurasia/India
Mandarin Chinese	Sino-Tibetan	Isolating/analytic	SE Asia and Oceania/China
Māori	Austronesian	Isolating	SE Asia and Oceania/New Zealand
Marathi	Indo-European	Inflectional/ polysynthetic	Eurasia/India
Movima	Movima	Agglutinative	South America/Bolivia

Language	Family	Morphological type	Area
Nelemwa	Austronesian	Isolating	SE Asia and Oceania/New Caledonia
Pipil	Uto-Aztecan	Agglutinative	North America/El Salvador
Slavey	Na-Dene	Polysynthetic	North America/Northwest Territories
Slovak	Indo-European	Inflectional	Eurasia/Slovakia
Spanish	Indo-European	Inflectional	Eurasia/Spain
Swahili	Niger-Congo	Agglutinative	Africa/Tanzania
Tamil	Dravidian	Agglutinative	Eurasia/Tamil Nadu
Tatar	Altaic	Agglutinative	Eurasia/Russia
Telugu	Dravidian	Agglutinative	Eurasia/India
Tibetan	Sino-Tibetan	Inflectional/ agglutinative	SE Asia and Oceania/China
Totonac	Totonacan	Agglutinative/ polysynthetic	North America/Mexico
Tzotzil	Mayan	Agglutinative/ polysynthetic	North America/Mexico
Udihe	Altaic	Agglutinative	Eurasia/Russia
Vietnamese	Austro-Asiatic	Isolating	SE Asia and Oceania/Vietnam
West Greenlandic	Eskimo-Aleut	Polysynthetic	North America/Greenland
Wichí	Matacoan	Agglutinative	South America/Argentina and Bolivia
Yoruba	Niger-Congo	Isolating	Africa/Benin, Nigeria
Zulu	Niger-Congo	Agglutinative	Africa/South Africa

The structure of the book

The book is divided into two parts. Part I contains chapter 1 and chapter 2. Chapter 1 discusses the scope of word-formation with regard to inflection (1.1). It is pointed out that any and all criteria proposed for the distinction between inflection and derivation (word-formation) primarily apply to prototypical cases of inflection and derivation, but can hardly help morphologists to dispose of all the ambiguities. Almost each of the criteria proposed in the literature faces counter-examples. This indicates that the clean and lucid Aristotelian classification of linguistic categories is just a desired ideal, if anything at all. Language at all of its levels is fraught with overlapping cases and fuzzy limits, categories, processes and relations. This is illustrated with respect to three phenomena falling within what is labelled here as the *supercategory of quantity*, in particular, the categories of evaluative morphology (1.1.3.1), aspect/Aktionsart (1.1.3.2) and plurality (1.1.3.3). The discussion is supported with evidence provided by the informants.

Chapter 2 takes up the issue of the boundaries of word-formation with respect to syntax in order to show that this interface is equally complicated and fuzzy, largely as a result of the vague concept of *word* (2.1). The well-known fact that the notion of *word* cannot be defined universally and that what counts as a sentence in one language may count as a single word in the system of another language is also illustrated by a number of examples from the languages sampled. Chapter 2 discusses in detail compounding (2.2) and its special case labelled as *noun incorporation* (2.3) because the status of compounds is one of the most ambiguous issues in the word-formation/syntax relation.

Part II describes the results of the cross-linguistic research and contains two types of information on various formal and/or semantic characteristics of a particular word-formation process or word-formation category, with focus on cross-linguistic diversity, and data concerning any major associations which can be observed between the independent variables and the word-formation processes and categories for the language sample.

Part II comprises chapters 3 to 7. Chapter 3 is a review of the word-formation processes combining free morphemes, namely compounding (3.1), reduplication (3.2) and blending (3.3). Reduplication and blending are discussed in this chapter for their similarities with compounding, again with focus on the former. This chapter also lays emphasis on compounding, therefore it discusses the types of compounds which have been recorded for the language sample and, from the point of view of processes, focuses on recursiveness (3.1.2), and on base modification in compounding (3.1.3).

Chapter 4 analyzes word-formation processes with bound morphemes. It reviews affixation (4.1), with emphasis on recursiveness (4.1.1.1) and base modification (4.1.1.2). It also examines one-to-many (4.1.2) and many-to-one relations (4.1.3) in affixation. This chapter leaves minor types of affixation for a separate section (4.2): infixation (4.2.1), prefixal–suffixal derivation (4.2.2), circumfixation (4.2.3) and prefixal–infixal and infixal–suffixal derivation (4.2.4).

Chapter 5 discusses word-formation processes which do not involve additional derivational material (5.1), along with subtractive word-formation processes (5.2). This brings together, for convenience, conversion (5.1.1), stress (5.1.2), tone/pitch (5.1.3) and internal modification on the one hand (5.1.4), and then back-formation on the other (5.2.1).

Chapter 6 examines the prototypical word-formation processes employed in individual languages to express semantic categories. The main focus is on the prevailing cross-linguistic tendencies in selected semantic categories and on illustrating the principle of diversity in unity. The latter objective is supported by numerous examples from the sample languages, with special emphasis on less common manifestations of the examined categories. This chapter groups the categories as nominal (6.2), evaluative (6.3), verbal (6.4) and word-class changing categories (6.5).

Chapter 7 gives an overview of the results obtained from statistical analysis of the data obtained. It presents the method used (7.1.1) and its conclusions and lays emphasis on the difficulty of identifying certain word-formation processes cross-linguistically, on the role of certain word-formation processes and on the import of the associations found in the statistical analysis (7.2).

Two appendices are included: one summarizes the relation between the languages of the study sample with word-formation processes and with semantic roles (Appendix I) and the other gives the questionnaire used in this book (Appendix II).

PART I

The field of word-formation

1 The scope of word-formation

> Cross-linguistic comparisons are thus difficult since the same category (e.g. diminutive) may be inflectional in one language but derivational in another. We cannot assume that, if a category is treated as an inflection in one language, it will be inflectional in the next language we encounter. To complicate matters further, within the same language the same affix may have both inflectional and derivational uses.   (Katamba 1993: 212)

This chapter outlines the scope of word-formation as it came to be understood in recent decades and shows how, rather than being clearly defined, the boundaries between derivation on the one hand, and inflection and syntax on the other, are fuzzy, and also that the same morphological category may be derivational in one language and inflectional in another. Therefore, the examined relation of word-formation to inflection and syntax should be perceived as a cline with prototypical and less prototypical cases, especially if the scope of study is cross-linguistic. It is the prototypical, i.e. productive word-formation processes and rules that are the focus of our cross-linguistic study of word-formation.

Section 1.1 discusses the relation between inflection and derivation (1.1.1). The problems connected with the delimitation of the scope of word-formation (1.1.2) are illustrated by means of three different linguistic phenomena (1.1.3), in particular, evaluative morphology (1.1.3.1), aspect/Aktionsart (1.1.3.2) and plurality (1.1.3.3).

1.1 Inflection vs derivation

1.1.1 General

The reflection of the opening motto is shared by many morphologists. It seems particularly relevant for this book, because it shows one of the major problems of research into universals and typological classification of languages from the perspective of word-formation or derivational morphology: the limits of the field under study. The difficulty inherent in the issue of the limits of word-formation across languages is aptly expressed by Laca (2001: 1215):

> It is somewhat of an irony that the best known universal generalizations concerning derivation, Greenberg's Universals 28 ('If both the derivation and the inflection follow the root, or they both precede the root, the derivation is always between the root and the inflection') and 29

('If a language has inflection, it always has derivation') (Greenberg 1963: 90), hinge upon the distinction between derivation and inflection, since this distinction has proven particularly elusive.

Thus, while one feels the need to distinguish between inflectional and derivational morphology in order to identify the scope of research, it is generally recognized that the borderline is rather blurred and, more important, that it may not coincide across languages.

Cross-linguistic data offer a wealth of examples illustrating this situation. One of them is the so-called D-element in Na-Dene languages (C. Thompson 1996). The D-element stands for prefixes, also called *classifiers* even if, as explained by Thompson, they do not actually classify anything. Thompson (1996: 353) maintains that they are to a large extent 'derivational and not always meaningful in modern Athapaskan languages'. In some languages, such as Hupa, a Na-Dene language spoken in North America, the D-element is mostly derivational, while in others, such as Koyukon, another Na-Dene language, it is more inflectional and productive. Even in Koyukon, however, it is clearly derivational in some cases (Thompson, pers. comm.). This account in itself is sufficient to suggest an ambiguous status of the D-element, which is mostly used in the formation of 'reflexives, reciprocals, agentless passives, anticausatives, antipassives, incorporation of body parts into the verb, erratives (with suppressed agency), impersonal subjects, and intransitive antitelic and iterative verbs' (Thompson 1996: 353).

Passivization in Udihe by the suffix -*u* (Nikolaeva and Tolskaya 2001: 287, 307ff.) is another example. Passive is commonly treated as an inflectional category, but in Udihe it is formed by derivation from a restricted class of transitive verbs:

(1)   Udihe   *ana-u*   <   *ana-*
                'be pushed'   'push.v'

(2)   Udihe   *umi-wu-*   <   *umi-*
                'be drunk'   'drink.v'

Another example is negation by circumfixation in Wichí within a regular inflectional paradigm (Nercesian, pers. comm.). Negation in Wichí is bound to modality and evidentiality. There are two possibilities:

(a)   the coding of an event or a state in the negative form is the result of inferential evidence, i.e. the knowledge of the event is obtained by inference from certain evidences, and

(b)   experiential evidence, i.e. the knowledge of the event is obtained by direct experience and it is therefore more certain than that obtained by inference.

Negative inferential is an amalgamated form that conflates negation, inferential evidentiality and person. The entire paradigm is *nam...a* for the first person, *ka...a* for the second person and *ni...a* for the third person. The negative form *ha...hi* (experiential evidentiality) is the same for all three grammatical persons:

(3) Wichí *ni-lofwel-a*
              NEG.INF.3SBJ-be.fast-NEG.INF
              'It is not fast'[1]

(4) Wichí *ha-'i-lofwen-hi*
              NEG.EXP-3SBJ-be.fast-NEG.EXP
              'It is not fast'

Gender in Slovak, where one and the same category can be both derivational and inflectional, is another example. In Slovak, the inflectional category of the gender of nouns is purely formal. This means that each noun belongs to one of the twelve basic formal paradigms (four paradigms per gender – masculine, feminine and neuter) and is declined for seven cases of singular and seven cases of plural depending on its membership in the formal gender paradigm. On the other hand, gender in the derivational system is determined by a derivational suffix:

(5) Slovak *vŕtať*   *vrt-ák*   *vŕtač-ka*
              'drill.v'   'driller.M'   'drilling machine.F'

(6) Slovak *striekať*   *striekač-ka*
              'spray.v'   'sprayer, syringe'

The last example cited here for the difficulty in separating inflectional and derivational morphology concerns a number of suffixes in Kwakw'ala which have a highly specialized meaning. Boas (1947: 225–6) maintains that the demarcations between the suffixes which merely complete the stem without adding any material concept to it, the suffixes indicating the syntactic function, and the suffixes which add new material concepts

> are somewhat arbitrary because they are fundamentally based on the structure of European languages. To us the concept of time is a functional element modifying the stem and not adding a new material concept; for there is no verbal expression that does not imply time, as permanent existence, present, past or future. In Kwakiutl such time concepts are treated like other material concepts.

This is illustrated in the following examples (Boas 1947: 240–1):

(7) Kwakw'ala *-oł, wEł*   *ᵋō'mpᵋwEł*
                 'remote past'   'the late father'

(8) Kwakw'ala *=a(y)agˑoł*   *le'gayagˑoł*
                 'have been done' 'one who had made a canoe'

---

[1] I.e. 'It is slow'.

Affixes with a highly specialized meaning can also be found in Japanese, where Kageyama (1982: 226) remarks that 'it is sometimes difficult to determine whether these are really prefixes or bound morphemes for compounding'. In general, this kind of meaning is a feature of polysynthetic languages where these affixes 'are used to express meanings that in most languages would be expressed through free lexical or grammatical morphemes in syntactic phrases' (Hall 2000: 538). Be that as it may, the fact is that they present features which are not in line with the general understanding of affixes.

While in most languages the inflection vs derivation ambiguities are restricted to individual cases or categories, as in the former examples, in others it is the whole morphological system that seems to be ambiguous in terms of the distinction in question. This has been claimed of Ket and the other Yeniseian languages (Werner 1998: 133) to the extent that, rather than separate processes, inflection and derivation are in these languages a single process of forming new lexical units (Belimov 1991: 25). Thus, Werner (1998: 135) mentions verbs in Ket which have complete inflectional paradigms but lack any infinitive as a basic citation form. As he shows, infixation of determinative, temporal and aspectual affixes may give rise to verb forms which might be considered to be new lexical units lacking any infinitive form:

(9)   Ket   *ti<j>vij*   *ц<j-l'>vij*
                  'southerly wind blows'   'southerly wind blew'

(10)   Ket   *ur<a>vij*   *ur<ɔ-n'>vij*
                  'northerly wind blows'   'northerly wind blew'

'Wind' can occur in verb forms as in (11) and (12):

(11)   Ket $^2du^\text{?}$ *ɛs'-k-u-vij*
                  the smoke comes
                  'The smoke turns upwards'

(12)   Ket $^2du^\text{?}$ *ɛs'-k-u-l'-bij*
                  the smoke came
                  'The smoke turned upwards'

Some existing infinitives are not present in the corresponding verb paradigms. This can be illustrated by the paradigm of the Ket verb *qʌr'eŋ/qʌr'eŋbet* 'give' (Werner 1998: 134). The following examples express the momentaneous Aktionsart in the left-hand column and the iterative Aktionsart in the right-hand column:

(13)   Ket   a.   *kbir-aq*   *kban'b-ɔ*
                    'you give me'   'you give me (always)'
               b.   *kbur-aq*   *kban'bil-ɔ*
                    'you gave me'   'you gave me (always)'

c.	*kab-aq*	*kan'b-ɔ*
	'you give him'	'you give him (always)'
d.	*kɔvij-aq*	*kan'bil-ɔ*
	'you gave him'	'you gave him (always)'
e.	*kiv-aq*	*kin'b-ɔ*
	'you give her'	'you give her (always)'

Werner (1998: 138) also draws attention to the questionable status (i.e. inflectional vs derivational) of verbal incorporation complexes in Yeniseian languages and speaks of a 'word-formation/form-formation' process, because in a number of cases the two processes are interspersed to a considerable degree. A change of root or determinative morpheme in a particular position of a verb form may distinguish various grammatical forms:

(14) Ket *baɣ d-un'-aptet*   *baɣ d-us'n-aptet*
           'I cut wood (in two parts)' 'I cut wood (in several parts)'[2]

Overall, as remarked by Haspelmath (1996: 47), the distinction inflection/ derivation 'is not absolute but allows for gradience and fuzzy boundaries ... we are dealing with a continuum from clear inflection to clear derivation with ambiguous cases in between'. This has also been borne out by Plank's (1994) analysis of twenty-eight criteria applied to six morphological categories in English. Plank maintains that the third person singular in English is most inflectional of all, more than plural. At the other end, there are the categories of diminutiveness in nouns and state–position of adjectives or adverbs, which are more derivational than the category of process–result of nouns, and this, in turn, is more derivational than the category of inchoative–causative. Neither of the polar (most typical) categories is absolutely inflectional or derivational but each of the six categories examined is dominated by inflectional or derivational features.

This observation can be geared towards the general principles of cognitive linguistics drawing our attention to prototypical cases, also expressed in Dressler's (2000: 7) proposal to distinguish between prototypical inflection and prototypical derivation. In the context of cross-linguistic research, the following conclusion by Dressler (2000: 7) is even more important:

> Degree of marginality may differ cross-linguistically ... Discrete boundaries between subcomponents or submodules are easier to draw within single languages than on a universal basis, but boundaries within one language often do not correspond to boundaries within another language.

---

[2] More examples of the fuzzy limit between inflection and derivation in Yeniseian languages, including incorporation complexes, causatives, aspectual forms, etc., can be found in Werner (1998: 137ff.).

1.1.2   The scope of word-formation

In 1962 and 1997, Dokulil defined the scope of word-formation by means of onomasiological categories (1997: 187):[3]

> The phenomenon to be named is, first, classed with a certain conceptual group possessing its categorical expression in the given language, and then, within the limits of this group, it is determined by a certain mark ... The conceptual group enters the onomasiological structure of the concept as a determined component (the onomasiological base), the mark enters it as a determining component (the onomasiological mark).

This delimitation of the scope of word-formation is a cognitive counterpart to the Marchandean, more formally grounded concept of the word-formation syntagma based on the *determinant–determinatum* structure. In this structure, both the *determinant* and the *determinatum* must be full linguistic signs (Marchand 1960). The *determinatum* can stand for the whole syntagma in all positions (the *determinant* cannot) and is thus the basic part of the word-formation syntagma about which a statement is made by the *determinant*: 'in the logical relation "species-genus", only the word denoting the genus can become the *determinant*' (Marchand 1974: 304).

Word-formation processes that meet this double condition include affixation, compounding, reduplication, conversion (if accounted for as zero-derivation),[4] back-formation (if synchronically analyzed as zero-derivation) and (noun) incorporation. This list of word-formation processes should be completed with root-and-pattern, stem vowel modification, consonant alternation, circumfixation, derivation processes combining two affixes (prefixes, suffixes and infixes), combinations of affixation and vowel alternation and also blending. Clipping and acronymization are not considered word-formation processes here on the grounds that they do not meet the fundamental conditions of word-formation, i.e. that their primary function is not the naming of new objects of extra-linguistic reality.

However, from the formal point of view, the above delimitation of the scope of word-formation does not contribute much to the distinction between inflection and derivation, because formal techniques like affixation, root-and-pattern, reduplication and stem modification, among others, are used for both inflection and derivation.

A number of linguists after Dokulil and Marchand have proposed criteria for the distinction between inflection and derivation in various theoretical frameworks. Unfortunately, none of these criteria can be considered a hard-and-fast rule guaranteeing a cross-linguistically clear-cut distinction. The literature shows that the classification of categories based on the

---

[3] Onomasiological categories are here understood as the 'types of [the] inner structuring of the concept, in view of its expression in the given language' (Dokulil 1997: 187).

[4] Cf. Štekauer (1996, 2005) for an onomasiological account of conversion as conceptual recategorization.

disjunctive, either–or, principle finds limitations in this and other branches of linguistics.

The split morphology view has both advocates (e.g. Perlmutter 1988; Anderson 1992) and opponents (e.g. Halle 1973; Williams 1981; Lieber 1981, 1992; Kiparsky 1982a, 1982b; Guerssel 1983; Mohanan 1986; Booij 1994, 1995; van Marle 1995).[5] The former believe that the distinction between inflection and derivation is robust enough as a tendency and that counter-examples are exceptional and can be easily explained (e.g. Baker 1988; Laca 2001: 1215). The latter prefer to view inflection and derivation as a continuum (e.g. Bybee 1985; Dressler 1989; Booij 1994; Haspelmath 1996). The cognitive approach to linguistics has also unambiguously manifested that the categories of linguistic disciplines are based on the fuzziness principle (cf. Aarts, Denison, Keizer and Popova 2004) and that, therefore, inflection and derivation belong in a cline rather than in a dichotomy (Katamba 1993: 217).

In between the ends of the inflection/derivation gradient, ambiguous cases can be found which challenge the classical view of split morphology, such as the *quasi-inflectional affixes*. These affixes display typical features of inflectional affixes, are fully productive and do not express obligatory morphological categories but, unlike prototypical inflectional morphemes, they do not constitute a paradigm. These types of units can be found, e.g. in Totonac (Beck 2004), where they can express a number of semantic nuances like distribution, manner or direction of motion, repetition, simultaneity, etc.

It may be claimed that, given the absence of unambiguous formal and semantic criteria, the functional difference between inflectional and derivational morphology is crucial for their separation. Such a difference manifests itself as an opposition between two morphologies whose main fields of operation, the field of semiotics and the field of communication, are different but complementary. Word-formation (derivational morphology) is the field whose function is inherently semiotic. Its rules are used for giving names to entities of extra-linguistic reality, ranging over the conceptual categories of substance, action, quality and circumstance. Through the semiotic function, word-formation enters into contact with extra-linguistic reality.[6] Inflectional morphology does not have such a direct relation to the

---

[5] Van Marle (1995) argues against the strict division of inflection and derivation based on examples of Dutch which, in his view, demonstrate that derivational forms may develop inflection-like properties, while inflectional forms may display derivation-like properties. Therefore, van Marle speaks of the 'interwoven' character of inflectional and derivational properties: 'derivation and inflection bear upon two distinct aspects of words: their lexical-semantic dimension and their syntax-oriented dimension. Typical of word structure seems to be, then, that these two dimensions are often entangled ... Evidently, this means that both dimensions of the word – i.e. the lexical semantic and the syntax-oriented – constitute a unity which is much closer than is often assumed' (1995: 78–9).

[6] As noted elsewhere (Štekauer 2005), word-formation is a part of an important semiotic triad: (i) object (of an extra-linguistic reality) to be named, (ii) language user (as a coiner of a new linguistic sign, i.e. new naming unit), and (iii) linguistic sign itself as a new candidate for membership in the system of language (*langue*).

language user or to extra-linguistic reality. Inflectional rules apply automatically, without any creative involvement of language users. The conditions for their operation are pre-determined in the semiotic act of coining new complex words. Functionally, inflectional morphology is mainly a resource that enables the language user to express relations between units in sentences in the communication process. The naming function of word-formation is thus complemented with the relational function of inflectional morphology.

This apparently unambiguous functional difference is, however, hard to observe in all cases of inflection and/or derivation. By way of an example of how fuzzy the field can be, let us point out that inflection may sometimes have a naming function, such as the word-forming function of inflectional paradigms in conversion (transflexion) in Slavic languages (cf. Smirnickij 1953, 1954; Dokulil 1968, 1982; Furdík 2004), as in (15) and (16):

(15)   Slovak   *beža-t'*.V   >   *beh*.N
                          'run.v'   'run.n'

(16)   Slovak   *červen-ý*.ADJ   >   *červen-ý*.SG.N
                          'red.ADJ'   'red.N'

Also, the delimitation of a new object is not so obvious as might be expected. Thus, we may ask whether the quantity-based categories of language are new objects of naming: while simple plural, as in English *boy* vs *boy-s* or its Slovak equivalents *chlapec* vs *chlapc-i*, seems to keep a word within the limits of an originally named object, it may be shown that, cross-linguistically, there are multiple and diverse manifestations of plurality which go beyond the limits of a single word. Similarly, are augmentatives and diminutives new objects, new linguistic signs, or extensions of the meanings of the existing objects?[7] Different answers can be given according to opposite evidence and arguments. The following section examines three borderline cases related to the supercategory of quantity in order to illustrate the difficulty inherent in the inflection vs derivation distinction from a cross-linguistic perspective.

1.1.3   Ambiguities in the supercategory of quantity

1.1.3.1   Evaluative morphology

This chapter opens with a quotation from Katamba's (1993: 212) discussion of the sometimes inflectional and sometimes derivational nature of diminutives. Katamba notes that, in many African languages, augmentatives and diminutives are marked by affixes that are at the heart of the inflectional system. Thus, in Luganda the prefixes *ka-/bu* may function as unmarked inflectional singular/plural markers as in *ka-solya* 'roof' vs *bu-solya* 'roofs',

---

[7] This question does not apply to unambiguous cases of changed denotation, like those given by Kryk-Kastovsky (2000), e.g. (Viennese) German *Krüg-erl Bier* ([pint-DIM]) 'pint of beer', Italian *libretto* ([book-DIM]) 'opera libretto' and Polish *łyż-ecz-ka* ([spoon-DIM]) 'teaspoon'.

but also as derivational diminutive prefixes as in *mu-kazi* 'woman' vs *ka-kazi* 'little woman' and *ba-kazi* 'women' vs *bu-kazi* 'little women'. Similarly, *bi-* and *ki-* are unmarked inflectional singular/plural markers in *ki-sero* 'basket' vs *bi-sero* 'baskets', but derivational augmentative prefixes in *ki-kazi* 'large woman' and *bi-kazi* 'large women' (Katamba 1993: 211).

As a confirmation of Katamba, Anderson (1992: 80ff.), in reference to diminutive affixes in Fula, a Niger-Congo language spoken in Africa, argues that, while diminutive formation is derivational in many languages, diminutives in Fula are integrated into the paradigmatic system as the marking of number, and that this paradigmatic system takes part in the syntactic relation of agreement, which is a major inflectional feature.

By contrast, Brown and Dryer (unpublished manuscript) give evidence that the category of diminutiveness in Walman, a language of the Torricelli family spoken in Australia-New Guinea, is inflectional. Similarly, Contini-Morava (pers. com.) shows that diminutives in Swahili are formed by replacing the noun class prefix with *ki-* (Class 7) and *vi-* (plural, Class 8), as in (17), and augmentatives are formed by replacing the noun class prefix with zero (Class 5) and *ma-* (plural, Class 6), as in (18):

(17)   Swahili   *kitoto*   <   *mtoto*
                     'small child, infant'   'child'

(18)   Swahili   *toto*   <   *mtoto*
                     'large, ungainly child'   'child'

Halfway between these two positions, Scalise (1984) describes evaluative morphology as a third level of morphology different from both inflectional and derivational morphology. Based on examples from Italian, Scalise shows that evaluative suffixes:

(a)   violate the Unitary Output Hypothesis,
(b)   are transparent with regard to the lexical category (the category is always that of the base) and to the syntactic features,
(c)   may be attached to more than one lexical category,
(d)   change the semantics of the base,
(e)   allow repeated application, and
(f)   are always peripheral with regard to genuine derivational suffixes and internal with regard to inflectional morphemes.

However, Scalise's claims are not universal. Thus, diminutive suffixes may change the lexical category of the base in Slovak: the masculine gender of *medveď* 'bear' changes to neuter in one of its diminutive forms, *medvieďa*, and the feminine gender of *žena* 'woman' changes to neuter in the diminutive *žieňa*. Similar cases abound. While the language-specific nature of Scalise's account of evaluative morphology was demonstrated by Stump (1993), augmentatives and diminutives are intriguing for their relation to inflection and derivation (cf. Dressler 1997: 1403, 1406).

1.1.3.2   Aspect/Aktionsart

Aspect/Aktionsart is further evidence of the vague borderline between inflection and derivation, and has been discussed in the literature accordingly (Spencer 2004: 1–2):

> there are numerous cases in which we wish to say that a semantic predicate is added to a word without changing the word class, for example, Aktionsart markers. These cases are notoriously difficult to classify as inflection or derivation and I argue that they represent the final type of category mixing, asyntactic derivation.

The problem concerning the nature of aspect/Aktionsart has a terminological, a semantic and a formal side. Terminologically, there does not seem to be a unified use of the term *aspect*. In the English-written literature there is usually no distinction between aspect and Aktionsart. It is only recently that this distinction came to be drawn, in particular, between more or less grammatical aspect (covering notions like perfectivity) and more or less lexical (which presumably implies derivational) Aktionsart (covering various *aspects* of action, such as iterativity, durativity, inchoativity, habituality, telicity, etc.). According to Dressler (1968: 40), this distinction dates back to Agrell (1908).

Boogaart (2000: 1166) distinguishes between lexical aspect and grammatical aspect, thus reflecting the difference between Aktionsart as a lexical–derivational property of verbs and aspect *per se* expressed grammatically. Boogaart (2000: 1167) points out problems with this distinction, like the fact that Aktionsart is in many languages expressed by grammatical means. A case in point is Jaqaru. Hardman (2000: 59) reports that the iterative suffix -*q"a* 'is considered a part of the inflectional system because its use is obligatory, because it does not enter into lexicalizations (its meaning is always predictable) and morphologically it forms an integral part of the marking within the person/tense system'. However, the fact that the suffix in question is integrated in the stem seems to argue against its treatment as an inflectional suffix.

But the crux of the matter here is, again, semantic: What actually is a new word, i.e. when can we speak about a new word? Boogaart (2000: 1167) tackles the issue in the discussion of the perfective verb in Slavic languages, which are reputedly true aspectual languages: 'the distinction is obligatory and it is independent of tense. However, it is a matter of some debate to what extent the perfectivizing prefixes of Russian in fact derive perfective verbs with a different lexical content, i.e. with a different Aktionsart.' As grammatical markers usually develop from lexical units, it is not always possible to classify aspectual forms as belonging either to the lexicon or to the grammar. Dressler (1968: 49) maintains that a number of Aktionsarten feature close semantic affinity to aspect and they usually incline to either perfective or imperfective aspect. Specifically, Dressler notes that this interconnection of aspect and Aktionsart is so strong in Slavic languages that 'most of the Aktionsarten are exclusively bound to a single aspect'.[8]

---

[8] Translation by Pavol Štekauer.

Table 2.1 shows the extensive possibilities of prefixation in German, Latin and Slovak. Many of these prefixes combine the aspect-related and the Aktionsart-related effects. Thus, when the prefix *pre-* is attached to the imperfective Slovak verb *písať* 'write', its meaning acquires a perfective nuance and, at the same time, changes into 'rewrite'. The Slovak verb *niesť* 'carry' is imperfective but, when the prefix *pri-* is attached, it becomes perfective and its meaning changes to 'bring' and, when the prefix *za-* is attached, the same base takes on the (perfective) meaning 'take it to (somebody)/(somewhere)'. This type of modification is extremely common in Slavic languages and turns imperfective into perfective verbs, usually altering the original meaning of the base and, thereby, producing new words.

An even more problematic side of the category of aspect/Aktionsart is habituality and iterativity. These are further subcategories of the supercategory of quantity and it is disputable whether affixation of this type keeps the verb within the original framework of the base or whether it produces a new verb.

Various positions can be found in the literature in this respect: Anderson (1985: 7–8) describes features of aspect in Russian in terms of derivation rather than of inflection and Hardman (2000: 59) points out the ambiguous nature of the category of iterativity in Jaqaru. Štasni (pers. comm.) treats the Serbian-Croatian verb *do-pis-iva-ti* 'add (in writing)', where *-iva* expresses iterativity, as a case of derivation, and so do Horecký and Ološtiak (pers. comm.) with regard to its Slovak counterpart *dopisovať*.[9] Similarly, Fortescue (1984) considers the West Greenlandic aspectual affix *-sar* of repetition as a derivational one and Nikolaeva and Tolskaya (2001: 308–9) also view deverbal aspectual affixes in Udihe as derivational.

Other examples of derivation expressed by aspectual markers are the momentaneous (semelfactive) aspect in Ket and other Yeniseian languages, which may refer to a single, unrepeated action, and the iterative aspect which refers to an ongoing action. According to Werner (1998: 146), the two aspects[10] may differ from each other by referring to either one or several objects. With verbs of motion, the aspectual forms also refer to the length of action. Finally, in Malayalam, the first constituent of verb + verb compounds always takes the form of an adverbial participle. Asher and Kumari (1997: 401) make explicit mention of the borderline nature of this structure, as in (19):

(19)   Malayalam   a.   *koṇṭu-varika*
                         take.hold.of-come
                         'bring'
             b.   *nookkikkaa·uka*
                  look-see
                  'look at admiringly'

---

[9] Both Serbian-Croatian *-iva* and Slovak *-ov* derive an imperfective, iterative/durative verb from a perfective verb.

[10] From what is said above, we would rather speak of Aktionsart in these cases.

c.   *ka.ttupitikkuka*
see-grasp
'find out'

The above can be interpreted as evidence that at least those subcategories of Aktionsart which fall under the supercategory of quantity are, by analogy to plurality, more derivation-like than other subcategories of aspect and Aktionsart, because they contribute to the lexical meaning of the motivating words in one or the other way. This is also in line with Kiefer's (1999) view of Aktionsart as 'the meaning of a morphologically complex verb introduced by morphological means which adds a semantic feature to the meaning of the base verb'.[11]

1.1.3.3   Plurality

Arguments have been raised in the literature concerning the derivational status of what has traditionally been considered an integral part of the inflectional system of language, as is number (cf., among others, Plank 1994: 1672; van Marle 1995: 74). Beard (1982) lists several similarities between pluralization and derivational processes:

(a)   formal and semantic irregularities (e.g. English *deer, salmon*, etc., and English *skies, heavens*, etc., respectively). Similarly, Russian gender distinction of singular paradigms is lost in the plural and Slovak collective nouns derived from a singular noun yield neuter gender from the masculine and, as the new noun behaves as a singular, a new inflectional paradigm,[12]

(b)   lexical constraints, as numerous nouns cannot be pluralized or cannot take the singular form,

(c)   preservation of number markings even where inflection completely disappears in the historical development of a language (e.g. in Bulgarian, English and Hindi), and

(d)   use of borrowings and agreement with lexical gender rather than with inflectional case in the relative pronoun of inflectional languages like Russian.

---

[11] Kiefer, F. 1999. 'Aktionsart-formation', paper presented at the MMM2 conference, 10–12 September 1999, Lija, Malta.

[12] These features confirm the existence of a new word. This is accompanied by stem vowel alternation, as in Slovak *list* 'leaf':

	Singular	Plural	Collective
Nominative	*list.*M	*líst-y*	*líst-ie*
Genitive	*list-a*	*líst-ov*	*líst-ia*
Dative	*list-u*	*líst-om*	*líst-iu*
Accusative	*list-Ø*	*líst-y*	*líst-ie*
Locative	*list-e*	*líst-och*	*líst-í*
Instrumental	*list-om*	*líst-ami*	*líst-im*

Similarly, Kießling (pers. comm.) assumes that plural formation in Datooga and other Southern Nilotic languages is derivational because it belongs to a larger number reference system in nouns where plural and singulative are just two categories: many nouns show a tripartite distinction of the basic form with collective or generic reference, a singular reference form (singulative) and a multiple reference form (plural). All three forms could be morphologically derived, but the capacity to derive two or three forms and the selection of plural and singulative markers largely depends on the lexical root and is not predictable by phonological or morphological criteria. Therefore, plurals and singulatives should be viewed as part of the lexicon and, thus, of word-formation.

The derivational pole of the category of plurality may also be illustrated by the so-called pluractional verbs in Hausa as discussed by Newman (2000: 423–9). Pluractional verbs in Hausa indicate the plurality of action and are derived productively from corresponding non-pluractional verb stems by reduplication. Their meaning can concern a multiple, iterative, frequentative, distributive or extensive action. (20a) and (20b) are two of Newman's examples, both based on preposing reduplication:

(20)   Hausa   a.   *tun~tùnā*
                              RED~tunàa
                              PL/ITE~remind
                              'remind many or often'
                      b.   *hàhhaifàa*
                              RED~hàifā
                              PL/ITE~give.birth
                              'give birth many times or to many children'

A similar point can be made of Kwakw'ala, where plurality is a derivational category. According to Boas (1947: 246), this category may express repetition (21a), several subjects (21b) or simultaneous action (21c) in different parts of a unit:

(21)   Kwakw'ala   a.   *mɛdɛˈlxu~mɛdɛˈlqwɛla*
                                 'It is boiling repeatedly'
                          b.   *mə̃ᵋ~mɛdɛˈlqwɛla*
                                 'Many are boiling'
                          c.   *mãᵋɛˈ~mdɛlqwɛla*
                                 'It is boiling in all of its parts'

The three different plural formations in Kwakw'ala resemble the plural system in Hausa. According to Anderson (1985: 30), the derivational status of at least the temporal, aspectual and plural groups is indicated by their being 'optional, and present only where necessary for emphasis or disambiguation; and ... equally applicable to words of any syntactic function or word class'.

While these facts argue for a case of pluractional markers as derivational in nature, this is not so in every language. A case in point is Karitiâna, an Arikem language spoken in South America. Sánchez-Mendes and Müller (2007) provide conclusive evidence that pluractionality excludes all singular, atomic events from the denotation of their verbs and thus behaves like the plural affix for nouns: its basic meaning is 'more than one event'. Consequently, pluractionality in Karitiâna cannot, among other things, express distributive meaning (the distributive meaning postulates the distribution of singular events, which are, however, not in the denotation of pluractional predicates). This point has been raised in reference to another language, Ket, where an inflectional suffix with plural meaning becomes a derivational one. Werner (1998: 41ff.) shows that the derivational suffix -η goes back to the plural suffix -η. (22) and (23) are examples of the acquired derivational status of -η:

(22)   Ket   *al'eη*   <   *al* + *-η*
               'trousers'   'half' + PL

(23)   Ket   *²ti²η*   <   *¹ti.k* + *-η*
               'hoarfrost'   'snow' + PL

In many cases the lexicalized plural forms are collective nouns which have developed a secondary plural form, such as those in (24):

(24)   Ket   *¹qə.n*   *qənten*   *qəntenəη*
               primary PL   secondary PL   'ant'

However, as noted by Werner (1998: 46), the derivational status of the original plural suffixes -η and -s'in may be called into question, because they are preceded by a plural suffix:

(25)   Ket   *⁴qä-s',*   >   *qe-η-s'in*
               'superior.N'   'superiors.N'

Werner refers to a similar observation by Bloomfield about German, where the plural of the diminutive *Kindchen* 'small child' is formed from the plural form of the non-diminutive base, i.e. *Kinder* yielding *Kinderchen*. As noted by Bloomfield (1933: 226), 'if a language contained too many cases of this sort, we should simply say that it did not distinguish such morphologic layers as are denoted by the terms "inflection" and "word-formation".'

A different piece of evidence is the participation of derivational affixes in inflectional paradigms, as in Breton (Stump 2005: 61–4), where the highly productive suffix *-enn* attaches to collectives. The resulting word is in the singular:

(26)   Breton   a.   *melien*   >   *melienenn*
                        'ants.COL'   'ant.SGT'
                  b.   *gwez*   >   *gwezenn*
                        'trees.COL'   'tree.SGT'
                  c.   *sivi*   >   *sivienn*
                        'strawberries.COL'   'strawberry.SGT'

This suffix can derive countable nouns from mass nouns and also be attached to a count noun or an adjective to produce a semantically related noun. All the derivations are of a feminine gender regardless of the properties of the base. The ability to change word-class and to determine the gender of the resulting formation and also other facts (e.g. *-enn* can be followed by another derivational suffix) suggest a derivational status for *-enn*, whereas the fact that the choice of the form (singulative or collective) is determined by the syntactic context[13] suggests inflectional status of *-enn*, because selection of inflectional forms for the sake of grammatical agreement is a typically inflectional property.

A final argument for the derivational nature of various aspects of plurality is its additional semantic content beyond the basic meaning of plural 'more than one'. When simple plural, as in prototypical inflectional paradigms, is compared with various meanings of plurality, a substantial difference between plural and plurality follows from the inclusion in the latter of additional semantic information represented by categories like collectivity, discontinuity, distribution, iterativity, quantitativeness, simultaneity, totality, etc.[14] The word-formation meaning of plurality thus follows from the additional semantic content added to the simple concept of 'more than one item or action' by the various plurality categories, as shown in Table 1.1:

Table 1.1. *A range of semantic categories within plurality*

(27)	Collectivity	'more than one + holistic perception of substance'	West Greenlandic *inu-aluit* person-COL 'group of people' (Fortescue 1984: 317)
(28)	Discontinuity[15]	'more than one + irregular frequency of action'	Hungarian *ki~ki-néz* DIS~look-out 'look out from time to time'

[13] Thus, the syntactic context that determines the selection between the singulative noun *sivienn* 'strawberry' and the collective *sivi* 'strawberries' likewise determines the selection between the singular noun *potr* 'boy' and the plural form *potred* 'boys' (Stump 2005: 63).

[14] Finer semantic distinctions are also possible: within the category of iterativity, E. Gruzdeva (2007. 'Distributive plurality in Nivkh', paper presented at the Workshop on Nominal and Verbal Plurality, 9–10 November, 2007, Paris) shows that in Nivkh, a language of the Nivkh family spoken in Eurasia, it is possible to distinguish between the so-called multiplicative plurality expressing repeated situations performed at the same period of time by identical participants, as in the first example below, and iterative plurality itself in which repeated situations are performed at different periods of time by identical participants, as in the second example below:

> Nivkh *Ñ-aqi*   *p-'aχṭa-za-d*
>   1SG-elder.brother   window-knock-ITE-IND
>   'My elder brother knocked (many times) at the window'

> Nivkh *Añ-añ-ŋara*   *nanq*   *eɣlŋ-badu-řa-d*
>   year-year-ITE   elder.sister child-give.birth-ITE-IND
>   'The elder sister gives/gave birth to a baby from year to year'

[15] We opt for this term in accordance with Dressler (1968: 63), who defines *discontinuative* as a function denoting a rare repetition of an action, with the emphasis on the pauses between individual repetitions. Dressler (1968) provides a subtle classification of various shades of the category of plurality.

(29)	Distribution	'more than one + distribution of elements/action'	Georgian	ხსა-ხსა-ο sam~sam-i DTB~three-NOM 'three each'
(30)	Indeterminate plurality/ diversity	'more than one + indeterminate number/volume/ extent of diverse elements'	Gã	jò~jò-ó-ì DIV-dance-ITE-PL 'dance at various places'
(31)	Iterativity	'more than one + repetition of action'	Datooga	gul-~gul ITE~knock 'knock repeatedly'
(32)	Quantitativeness	'more than one + extent/degree'	Breton	dorn-ad hand-QNT 'handful'
(33)	Reciprocal plurality	'more than one + reciprocal action/ relation'	Karao a.	manbakal man-bakal RCP.IPF-fight 'fight each other'[16]
			b.	man<ba>bakal RCP.IPF-<PL>-fight 'fight each other'[17]
(34)	Restricted applicability	'more than one + restriction'[18]	Ilocano	sik~sika RDP-you 'only you'
(35)	Simultaneity	'more than one + simultaneous action'	Amele	ta~tanaw-en[19] SIM~make.peace-3SG.PST 'as he made peace'
(36)	Totality	'more than one + all-inclusiveness'	Jaqaru	Narq atx'-ir-kuna canal clean-AG-TOT 'all the canal cleaners' (Hardman 2000: 11)

Additional examples can be found in several other languages. Campbell (1985: 46) states that some plural forms in Pipil take the suffix -wan when they are possessed. The suffix -wan expresses inalienable possession, usually with kinship terms or other closely related terms:

(37)   Pipil   -manuh-wan
                   'brothers'

---

[16] With two participants.
[17] With more than two participants.
[18] The extreme case being absence of plurality.
[19] From tanaw-ec 'make peace'.

(38)   Pipil   *-miyak-wan*
                     'family'[20]

Cowan (1969: 108) characterizes the Tzotzil suffix *-an* with the meaning 'multiple action of the same kind' as a derivational suffix:

(39)   Tzotzil   *mǐl-an*
                     kill.it-PL
                     'do a lot of killing to them'

Finally, Rubino (2005a: 115) points out that in Luiseño, a Uto-Aztecan language spoken in North America, different variants of reduplication can denote various plural actions: *lawi* means 'make a hole' while *law-lawi* means 'make two holes, make a hole twice' and *lawa-láwi* 'make many holes, more than two'.

The evidence and the arguments cited above do not conclude for or against the derivational nature of the traditionally inflectional category of number. However, they suggest that there seem to be enough grounds to separate, in cross-linguistic characterizations, the category of plural as an inflectional category from the conceptually/semantically more complex category of plurality, and that the latter of these would fall within the scope of word-formation.

1.1.4   Summary

      This chapter is not intended to analyze all of the criteria proposed for the distinction between inflection and derivation in the literature, but the cases discussed here may illustrate the overall situation in the field. Extensive discussion on this issue can be found, among others, in Scalise (1988), Dressler (1989), Plank (1994), van Marle (1995), Haspelmath (1996), Booij (2006) and Aikhenwald (2007). These and other works give support to the assumption that the majority of the inflection vs derivation criteria are based on the principle of a continuum with typical cases of inflection at one end, typical cases of derivation at the other and numerous intermediate cases which show features of both inflection and derivation.

---

[20] The hyphen at the beginning indicates that the noun is used with a possessive pronominal prefix, e.g. *nu-mu:n-wan* 'my brothers-in-law'.

2   Word-formation vs syntax

> [N]one of the possible criteria give a reliable distinction between two
> types of construction. The implication is that any distinction drawn
> on the basis of just one of these criteria is simply a random division
> of noun + noun constructions, not a strongly motivated borderline
> between syntax and the lexicon.   (L. Bauer 1998: 78)

If we wish to delineate the scope of word-formation we are, among other
things, expected to identify its basic unit, i.e. the linguistic sign resulting from
a process of word-formation. This is important in terms of the separation
between word-formation and syntactic structures, but it is particularly relevant with respect to word-formation processes combining free morphemes.
These include compounding, noun incorporation, reduplication (partial
reduplication being an exception) and blending. With the exception of the
last, these processes usually rank among the major word-formation processes, which means that they are fairly widespread cross-linguistically and,
in individual languages, they are usually among the most productive word-
formation processes. These word-formation processes also coincide with
what is labelled as *natural* word-formation processes in Natural Morphology,
i.e they are based on the principle of constructional iconicity.

This chapter reviews the main pitfalls in the effort to draw a borderline
between word-formation and syntax, i.e. the concept of wordhood (2.1),
and the status of compounds (2.2). Section 2.3 is devoted to the process of
(noun) incorporation and is taken as an illustrative example of a linguistic
phenomenon for whose lexical (word-formation) nature there are arguments
in favour and against.

2.1   Different notions of word

It is not easy to identify what language users intuitively have in mind
when we talk about words. This can be seen in the discussion of this issue by Di
Sciullo and Williams (1987) and also in Dixon and Aikhenvald (2002). Several
theoretical distinctions have been introduced to clarify the issue, like the separation of different *words*, i.e. words from the orthographical, phonological,
lexical, morphological, grammatical and syntactic points of view.

This distinction does not solve the problem of word-formation and the
units identified as words on the basis of one of these criteria need not

necessarily coincide with what are words according to another (Julien 2006: 617–18). This can be illustrated with Jaqaru, in which it is convenient to distinguish between morphological words, i.e. plain roots and roots with verbal and/or nominal suffixes (including thematic morphemes, (1) and (2), and syntactic words, which also contain 'suffixes which tie them into the sentence structure', (3) and (4); Hardman 2000: 8):

(1)   Jaqaru   *qumpishi*
                       'girdle, support worn inside the Tupe belt (*wak'a*)'

(2)   Jaqaru   *quqimi*
                       'dried ear of corn stored with the leaves'

(3)   Jaqaru   *qumpshi-wa*
                       'It is a girdle support'

(4)   Jaqaru   *quqmi-wa*
                       'It is a dried corn ear'

A number of replacement terms for *word* have been made available in the literature, such as *lexical unit* (Cruse 1986), *listeme* (Di Sciullo and Williams 1987: 3) or *naming unit* (Štekauer 1998, drawing on Mathesius 1975). Each of these and others which are not mentioned here, have far-reaching theoretical implications. Thus, the *listeme* is defined as a unit *listed* in the lexicon, i.e. stored in the mental lexicon of a language user. Importantly, Di Sciullo and Williams (1987) explicitly emphasize the difference between listedness (listing a unit in the lexicon) and *wordhood*: not only words, but also morphemes, idioms, phrases and even sentences like English *How do you do?* are listed, because they do not have any internal structure to predict their semantic or grammatical behaviour and, therefore, must be memorized and stored in the lexicon. The lexicon is thus presented as a set of irregularities: 'a collection of the lawless' (Di Sciullo and Williams 1987: 4). Yet, a great number of complex words are not listed, specifically those based on regular and productive word-formation rules. In other terms, it is not the word but the particular word-formation rule that is stored.

Listedness raises the issue of whether the various forms of words, the *word-forms* which are produced for categories like case, number, gender, person, tense and a number of other categories in inflectional languages are stored in the lexicon. It could be argued that they are stored and that, therefore, they should be considered listemes and, consequently, words. However, it can also be said that, as with productively coined words, a paradigm is identified with a word stored in the lexicon and the individual forms are generated for the purpose of syntax. It may even be the case that different inflected forms are dealt with differently. Julien (2006: 618) gives an example from Northern Saami, a Uralic language spoken in Eurasia: while it may be assumed that *beana* 'dog.NOM' and *beatnaga* 'dog.ACC' are both listed, the listedness of *beatnagiidisctguin* 'with their (own) dogs' is questionable.

Listedness is also difficult to apply to idioms: while they are semantically idiosyncratic and therefore should be listed (by the criteria given by Di Sciullo and Williams 1987), they are also analyzable and therefore should not be listed (by the criteria given by Lieber 1981). The confusion is aggravated by the scalar nature of the compound vs idiom relationship, where compounds and idioms form a continuum of different degrees of transparency/opacity (cf. Kavka 2003, 2009; Fernández-Domínguez 2009: 68). This discussion thus leads to the question of whether compounds should be listed or not and, if so, which compounds should be, which should not be and why.

Since, however, the linguistic signs which fall within the scope of word-formation are of a highly diverse nature, both cross-linguistically and not infrequently within one and the same language, linguists came to be rather uncertain as to what actually is a word and what is not. The following examples from several languages of a number of language families show that what is a word in one language can correspond to a sentence in another, in this case in English:

(5)   Clallam   *nǝ-sxʷčɬ-ɬqčɬšáʔ*
                      my-CAU-ADV-affect-fifty
                      'Fifty of them got me'

(6)   Georgian   გა-მ-ა-კეთ-ებ-ინ-ებ-დ-ე-ს-ო
                      ga-m-a-k'et-eb-in-eb-d-e-s-o
                      PREVERB-V-IO1.SG-version-do-THM-CAU-IPF-SBJ-S3.SG-QUO
                      '[If/when] s/he would make me do it, s/he says/said'

(7)   Ket   *da-u-g-d-o-v-il-tang*
                      3F.SBJ-3N.TR.OBJ-ABL-across-THM-INS.APP-PST-drag
                      'She dragged it (using a conveyance)'

(8)   Nelemwa   *u-paare-a-r-I na*
                      way.of-tell-DET-*it-of*-me
                      (lit. 'way of telling of it of me')
                      '[It's] my way of telling it'

(9)   Totonac   *na-kin-ka:-ta-la'h-x'a:-te:lha-ni-ya:-n-tunká*
                      FUT-1OBJ-PL.OBJ-3PL.SBJ-DST-husk.corn-AMB-BEN-IPF-2OBJ-very
                      'They will go around husking lots of corn for us'

(10)   Zulu   *be-si-nga-sa-zu-m-biz-a*
                                      PST-we-NEG-still-FUT-him/her-call-v
                                      'We were no longer going to call him/her'

Fortescue (1980: 260) demonstrates for West Greenlandic that the *sentence words* of (5) to (10)[1] should be viewed as real polysynthetic words rather than as strings of analytic words (cf. in this respect Anderson 1985: 32–3, in reference to the polysynthetic language Kwakw'ala). Thus, the status of some sequences can be other than words or sentences by falling between the two in some ways. Schiffman (1996) notes that Tamil can combine nouns with verbs and make *compound verbs*, i.e. verbs that are equivalent to a verb in another language. The nominal part of this compound is not marked for case, though it may in fact be the semantic object of the verbal action.

The notion of *compound* makes the point at issue even more difficult to handle. Specifically, the separation of compounds from phrases has been described as 'one of the more vexed problems in morphological theory, particularly in languages which are relatively poor in agreement morphology' (Spencer 2000: 315; cf. also Giegerich 2004, 2009 on English; Booij 2009 on Greek and Dutch; Schäfer 2009 on Mandarin Chinese; van Goethem 2009 on Romance and Germanic languages). This is the result not only of the vagueness of the notions under discussion and of the different theoretical positions that can be taken with respect to them, but also of the fact that a number of compounds develop from phrases.

The concept *word* is thus a fuzzy notion covering a range of various referents. In addition, the issue of wordhood is further obscured by the status of some bound elements which semantically behave as free morphemes and therefore remind us of Beard's (1981) forty-four cognitive categories which can be potentially expressed by both inflection and derivation. From this it follows that there is a large number of elements which have identical cognitive bases and unequal status in terms of wordhood. Malkiel (1978: 127) gives examples of this well-known Indo-European phenomenon from German and Latin, but this is also common in Slavic languages as seen in Table 2.1.

Table 2.1. *Examples of bound elements in German, Latin and Slovak*

German	Latin	Slovak	
(11) a. *durch-*	(12) a. *ē-/ex-*	(13) a. *od-* >	*odhodiť*
'through'	'out'	'from'	'throw away'
b. *gegen-*	b. *inter-*	b. *do-* >	*dobehnúť*
'against'	'between'	'to'	'run to a place.PFV'

---

[1] As noted by Fortescue (1980: 261), 'at least a dozen affixal morphemes can be found in single verb forms, and sometimes up to four of the same category ... can be encountered successively'.

German	Latin	Slovak		
c. *über-*	c. *per-*	c. *v-*	>	*vbehnúť*
'above, beyond'	'through'	'in(to)'		'run into'
d. *wieder-*	d. *prō-*	d. *z-*	>	*zbehnúť*
'again'	'before'	'from'		'desert.v'
e. *zurück-*	e. *sub-*	e. *na-*	>	*nasadiť*
'back'	'under'	'on'		'put onto'
		f. *nad-*	>	*nadhodiť*
		'above'		'throw up'

Similar cases exist beyond the Indo-European linguistic area too. As noted by Dixit (pers. comm.), attachment of postpositions or adverbs to the stem is the crucial process of word-formation in Marathi. It is applicable to nouns, pronouns, adjectives, postpositions, adverbs and verbs, and produces adverbs, adjectives and conjunctions. Laca (2001: 1219) also mentions formatives that have freely occurring particles but do not qualify automatically as lexemes:

(a)   adpositional or adverbial particles that play a role both in phrase and in lexeme formation, mostly as prefixes, e.g. German *gegen* 'against', *gegen mich* 'against me' vs *Gegenteil* 'opposite' or *vor* 'before, in front of', *vor ihm* 'before him' vs *vorkommen* 'happen',

(b)   lexemes belonging to major lexical categories that are being grammaticalized as derivational affixes by a well documented diachronic process in which derivational patterns emerge from series of compounds (or of set phrases that have been subject to univerbation). Thus, the status of German *frei* 'free', *voll* 'full' and *arm* 'poor', in *risikofrei* 'free from risk', *angstvoll* 'fearful' and *gefühlsarm* 'showing little feeling, insensitive' is doubtful. In such cases, affixal status only becomes certain when the corresponding lexeme disappears (as in the case of German *-heit*; cf. also English suffixes developed from lexemes) or when a clear semantic and/or formal split intervenes that disrupts the etymological connection (English *full* vs reduced and unstressed *-ful*, Spanish *mente* 'mind' vs the adverbial suffix *-mente*).

As in other issues, a continuum is assumed to exist between affixes (bound units) and words (free units), with different sorts of units between them, like various types of clitics (Zwicky 1977). Thus, in describing Chalcatongo Mixtec, an Oto-Manguean language spoken in North America, Macaulay (1996: 14) refers to the category of phrasal affixes (i.e. affixes attached to phrases) and maintains that they are affix-like in terms of dependence and word-like in terms of placement.

2.2   The status of compounds

A number of criteria have been proposed in the literature for the identification of compounds. These criteria may have to be applied differently in different languages, as Plank (1994: 1672) proposed for the opposition inflection vs derivation, or each language may have additional criteria bound to its specific system: besides the difficulty inherent in the concept of compounding, the cross-linguistic study of compounding is further complicated by the fact that some languages may accept as compounds units which would not be accepted as such in other languages,[2] or by the fact that they just do not exist in all languages (L. Bauer 2006: 721–2).[3] A similar picture is obtained for noun incorporation, where opposing views and varied cross-linguistic evidence make it difficult to go beyond a rather general description.

Leaving aside the sentence-like words illustrated in (5) to (10), one of the central problems of word-formation is the position of compounds and their relation to syntactic phrases. The special position of compounds may be seen from their treatment or, rather, lack of any treatment, in early lexicalist works. Neither Halle (1973), in the first programmatic paper on generative word-formation, nor Aronoff in his breakthrough monograph of generative word-formation (1976), deal with compounds. Halle speaks of two types of word-formation rules, those combining stems and affixes, and those combining words and affixes. Aronoff's word-formation rule is a phonological operation on the base which consists in attaching an affix.

In the transformationalist tradition, compounds are generated from kernel sentences and are treated as syntactic structures (Lees 1960, 1970; Marchand 1965a, 1965b; Kastovsky 1969; Li 1971;[4] Levi 1978; Roeper and Siegel 1978).

Compounds are assigned a special status by, among others, Strauss (1982) and Anderson (1992), who identify three components of morphology (inflection, derivation and compounding), and also by Jackendoff (2009: 113) in his conception of protolanguage as cognitive scaffolding on which modern language is built:

> relics of earlier stages of the language capacity remain as pockets within modern language. These relics would have only rudimentary grammatical structure, and such grammatical structure as there is would not do much to shape semantic interpretation. Rather, we would expect

---

[2] L. Bauer cites Glinert (1989), who labels as *compounds* those units that an English-focused morphologist would identify as blends. Other examples cited by Bauer are French *chemin de fer* 'way of iron', i.e. 'railway', and *pomme de terre* 'apple of earth', i.e. 'potato'.

[3] Compounding has been reported here not to exist in Dangaléat, in Diola-Fogny, in Karao and in West Greenlandic, and the data for Kwakw'ala (Boas 1947) indicate that compounding does not exist in this language as a productive word-formation process either.

[4] Li, C. 1971. 'Semantics and structure of compounds in Chinese'. PhD thesis, University of California, Berkeley, CA.

semantic interpretation to be highly dependent on the pragmatics of the words being combined and on the contextual specifics of use. I suggest that compounding fills the bill completely.

No matter which of the numerous positions we adhere to, it is necessary to admit the diversity of views reflecting the diversity of the phenomenon of compounding, a word-formation process that is far from homogeneous. A case in point is Tzotzil, in which compounding admits four different types of stems (Cowan 1969: 89ff.):

(a)   root (i.e. one morpheme),
(b)   radical (root + one or more derivational affixes),
(c)   compound itself, and
(d)   compound radical (compound + one or more derivational affixes).

This gives rise to a number of combinations which are summarized in Table 2.2.

Table 2.2. *Some combinations of the internal structure of compounds in Tzotzil*

Root + root	(14) Tzotzil	*pĭš-xól* wrap-head 'hat'
Root + radical	(15) Tzotzil	*mé²-[kʼĭn-ob-al]* mother-mist 'rainbow'
Radical + root	(16) Tzotzil	*[tʼsúb-il]-lúm* powder-ground 'dust'
Radical + radical	(17) Tzotzil	*[sĭk-il]-[tšám-el]* cold-quality-sickness 'malaria'
Root + compound	(18) Tzotzil	*tĭ²-[mák-té²]* opening-[enclosure-wood] 'fence gate'
Radical + compound	(19) Tzotzil	*[kʼán-al]-[²óʼn-ton]* [yellow-quality]-[heart-stone] 'bird with yellow breast'
Compound + radical	(20) Tzotzil	*[tóx-tóx]-[tšám-el]* [straight-straight]-[act of dying] 'die very quickly'

A number of references can be found in the literature on the identification of compounds (Marchand 1969; Adams 1973, 2001; L. Bauer 2001; Donalies 2004). One of the most recent ones, Lieber and Štekauer (2009), discusses various aspects of compoundhood (wordhood) and maps the state of the art in the field from the perspective of various theoretical approaches as well as by describing the process of compounding in various languages of the world. In the following we confine ourselves to the illustration of the word-formation/syntax problem by discussing the status of noun incorporation.

2.3   Compounding and noun incorporation

Like compounding, noun incorporation appears as one of the most problematic areas at the word-formation/syntax interface. Noun incorporation is here understood as a verb-forming process whereby a nominal stem is fused with a verbal stem to yield a larger, derived verbal stem. In noun incorporation, the incorporated noun functions as an argument (usually object) of the predicative verb. This is a definition of prototypical cases of noun incorporation, but this definition is not an all-encompassing one.[5] Sadock (2006: 585) shows that the scope of the concept of incorporation varies considerably, ranging from the original, narrowly defined noun incorporation up to any juxtaposition of two functional or lexical categories (Baker 1988).

Thus, while incorporation usually makes use of full words, there are also cases in which incorporation is based on an affix, like nominal stems fused with an affix. Recognizing an affix-based incorporation can be, according to de Reuse (1994: 200), traced back to Kroeber (1910). In West Greenlandic there are many bound verbal suffixes, such as -qar 'have', -si 'get', -lisaar 'wear', -tur 'eat/drink', -liur 'make' and -ssaaliqi 'lack' (Fortescue 1984: 82):

(21)   West Greenlandic   *nutaa-mik umiarsuar-nut talittarvi-qar-puq*
                            new-INS ship-all.PL   harbour-have.3SG.IND
                            'There is a new harbour for ships'

(22)   West Greenlandic   *kissartu-mik kavvi-sur-put*
                            hot-INS   coffee-drink-3.IND
                            'They drank hot coffee'
                            (Fortescue 1984: 83)

Fortescue (1984: 84) wonders 'whether "incorporation" is the best term to use here, since all verbalizing affixes like *qar* are bound forms, never stems'. In fact, as argued by Malouf (1999), while the resulting denominal verb has the full syntactic and morphological distribution of any verb in West Greenlandic and retains some of the properties of the incorporated nominal, it has little in common with noun incorporation constructions in languages

---

5   According to Sadock (2006: 585), 'it was in this sense that the word *Einverleibung* was originally used in describing facts of "Mexican" (Nahuatl) by von Humboldt, who contrasted a sentence with an independent verb and object: *ni-c-qua in nacatl* "I-it-eat the meat" with the incorporated form *ni-naca-qua* "I-meat-eat"'.

like Mohawk, an Iroquoian language spoken in North America, or in Southern Tiwa, a Kiowa-Tanoan language also spoken in North America.

This case is not unique: Mithun (1984: 885) reports on languages that 'contain affixes which function much like I[ncorporated]N[oun]'s, often highly productively. Others contain affixes which function much like incorporating V[erb]'s, again often very productively.' Similarly, Gerdts (1998: 94–7) refers to the abundance of the so-called lexical suffixes in Salishan, Wakashan and other northwestern Amerindian languages which carry a nominal meaning denoting body parts, environmental concepts, cultural items and human terms.[6] These suffixes undergo the same kind of incorporation as nouns and establish the same kind of relations as stem-based noun incorporation. In Gerdts' view, 'lexical suffixes can be regarded as incorporated nouns that have lost their status as free-standing nominals' (1998: 97).

A different case is offered by noun-stripping-based incorporation in Lakhota,[7] in which a noun is followed by an adjectival modifier:

(23)   Lakhota   *hayáke   waštéšte   khoyáka*
                        clothes   good-RDP   ST-s0-A0-wear
                        'He wore nice clothes'
                        (de Reuse 1994: 207)

The usual objection is that a noun cannot be considered stripped if followed by an adjectival modifier. De Reuse argues, however, that the noun and the adjective are not a phrase. Instead they form a syntactic compound with its characteristic stress (i.e. main stress on the second syllable of the first constituent and secondary stress on the second syllable of the second constituent).

Mithun (1984: 847) points out that 'noun incorporation is perhaps the most nearly syntactic of all morphological processes' and Katamba (1993: 287) adds that it 'obscures the boundary between syntax and morphology'. This is clear in borderline cases like the following from Udihe, where the bond between the verb *b'a-* 'get' and the incorporated noun in accusative is rather loose (Nikolaeva and Tolskaya 2001: 326ff.), and the latter may be

---

[6] Examples from Kwakw'ala follow (Boas 1947: 238–40):

       Kwakw'ala   =*ił*   *ᵋăxᵋā'lił*
                 'floor of house, in house'   'put on floor'

       Kwakw'ala   -*!xo*   *qɛnxâ'la*
                 'neck'   'have around neck'

[7] According to Gerdts (1998: 93–4), noun stripping (deletion of usual case markings or determiners of the noun phrase) differs from incorporation on the ground that the juxtaposed constituents preserve their phonological features, such as stress. On the other hand, 'like incorporation, noun stripping is almost always limited to objects and to subjects of inactive verbs. Prototypical stripped nouns are indeterminate and inanimate' (Gerdts 1998: 94).

modified by an adjective (24) and may even be separated from the governing
verb (25) (Nikolaeva and Tolskaya 2001: 327):

(24)   Udihe   *Sagdi   baita-wa   b'a-ni*
                     Big   trouble-ACC   get.PST-3SG
                     'He got into big trouble'

(25)   Udihe   *Ali   b'a-ni   uti   zuge-we?*
                     When   get.PST-3SG   that   trouble-ACC
                     'When did this misfortune happen to him?'[8]

In principle, there are two major positions on the status of (noun) incorporation: the syntactic position, which explains noun incorporation by a movement operation in syntax, and the lexical/word-formation position. In Leza's
(2001: 714) view, neither the proponents of a syntactic approach nor those
of a morphological (i.e. lexical) approach have argued unambiguously and
compellingly in favour of their respective positions.

The syntactic approach to noun incorporation goes back to Mardirussian
(1975) but was primarily developed by Sadock (1980, 1985, 1986) and Baker
(1983, 1985, 1988).[9] The argument is that noun incorporation is basically a
syntactic process. In Katamba's (1993: 283) words it is 'a productive syntactic rule that builds a special type of compound verb'. Baker makes use of
his Mirror Principle to suggest that the processes employed in generating
a complex form by noun incorporation mirror the syntactic processes. In
his view, noun incorporation is based on the movement of a word from its
position in a noun phrase of a sentence to a position inside a verb. Thus,
Kageyama (1982: 243) treats noun incorporation like Japanese 腰掛ける
(kosi-kakeru) 'sit down' (lit. 'put one's buttocks'),手間取る (tema-doru)
'take time', 物言う (mono-yuu) 'say (something)', etc. as nominalization
compounds 'derived from their paraphrasing sentential constructions' by
movement transformation. Baker argues in favour of a syntactic nature of
noun incorporation by assuming that:

(a)   incorporation can leave behind the non-head portions of the
          noun phrase,
(b)   a copy may be left behind,
(c)   only objects and subjects of intransitives can be incorporated,
          this being a syntactic specification, and

---

[8] Even so, certain features separate these instances of noun incorporation from syntactic
     structures: 'The object in them does not passivize, does not control depictives and does not
     relativize, unlike a regular direct object ... Unlike other objects, these compounds cannot be
     coordinated without repeating the verb ... These properties suggest that we are here dealing
     with an object characterized by a certain degree of incorporation, and that the compound
     expressions ... [in (24) and (25)] are transitional in character, being somewhere between a
     syntactic phrase and a lexical element' (Nikolaeva and Tolskaya 2001: 327–8).
[9] Baker, M. 1983. 'Noun incorporation in Iroquoian'. Manuscript. Cambridge, MA: MIT.

(d)   incorporated nouns may introduce new discourse referents (cf. Di Sciullo and Williams 1987).

Syntactic arguments were called into question by Mithun (1984), Di Sciullo and Williams (1987: 63–9) and Spencer (1995, 2000). Mithun (1984, 1986), Rosen (1989), Anderson (1992: 267–9) and Gerdts (1998) propose a lexical approach instead, and treat noun incorporation as a lexical process, specifically as a special case of compounding. Thus, Gerdts (1998: 84) defines noun incorporation as 'the compounding of a noun stem and a verb (or adjective) to yield a complex form that serves as the predicate of a clause'.[10]

The proponents of the lexical/word-formation approach to noun incorporation agree on its general compounding principle, but the details and foci of their respective treatments of noun incorporation differ. Thus, Mithun (1984) distinguishes four noun incorporation types primarily on the basis of various (discourse) functions and Rosen (1989) classifies noun incorporations according to their syntactic features as two groups:

(a)   those which preserve the argument structure of the incorporating verb intact ('classifier N[oun] I[ncorporation]'),[11] and
(b)   those in which one argument of the verb is satisfied with the complex verb which results in turning a transitive verb into an intransitive one ('compound N[oun] I[ncorporation]').

Noun incorporation is, in the vast majority of cases, connected with incorporating a single noun. Yet, a rare case of two incorporated nouns, mostly combined with locative and instrumental prefixes, can be found in Lakhota. One such example, whose structure is [N+[Loc+[N+[Loc+[Loc+V]]]]], is given in de Reuse (1994: 216):

(26)   Lakhota   *xta'ómakhiyokpazA*
                      evening-LOC-earth-LOC-LOC-be.dark
                      'grow dusk'

De Reuse (1994: 202) also shows that, in addition to an incorporated noun stem, Lakhota stative verbs can incorporate a pronominal prefix too. Thus, the stative verb *chóla* 'be missing' in (27) below has two arguments after noun incorporation: the stative pronominal prefix *ma-* 'first person' and the incorporated noun *sí* 'foot':

---

[10] Gerdts (1998: 88), however, acknowledges the unique nature of this type of compounding because 'in noun incorporation ... the stem that results from the compounding of a noun stem and a verb serves a dual role in the clause: it is both the verb and one of the arguments of a verb'.

[11] The term *classifier* reflects the fact that the incorporated noun classifies the object noun. In other words, the incorporated noun must be more general than the object NP. Therefore, as exemplified by Rosen (1989: 297), while 'I animal-bought a dog' is acceptable, 'I dog-bought an animal' is not.

(27)   Lakhota   *sí ma-čhóla*
                         foot s1-lack
                         'I lack feet'

The inclusion or not of noun incorporation in the field of word-formation is just one example of how relevant theoretical frameworks can prove in typological research. It also illustrates that, in some cases, theory-independent approaches in typological research are just not possible.

Another point concerns the internal relations in word-formation itself. If we admit that noun incorporation is a word-formation process, we are then probably expected to decide on such borderline cases as represented by this phenomenon in English. It has long been assumed by the majority of morphologists that examples like English *to chain-smoke, to sleep-walk*, etc. are back-formations from the corresponding verbal compounds. The arguments are based mainly on the diachronic data indicating that the longer forms appeared historically before the shorter ones.

Not only does this sort of argument not seem to be sufficiently reliable to justify the claim concerning the nature of a word-formation process, but it may also be argued that the original process of back-formation in English gave rise to numerous analogical formations which did not rely on longer counterparts any more. The growing number of such formations[12] may have triggered a synchronically productive process of noun incorporation. This account is favoured in Kiparsky's approach (1982a), which explains the generation of this class of expressions as compounding, based on the rule $[Y\ Z]_X$ (where X stands for a verb). An even stronger claim in this line was made by Kastovsky (1986: 419), when he predicted the gradual development of a productive process of noun incorporation. Kastovsky (2009: 338) recently strengthened this claim by arguing that 'this type has become rather popular in Modern English as a result of the re-interpretation of denominal back-formations'. The position presented here, as in the opening lines of this section, is in accordance with E. Sapir (1921), who also treats this kind of complex words as cases of noun incorporation: noun incorporation is thus viewed as compounding, i.e. a process controlled by word-formation rules (cf. Štekauer 1998 and 2005).

2.4   Summary

Compounding and noun incorporation lie at the interface of word-formation and syntax and show that similar problems to the ones discussed in chapter 1 on the limit between inflection and derivation can be found between word-formation and syntax. In this respect, word-formation is no exception to the general fuzzy nature of linguistics. Partly for this

---

[12] Cf., among others, Szymanek (2005: 434), who maintains that this pattern 'has been marked by considerable growth over recent years'.

reason, derivation, like inflection, is best described in terms of prototypical characteristics or, maybe, it can be described only in terms of prototypes. Unlike what happens in inflection and derivation, where the separation is presented as a gradient both by the literature (among others, Bybee 1985: 5; Plank 1994: 1672) and by a review of language systems, the separation between compounding or noun incorporation and syntactic structures is much more difficult to express even in a gradient.

The implications for word-formation typology and universals are that decisions concerning the selection of the categories considered to be word-formation may be called into question. The range of ambiguous categories is relatively large. What seems therefore necessary is to focus on the pro-totypical and most productive instances of the individual word-formation processes. With such an approach (cf. also Booij 2006: 654), there may still be a substantial space of uniqueness pertaining to both formal and semantic characteristics of the individual word-formation processes and categories and, first and foremost, to their respective functions.

PART II

Cross-linguistic analysis

3   Word-formation processes combining free morphemes

> The study of language universals has been a major focus of modern
> linguistics for at least the past three decades.   (Hawkins 1988: 3)

If the above quotation holds true, at present we may extend the period of
intensive research into language universals and language typology to fifty
years. Of that, comparatively little attention has been devoted to word-
formation. In our research into typology in word-formation we primarily
follow Anderson's (1985: 9) view of typological studies (cf. 'Antecedents' in
the 'Introduction'). For this reason, one of our objectives has been to identify/
verify associations between language families, inflectional types, and word
order with respect to word-formation processes and categories.

This chapter focuses on word-formation processes combining morphemes
and devotes a section to compounding (3.1), reduplication (3.2) and blending (3.3). Emphasis is laid on compounding, with a review of different types
and processes within compounding.

3.1   Compounding

Libben (2006: 2) considers compounding a language universal,
and in some languages compounding is reported to be extremely productive:
according to the data in Ceccagno and Basciano (2009), approximately 80
per cent of Chinese words are compounds and over 90 per cent of all new
words in *The Contemporary Chinese Dictionary* (Yuan, Zhang and Chen
2002) are compounds. In the study sample, compounding is recorded in the
languages shown in Table 3.1 (90.91 per cent in the study sample):

Table 3.1. *Compounding in the study sample*

Language	Family	Morphological type	Area
Amele	Trans-New Guinea	Polysynthetic/synthetic	Australia-New Guinea/Madang
Amharic	Afro-Asiatic	Inflectional	Africa/Ethiopia
Anejom	Austronesian	Agglutinative	SE Asia and Oceania/Vanuatu
Bardi	Australian	Fusional	Australia-New Guinea/Australia
Breton	Indo-European	Fusional	Eurasia/France
Cirecire	Khoisan	Isolating	Africa/Botswana
Clallam	Salishan	Polysynthetic	North America/USA

Language	Family	Morphological type	Area
Datooga	Nilo-Saharan	Agglutinative/ fusional	Africa/Tanzania
English	Indo-European	Isolating	Eurasia/Ireland and UK
Estonian	Uralic	Agglutinative/fusional	Eurasia/Estonia
Finnish	Uralic	Agglutinative	Eurasia/Finland
Gã	Niger-Congo	Agglutinative	Africa/Ghana
Georgian	Kartvelian	Inflectional/ agglutinative	Eurasia/Georgia
Greek	Indo-European	Fusional	Eurasia/Greece
Hausa	Afro-Asiatic	Fusional	Africa/Niger, Nigeria
Hebrew	Afro-Asiatic	Inflectional	Africa/Israel
Hungarian	Uralic	Agglutinative	Eurasia/Hungary
Ilocano	Austronesian	Agglutinative	SE Asia and Oceania/Philippines
Indonesian	Austronesian	Agglutinative	SE Asia and Oceania/Indonesia
Japanese	Japanese	Agglutinative	Eurasia/Japan
Jaqaru	Aymaran	Agglutinative	South America/Peru
Kalkatungu	Australian- Aboriginal	Agglutinative	Australia-New Guinea/Australia
Ket	Yeniseian	Agglutinative	Eurasia/Russia
Konni	Niger-Congo	Agglutinative	Africa/Ghana
Lakhota	Siouan	Synthetic/ polysynthetic	North America/USA
Luganda	Niger-Congo	Agglutinative	Africa/Uganda
Luo	Nilo-Saharan	Agglutinative	Africa/Kenya, Tanzania
Maipure	Arawakan	Agglutinative	South America/Venezuela
Malayalam	Dravidian	Agglutinative	Eurasia/India
Mandarin Chinese	Sino-Tibetan	Isolating/analytic	SE Asia and Oceania/China
Māori	Austronesian	Isolating	SE Asia and Oceania/New Zealand
Marathi	Indo-European	Inflectional/ polysynthetic	Eurasia/India
Movima	Movima	Agglutinative	South America/Bolivia
Nelemwa	Austronesian	Isolating	SE Asia and Oceania/New Caledonia
Pipil	Uto-Aztecan	Agglutinative	North America/El Salvador
Slavey	Na-Dene	Polysynthetic	North America/Northwest Territories
Slovak	Indo-European	Inflectional	Eurasia/Slovakia
Spanish	Indo-European	Inflectional	Eurasia/Spain
Swahili	Niger-Congo	Agglutinative	Africa/Tanzania
Tamil	Dravidian	Agglutinative	Eurasia/Tamil Nadu
Tatar	Altaic	Agglutinative	Eurasia/Russia
Telugu	Dravidian	Agglutinative	Eurasia/India

Language	Family	Morphological type	Area
Tibetan	Sino-Tibetan	Inflectional/ agglutinative	SE Asia and Oceania/China
Totonac	Totonacan	Agglutinative/ polysynthetic	North America/Mexico
Tzotzil	Mayan	Polysynthetic/ agglutinative	North America/Mexico
Udihe	Altaic	Agglutinative	Eurasia/Russia
Vietnamese	Austro-Asiatic	Isolating	SE Asia and Oceania/Vietnam
Wichí	Matacoan	Agglutinative	South America/Argentina and Bolivia
Yoruba	Niger-Congo	Isolating	Africa/Benin, Nigeria
Zulu	Niger-Congo	Agglutinative	Africa/South Africa

3.1.1   Types of compounds

The scope of the book does not allow the survey of all possible types of compounds here. Therefore, focus is on the most widespread types: adjective + adjective compounds (3.1.1.1), compound verbs (3.1.1.2) and noun + noun compounds (3.1.1.4).

3.1.1.1   Adjective + adjective compounds

Adjective + adjective compounds have been recorded in the languages shown in Table 3.2.

Table 3.2. *Adjective + adjective compounding in the study sample*

Language	Family	Morphological type	Area
Amele	Trans-New Guinea	Polysynthetic/synthetic	Australia-New Guinea/ Madang
Breton	Indo-European	Fusional	Eurasia/France
Cirecire	Khoisan	Isolating	Africa/Botswana
English	Indo-European	Isolating	Eurasia/Ireland and UK
Estonian	Uralic	Agglutinative/fusional	Eurasia/Estonia
Finnish	Uralic	Agglutinative	Eurasia/Finland
Georgian	Kartvelian	Inflectional/agglutinative	Eurasia/Georgia
Greek	Indo-European	Fusional	Eurasia/Greece
Hausa	Afro-Asiatic	Fusional	Africa/Niger, Nigeria
Indonesian	Austronesian	Agglutinative	SE Asia and Oceania/ Indonesia
Japanese	Japanese	Agglutinative	Eurasia/Japan
Lakhota	Siouan	Synthetic/polysynthetic	North America/USA
Mandarin Chinese	Sino-Tibetan	Isolating/analytic	SE Asia and Oceania/China

Language	Family	Morphological type	Area
Marathi	Indo-European	Inflectional/polysynthetic	Eurasia/India
Slovak	Indo-European	Inflectional	Eurasia/Slovakia
Spanish	Indo-European	Inflectional	Eurasia/Spain
Tibetan	Sino-Tibetan	Inflectional/agglutinative	SE Asia and Oceania/China
Udihe	Altaic	Agglutinative	Eurasia/Russia
Vietnamese	Austro-Asiatic	Isolating	SE Asia and Oceania/Vietnam

3.1.1.1.1 Formal characteristics Formally, adjective + adjective compounds can occur without and with a linking element. Examples are given in Table 3.3.[1]

Table 3.3. *Adjective + adjective compounding with/out a linking element*

	Without a linking element			With a linking element	
(1)	Amele	*ben nag* big-small 'a little bit big'	(2)	Belorussian	чорн-а-зялёны chornazjal'jony 'black-green'
(3)	Estonian	*pisi-tilluke* 'little tiny'	(4)	Greek	μαυρόασπρος mavr-o-aspros 'black and white'
(5)	Finnish	*syvä-puhdas* deep-clean 'very clean' (Koivisto)	(6)	Romanian	*fizic-o-chimic* 'physical-chemical'
(7)	Hindi	*lal-pīla* 'red and yellow; colourful' (Kachru 2006: 120)	(8)	Serbian-Croatian	*mlad-o-bosanski* 'young Bosnian'
			(9)	Slovak	*svetl-o-modrý* 'light blue'
			(10)	Ukrainian	жовт-о-зелений zhovtozelenij 'yellow-green'

The members of the compounds can be stems, but also inflected forms, as in Finnish (11) and Udihe (12) and (13). The latter can combine a content element and the copula verb *bi-* 'be' and, sometimes, also *ede-* 'become' in the corresponding form. The content element may be an adverb, a derived adjective or an ideophonic adverb:

---

[1] Here exemplified with a common linking element in Indo-European languages: *-o-*.

(11)   Finnish   *vaalea-n-sininen*
                    light-GEN-blue
                    'light blue'
                    (Laakso)

(12)   Udihe   *bei-bi-*
                 in.vain-be
                 'simple'

(13)   Udihe   *täsi bi-*
                 very.much-be
                 'full'
                 (Nikolaeva and Tolskaya 2001: 200)

Adjective + adjective compounds can be, to use Scalise and Bisetto's (2009) terminology, attributive (14) and coordinate (15):

(14)   Serbian-Croatian   *svetloplav*
                            'light blue'

(15)   Spanish   *italo-argentino*
                   'Italian-Argentinean'

Subordinative compounds usually present a structure of modifier + head sequence, but the opposite is also possible, as illustrated in (16):

(16)   Romanian   *galben-auriu*
                    yellow-golden
                    'golden-yellow'

3.1.1.1.2 *Semantic characteristics* Semantically, three types of meaning have been identified in the study sample: a purely compositional meaning,[2] a modified meaning,[3] and a new concept motivated by the adjectival constituents, as shown in Table 3.4:

---

[2] Interestingly, the majority of examples in our sample denote colours. According to Newman, about half of twenty compound adjectives in Hausa have the structure *ruwan X* 'colour-of-X':

   Hausa   *ruwan tōkaà*
            colour.of-ash
            'grey'

[3] Let us also mention the noun + adjective compound type in Udihe (Nikolaeva and Tolskaya 2001: 200), which combines a noun and a semantically light (quantifying) adjective, e.g. *egdi* 'many' or *maŋga* 'strong, very much', with intensifying meaning:

   Udihe   *meje egdi*
            'clever, intelligent'
   Udihe   *kui(-ni) maŋga*
            'strong'

Table 3.4. *Semantic types in adjective + adjective compounding*

	Compositional meaning		Modified meaning		New concept
(17) Afrikaans	*diep-rooi* deep-red 'scarlet'	(18) Dutch	*blauw groen* blue-green 'bluish green'	(19) Indonesian	*lemah-lembut* weak-soft 'gentle'
(20) Georgian	შავთეთრი šav-tetr-i black-white 'black-white'	(21) Finnish	*sini-vihreä* blue-green 'bluish green' (Koivisto)	(22) Lakhota	*zi-thó* yellow-blue 'green'
(23) Italian	*rosso-blu* 'red-blue'			(24) Mandarin Chinese	美好 měi-hǎo beautiful-good 'lovely, fine'
(25) Mandarin Chinese	藍紫 lánzǐ 'blue-violet'			(26) Marathi	लहानथोर lahaana-thora common/younger-great/ elder 'including all types of persons'
(27) Russian	син-е-зелён-ый sin-e-zel'jon-y blue-LNK-green- NOM.SG.M 'blue-green'				
(28) Serbian- Croatian	*crno-belo* 'black-white'				

Māori presents an ambiguous case: according to Harlow (pers. comm.), there is only one example of adjective + adjective compound in this language (29) and even this seems to be questionable:

(29)   Māori   *hari-koa*
                       happy-happy
                       'happy, pleased'

According to W. Bauer (1997: 77), Māori does not have the word-class adjective, which in this language is rather a class of verbs.[4] These verbs can occur as modifiers in post-nuclear position in noun phrases, as in (30) (W. Bauer 1997: 303):

(30)   Māori   *Ka   pātai   mai   a   Pou, "He   wāhi   pai   anō?"*
                       TAM ask   hither PER   Pou   CLS   PLC   good   again
                       'Pou asked, "Is it a nice place, too?"'

3.1.1.2   Compound verbs

Compound verbs, i.e. compounds whose head is verb, as in *to spotlight* or *to stagemanage*, are a controversial case in word-formation in languages like English. While the status of nominal and adjectival compounds is relatively clear, the existence of compound verbs in English has been called into question by a considerable number of morphologists, like Marchand (1960) or Lieber (2004: 48). The former calls this type of structure *pseudocompounds* and explains their formation by processes other than compounding. This is common in the literature and a number of sources have been cited for the alleged compound verbs, e.g. back-formation from other compounds (Marchand 1960: 59; Adams 1973; Allen 1978: 214), zero-derivation from other compounds (Marchand 1960: 59; Adams 1973, 2001: 101)[5] or noun incorporation (Štekauer 2009: 282).[6]

Interestingly, Adams (1973) cites Pennanen (1966: 7.5)[7] in support of her view that compound verbs may be based on analogical formation, while her 2001 revision (Adams 2001: 109) assumes that 'genuine verb compounding is not likely to develop in modern English'. The controversy on the existence of a verb-forming process of compounding in English is unavoidable when

---

[4] According to Lynch (pers. comm.), Anejom does not have adjectives either.
[5] Compound verbs formed by back-formation, such as *globe-trot* from *globetrotter*, or *globetrotting*, are explained by Adams (1973: 106) as a reinterpretation of their constituent structure, e.g. from [*globe*] + [*trot*[*ter*]] to [*globe*] + [*trot*] + *er*. As a result, the suffix *-er* does not belong to the stem *trot-*, but to the compound stem *globe-trot-*, and can be removed leaving the compound verb *globe-trot*. Other examples are the verbs *brainwash*, *computer-generate*, etc. (Adams 2001: 101).
[6] Cf. Chung (2006) on verbal compounds in Mandarin Chinese and Ralli (2009) in Greek.
[7] 'The reciprocal influence of the various patterns of word-formation plays an important role. The existence of composite verbs of a given type, formed for instance by retrograde derivation, will encourage and facilitate the formation of similar verbs by other means of word-formation, for instance by conversion or compounding, and vice versa' (Pennanen 1966: 7.5). Thus, *chainsmoke* is a back-formation from *chain-smoker* but *chain-drink* (1958) is an analogical formation.

L. Bauer and Renouf (2001: 110) identify neologisms such as *dry-burn*, *test-release*, *thumb-strum* and *slow-bake* as compound verbs. Kiparsky (1982a: 16) considers compound verbs with adverbials as left-hand constituents (English *hand-pick*, *sun-dry*, etc.) to be a class of systematic exceptions to the First Sister Principle. Kiparsky emphasizes that 'the process which derives these compound verbs ... e.g. *air-condition*, is the same which forms all compounds including synthetic compounds' (1982a: 19). This process is based on the rule $[Y \ Z]_X$, with X being a verb.

Compound verbs are recorded in the languages shown in Table 3.5.

Table 3.5. *Verb + verb compounding in the study sample*

Language	Family	Morphological type	Area
Amele	Trans-New Guinea	Polysynthetic/synthetic	Australia-New Guinea/Madang
Amharic	Afro-Asiatic	Inflectional	Africa/Ethiopia
Anejom	Austronesian	Agglutinative	SE Asia and Oceania/Vanuatu
Cirecire	Khoisan	Isolating	Africa/Botswana
Georgian	Kartvelian	Inflectional/agglutinative	Eurasia/Georgia
Greek	Indo-European	Fusional	Eurasia/Greece
Ilocano	Austronesian	Agglutinative	SE Asia and Oceania/ Philippines
Japanese	Japanese	Agglutinative	Eurasia/Japan
Ket	Yeniseian	Agglutinative	Eurasia/Russia
Luganda	Niger-Congo	Agglutinative	Africa/Uganda
Malayalam	Dravidian	Agglutinative	Eurasia/India
Mandarin Chinese	Sino-Tibetan	Isolating/analytic	SE Asia and Oceania/China
Marathi	Indo-European	Inflectional/polysynthetic	Eurasia/India
Movima	Movima	Agglutinative	South America/Bolivia
Nelemwa	Austronesian	Isolating	SE Asia and Oceania/New Caledonia
Tamil	Dravidian	Agglutinative	Eurasia/Tamil Nadu
Telugu	Dravidian	Agglutinative	Eurasia/India
Tibetan	Sino-Tibetan	Inflectional/agglutinative	SE Asia and Oceania/China
Totonac	Totonacan	Agglutinative/ polysynthetic	North America/Mexico
Tzotzil	Mayan	Agglutinative/polysynthetic	North America/Mexico
Udihe	Altaic	Agglutinative	Eurasia/Russia
Vietnamese	Austro-Asiatic	Isolating	SE Asia and Oceania/Vietnam

3.1.1.2.1 Formal characteristics Leaving aside noun incorporation (which produces verbal compounds with a noun as an argument of the incorporating verb), verbal compounds mostly include combinations of two verbs (cf. left column in Table 3.6). Following Scalise and Bisetto (2009), these can be classified as two types:

(a)   the two verbs associate two individual elements without reference to any of them as a separate entity, as in true dvandva compounds in the left column of Table 3.6, or

(b)   they express two properties associated with an entity, in this case, two aspects of action, as in the right column of Table 3.6.

Table 3.6. *Two types of reference in compound verbs*

Two elements without reference to any as a separate entity		Two properties associated with an entity	
(31) Afrikaans	*ry-loop* ride-walk 'hitchhike.v'	(32) Georgian	წა-ვიდ-წამო-ვიდ-ა c'a-vid-c'amo-vid-a PREVERB-move-PREVERB-move-S3.SG s/he-went-came 'S/he went away and returned'
(33) Ilocano	*sumurok-kumurang* go.beyond-have.less 'more or less'	(34) German	*fliesspressen* 'flow-press'[8]
(35) Nelemwa	*tâlâ-mwemwelî* hear/smell/feel- know/remember 'understand.v'	(36) Japanese	走り出る hasiri-deru run-go.out 'run out' (Kageyama 2009: 513)
(37) Vietnamese	*an³³ uəŋ³⁵* ăn uống eat-drink 'consume.v' (Thái Ân)	(38) Luganda	*so kazi* do-work 'work.v'
		(39) Marathi	करून थकलो karuuna thakalo did/done-tired 'tired of doing/tired because of doing'
		(40) Nelemwa	*fwayi tôôle* peel/skin-break the head of the fish backwards/do in the reverse sense 'skin backwards'

In Amele, these structures, very common with the verbs *q-oc* 'hit' and *m-ec* 'put', represent a borderline case. Roberts (1987: 309) maintains that, while this sort of verbal compound often has an idiomatic meaning which cannot be determined from the meanings of the constituents, *q-oc* and *m-ec* function in such expressions rather as copula verbs, because they can combine

---

[8] In technical language only (Dalton-Puffer, pers. comm.).

productively with almost any nominal and adjectival element. Examples of combinations of these verbs with another verb are shown in (41) to (43):

(41)   Amele   *cahug q-oc*
                       smell-hit
                       'be smelly'

(42)   Amele   *qel-I q-oc*
                       throw hit
                       'thunder.v'

(43)   Amele   *sanan m-ec*
                       start-put
                       'start.v'
                       (Roberts 1987: 310–12)

Hudson (pers. com.) describes a very productive process of formation of compound verbs in Amharic. The so-called *say*-composite verbs are formed with a particular form of the verb 'say' and a word of indefinite word-class (used only in these compounds and uninflected) regularly derived from another verb:

(44)   Amharic   ከፈት አለ
                       käfätt alä'
                       open-it/he.said
                       'It opened gradually'

This compound is based on the root *k-f-t* 'open' and the past tense form of the verb 'say', *alä* 'he said'. Literally, it means 'it/he said "käfätt"', where *käfätt* is not translatable alone.

In Malayalam, a highly productive process of verb + verb compounding produces 'hybrid compounds', combining an English verb and Malayalam *ceyyuka* 'do' (Asher and Kumari 1997: 404). A sort of borderline case is represented by those noun + verb compounds in Malayalam whose verbal constituent may be treated, according to Asher and Kumari (1997: 403), as a lexical or grammatical element. The source is always an abstract noun which usually expresses emotion. Verbs are formed by addition of *peṭuka* 'fall' or 'get into or under':

(45)   Malayalam   a.   *bhayappeṭuka*
                            bhayam-peṭuka
                            fear-fall
                            'be afraid'
                       b.   *aaʃappeṭuka*
                            aaʃa-peṭuka
                            desire-fall
                            'long for'
                            (Asher and Kumari 1997: 389)

Adjective + verb structures are also common in other languages:

(46)   Amele   *meeg m-ec*
dry-put
'become dry'
(Roberts 1987: 310–11)

(47)   Catalan   *malparlar*
ill-speak
'speak ill'

(48)   Japanese   近寄る
tika-yoru
near-approach
'go near'
(Kageyama 2009: 513)

Japanese also offers a variant of the adjective + verb compound. Kageyama (2009: 513) refers to AN + V compounds, where AN stands for *adjectival noun*, i.e. 'noun-like adjectives that take the *-na* inflection instead of the adjectival inflection *-i* in pronominal position' as in (49):

(49)   Japanese   高価過ぎる
kooka-sugiru
expensive-exceed
'be too expensive'

While the majority of verbal compounds leave the form of motivating constituents intact, modifications of the first stem may occur, as exemplified by Amele:

(50)   Amele   *ji fec*
jec-fec
eat-see
'taste.v'

Apart from prototypical cases characterized by the combination of two verbal stems (if we disregard noun incorporation) which also exist as independent words of a language without formal modification of the constituent stems, there are also peripheral instances of verbal compounds. Two types will be mentioned here. One is eroded roots in Ket: many finite verbs in Ket consist of an infinitive in the *incorporate* slot and a semantically eroded morpheme in the *root* slot which conveys some notion of aspect. These could be considered verbal compounds, as in (51):

(51)   Ket   *il-ba-g-a-qan*
singing-1SG.SBJ-ADE-THM-ICP
'I begin to sing'

The other peripheral case is verbal compounds in Cirecire, which can come into existence by reduplication of verbal stems, as in (52):

(52)   Cirecire   *quu~quu*
                       go/move~RDP
                       'look around, hunt'

3.1.1.2.2 Semantic characteristics As with any other type of compounds, the meaning of verbal compounds can be based on the principle of compositionality or it can be more than a mere sum of the meanings of the motivating constituents, as shown in Table 3.7.

Table 3.7. *Compositional and non-compositional meaning in verbal compounding*

Compositional meaning		Non-compositional meaning	
(53) Japanese	忌み嫌う imi-kirau detest-hate 'detest and hate' (Kageyama 2009: 514)	(54) Japanese	食べ過ぎる tabe-sugiru eat-pass.beyond 'overeat.v'
(55) Mandarin Chinese	維修 wéixiū maintain-repair 'maintain and repair'	(56) Marathi	करून बसलो karuuna basalo did/done-sit 'done (something) which is not under control after doing it'[9]

3.1.1.3 Noun incorporation

Noun incorporation is recorded in the languages shown in Table 3.8. (38.18 per cent in the study sample):

Table 3.8. *Noun incorporation in the study sample*

Language	Family	Morphological type	Area
Amele	Trans-New Guinea	Polysynthetic/synthetic	Australia-New Guinea/Madang
Anejom	Austronesian	Agglutinative	SE Asia and Oceania/Vanuatu
Clallam	Salishan	Polysynthetic	North America/USA
English	Indo-European	Isolating	Eurasia/Ireland and UK
Estonian	Uralic	Agglutinative/fusional	Eurasia/Estonia
Hebrew	Afro-Asiatic	Inflectional	Africa/Israel

[9] Meaning 'a situation beyond control'.

Language	Family	Morphological type	Area
Ket	Yeniseian	Agglutinative	Eurasia/Russia
Konni	Niger-Congo	Agglutinative	Africa/Ghana
Lakhota	Siouan	Synthetic/polysynthetic	North America/USA
Mandarin Chinese	Sino-Tibetan	Isolating/analytic	SE Asia and Oceania/China
Movima	Movima	Agglutinative	South America/Bolivia
Nelemwa	Austronesian	Isolating	SE Asia and Oceania/New Caledonia
Pipil	Uto-Aztecan	Agglutinative	North America/El Salvador
Slavey	Na-Dene	Polysynthetic	North America/Northwest Territories
Tamil	Dravidian	Agglutinative	Eurasia/Tamil Nadu
Telugu	Dravidian	Agglutinative	Eurasia/India
Totonac	Totonacan	Agglutinative/ polysynthetic	North America/Mexico
Tzotzil	Mayan	Agglutinative/ polysynthetic	North America/Mexico
Udihe	Altaic	Agglutinative	Eurasia/Russia
Wichí	Matacoan	Agglutinative	South America/Argentina and Bolivia
Yoruba	Niger-Congo	Isolating	Africa/Benin, Nigeria

Incorporation is considered here a verb-forming process whereby a nominal stem is fused with a verbal stem to yield a larger, derived verbal stem, according to the definition proposed for the purposes of our research by L. Bauer (pers. comm.). Noun incorporation follows after the section of compound verbs (3.1.1.2) because instances of noun incorporation are prevailingly viewed as compound verbs.

While a broad approach to incorporation does not seem to make a distinction between incorporation and polysynthetism, our findings are in accordance with Aikhenvald's (2007: 6, 12) observation that not all polysynthetic languages have noun incorporation and languages with incorporation need not be polysynthetic.

On the other hand, the non-existence of compounding in these languages is confirmed by the absence of incorporation. This observation corresponds with what is assumed by Leza (2001: 718), according to whom not all Amerindian languages feature noun incorporation even if they are polysynthetic. Noun incorporation is productively used in many non-polysynthetic languages.

3.1.1.3.1 Formal characteristics While the prototypical case of incorporation is nominal incorporation, specifically one in which the incorporated noun functions as an object argument of the verb, a number

of peripheral types of incorporation have been reported in the literature and
have been found in the languages sampled here.

Thus, Werner (1998: 58ff.) demonstrates that languages like Ket, Kott
and Yugh, which are Yeniseian languages spoken in Eurasia, make use of
'nominal incorporation' in which a compound adjective in the function of
the modifier and a noun as the head form a unity. The view that these expressions involve noun incorporation is supported by their ability to include possessive prefixes which are usually combined with nouns and, in certain cases,
also with verbs. Examples of this kind of nominal incorporation are given in
(57) and (58):

(57)   Ket   *qä-γit,*
                  ^{4}qä-^{2}ki$^?$t
                  big-price
                  'expensive'

(58)   Yugh   *χɛgit*
                  ^{2}χɛ$^?$-^{2}ki$^?$t'
                  big-price
                  'expensive'

Adjective incorporation also occurs in Pipil, although it is reportedly rare:

(59)   Pipil   *sek-kalaki*
                  cold-enter
                  'get cold'

A similar case occurs in Estonian, where a small group of verbs formed by
incorporation usually have as the first component an adjective stem, but a
noun is also possible. Estonian syntax prefers to express the meanings of
such nominal stems as adverbials. Thus, (60a) is more marked than (60b):

(60)   Estonian   a. *sügav-künd-ma*
                         deep-plough.v-SUP
                         'plough deep.v'
                      b. *sügavalt.*ADR *kündma.*V
                         deeply-plough.v-SUP
                         'plough deep.v'

Examples of frequently used Estonian incorporated verbs are:

(61)   Estonian *kuri-tarvita-ma*
                  evil-use-SUP
                  'abuse.v'

(62)   Estonian *häda-maandu-ma*
                  hardship-land.v-SUP
                  'force-land, make emergency landing'

Lakhota is a source of insights into various aspects of noun incorporation. The following is based on de Reuse's (1994) account of this Siouan language. In Lakhota noun incorporation is treated as a type of compounding with which it also shares phonological properties, like the following three different stress patterns:

(a)   noun incorporations with a single main stress (labelled *lexical compounds*) are controlled by the Dakota Accent Rule, which places stress on the second syllable of a word regardless of whether this syllable is a part of the first or of the second compound constituent. This type of noun incorporation is, phonologically, a tight unit, often with lexicalized meaning, and its productivity is low compared to so-called syntactic compounds,

(b)   noun incorporation with stress weakening on the second syllable of the second constituent imposed on it (as well as on the first constituent by the Dakota Accent Rule before the process of incorporation). This type is semantically more transparent and more productive. Since the former, the lexical compound type of noun incorporation, is phonologically very tight, the noun stem undergoes various phonological modifications (truncation), like voicing of the final stop (final /t/ and /č/ become /l/) and devoicing of a final fricative. Cases of coalescence of the final vowel of the first constituent and the initial vowel of the second constituent accompany both types of noun incorporation, as shown in Table 3.9.

Table 3.9. *Noun incorporation with truncation and with coalescence in Lakhota*

Noun incorporation with truncation	Noun incorporation with coalescence
(63) Lakhota *pheľiška̧* phéta-iška̧ fire-move.v.near 'be active around the fire'	(64) Lakhota *phetiška* phéta-iška̧ fire-move.v.near 'come near the fire, draw up to the fire, to warm oneself' (de Reuse 1994: 205)

(c)   noun incorporation which maps compounding, labelled *noun stripping*, because the noun 'is stripped of the articles, determiners, and case-marking elements that usually accompany it, and then juxtaposed to the verb' (de Reuse 1994: 206):

(65)   Lakhota   *napé yúzA*
          hand.INS-take.hold
          'shake hands'

(66)   Lakhota   *phá kaksÁ*
                       head.INS-cut
                       'behead.v'
                       (de Reuse 1994: 209)

Noun incorporation need not be restricted to the left-hand position of
the incorporated noun. In Clallam (68) the nominal object, expressed by
a *lexical suffix* rather than by a root, takes right-hand position. Examples
where the incorporated noun takes right-hand position can be found in other
languages too:

(67)   Anejom   *esjaalak*
                       esjañ-nalak
                       put.down-roller
                       'put down rollers (for a canoe)'

(68)   Clallam   *λəmé$?q^w$*
                       λɜm'-e$?q^w$
                       be bumped-head
                       'get bumped on the head'

(69)   Nelemwa   *thu-naar-e*
                       do-oven-TR
                       'cook it in the oven'

The position of the incorporated noun in these languages matches
Mardirussian's (1975: 384) observation that the incorporated noun attaches
to the right of the verb in verb-initial languages. Word order in Clallam is
VSO, VOS in Anejom and, in Nelemwa, 'nominal arguments come after the
predicate, either as VS (where [S] is the absolutive nominal argument of an
intransitive verb) or VOA (where O stands for the second argument/patient
and A for the agent of a transitive verb)' (Bril 2004: 500). Interestingly, the
examples from Anejom, Clallam and Nelemwa contradict the generalization
made by Caballero *et al.* (2006), according to which the order of noun and
verb in languages with unproductive noun incorporation is noun + verb,
while in languages with productive noun incorporation it follows the order
of words in syntax.[10]

3.1.1.3.2 Semantic characteristics The description of noun incorporation
mentions that an incorporated noun functions as an argument (usually
object) of the predicative verb. Remarkably, in none of the latter examples

---

[10] Caballero, G., Houser, M. J., Marcus, N., McFarland, T., Pycha, A., Toosarvandani, M.,
Wilhite, S. and Nichols, J. 2006. 'Nonsyntactic ordering effects in syntactic noun incorporation'. Manuscript. University of California at Berkeley CA.

does the noun function as an object: instead it identifies location. This has been reported in the literature both in general and in a number of languages. According to Gerdts (1998: 87), while incorporated nouns are typically related to objects or to subjects of inactive predicates,[11] they can also express locatives, instruments or passive agents and they do not generally correspond to subjects of active intransitives or transitives, to indirect objects or to benefactives. Mithun (2009: 576) remarks that the variety of relations that hold in Mohawk between the noun incorporation members is much like what we find with noun + noun compounds in English and that 'the same Mohawk verb root can ... occur with incorporated nouns with quite different semantic roles'. Similarly, Kageyama (1982: 244) claims that the incorporated noun functions as a direct object in about 50 per cent of this type of Japanese compound verbs ((70) and (73)), as an adverbial in about 25 per cent ((71) and (74)), and as a subject of intransitive predicates in about 25 per cent ((72) and (75)) (see Table 3.10).

Table 3.10. *Incorporated noun as direct object, as adverbial and as subject in Japanese*

Incorporated noun as direct object		Incorporated noun as adverbial		Incorporated noun as subject	
(70)	Japanese 骨折る hone-oru 'take pains'	(71)	Japanese 旅立つ tabi-datu 'go on a journey'	(72)	Japanese 腹立つ hara-datu 'get angry'
(73)	Japanese 手間取る tema-doru 'take time'	(74)	Japanese 背負う se-ou 'carry on one's back'	(75)	Japanese 仕方ない sikata-nai 'there is no other choice'

In line with the above, the languages sampled here show that it is not only internal arguments of verbs that can be incorporated. In Mandarin Chinese, where noun incorporation is reportedly very productive, there are, beside the default cases of object, numerous instances of the incorporated noun in other functions, as shown in Table 3.11.

---

[11] Inactive predicates are process verbs, stative verbs or adjectives (Gerdts 1998: 87).

Table 3.11. *Incorporated nouns as other than object in Lakhota and Mandarin Chinese*

Agentive subject	(76)	Lakhota	*maxpíya naxléčA wakịyą akù* (lit. 'for Thunder Beings to return') 'for a cloud to burst (the sky tears)' 'for a storm to come up in springtime' (de Reuse 1994: 221)
Goal[12]	(77)	Lakhota	*šų(g)mník²u* dog-water-give 'water horses' (de Reuse 1994: 215)
Manner	(78)	Mandarin Chinese	油 yóuzhá-yóuzhà[13] oil-fry 'deep-fry.v'
Manner adverb	(79)	Lakhota	*hịhą́ hothị̀* owl-voice-have 'hoot.v' (de Reuse 1994: 215)
Patient	(80)	Lakhota	*šųgsóta* dog-be.used.up 'for horses to die off' (de Reuse 1994: 220)
Pattern	(81)	Mandarin Chinese	瓜分 guāfēn[14] melon-divide 'divide up.v (as though cutting up a melon)'
Time adverb	(82)	Lakhota	*hą²ómani* night-LOC-ST-walk 'walk at night' (de Reuse 1994: 211)

Pipil offers examples where the incorporated noun performs the function of an instrumental prefix (83), as well as standard examples (84):[15]

[12] With two incorporated nouns.

[13] Literal.

[14] Metaphorical.

[15] Such a prefix 'is basically an incorporated noun, usually a body-part term, which semantically signals instrument by which the action of the verb is realized. These have been called instrumental prefixes because in some languages the incorporated elements appear in a changed, abbreviated form somewhat different from the full nouns from which they are derived' (Campbell 1985: 96).

Pipil is also interesting for the concentration of the most productive noun incorporation within the lexical field of body parts (cf. Mithun 1984: 860):

Pipil   *ta-teːn-naːmiki*
RDP.ITE-mouth-meet/encounter
'kiss.v'
(Campbell 1985: 98–100)

(83)   Pipil   *tan-kwa*
                    tooth-eat
                    'bite.v'
                    (Campbell 1985: 96)

(84)   Pipil   *ku:-tapa:na*
                    wood-break.v.open
                    'split firewood.v'
                    (Campbell 1985: 97)

These examples of Pipil lead to the role of locative and instrumental prefixes in noun incorporation in Lakhota. According to de Reuse (1994:
210ff.), incorporations of the structure [N+[LOC+V]] and [N+[INS+V]] are very
common. They usually co-exist parallel to prefixless noun incorporations.
The prefixed and prefixless constructions may differ in valence and meaning.
Table 3.12 presents various combinations of locative and instrumental
arguments and prefixes in Lakhota:

Table 3.12. *Combinations of noun incorporation in Lakhota*

	Without a prefix	With one prefix	With two prefixes
LOC	(85) Lakhota *čhabkhúwa* beaver-hunt 'hunt beaver'	(86) Lakhota *čhab ʔókhuwa* beaver-LOC- hunt 'hunt beaver'	
INS	(87) Lakhota *čhąté t ʔ į zA* heart-be.firm 'be stout- hearted, to be firm of heart'		(88) Lakhota *čhąté kat ʔ įzA* heart-INS-be. firm 'make one fearless'

Constructions with both locative and instrumental prefixes incorporated
by a verb (N+[LOC+[INS+V]]) are also possible (de Reuse 1994: 212):

(89)   Lakhota   *wé ayúš ʔe*
                    blood-LOC-INS-drop
                    'drop blood on (somebody)'

While noun incorporation is connected with incorporating a single noun in
the vast majority of cases, Lakhota also allows a rare case of two incorporated nouns, mostly combined with locative and instrumental prefixes. One
such example, whose structure is [N+[LOC+[N+[LOC+[LOC+V]]]]], is given
in (90):[16]

---

[16] For examples of multiple incorporation with causatives, cf. Gerdts (1998: 87).

(90)   Lakhota   *xta ʔómakhiyokpazA*
                        evening-LOC-earth-LOC-LOC-be.dark
                        'grow dusk'

In Ket (Vajda, pers. comm.), noun incorporation is limited to a handful of verb stems like *eat, make, pour* or *have*:

(91)   Ket   *d-qus-i-bet*
                        1SG.SBJ-tent-THM-make
                        'I engage in tent-making'

(92)   Ket   *san-nɔ*
                        ^{2}saʔq-^{3}qɔ:
                        squirrel-kill/die
                        'hunt squirrels'
                        (Werner 1998: 99)

What makes noun incorporation in Yeniseian languages attractive is that in the finite verb form these nominal incorporations are split into two parts: the determining constituent always assumes position 12 and the basic constituent the zero position. If the determining constituent is a compound itself, the first constituent takes position 13 and the second constituent takes position 12 (Werner 1998: 99).[17]

Noun incorporation is productive in Tamil. According to Schiffman (1996), the commonest and most general of the incorporating verbs is ஸ்ரப்ணை (*pannu*) 'make, do'. It can be added to a noun to make a verb. This is the most common way of making verbs out of borrowed English words. Sometimes Tamil even borrows words for lexical items which are already available in the language:

---

[17] Ket is characterized by a rigid template of prefix and suffix position classes, with each position reserved for a particular grammatical category. The following is a template of prefix position classes:

Prefix	Position
Subject	8
Incorporated root	7
Subject or object	6
Derivational consonant	5
Tense/mood affix	4
Neuter class subject or object	3
Tense/mood consonant	2
Subject or object affix	1
Verb root	0

However, various sources give different numbers of positions. Werner's (1998) 'maximum model' of verbal forms in Ket distinguishes 14 positions. This maximum model varies according to the specific type of verb.

(93)   Tamil   •எருஞ்சை டிரஹஉன
                    draiv pannu
                    'drive (a car)'

(94)   Tamil   னு'ன்டு'வ டிரஹஉன
                    vaakking pannu
                    'take a walk, go walking'

Schiffman explains that டிரஹஉன (*pannu*) can be attached to both nouns and verbs (usually borrowed from English), but always with the effect of having been added to nouns, i.e. what precedes *pannu* is a noun phrase in Tamil, regardless of whether it is a noun phrase or a verb phrase in English. Thus, •எருஞ்சை *draiv* in (93), though a verb in English 'drive.v', is treated as a noun in Tamil.

Noun incorporation in Slavey may be illustrated with a set of three examples (Rice, pers. comm.). In the first (95), the pre-verb and stem together mean 'sg.stand', the incorporate is -*tse* 'cry.N' and *d-* is a prefix that occurs with an incorporate indicating an oral activity. In the second, (96), the noun stem *tthí* 'head' is incorporated, the verb stem is -*chu* and the prefix *e-* is required with this. This verb without the incorporate means 'handle sg.object around'. Finally, in the third example, (97), the incorporate is *shé* 'food', because this stem does not occur independently:

(95)   Slavey   *ná-tse-de-we*
                     PREVERB-cry-QUALIFIER-STM
                     'S/he stands crying'

(96)   Slavey   *k'e-tthí-e-chu*
                     around-head-QUALIFIER-STM
                     'S/he turns his/her head'

(97)   Slavey   *shé-tiN*
                     food-STM
                     'S/he eats'

This is similar to Kwakw'ala, where there is a group of incorporating verbs that only occur with their objects incorporated (Anderson 1992: 269).

According to Pingali, in addition to prototypical incorporation in Telugu (98), a set of auxiliary verbs participate in constructing what Pingali calls 'quasi-compounds'. Auxiliary verbs also attach to English borrowings, as in (99) and (100):

(98)   Telugu   పురుగు పట్టు
                     purugu paTTu
                     insect-catch
                     'be infested by insects'

(99)   Telugu   డ్రెస్ అవ్వు
                          dress avvu
                          dress-happen
                          'get dressed'

(100)   Telugu   స్విం చేయి
                          swim ceeyi
                          swim-do
                          'swim.v'

Examples of noun incorporation in other languages are shown in (101) to (106):

(101)   Catalan   *cama-trencar*
                          leg-break-INF
                          'cause (something) to break its leg'

(102)   Greek   αφισοκολλώ
                          afis-o-kolo
                          poster-stick
                          'stick posters (on the wall)'

(103)   Tibetan   ལུག་རྫི
                          lug-rdzi
                          sheep-tend
                          'shepherd.v'

(104)   Totonac   *laka-lás-a*
                          face-slap-IPF
                          'slap (somebody) in the face'

(105)   Tzotzil   *t'šút'š-ul púšil-an*
                          small.pieces-fold.repeatedly
                          'fold (something) smaller and smaller'
                          (Cowan 1969: 95)

(106)   Wichí   *yenlhipeya*
                          o-yen-lhip-ey-a
                          3SBJ-make-piece-PL-ACC
                          make-pieces
                          'S/he chops'

3.1.1.4   Noun + noun compounds

Noun + noun compounding is recorded in the languages shown in Table 3.13.

Table 3.13. *Noun + noun compounding in the study sample*

Language	Family	Morphological type	Area
Amele	Trans-New Guinea	Polysynthetic/synthetic	Australia-New Guinea/ Madang
Amharic	Afro-Asiatic	Inflectional	Africa/Ethiopia
Anejom	Austronesian	Agglutinative	SE Asia and Oceania/ Vanuatu
Bardi	Australian	Fusional	Australia-New Guinea/ Australia
Breton	Indo-European	Fusional	Eurasia/France
Cirecire	Khoisan	Isolating	Africa/Botswana
Datooga	Nilo-Saharan	Agglutinative/fusional	Africa/Tanzania
English	Indo-European	Isolating	Eurasia/Ireland and UK
Estonian	Uralic	Agglutinative/fusional	Eurasia/Estonia
Finnish	Uralic	Agglutinative	Eurasia/Finland
Gã	Niger-Congo	Agglutinative	Africa/Ghana
Georgian	Kartvelian	Inflectional/agglutinative	Eurasia/Georgia
Greek	Indo-European	Fusional	Eurasia/Greece
Hausa	Afro-Asiatic	Fusional	Africa/Niger, Nigeria
Hebrew	Afro-Asiatic	Inflectional	Africa/Israel
Hungarian	Uralic	Agglutinative	Eurasia/Hungary
Ilocano	Austronesian	Agglutinative	SE Asia and Oceania/ Philippines
Indonesian	Austronesian	Agglutinative	SE Asia and Oceania/ Indonesia
Japanese	Japanese	Agglutinative	Eurasia/Japan
Jaqaru	Aymaran	Agglutinative	South America/Peru
Ket	Yeniseian	Agglutinative	Eurasia/Russia
Konni	Niger-Congo	Agglutinative	Africa/Ghana
Lakhota	Siouan	Synthetic/polysynthetic	North America/USA
Luganda	Niger-Congo	Agglutinative	Africa/Uganda
Maipure	Arawakan	Agglutinative	South America/Venezuela
Malayalam	Dravidian	Agglutinative	Eurasia/India
Mandarin Chinese	Sino-Tibetan	Isolating/analytic	SE Asia and Oceania/China
Māori	Austronesian	Isolating	SE Asia and Oceania/New Zealand
Marathi	Indo-European	Inflectional/polysynthetic	Eurasia/India
Movima	Movima	Agglutinative	South America/Bolivia
Nelemwa	Austronesian	Isolating	SE Asia and Oceania/New Caledonia

Language	Family	Morphological type	Area
Slavey	Na-Dene	Polysynthetic	North America/Northwest Territories
Slovak	Indo-European	Inflectional	Eurasia/Slovakia
Spanish	Indo-European	Inflectional	Eurasia/Spain
Swahili	Niger-Congo	Agglutinative	Africa/Tanzania
Tamil	Dravidian	Agglutinative	Eurasia/Tamil Nadu
Tatar	Altaic	Agglutinative	Eurasia/Russia
Telugu	Dravidian	Agglutinative	Eurasia/India
Tibetan	Sino-Tibetan	Inflectional/agglutinative	SE Asia and Oceania/China
Tzotzil	Mayan	Agglutinative/polysynthetic	North America/Mexico
Vietnamese	Austro-Asiatic	Isolating	SE Asia and Oceania/ Vietnam
Wichí	Matacoan	Agglutinative	South America/Argentina and Bolivia
Yoruba	Niger-Congo	Isolating	Africa/Benin, Nigeria
Zulu	Niger-Congo	Agglutinative	Africa/South Africa

Noun + noun compounds may appear without a linking element and with a linking element, as shown in Table 3.14.

Table 3.14. *Noun + noun compounding with/out a linking element*

Without a linking element		With a linking element		
(107)	Cirecire	*dju-bee* house-animal 'cow'	(108)	Hausa	*gida-n-saurō* mosquito-LNK-net 'mosquito net'
(109)	Finnish	*ruoka-pöytä* food-table 'dining-room' (Koivisto)	(110)	Ilocano	*bato-n-lagip* stone-LNK-memory 'monument'
(111)	Georgian	ვაჟი-შვილ- *važi-švil-* boy-child 'son' (Cherchi 1999: 4)	(112)	Māori	*waiata-ā-ringa* song-LNK-hands 'action song'[18]
(113)	Jaqaru	*wajr-qucxa* wajra-qucxa horn-lake 'horn lake'[19] (Hardman 2000: 46)	(114)	Movima	*jo'me-m-baːri* bird-LNK-ankle 'chicken foot'

[18] A song accompanied by hand and body actions.
[19] A toponym. There are many toponyms among noun + noun compounds in Jaqaru.

Without a linking element			With a linking element	
(115)	Marathi	मसाले भात masaale bhaata spices-cooked.rice 'spiced rice'	(116) Slovak	*vzduch-o-lod'* air-LNK-ship 'airship'
(117)	Spanish	*casaquinta* house-villa 'country house'	(118) Swedish	*möte-s-plats* meet-LNK-place 'meeting place'
(119)	Tatar	*esh-kuvar* work-pursuer 'businessman' (Schamiloglu)	(120) Telugu	పెంకు-టి-ఇల్లు penku-LNK-illu tile-LNK-house 'tiled house'
(121)	Tzotzil	*nukul moral* leather-bag 'leather bag' (Haviland 1980)	(122) Ukrainian	пар-о-воз par-o-voz steam-LNK-carrier 'steam engine'

This section now reviews first noun + noun compounds without a linking element and then noun + noun compounds with a linking element.

3.1.1.4.1 Formal characteristics of noun + noun compounds without a linking element In nominal compounding, the left-hand position of the modifying noun is a default case. However, the languages sampled offer alternative distributions, like right-hand position for the modifier or either position, i.e with the modifier in the left-hand position or in the right-hand position, as in the Hindi and Vietnamese examples in Table 3.15.

Table 3.15. *Modifier position in noun + noun compounding*

Modifier in right-hand position			Modifier in either position
(123)	Anejom	*inwau-kava* vine-kava 'kind of vine with leaves like those of kava'	
(124)	Indonesian	*toko buku* store-book 'bookstore' (Müller)	
(125)	Luganda	*rutan Swahili* language-Swahili (as a people) 'Swahili language'	

Modifier in right-hand position		Modifier in either position	
(126) Hindi	छाया-तरु chaya-təru shade-tree 'shade tree'	(127) Hindi	चरण - कमल cərəŋ-kəməl feet-lotus 'lotus feet' (Kachru 2006: 120)
(128) Vietnamese	$s\varepsilon^{33}\ l\mu\partial^{313}$ xe lửa vehicle-fire 'train' (Alves)	(129) Vietnamese	$th\mu\partial\eta^{33}\ x\partial w^{313}$ thương khẩu commerce-port 'commercial port' (Thái Ân)

Modifiers in compounds therefore do not always seem to be restricted to one position. Position is, however, used for a classification in some languages, like Breton, where strict compounds are right-headed (130) and loose compounds are left-headed (131) (see Table 3.16).

Table 3.16. *Strict (right-headed) vs loose (left-headed) compounding in Breton*

Strict compound (right-headed)		Loose compound (left-headed)	
(130) Breton	*morvran* mor-bran sea-crow 'cormorant'	(131) Breton	*kaz-koad* cat-wood 'squirrel'

3.1.1.4.2 Semantic characteristics of compounds without a linking element
Section 3.1.1.2 shows that the non-applicability of the principle of compositionality is not a universal feature of compounds. Further examples of noun + noun compounds whose meanings can be computed as a sum of the meanings of their constituents and which are figurative meanings are given in Table 3.17. In the table, (132) and (138) are instances of the so-called pleonastic compounds, where the head is a hyperonym of the non-head.

Table 3.17. *Compositional and figurative meaning in noun + noun compounding*

Compositional meaning		Figurative meaning	
(132) Malayalam	*roojaappuuvə* roojaa-puuvə rose-flower 'rose'	(133) Amele	*cabi gel* garden-fence 'year'

	Compositional meaning		Figurative meaning
(134) Serbian-Croatian	*krem-pita* cream-cake 'cream cake'	(135) Hausa	*birìi-bōkòo* monkey-trickery 'big but ineffective person or thing'
(136) Slovak	*zbormajster* chorus-master 'chorus conductor'	(137) Ket	*mamul* ²ma²m-¹u.l breast-water 'milk' (Werner 1998: 49–50)
(138) Telugu[20]	కొబ్బరికాయ kobbari kaaya coconut fruit 'coconut'	(139) Konni	*tɔn-yll-ŋ* bow-nail-SG 'arrow'
(140) Tibetan	སྤུ་གྲི spu-gri hair-knife 'razor'	(141) Slavey	*ta-ghú* water-tooth 'white cap'
(142) Ukrainian	*півкруг* pivkrug half-circle 'semicircle'	(143) Wichí	*poy'i-fwes* frog's-fingers 'fork'

Typical dvandva compounds in the field of kinship terms are offered by Georgian (144) and Maipure (145):

(144)   Georgian   დედ-მამ
ded-mama
father-mother
'parents'

(145)   Maipure   *ani-kiwakané*
son-father
'husband'

3.1.1.4.3 *Formal characteristics of compounds with a linking element*
Compounding with a linking element is recorded in the languages shown in Table 3.18.

---

[20] According to Pingali (pers. comm.), noun + noun compounds in Telugu also have a plural suffix inside them.

Table 3.18. *Compounding with a linking element in the study sample*

Language	Family	Morphological type	Area
Cirecire	Khoisan	Isolating	Africa/Botswana
Finnish	Uralic	Agglutinative	Eurasia/Finland
Greek	Indo-European	Fusional	Eurasia/Greece
Hausa	Afro-Asiatic	Fusional	Africa/Niger, Nigeria
Hebrew	Afro-Asiatic	Inflectional	Africa/Israel
Ilocano	Austronesian	Agglutinative	SE Asia and Oceania/Philippines
Ket	Yeniseian	Agglutinative	Eurasia/Russia
Luganda	Niger-Congo	Agglutinative	Africa/Uganda
Māori	Austronesian	Isolating	SE Asia and Oceania/New Zealand
Movima	Movima	Agglutinative	South America/Bolivia
Slavey	Na-Dene	Polysynthetic	North America/Northwest Territories
Slovak	Indo-European	Inflectional	Eurasia/Slovakia
Telugu	Dravidian	Agglutinative	Eurasia/India

Perhaps the best-known and theoretically most extensively discussed linking elements of compounding are in German, as in *Arbeitslohn*, *Alterungsprozess*, etc. The discussion about this issue usually concerns the status of *-s-*, *-n-*, *-e* and of other linking elements that are historically developed from genitive and plural morphemes (Neef 2009).[21]

However, linking elements are not an exclusive feature of a particular genetically related group of languages, in this case the Germanic genus,[22] or of a particular inflectional type or geographic area. Admittedly, links are not equally frequent in all linking languages. Thus, although they are rare in the Dravidian language Telugu, they can still be found in such languages, as shown in (146):

(146)   Telugu   పెంకుటిల్లు
         penk-u-Tillu
         tile-LNK-house
         'tiled house'

---

[21] Kastovsky (2009: 331) stresses the fact that these linking elements acted in Indo-European compounds as stem formatives and inflectional endings. In the course of time, they lost their original morphological status and developed into a purely formal compound marker. This is proved, Kastovsky notes, by modern examples where the linking elements cannot be the appropriate inflectional ending, e.g. *Liebesdienst* 'favour' (lit. 'service out of love') or *Universitätsbibliothek* 'university library', because neither *Liebes* nor *Universitäts* are genitives of feminine *Liebe* and *Universität*, respectively. For discussion on linking elements in German cf. also Lieber (1981), Becker (1992), Anderson (1992), Beard (1995), Wegener (2003), Barz (2005) or Neef (2009).

[22] L. Bauer (2009a: 406) shows that the left-hand element of Danish compounds selects a particular linking element. While rare, there are instances of two different linking elements distinguishing the meaning of otherwise identical compounds, e.g. *landmand* 'farmer' (lit. 'land-man') vs *landsmand* 'fellow countryman'.

Links appear to be mainly single-phoneme elements, either vowels or consonants. If an interfix is formed by a vowel, then it is usually a back vowel (low or mid), while for consonants there does not seem to be any pattern. Examples are given in Table 3.19.

Table 3.19. *Vocalic and consonantal links in compounding*

Vocalic link		Consonantal link	
(147)	Afrikaans	*hond-e-hok*	(148)	Ilocano	*bato-n-lagip*
		dog-LNK-cage			stone-LNK-memory
		'dog house'			'monument'
(149)	Belorussian	*краявід*	(150)	Ket	*des-t-hyʄ*[23]
		край-а-віd			eye-LNK-stomach
		krajavid			'eye socket'
		land-LNK-sight			
		'landscape'			
(151)	Greek	*λουλουδότοπος*	(152)	Slavey	*ledî-h-tene*
		lulud-ó-topos			tea-LNK-pot
		flower-LNK-place[24]			'teapot'
		'flower place'			
(153)	Māori	*waiata-ā-ringa*	(154)	Swedish	*möte-s-plats*
		song-LNK-hands			meet-LNK-place
		'action song'			'meeting place'
(155)	Serbian-	*blat-o-bran*			
	Croatian	mud-LNK-protect			
		'(car) fender'			

3.1.1.5   Exocentric compounds

Exocentric compounding is recorded in the languages shown in Table 3.20.

Table 3.20. *Exocentric compounding in the study sample*

Language	Family	Morphological type	Area
Anejom	Austronesian	Agglutinative	SE Asia and Oceania/Vanuatu
Bardi	Australian	Fusional	Australia-New Guinea/Australia
Breton	Indo-European	Fusional	Eurasia/France
Cirecire	Khoisan	Isolating	Africa/Botswana

[23] The link is an etymological possessive clitic.

[24] As noted by Ralli (pers. comm.), Greek compounds have stems as their first member. Their structure is stem + stem or stem + word and they also include a linking element -*o*- between the first and the second member. However, there are also some loose multi-word compounds, the structure of which is word + word. This category does not have linking elements.

Language	Family	Morphological type	Area
English	Indo-European	Isolating	Eurasia/Ireland and UK
Estonian	Uralic	Agglutinative/ fusional	Eurasia/Estonia
Finnish	Uralic	Agglutinative	Eurasia/Finland
Georgian	Kartvelian	Inflectional/ agglutinative	Eurasia/Georgia
Greek	Indo-European	Fusional	Eurasia/Greece
Hausa	Afro-Asiatic	Fusional	Africa/Niger, Nigeria
Hebrew	Afro-Asiatic	Inflectional	Africa/Israel
Hungarian	Uralic	Agglutinative	Eurasia/Hungary
Ilocano	Austronesian	Agglutinative	SE Asia and Oceania/Philippines
Japanese	Japanese	Agglutinative	Eurasia/Japan
Jaqaru	Aymaran	Agglutinative	South America/Peru
Lakhota	Siouan	Synthetic/ polysynthetic	North America/USA
Luganda	Niger-Congo	Agglutinative	Africa/Uganda
Maipure	Arawakan	Agglutinative	South America/Venezuela
Mandarin Chinese	Sino-Tibetan	Isolating/analytic	SE Asia and Oceania/China
Māori	Austronesian	Isolating	SE Asia and Oceania/New Zealand
Marathi	Indo-European	Inflectional/ polysynthetic	Eurasia/India
Nelemwa	Austronesian	Isolating	SE Asia and Oceania/New Caledonia
Slovak	Indo-European	Inflectional	Eurasia/Slovakia
Spanish	Indo-European	Inflectional	Eurasia/Spain
Swahili	Niger-Congo	Agglutinative	Africa/Tanzania
Telugu	Dravidian	Agglutinative	Eurasia/India
Tibetan	Sino-Tibetan	Inflectional/ agglutinative	SE Asia and Oceania/China
Tzotzil	Mayan	Agglutinative/ polysynthetic	North America/Mexico
Wichí	Matacoan	Agglutinative	South America/Argentina and Bolivia
Zulu	Niger-Congo	Agglutinative	Africa/South Africa

Compounds have traditionally been divided into endocentric and exocentric. The former are characterized by the binary structure of *determinant–determinatum* with the compound being a hyponym of its *determinatum* (head). The latter are said to have no head constituent (cf., among others, Scalise and Bisetto 2009) or zero *determinatum* (i.e. one lying outside the compound; Marchand 1960: 11) and, therefore, the compound cannot be a hyponym of the *determinatum*, e.g. English *paleface*, *redskin*, etc.

This classification has raised much debate. In this respect, the position of this book is one that these compounds are generated in the same way as endocentric compounds. Two arguments can be raised:

(a)   the psychological reasons can be found in both classical structuralist and onomasiological approaches. Marchand (1960: 11) points out the general tendency of speakers 'to see a thing identical with another already existing and at the same time different from it'. This principle, which Kastovsky (1982: 152) calls the 'identification-specification scheme' is a key to one of the fundamental principles of Marchand's and Kastovsky's theories based on the binary, syntagmatic structure of motivated words: each word-formation syntagma is based on the *determinant–determinatum* relation, where the latter identifies and the former specifies (cf. 1.1.2.). The same principle underlies the onomasiological conception[25] and Natural Morphology, although in a different way in the latter: the most natural coinages are the most diagrammatic (a new meaning is accompanied with a new form), e.g. *read-er*, where there is 'a diagrammatic analogy between semantic and morphotactic compositionality (or transparency)' (Dressler, Mayerthaler, Panagl and Wurzel 1987: 102), and

(b)   there is no reason to surmise that there is any other cognitive process underlying a small group of exocentric compounds deviating from the identification–specification scheme, because this way of conceptual analysis is the essence of naming in general. Štekauer (1998) explains exocentric compounds as a two-step process in which only the first step has word-formation relevance. It consists in the formation of an auxiliary, onomasiologically complete (i.e. with both the base and the mark included), compound complex word. The second step is based on shortening, which is sometimes not considered to be a word-formation process. By implication, this type of complex word can be analyzed on a par with the underlying full, auxiliary, version, although the latter has not come to be used (institutionalized). Hence, *redskin* can be analyzed as 'redskin + person', *sabretooth* as 'sabretooth + tiger', *garde-manger* as 'garde-manger + place' and *killjoy* as 'killjoy + person'.

    Ten Hacken (2000: 358) maintains that 'in view of their problematic nature, it is not surprising that it has sometimes been proposed that exocentric compounds are irregular and unproductive'. Contrary to this assumption, Ten Hacken (2000: 358) maintains that the English possessive adjective + noun type of exocentric compound does 'not constitute a closed class and new

---

[25] 'The phenomenon to be named is usually identified with a specific conceptual class having its categorial expression in the particular language and subsequently, within the limits of this class, it is determined by a mark. The conceptual class enters the onomasiological structure as a determined constituent – the onomasiological base, the mark as a determining constituent – the onomasiological mark. The onomasiological base may stand for a conceptual genus or a more general conceptual class' (Dokulil 1962: 29).

coinages can be interpreted on a regular basis' and the verb + noun type 'is productive in Romance languages'.

The data used here bear witness to:

(a)   a relatively strong position of figurativeness in natural languages, and

(b)   the universal tendency to a speaker-friendly (but not listener-friendly) economy of expression which at all language levels struggles with the listener-friendly and not speaker-friendly tendency towards clarity of expression.

The relative popularity of this word-formation process means that, in this particular case, the tendency towards the economy of expression overpowers the opposite trend towards the clarity of expression, even if the cumulative meaning of the constituents of many exocentric compounds is indicative of their final meaning.

Our questionnaire examined the occurrence of two different types of exocentric compounds:

(a)   the *redskin* type (meaning a 'person with a red skin' or a 'potato with a red skin'), in which the expressed constituents identify the feature of the unexpressed head (base, *determinatum*), and

(b)   the *garde-manger* type (lit. 'keep food', i.e. 'pantry'), where a verb and its object are used to denote an entity with a new meaning.

Exocentric compounding of the *redskin* type is recorded in all the languages listed in Table 3.20 except Maipure and Swahili. Exocentric compounding of the *garde-manger* type is recorded in the languages shown in Table 3.21.

Table 3.21. *Exocentric compounding of the* garde-manger *type in the study sample*

Language	Family	Morphological type	Area
Amele	Trans-New Guinea	Polysynthetic/ synthetic	Australia-New Guinea/ Madang
Amharic	Afro-Asiatic	Inflectional	Africa/Ethiopia
Breton	Indo-European	Fusional	Eurasia/France
Cirecire	Khoisan	Isolating	Africa/Botswana
Clallam	Salishan	Polysynthetic	North America/USA
Diola-Fogny	Niger-Congo	Agglutinative	Africa/Gambia, Senegal
Finnish	Uralic	Agglutinative	Eurasia/Finland
Gã	Niger-Congo	Agglutinative	Africa/Ghana
Hebrew	Afro-Asiatic	Inflectional	Africa/Israel
Japanese	Japanese	Agglutinative	Eurasia/Japan
Jaqaru	Aymaran	Agglutinative	South America/Peru
Kwakw'ala	Wakashan	Polysynthetic	North America/Canada

Language	Family	Morphological type	Area
Luo	Nilo-Saharan	Agglutinative	Africa/Kenya, Tanzania
Maipure	Arawakan	Agglutinative	South America/Venezuela
Mandarin Chinese	Sino-Tibetan	Isolating/analytic	SE Asia and Oceania/China
Nelemwa	Austronesian	Isolating	SE Asia and Oceania/ New Caledonia
Slovak	Indo-European	Inflectional	Eurasia/Slovakia
Spanish	Indo-European	Inflectional	Eurasia/Spain
Tibetan	Sino-Tibetan	Inflectional/ agglutinative	SE Asia and Oceania/China
Udihe	Altaic	Agglutinative	Eurasia/Russia
Yoruba	Niger-Congo	Isolating	Africa/Benin, Nigeria
Zulu	Niger-Congo	Agglutinative	Africa/South Africa

3.1.1.5.1 Formal characteristics Chung (1994) discusses verb + noun compounds, i.e. exocentric compounds of the *garde-manger* type, in Chinese, French and Spanish. She argues that Spanish has two predictable and invariable forms of this type of compound: the third person singular indicative form of a verb plus a plural noun (156) and the second element is not in plural. Chung, however, notes that some exocentric compounds of this type have an alternate form with a pluralized nominal constituent:

(156)   a.   Spanish   *limpiadientes*
                                  cleans-teeth
                                  'toothpick.INS'
                                  (Chung 1994: 4)
                French   *couvre-lit*
                                  covers-bed
                                  'bedspread'
                                  (Chung 1994: 10)
        b.   Spanish   *lavaplatos*
                                  washes-dishes
                                  'dishwasher.AG'
                                  (Chung 1994: 7)
                French   *garde-malade*
                                  watches-sick.person
                                  'nurse.N'
                                  (Chung 1994: 10)
        c.   Spanish   *saltamontes*
                                  jumps.over-hills
                                  'grasshopper'[26]
                                  (Chung 1994: 7)

[26] An animal.

In either case, the principles postulated by level-ordering models are vio-
lated, because inflection precedes the word-formation process of compounding. According to Spencer (2005: 74), this is frequent in Romance
languages:

(157)   Catalan   *eixugamà*
                    dries-hand
                    'towel'

(158)   Italian   *porta-lettere*
                    carries-letters
                    'postman, mailman'

(159)   Portuguese   *guarda-roupa*
                        keeps-clothings
                        'piece of furniture used to keep the clothes'

(160)   Romanian   *pierde-vară*
                     loses-summer
                     'dawdler, slowcoach'

While the number of exocentric compounds of the *garde-manger* type
is much smaller in Mandarin Chinese than in French and Spanish, their
semantics map the three basic groups identified for the latter two languages
(agents,[27] instruments and animals/plants), even if such compounds in
Chinese are 'often semantically more opaque – even to a native speaker –
than in e.g. Spanish and French' (Chung 1994: 14) (see Table 3.22).

Table 3.22. *Agents, instruments and animals/plants exocentric compounding
of the* garde-manger *type in Mandarin Chinese*

Agents	Instruments	Animals/plants

(161) Mandarin 領路
    Chinese lǐnglù
        lead-road
        'guide'
        (Chung
        1994: 20)
	(162) Mandarin 護面
	    Chinese hùmiàn
	        protect-
	        face
	        'protective
	        mask'
	        (Chung
	        1994: 14)
		(163) Mandarin 忍冬
		    Chinese rěndōng
		        endure-winter
		        'honeysuckle'[28]

---

[27] Agent nouns of this type are mainly generated by means of two productive verb elements, *sī*
'manage.v, control.v' and *lǐng* 'lead.v'.

[28] A plant that can withstand low temperatures.

Agents	Instruments	Animals/plants
(164) Mandarin 推事 Chinese tuīshì deduce- affair 'judge' (Chung 1994: 20)	(165) Mandarin 束胸 Chinese shùxiōng bind-chest 'bra' (Chung 1994: 15)	(166) Mandarin 宮 Chinese shǒugōng guard-palace 'gecko'[29] (Chung 1994: 22)

According to Berman (pers. comm.), verb + object compounds are common in Hebrew, but restricted to verbs in the so-called *benoni* form, which functions as a participial and as a present tense verb and is often lexicalized as a noun (either agent or instrument). However, it is more usual for verbs to be in an exclusively nominal pattern.

Interestingly, as noted by Chung, some Spanish exocentric compounds of this type can become a part of a new compound of the same type:

(167)   Spanish   *portaparaguas*
          (porta + [par(a) + aguas])
          holds-stops-waters
          'umbrella stand'
          (Chung 1994: 9)

Exocentric compounds are quite common in Indian languages like Malayalam (here, only of the *garde-manger* type) (168) and Marathi (169):

(168)   Malayalam   *kuttuvaakkə*
          kuttuka-vaakkə
          pierce.v-word
          'taunt.v'
          (Asher and Kumari 1997: 400)

(169)   Marathi   पिकले पान
          pikale paana
          matured-leaf
          'a person likely to die due to age'

Comrie (1989: 26ff.) maintains that the morphology of a language reflects its syntax. Chung's analysis confirms this assumption in terms of the order of the constituents of the examined compounds, i.e. the verb is followed by the noun in the SVO type of the languages examined. By contrast, in Burmese, a Sino-Tibetan language spoken in South East Asia and Oceania, and Persian, an Indo-European language spoken in Eurasia, the order of constituents in

---

[29] I.e. it protects the place it inhabits by eating insect pests.

compounds of this type is reversed, which reflects the Burmese (170) and Persian (171) SOV syntax:

(170)   Burmese   *htamin-hce*
                      rice-cook.v
                      'cook.v'
                      (Chung 1994: 23)

(171)   Persian   *jibbor*
                      pocket-take.away
                      'pickpocket'
                      (Chung 1994: 23)

Table 3.23 reviews exocentric compounds of the *redskin* and *garde-manger* types.

Table 3.23. *Exocentric compounding of the* redskin *and* garde-manger *type*

	Redskin compounds			*Garde-manger* compounds
(172)	Breton	*askell-groc'hen* wing-skin 'bat'	(173) Breton	*torr-penn* break-head 'puzzle, headache'
(174)	French	*rouge-gorge* red-throat 'robin'	(175) French	*garde-manger* keep-food 'pantry'
(176)	Greek	κοκκινομάλλης kokin-o-malis red-LNK-hair 'a person with red hair'	(177) Greek	μισογύνης mis-o-jinis hates-LNK-women 'woman hater'
(178)	Italian	*pelle-rossa* skin-red 'redskin'	(179) Italian	*porta-lettere* carry-letters 'mailman'
(180)	Hebrew	קלתדעת qalat da'at light.F.GEN-thought 'light-headed, frivolous'	(181) Hebrew	גורד שחקים gored shexakim scrapes heights 'skyscraper'
(182)	Jaqaru	*namp'-janhq'u* namp'a-janhq'u head-white 'head white'[30] (Hardman 2000: 46)	(183) Jaqaru	*um-nqu-nushu* uma-nuqu-nushu drink.v-a.lot-pur 'watering hole'[31] (Hardman 2000: 47)
(184)	Hausa	*jan-baki* red.LNK-mouth 'lipstick'	(185) Hausa	*kàs-gaushì* kill.v-embers 'fat meat'

---

[30] A corn species.
[31] A toponym.

Redskin compounds			*Garde-manger* compounds		
(186)	Lakhota	*zí-skopa* yellow-bent 'banana'	(187)	Lakhota	*blo-'í-yublu* potato-at-plough 'tractor'
(188)	Nelemwa	*bwaa nok* head-fish 'piece of wood to measure the size of the mesh'	(189)	Nelemwa	*ni thu maak* do-be.dead, death (lit. 'in do funerals') 'during the funerals'
(190)	Serbian- Croatian	*pali-drvce* burns-wood 'lucifer match'	(191)	Serbian- Croatian	*nezna-bog* not-knows-god 'non-believer'
(192)	Spanish	*cara-pintada* face-painted[32]	(193)	Spanish	*saca-corchos* pulls-corks 'corkscrew'
(194)	Tibetan	ริ་བཟང dri-bzang good-smell 'saffron'	(195)	Tibetan	རྡོ་བཟོ rdo-bzo stone-work 'mason'
(196)	Wichí	*to-fwefw-t'oj* POS.IDF-finger-hide 'finger nail'	(197)	Wichí	*chos-tilhoj* tail-carry 'scorpion'

3.1.1.5.2   Semantic characteristics The languages sampled indicate that the prototypical semantics of exocentric compounds encompasses first, human beings, animals and plants whose explicit part (i.e. surface name) refers to the characteristic quality and, second, instruments of action. This is in accordance with Chung's observation (1994) that compounds of the *garde-manger* type usually denote agents (specialized professions), instruments and animals and plants as in Table 3.23. It follows from her analysis that many exocentric compounds of this type have isomorphic equivalents in other languages. This does not mean that other meanings might not occur (see Table 3.24).

Table 3.24. *Semantic diversity in exocentric compounding*

Body part			
	(198)	Estonian	*kaksteist-sõrmik* twelve-glove 'duodenum'
	(199)	Luganda	*su ras* wool-head 'hair'
	(200)	Tzotzil	*bé-t'šit'š* trail-blood 'vein, artery'

[32] A military faction in Argentina.

Clothing item	(201)	Anejom	*incat-adgañ* pandanus-put.on.head 'hat'
Physical phenomenon	(202)	Cirecire	*xueen* thing-bright 'moon light'
Season	(203)	Hindi	पत-झड pət-jʰəɽ leaf-fall 'autumn'
State	(204)	Breton	*torr-penn* break-head 'puzzle, headache'

3.1.1.6   Coordinative compounds

Coordinative (copulative) compounds or co-compounds are in principle double-head structures, because their constituents are not related by semantic or structural subordination. Coordinative compounding of the noun + noun type is recorded in the languages shown in Table 3.25.

Table 3.25. *Coordinative compounding of the noun + noun type*

Language	Family	Morphological type	Area
Bardi	Australian	Fusional	Australia-New Guinea/ Australia
Cirecire	Khoisan	Isolating	Africa/Botswana
English	Indo-European	Isolating	Eurasia/Ireland and UK
Estonian	Uralic	Agglutinative/fusional	Eurasia/Estonia
Finnish	Uralic	Agglutinative	Eurasia/Finland
Georgian	Kartvelian	Inflectional/agglutinative	Eurasia/Georgia
Greek	Indo-European	Fusional	Eurasia/Greece
Hebrew	Afro-Asiatic	Inflectional	Africa/Israel
Japanese	Japanese	Agglutinative	Eurasia/Japan
Malayalam	Dravidian	Agglutinative	Eurasia/India

Mandarin
  Chinese
	Sino-Tibetan	Isolating/analytic	SE Asia and Oceania/
			  China

Nelemwa	Austronesian	Isolating	SE Asia and Oceania/ New Caledonia
Slovak	Indo-European	Inflectional	Eurasia/Slovakia
Spanish	Indo-European	Inflectional	Eurasia/Spain
Tatar	Altaic	Agglutinative	Eurasia/Russia
Telugu	Dravidian	Agglutinative	Eurasia/India
Tibetan	Sino-Tibetan	Inflectional/agglutinative	SE Asia and Oceania/China
Wichí	Matacoan	Agglutinative	South America/Argentina and Bolivia

Coordinative compounding of the adjective + adjective type is recorded in the languages shown in Table 3.26.

Table 3.26. *Coordinative compounding of the adjective + adjective type*

Language	Family	Morphological type	Area
Cirecire	Khoisan	Isolating	Africa/Botswana
English	Indo-European	Isolating	Eurasia/Ireland and UK
Estonian	Uralic	Agglutinative/fusional	Eurasia/Estonia
Finnish	Uralic	Agglutinative	Eurasia/Finland
Georgian	Kartvelian	Inflectional/agglutinative	Eurasia/Georgia
Greek	Indo-European	Fusional	Eurasia/Greece
Hebrew	Afro-Asiatic	Inflectional	Africa/Israel
Japanese	Japanese	Agglutinative	Eurasia/Japan
Lakhota	Siouan	Synthetic/polysynthetic	North America/USA
Mandarin Chinese	Sino-Tibetan	Isolating/analytic	SE Asia and Oceania/China
Marathi	Indo-European	Inflectional/polysynthetic	Eurasia/India
Nelemwa	Austronesian	Isolating	SE Asia and Oceania/ New Caledonia
Slovak	Indo-European	Inflectional	Eurasia/Slovakia
Spanish	Indo-European	Inflectional	Eurasia/Spain
Tatar	Altaic	Agglutinative	Eurasia/Russia

The contents of Table 3.25 and Table 3.26 comply with the observations of Wälchli (2005: 2), according to whom co-compounds are mainly found in the languages of Asia, easternmost Europe and New Guinea.

3.1.1.6.1 Formal characteristics Certain formal differences may occur between coordinative and other compound types, as in Malayalam. As pointed out by Fabb (1998: 67), coordinative compounds may have properties by which they differ from other types of compound, e.g. they do not accept gemination.

While dvandva compounds admit, theoretically, the reordering of their members without violating the meaning, the sequence of constituents is practically fixed. The fixed order is, according to Kageyama (1982: 236), determined by various linguistic, social and cultural factors.[33]

3.1.1.6.2 Semantic characteristics Semantically, not all coordinative compounds are equal in nature, with dvandva compounds representing a subclass of coordinative compounds. In spite of this, Scalise and Bisetto (2009: 36) point out that the Sanskrit term *dvandva* is often used inappropriately for the whole class of coordinative compounds. L. Bauer's

---

[33] E.g. meaning (positive comes before negative), sex (male before female), age (elder before younger) and other factors.

(2009b: 351–2) analysis of coordinative compounds distinguishes the following types (cf. also L. Bauer 2008):

(a)   translative, e.g. *Paris-Rome* [flight],
(b)   co-participant, e.g. *Russian-Turkish* [war],
(c)   appositional, e.g. *owner-director*,
(d)   compromise, e.g. *blue-green*,
(e)   generalizing, e.g. Mordvin, a Uralic language spoken in Eurasia, *t'ese-toso* (lit. 'here there', i.e. 'everywhere'), and
(f)   dvandva, which may be subclassified as additive, co-hyponymic, co-synonymic, approximate, and endocentric.

A different position is represented by Wälchli (2005), who takes inherence-based 'natural coordination'[34] as the criterion of co-compoundhood, and disregards copulative compounds which violate this principle. As a result, Wälchli eliminates from the scope of co-compoundhood types (a) to (d) of L. Bauer's classification. The analysis of co-compounds presented here is based on the approach represented by Bauer.

Thus, the meaning of coordinative compounds can be completely based on the principle of compositionality or the motivating constituents may develop a new quality. A source of the latter is Hindi, because the meaning of a number of coordinative compounds in Hindi is more than the mere sum of the meanings of their motivating words: they constitute a new conceptual meaning both in nominal and in adjectival compounds (see Table 3.27).

Table 3.27. *Non-compositional nominal and adjectival compounding in Hindi (examples by Kachru 2006: 119–20)*

Non-compositional nominal compounds		Non-compositional adjectival compounds	
(205) Hindi	गाय-बैल gay-bɛl cow-bullock 'cattle'	(206) Hindi	लाल-पीला lal-pīla red-yellow 'colourful'
(207) Hindi	माता-पिता mata-pita mother-father 'parents'	(208) Hindi	मोह-ताज moṭa-taza fat-fresh 'bulky'
(209) Hindi	दाल-भत dal-bʰat lentil-rice 'food'		

---

[34] Unlike 'accidental coordination', 'natural coordination' is the 'coordination of items which are expected to co-occur, which are closely related in meaning, and which form conceptual units' (Wälchli 2005: 5).

A similar technique can be found in other languages too:

(210)   Amele   *dana caja*
                        man-woman
                        'people'
                        (Roberts 1987: 86)

(211)   Telugu   తల్లితండ్రులు
                        tallitanDrulu
                        mother-father-PL
                        'parents'

(212)   Tibetan   ར་ལུག
                        ra-lug
                        goat-sheep
                        'domestic animals'

As noted by Kachru (2006: 120) 'a number of such compounds have one item from Indo-Aryan and one from Perso-Arabic source, both with identical meaning':

(213)   Hindi   धन-दौलत
                        dhǝn-dɔlǝt
                        'wealth'

(214)   Hindi   तन-बदन
                        tǝn-bǝdǝn
                        'body'

Conversely, the second member of some compounds may have an opposite meaning to that of the first constituent:

(215)   Hindi   देन-लेन
                        den-len
                        give-take
                        'reciprocity'

(216)   Hindi   आगा-पीछा
                        aga-pīcha
                        front-back
                        'future in light of past experience'
                        (Kachru 2006: 120)

Examples of coordinative compounds based on the compositional principle and of those which are not are given in Table 3.28.

Table 3.28. *Semantic diversity in coordinative compounding*

Coordinative compounding with compositional meaning		Coordinative compounding with non-compositional meaning	
(217)	Afrikaans	*skryfwer-skilder* 'writer-painter'	(218)	Afrikaans	*blou-pers* blue-purple 'indigo'
(219)	Bardi	*aala-bo* man's.child-woman's.child 'children'	(220)	Belorussian	генерал-маёр general-mayor 'major-general'
(221)	Belorussian	бел-а-ружовы belaruzhovy white-LNK-pink 'white-pink'	(222)	Estonian	*öö-päev* night-day 'day'[35]
(223)	Catalan	*sintactic-o-semàntic* syntactic-LNK-semantic 'syntactic-semantic'	(224)	French	*porte-fenêtre* door-window 'French window'
(225)	Dutch	*eigenaar-directeur* 'owner-director'	(226)	Hebrew	שושן פורים šušan purim old.city.in.Persia-Jewish.holiday 'purim celebrated in cities with walls'
(227)	Estonian	*must-valge* 'black-white'	(228)	Italian	*pesce-cane* fish-dog 'shark'
(229)	Finnish	*kanttori-urkuri* 'cantor-organist' (Laakso)	(230)	Lakhota	*zi-thó* yellow-blue 'green'
(231)	French	*sourd-muet* deaf-dumb 'deaf-and-dumb'	(232)	Mandarin Chinese	師兄 shīxiōng teacher-elder.brother 'senior fellow apprentice'[36]
(233)	Georgian	ზეინკალ-შემდუღებელ-ი zeink'al-šemdughebel-I mechanic-welder-NOM 'mechanic-welder'	(234)	Marathi	काळी-निळी kaaLii-niLii[37] black-blue 'black-and-blue'[38]
(235)	German	*Dichter-Sänger* 'poet-singer'	(236)	Nelemwa	*âlô ak* child/youth-man/male 'young man'

[35] Twenty-four hours.
[36] As a term of respect.
[37] L = retroflex 'l'.
[38] The colour of skin after hitting something.

Coordinative compounding with compositional meaning	Coordinative compounding with non-compositional meaning
(237) Greek *αλατοπίπερο* alat-o-pipero salt-LNK-pepper 'salt and pepper'	(238) Romanian *câine-lup* dog-wolf 'wolf hound'
(239) Hebrew ספרדית יהודית Sfaradit yehudit Spanish-Jewish 'Judeo-Spanish'	(240) Tatar *sawït-saba* container-vessel 'dishes' (Wertheim)
(241) Portuguese *bomba-relógio* 'bomb-watch'	
(242) Russian *город-герой* gorod-geroy 'city-hero'	
(243) Slovak *letec-inštruktor* 'pilot-instructor'	
(244) Spanish *mujer policía* woman-police 'police woman'	
(245) Swedish *kvinno-präst* 'woman-priest'	

Asher and Kumari (1997: 399) maintain that the compositional principle may be reflected in the attachment of the plural morpheme, as in Malayalam, where the coordinative compounds with the feature [+ HUMAN] are always in plural (suffix -*maar*). If the feature is [– HUMAN], the plural suffix -*kaḷ* is used:

(246)   Malayalam   *acchan-amma-maar*   vs   *aaṭumaaṭu(-kaḷ)*
            father-mother-PL   sheep-cattle-PL
            'parents'   'sheep and cattle'
            (Asher and Kumari 1997: 399)

3.1.2   Recursiveness in compounding

Recursive compounding is recorded in the languages shown in Table 3.29.

Table 3.29. *Recursive compounding in the study sample*

Language	Family	Morphological type	Area
Amele	Trans-New Guinea	Polysynthetic/synthetic	Australia-New Guinea/ Madang

Language	Family	Morphological type	Area
Breton	Indo-European	Fusional	Eurasia/France
English	Indo-European	Isolating	Eurasia/Ireland and UK
Estonian	Uralic	Agglutinative/fusional	Eurasia/Estonia
Finnish	Uralic	Agglutinative	Eurasia/Finland
Greek	Indo-European	Fusional	Eurasia/Greece
Hebrew	Afro-Asiatic	Inflectional	Africa/Israel
Hungarian	Uralic	Agglutinative	Eurasia/Hungary
Japanese	Japanese	Agglutinative	Eurasia/Japan
Jaqaru	Aymaran	Agglutinative	South America/Peru
Malayalam	Dravidian	Agglutinative	Eurasia/India
Mandarin Chinese	Sino-Tibetan	Isolating/analytic	SE Asia and Oceania/China
Movima	Movima	Agglutinative	South America/Bolivia
Slavey	Na-Dene	Polysynthetic	North America/Northwest Territories
Telugu	Dravidian	Agglutinative	Eurasia/India
Tibetan	Sino-Tibetan	Inflectional/agglutinative	SE Asia and Oceania/China
Totonac	Totonacan	Agglutinative/polysynthetic	North America/Mexico
Tzotzil	Mayan	Agglutinative/polysynthetic	North America/Mexico

We understand recursiveness as a repetition of a word-formation process, such as recursive conversion in (247), or a formally or semantically grounded word-formation rule, as in (248):[39]

(247)   English   *to sur'vey > a 'survey > to 'survey*
                      (L. Bauer and Valera 2005: 12)

(248)   Slovak   *mal<il><il><il>ink-ý*
                      small-DIM-DIM-DIM-DIM-M.SG.NOM
                      'very very very very small'

The latter example illustrates the repetition of a semantically based rule of diminutive-formation based on a combination of two different formally defined rules. The *-il* infixing rule is recursive and follows a single, non-recursive application of another diminutivizing rule which is based on the suffix *-ink*. Examples of recursive compounding are the following:

(249)   Afrikaans   *kat-kos-bak-winkel-venster*
                        cat-food-bowl-shop-window
                        'window of a shop that sells bowls for cat food'

---

[39] Cf. Mukai (2008) on recursive compounding and, for a comparison of English and Spanish, Bauer, L., Díaz-Negrillo, A. and Valera, S. 2009, 'Recursiveness in neoclassical compounds', paper presented at the SLE 42nd Annual Meeting, 9–12 September 2009, Lisbon.

(250)   Dutch   *hand-doeken-rek*
                          hand-towel-rack
                          'towel rack'

(251)   Estonian   *mets-maasika-moos*$_N$
                          forest-strawberry-jam
                          'wild strawberry jam'

(252)   Greek   *αγροτοελαιοκαλλιέργεια*
                          agrot-o-ele-o-kalierjia
                          farmer-LNK-olive-LNK-culture
                          'olive cultures by farmers'

(253)   Hungarian   *villany-szerelő-mester*
                          electricity-technician-master
                          'electrician'

(254)   Italian   *direzione ufficio acquisti*
                          direction-office-purchases
                          'management of the purchasing office'

(255)   Jaqaru   *wank-nayr-aqⁿi*
                          wanka-nayra-aqⁿi
                          person.from.Huancayo-eye-cave
                          'Cave of the Huanca eye'[40]
                          (Hardman 2000: 47)

(256)   Portuguese   *conta-poupança-habitação*
                          account-saving-inhabitation
                          'inhabitation saving account'

(257)   Slavey   *gah-wɛh-tlˡá-ˡe*
                          rabbit-skin-bottom-clothing
                          'rabbit skin pants'
                          (Rice 2009: 551)

(258)   Tzotzil   *pat mak na*
                          back-lid-house
                          'behind the door of the house'
                          (Haviland 1980)

Recursiveness is frequent in some languages and infrequent in others. In Germanic languages recursiveness frequently gives rise to long expressions:

[40] A toponym.

(259)   Dutch   *weersvoorspellingsdeskundigencongres*
'weather forecast experts conference'
(Don 2009: 370)

(260)   English   *bathroom towel rack*
(Selkirk 1982: 15)

(261)   German   *Riesentunnelbaumaschine*
'giant-tunnel-building-machine'

(262)   Swedish   *vägg-bok-hylle-bok-stöd*
(lit. 'wall-book-shelf-book-end')
'book end for a book-shelf on a wall'

Recursiveness is also common in languages of other families, like Malayalam, where 'native words of compounds can be combined with loans from Sanskrit, English or elsewhere' (Asher and Kumari 1997: 400):

(263)   Malayalam   *baalyakaalam*   >   *baalyakaalasakhi*
baalyam-kaalam   baalyakaalam-sakhi.F
childhood-time
'time of childhood'   'childhood friend'

(264)   Malayalam   *malakkaRi*   >   *malakkaritooʈʈam*
mala-kaṛi'   malakkaṛi-tooʈʈam
mountain-vegetable
'green vegetables'   'vegetable garden'

(265)   Malayalam   *kaiyezuttə*   +   *granthaʃaala* > *kaiyezuttə-granthaʃaala*
kai-yezuttə   grantham-ʃaala
hand-writing   book-hall
'manuscript'   'library'   'manuscript library'

Deviations from the prototypical case in our sample include:

(a)   a compound with verbal stems inserted between nominal stems:

(266)   Totonac   *kilhpi:li:tzi:lakamiyá:lh*
kilhpi:-li:tzí:n-laka-min-ya:lh
jawline-laugh-face-come-stand
'stand looking this way laughing out of the side of one's mouth'

(b)   a combination of verbal and nominal stems:

(267)   Mandarin Chinese   收音機開關
shōuyīnjīkāiguān
receive-sound-machine-open-close
'radio knob'

(c)   a combination of adjectival and nominal stems:

(268)   Tibetan   བོད་རྒྱ་ཚིག་མཛོད་
                        bod-rgya-tshig-mdzod
                        Tibetan-Chinese-Word-Treasury
                        'Tibetan–Chinese bilingual dictionary'

(d)   a present participle between nominal stems, the first of which is
               in genitive:

(269)   Finnish   *parran-ajo-kone*
                        beard-GEN-driving-machine
                        'razor'
                        (Koivisto)

(e)   a combination of various categories:

(270)   Hebrew   אַף עַל פִּי כֵן
                        'af 'al pi xen < 'af 'al pi < 'al pi
                        also-on-mouth-so < also on mouth < on-mouth
                        'nevertheless, all the more so'

(f)   a combination of an ordinal numeral with a nominal stem:

(271)   Serbian-Croatian   *prvo-bratučed*
                                 'first cousin'

(g)   one of the nouns in plural:

(272)   Telugu   ˇ కళ్ళజోడుపెట్ట
                        kaLLa jooDu peTTe
                        eyes-pair-box
                        'spectacle case'

While compounding is right-headed in the majority of languages, the most
productive compounding rule in Breton yields left-headed compounds. This
is also reflected in recursive application of such a compound rule (Stump,
pers. comm.):

(273)   Breton   *toull-maen-gad*
                       hole-stone-rabbit
                       'a vent-hole above the door in a traditional oven,
                       which was sometimes plugged with a rock called a
                       maen-gad [stone-rabbit]'

By contrast, recursiveness is strictly limited in Slavic languages, where recursive compounding is in principle unproductive and restricted to specific
cases, like copulative adjectives in Russian and Slovak:[41]

---

[41] In Dutch it is limited to noun + noun compounds and, under certain conditions, to verb +
      noun compounds.

(274)   Russian   *англо-немецко-японско-руско-венгерский словар*
anglo-nemecko-yaponsko-rusko-vengersky slovar
'English-German-Japanese-Russian-Hungarian
dictionary'

(275)   Slovak   *červeno-modro-biela* (*zástava*)
'red-blue-white (flag)'

In Konni, it is possible to add more than one adjective to a noun to form a compound. According to Cahill's (pers. comm.) data, three adjectives in a word is the maximum:

(276)   Konni   *jà-kù-yèelì-kpíí-'ká*
thing-old-white-big-the
'the old big white thing'
(Cahill 1999)[42]

Finally, in another non-recursive language, Spanish, recursiveness can be identified for some exocentric verb + noun compounds of the *garde-manger* type:

(277)   Spanish   *limpia-para-brisas*
limpia-[para-brisas]
cleans-stops-breeze
'windscreen wipers'

In some other languages, the productivity of recursive compounding is questionable, as in Lakhota, where recursiveness has been cited for noun incorporation allowing two incorporated nouns to produce the structure [N+[N+[V]]], as in (278) and (279):

(278)   Lakhota   *šų(g)mnik'u*
dog-water-give
'water houses'

(279)   Lakhota   *hįhá hothų*
owl.voice-have
'hoot.v'
(de Reuse 1994: 215)

However, these cases are controversial and, thus, Pustet (pers. comm.) maintains that cases of double incorporation as above do not appear in her database, nor in any other Lakhota source except in de Reuse's (1994) paper. Although the pattern exists, Pustet suspects that they may be idiosyncratic cases of lexicalization.

---

[42] Cahill, M. 1999. 'Aspects of the morphology and phonology of Konni'. PhD dissertation, Ohio State University, OH.

3.1.3   Word-formation base modification in compounding

Base modification in compounding is recorded in the languages shown in Table 3.30.

Table 3.30. *Base modification in compounding*

Language	Family	Morphological type	Area
Anejom	Austronesian	Agglutinative	SE Asia and Oceania/ Vanuatu
Breton	Indo-European	Fusional	Eurasia/France
Cirecire	Khoisan	Isolating	Africa/Botswana
Datooga	Nilo-Saharan	Agglutinative/fusional	Africa/Tanzania
Gã	Niger-Congo	Agglutinative	Africa/Ghana
Georgian	Kartvelian	Inflectional/ agglutinative	Eurasia/Georgia
Greek	Indo-European	Fusional	Eurasia/Greece
Hausa	Afro-Asiatic	Fusional	Africa/Niger, Nigeria
Hebrew	Afro-Asiatic	Inflectional	Africa/Israel
Japanese	Japanese	Agglutinative	Eurasia/Japan
Jaqaru	Aymaran	Agglutinative	South America/Peru
Ket	Yeniseian	Agglutinative	Eurasia/Russia
Konni	Niger-Congo	Agglutinative	Africa/Ghana
Malayalam	Dravidian	Agglutinative	Eurasia/India
Marathi	Indo-European	Inflectional/ polysynthetic	Eurasia/India
Movima	Movima	Agglutinative	South America/Bolivia
Nelemwa	Austronesian	Isolating	SE Asia and Oceania/New Caledonia
Slavey	Na-Dene	Polysynthetic	North America/Northwest Territories
Tamil	Dravidian	Agglutinative	Eurasia/Tamil Nadu

The nature of modifications varies and is manifested in diverse ways. Table 3.31 includes the types found here with examples.

Table 3.31. *Types of base modification in compounding*

Voicing of an initial fricative of the second constituent of a compound[43]	(280)	Japanese	秋空 aki-zora aki-sora 'fall-sky'

---

[43] This is true of Slavey subordinate compounds which share this feature with possessive constructions: an initial fricative of the possessed item is voiced (Rice 2009: 558).

Vowel modification in the first compound constituent, e.g. *o* to *a*	(281)	Belorussian	насаглотка nasaglotka 'nasopharix'	< *нос* nos 'nose'
Vowel change at the end of the first constituent	(282)	Georgian	ჭრელ-ა-ჭრულ-ა[44] č'rel-a-č'rul-a[44] č'rel-NMR-RDP-NMR 'colourful'[45]	
Merge of vowels	(283)	Hindi	पत्रोत्तर patrottar letter-reply (Pořízka 1972: 402)	< पत्र-उत्तर patra-uttara 'reply to a letter'
Loss of the final vowel in the first compound constituent	(284)	Swedish	*skol-hus* 'school house'	< *skola-hus*
Loss of the final consonant in the first compound constituent	(285)	Konni	*naa-bɩŋ-tɩ* cow-feces-PL 'cow faces'	< *naag-ɩŋ-tr*
Loss of the initial syllable of the second constituent	(286)	Anejom	*nataheñ-taketha* girl-woman 'young woman'	< *nataheñ-intaketha*
Shortening of the final long vowel in the first compound constituent	(287)	Cirecire	*qaretsii* foot-buttock 'heel'	< *qaree-tsii*
Regressive, manner assimilation of the consonant in the first constituent	(288)	Ket	*aqqut* lightning-road 'rainbow'	< *ekng-qot*
Regressive assimilation of place affecting the stem-final nasal consonant (ŋ) under the influence of the stem-initial consonant of the next stem	(289)	Malayalam	*aaɳ-kuʈʈi* male-child 'boy'	
Stem-final consonant doubling	(290)	Malayalam	*kaaʈʈaana* forest-elephant	< *kaaʈə-aana* 'wild elephant'
Devoicing	(291)	Tamil	விஇடடுக்காரர் viiTTukkaarar house-person 'landlord, husband'	< விஇடு-காரா viiTu-kaarar
Mutation in the second compound constituent caused by the first constituent	(292)	Breton	*morvran* sea-crow 'cormorant'[46]	< mor-bran

[44] As pointed out by Amiridze (pers. comm.), -*a* is probably a nominalizer/adjectivizer.
[45] With a negative reading, if used with clothes, when dressed tastelessly. However, with meadows full of flowers the reading of *č'rel-a-č'rul-a* is not negative.
[46] With lenition of *bran*.

Change in stress	(293)	Greek	λουλουδότοπος lulud-ó-topos 'flower place'	< lulúdi-tópos
Substitution of one liquid for another in the first compound constituent accompanied by the loss of the word-final -t in the same constituent	(294)	Nelemwa	ara-hoogo surface-mountain 'the mountain side'	< alat-hoogo
Combination of stress and tone changes	(295)	Hausa	gàashì-n-bàaki hair-LNK-mouth 'moustache'	< gaashì H-L-bàakii[47]

3.2   Reduplication

Reduplication is recorded in the languages shown in Table 3.32 (80 per cent of the study sample):

Table 3.32. *Reduplication in the study sample*

Language	Family	Morphological type	Area
Amele	Trans-New Guinea	Polysynthetic/ synthetic	Australia-New Guinea/ Madang
Amharic	Afro-Asiatic	Inflectional	Africa/Ethiopia
Anejom	Austronesian	Agglutinative	SE Asia and Oceania/ Vanuatu
Bardi	Australian	Fusional	Australia-New Guinea/ Australia
Breton	Indo-European	Fusional	Eurasia/France
Cirecire	Khoisan	Isolating	Africa/Botswana
Clallam	Salishan	Polysynthetic	North America/USA
Dangaléat	Afro-Asiatic	Agglutinative	Africa/Chad
Datooga	Nilo-Saharan	Agglutinative/ fusional	Africa/Tanzania
Diola-Fogny	Niger-Congo	Agglutinative	Africa/Gambia, Senegal
English	Indo-European	Isolating	Eurasia/Ireland and UK
Finnish	Uralic	Agglutinative	Eurasia/Finland
Gã	Niger-Congo	Agglutinative	Africa/Ghana
Georgian	Kartvelian	Inflectional/ agglutinative	Eurasia/Georgia
Hausa	Afro-Asiatic	Fusional	Africa/Niger, Nigeria

[47] I.e. with high (H) and low (L) tone.

Language	Family	Morphological type	Area
Hebrew	Afro-Asiatic	Inflectional	Africa/Israel
Ilocano	Austronesian	Agglutinative	SE Asia and Oceania/ Philippines
Indonesian	Austronesian	Agglutinative	SE Asia and Oceania/ Indonesia
Japanese	Japanese	Agglutinative	Eurasia/Japan
Jaqaru	Aymaran	Agglutinative	South America/Peru
Kalkatungu	Australian-Aboriginal	Agglutinative	Australia-New Guinea/ Australia
Karao	Austronesian	Inflectional/ polysynthetic	SE Asia and Oceania/ Philippines
Ket	Yeniseian	Agglutinative	Eurasia/Russia
Konni	Niger-Congo	Agglutinative	Africa/Ghana
Kwakw'ala	Wakashan	Polysynthetic	North America/Canada
Lakhota	Siouan	Synthetic to polysynthetic	North America/USA
Luganda	Niger-Congo	Agglutinative	Africa/Uganda
Luo	Nilo-Saharan	Agglutinative	Africa/Kenya, Tanzania
Mandarin Chinese	Sino-Tibetan	Isolating/analytic	SE Asia and Oceania/China
Māori	Austronesian	Isolating	SE Asia and Oceania/New Zealand
Marathi	Indo-European	Inflectional/ polysynthetic	Eurasia/India
Nelemwa	Austronesian	Isolating	SE Asia and Oceania/New Caledonia
Pipil	Uto-Aztecan	Agglutinative	North America/El Salvador
Slovak	Indo-European	Inflectional	Eurasia/Slovakia
Swahili	Niger-Congo	Agglutinative	Africa/Tanzania
Tamil	Dravidian	Agglutinative	Eurasia/Tamil Nadu
Tatar	Altaic	Agglutinative	Eurasia/Russia
Telugu	Dravidian	Agglutinative	Eurasia/India
Tibetan	Sino-Tibetan	Inflectional/ agglutinative	SE Asia and Oceania/China
Totonac	Totonacan	Agglutinative/ polysynthetic	North America/Mexico
Tzotzil	Mayan	Agglutinative/ polysynthetic	North America/Mexico
Udihe	Altaic	Agglutinative	Eurasia/Russia
Vietnamese	Austro-Asiatic	Isolating	SE Asia and Oceania/ Vietnam
West Greenlandic	Eskimo-Aleut	Polysynthetic	North America/Greenland
Wichí	Matacoan	Agglutinative	South America/Argentina and Bolivia
Yoruba	Niger-Congo	Isolating	Africa/Benin, Nigeria
Zulu	Niger-Congo	Agglutinative	Africa/South Africa

Reduplication can be both inflectional and derivational, although the latter is more frequent (Bybee 1985: 97).[48] Wiltshire and Marantz (2000: 557) define reduplication as a type of affixation 'in which the phonological form of an affix is determined in whole or in part by the phonological form of the base to which it attaches'. Example (296) compares non-reduplicated and reduplicated forms:

(296)   Karao   *man~bakal*   vs   *man~ba~bakal*
                            RCP.IPF-fight   RCP.IPF~PL~fight
                            'fight each other'[49]   'fight each other'[50]

A disputable point of this definition is the term *affix*, because in full reduplication it is the base that is reduplicated and, therefore, it can hardly be considered to function as an affix. Another reason why use of the term *affix* for the definition of reduplication is controversial is that each affix is a generalization in terms of the meaning applicable to a (relatively) high number of word-formation bases, unlike reduplicated elements of partial reduplication.

As a result, a number of approaches have arisen which propose alternative views. Inkelas and Zoll (2005), among others, treat reduplication as morphological copying, which brings full reduplication closer to compounding. Others (McCarthy and Prince 1994; Urbanczyk 2001) distinguish between affix-like and compound-like reduplication. The latter approach seems to be reasonable, because what is covered by the term *reduplication* are processes of a different nature. The repetition of a stem, i.e. a bilateral sign, is different from making use of a combination of phonemes which do not carry any meaning in isolation.

Himmelmann (2005: 121) states that 'reduplication is probably the most pervasive morphological process in western Austronesian languages in that it is a productive process in all of them'. Similarly, Wiltshire and Marantz (2000: 561) argue that 'reduplication plays a major role in the formation of words in members of the Austronesian family ..., while it is less common in the Indo-European family members' and that 'reduplication also seems to be found in languages of all morphological types'.

A question may be raised how to qualify languages like English in terms of reduplication. The existence of full reduplication is sometimes denied in English and only constructions of the type *helter-skelter* are cited

---

[48] In accordance with Moravcsik (1978: 301), our analysis ignores syntactic cases of the type 'very very bright'. It also ignores onomatopoetic reduplications, as in the examples below:

Hindi   *cẽ~cẽ*
            'chirping'
Hindi   *bhən~bhən*
            'buzzing'
            (Kachru 2006: 127).

[49] With two participants.

[50] With more than two participants. Cf. also example (306) for a combined reduplication–affixation process.

(Carstairs-McCarthy, pers. comm.). Formations of precisely this type are treated by Marchand (1960: 345ff.) as pseudocompounds and labelled as *rime combinations*. Marchand also identifies as reduplications so-called ablaut combinations like *chitchat* and *singsong*. Similar reduplications occur in other languages of our sample too, e.g. in German, as in *Heckmeck* 'fuss' and *ruckzuck* 'very quickly'.

Carstairs-McCarthy's position means that he disregards the existence in English of cases of complete (total) reduplications, each of whose individual parts carries a meaning of its own and contributes to the overall meaning of the complex word. In his (2004) analysis, Hohenhaus discusses cases like *job-job*, *jealous-jealous*, and others under the label *identical constituent compounding*. Hohenhaus stresses two facts:

(a)   the reduplicated constituent contributes to the modification of the basic, prototypical meaning of the simple word, and

(b)   reduplication is a genuine word-formation process.[51]

Hohenhaus also shows that the common semantic pattern for identical compounds in English is 'an XX is a proper/prototypical X' for nouns and 'XX = really/properly/extremely X' for adjectives, adverbs and verbs. Hohenhaus's review of the literature (specifically, Wierzbicka 1991 and Mau 2002) shows that this phenomenon is vivid in other languages. The sample studied here provides examples of reduplication inside and outside the Indo-European family:

(297)   Italian   *neri neri*
          'really black, very black, jet black'

(298)   Kwakw'ala   *xwɛ~xwa'k!wɛm*   <   *xwa'k!wɛna*
          'real canoe'   'canoe'

By contrast, some examples from the literature raise questions, e.g. Spanish *mina mina* and *cuidad cuidad* (Mau 2002): *mina* and *cuidad*, being noun and verb respectively, are hardly likely to be reduplicated, because they are not gradable or are not perceived as such by Spanish speakers. In fact, reduplication in Spanish is based on adjectives (301). Examples (299) and (300) illustrate a noun and a verb which could be reduplicated, even if this device is used rarely:

(299)   Spanish   *Es un coche~coche*
                      is-a-car~car
                      'It is a very good car'

(300)   Spanish   *?/*Hoy trabaja~trabaja*
                      today-work~work
                      'Today, work a lot'

---

[51] Hohenhaus is aware of the difficulties connected with distinguishing between reduplicated lexical units and mere repetition in syntax. He proposes two criteria: the contrastive frame '(I do) *not* (mean) YX, *but* XX', and interrogative co-text (Hohenhaus 2004: 305–6).

(301)   Spanish   *Es malo~malo*
                            is-bad~bad
                            'It is really bad'

These and other examples demonstrate that 'at least within the realm of Indo-European languages, including Germanic, Romance and Slavic languages, the phenomenon does have some footing' (Hohenhaus 2004: 319). What matters, however, is the cross-linguistic semantic unity of this type of reduplication, captured above.

Reduplication need not occur as the only word-formation process in a naming act (Inkelas 2006: 417). Table 3.33 shows several possibilities in which reduplication accompanies, or is accompanied by, another process in various languages.

Table 3.33. *Reduplication and affixation, and reduplication and compounding*

Reduplication and affixation[52]		Reduplication and compounding	
(302) Gã	*tsO-mO~tsO-mOi* [53] turn.over-ITE/PL~turn.over-ITE/PL 'turn over and over, many things in many places'	(303) Mandarin Chinese	小鞋鞋 xiǎoxiéxié [54] little-shoe(s)~shoe(s) 'shoesies'
(304) Indonesian	*buah~buah-an* < *buah* fruit~fruit-IFL 'various sorts of fruit' 'fruit'	(305) Tzotzil	*tĭʔ- tĭʔ-náb* edge~edge-deep.water 'lake shore, ocean shore' (Cowan 1969: 95)
(306) Karao	*t~<in>~oo-too* RDP<in>~too 'doll, statue' [55]		
(307) Konni	*di~digi-rú* RDP~cook-AG 'cook'		

---

[52] As observed by Cahill (1999: 58), agentive derivations in Konni take, besides the agentive suffix, 'a reduplicative prefix consisting of the first consonant of the stem and a high vowel that generally agrees in roundness (or the [dorsal] nature) ... and atr with the following stem'.

[53] The reduplicated element is an affixed stem: the suffix *-mO* is used to derive the iterative/pluractional form of the verb. The reduplicated form then takes the suffix *-i* (Kropp Dakubu, pers. comm.).

[54] Only in baby talk (Chung, pers. comm.).

[55] The root is *too* [toʔo] 'person'. In the case of *_tinootoo_*, the reduplicated portion appears to be the whole word. It should be noted that in Karao a sequence of vowels is always separated by a glottal stop, which is not represented orthographically because it is predictable. Therefore, *_too_* is phonetically [toʔo] (Brainard, pers. comm.).

In Tzotzil, reduplication may also be combined with a suffix attached to so-called stative stems. If a stative stem combines with the suffix *-tik* 'pretty ...', 'somewhat ...', it is always formed by root reduplication. Such a reduplicated form never occurs alone (308):

(308)   Tzotzil   *sák~sák-tik*
                      white~white-somewhat
                      'whitish'
                      (Cowan 1969: 103)

Tzotzil also provides an example of reduplication of an affixed stem, the so-called radical (309):

(309)   Tzotzil   *mákan~mákan*
                      repeatedly.close.off~repeatedly.close.off
                      'keep on taking over (as land)'

Reduplication in Jaqaru is interesting in several respects:

(a)   in all of its cases it is complete, but the morphophonological rule causes the last vowel in the reduplicated preposed constituent to drop,
(b)   it may be based on both roots (310) and stems (311), and
(c)   the reduplication of intensive adjectives includes a linking element *-y-* giving the structure C1V1C2V2*y*C1V1C2V2 (312), while the reduplication of intensive verbs includes the linking element *-x-* resulting in the structure C1V1C2V2*ch*C1V1C2V2 (313):

(310)   Jaqaru   *ut~uta*
                     RDP~house
                     'place where there are many houses'

(311)   Jaqaru   *taj-nuq~taj-nuqu*
                     RDP~step.on
                     'walk step by step, very carefully'

(312)   Jaqaru   *janhq'u~y~janhq'u*
                     white-LNK-white
                     'very white'

(313)   Jaqaru   *jayra~ch~jayra*
                     dance~LNK~dance
                     'dance untiringly'

3.2.1   Types of reduplication

Structurally, we distinguish two basic types of reduplication, complete and partial.[56] Complete reduplication is recorded in the languages shown in Table 3.34.

Table 3.34. *Complete reduplication in the study sample*

Language	Family	Morphological type	Area
Amele	Trans-New Guinea	Polysynthetic/synthetic	Australia-New Guinea/ Madang
Amharic	Afro-Asiatic	Inflectional	Africa/Ethiopia
Anejom	Austronesian	Agglutinative	SE Asia and Oceania/ Vanuatu
Bardi	Australian	Fusional	Australia-New Guinea/ Australia
Cirecire	Khoisan	Isolating	Africa/Botswana
Clallam	Salishan	Polysynthetic	North America/USA
Dangaléat	Afro-Asiatic	Agglutinative	Africa/Chad
Datooga	Nilo-Saharan	Agglutinative/fusional	Africa/Tanzania
Diola-Fogny	Niger-Congo	Agglutinative	Africa/Gambia, Senegal
English	Indo-European	Isolating	Eurasia/Ireland and UK
Gã	Niger-Congo	Agglutinative	Africa/Ghana
Georgian	Kartvelian	Inflectional/agglutinative	Eurasia/Georgia
Hausa	Afro-Asiatic	Fusional	Africa/Niger, Nigeria
Hebrew	Afro-Asiatic	Inflectional	Africa/Israel
Ilocano	Austronesian	Agglutinative	SE Asia and Oceania/ Philippines
Indonesian	Austronesian	Agglutinative	SE Asia and Oceania/ Indonesia
Japanese	Japanese	Agglutinative	Eurasia/Japan
Jaqaru	Aymaran	Agglutinative	South America/Peru
Kalkatungu	Australian- Aboriginal	Agglutinative	Australia-New Guinea/ Australia
Karao	Austronesian	Inflectional/polysynthetic	SE Asia and Oceania/ Philippines
Konni	Niger-Congo	Agglutinative	Africa/Ghana
Kwakw'ala	Wakashan	Polysynthetic	North America/Canada
Luganda	Niger-Congo	Agglutinative	Africa/Uganda
Luo	Nilo-Saharan	Agglutinative	Africa/Kenya, Tanzania
Mandarin Chinese	Sino-Tibetan	Isolating/analytic	SE Asia and Oceania/ China
Māori	Austronesian	Isolating	SE Asia and Oceania/ New Zealand

[56] Rubino (2005c) is a useful outline of various types and semantic functions of reduplication.

Language	Family	Morphological type	Area
Marathi	Indo-European	Inflectional/polysynthetic	Eurasia/India
Slovak	Indo-European	Inflectional	Eurasia/Slovakia
Swahili	Niger-Congo	Agglutinative	Africa/Tanzania
Tamil	Dravidian	Agglutinative	Eurasia/Tamil Nadu
Tatar	Altaic	Agglutinative	Eurasia/Russia
Telugu	Dravidian	Agglutinative	Eurasia/India
Tibetan	Sino-Tibetan	Inflectional/agglutinative	SE Asia and Oceania/ China
Tzotzil	Mayan	Agglutinative/polysynthetic	North America/Mexico
Udihe	Altaic	Agglutinative	Eurasia/Russia
Vietnamese	Austro-Asiatic	Isolating	SE Asia and Oceania/ Vietnam
Yoruba	Niger-Congo	Isolating	Africa/Benin, Nigeria
Zulu	Niger-Congo	Agglutinative	Africa/South Africa

Table 3.34 shows that complete reduplication is widespread in the sample. Bourchier (2008) also reports a high percentage (87 per cent) in her research into thirty languages.[57] As we will see with other reduplication data, our data and Bourchier's are very similar. What makes this agreement even more surprising is that her research encompasses both inflectional and derivational categories. It may therefore be assumed that, if present in a language, reduplication is used for both inflectional and derivational purposes.

Partial reduplication is recorded in the languages shown in Table 3.35.

Table 3.35. *Partial reduplication in the study sample*

Language	Family	Morphological type	Area
Amele	Trans-New Guinea	Polysynthetic/synthetic	Australia-New Guinea/ Madang
Amharic	Afro-Asiatic	Inflectional	Africa/Ethiopia
Anejom	Austronesian	Agglutinative	SE Asia and Oceania/ Vanuatu
Bardi	Australian	Fusional	Australia-New Guinea/ Australia
Cirecire	Khoisan	Isolating	Africa/Botswana
Clallam	Salishan	Polysynthetic	North America/USA
Dangaléat	Afro-Asiatic	Agglutinative	Africa/Chad
Datooga	Nilo-Saharan	Agglutinative/fusional	Africa/Tanzania
Diola-Fogny	Niger-Congo	Agglutinative	Africa/Gambia, Senegal
English	Indo-European	Isolating	Eurasia/Ireland and UK

[57] Bourchier, L. 2008. 'Re-dupli-ca-cate this'. Unpublished manuscript. Wellington: Victoria University.

Language	Family	Morphological type	Area
Gã	Niger-Congo	Agglutinative	Africa/Ghana
Georgian	Kartvelian	Inflectional/agglutinative	Eurasia/Georgia
Hausa	Afro-Asiatic	Fusional	Africa/Niger, Nigeria
Hebrew	Afro-Asiatic	Inflectional	Africa/Israel
Ilocano	Austronesian	Agglutinative	SE Asia and Oceania/ Philippines
Indonesian	Austronesian	Agglutinative	SE Asia and Oceania/ Indonesia
Kalkatungu	Australian- Aboriginal	Agglutinative	Australia-New Guinea/ Australia
Karao	Austronesian	Inflectional/polysynthetic	SE Asia and Oceania/ Philippines
Konni	Niger-Congo	Agglutinative	Africa/Ghana
Kwakw'ala	Wakashan	Polysynthetic	North America/Canada
Mandarin Chinese	Sino-Tibetan	Isolating/analytic	SE Asia and Oceania/ China
Māori	Austronesian	Isolating	SE Asia and Oceania/ New Zealand
Marathi	Indo-European	Inflectional/polysynthetic	Eurasia/India
Movima	Movima	Agglutinative	South America/Bolivia
Nelemwa	Austronesian	Isolating	SE Asia and Oceania/ New Caledonia
Pipil	Uto-Aztecan	Agglutinative	North America/El Salvador
Tamil	Dravidian	Agglutinative	Eurasia/Tamil Nadu
Tatar	Altaic	Agglutinative	Eurasia/Russia
Telugu	Dravidian	Agglutinative	Eurasia/India
Totonac	Totonacan	Agglutinative/polysynthetic	North America/Mexico
Vietnamese	Austro-Asiatic	Isolating	SE Asia and Oceania/ Vietnam
Yoruba	Niger-Congo	Isolating	Africa/Benin, Nigeria
Zulu	Niger-Congo	Agglutinative	Africa/South Africa

Specifically, partial preposing reduplication is recorded in the languages shown in Table 3.36.

Table 3.36. *Partial preposing reduplication in the study sample*

Language	Family	Morphological type	Area
Amele	Trans-New Guinea	Polysynthetic/synthetic	Australia-New Guinea/ Madang
Anejom	Austronesian	Agglutinative	SE Asia and Oceania/ Vanuatu

Language	Family	Morphological type	Area
Cirecire	Khoisan	Isolating	Africa/Botswana
Clallam	Salishan	Polysynthetic	North America/USA
Datooga	Nilo-Saharan	Agglutinative/fusional	Africa/Tanzania
Gã	Niger-Congo	Agglutinative	Africa/Ghana
Georgian	Kartvelian	Inflectional/agglutinative	Eurasia/Georgia
Hausa	Afro-Asiatic	Fusional	Africa/Niger, Nigeria
Ilocano	Austronesian	Agglutinative	SE Asia and Oceania/ Philippines
Indonesian	Austronesian	Agglutinative	SE Asia and Oceania/ Indonesia
Karao	Austronesian	Inflectional/polysynthetic	SE Asia and Oceania/ Philippines
Konni	Niger-Congo	Agglutinative	Africa/Ghana
Kwakw'ala	Wakashan	Polysynthetic	North America/Canada
Mandarin Chinese	Sino-Tibetan	Isolating/analytic	SE Asia and Oceania/ China
Māori	Austronesian	Isolating	SE Asia and Oceania/ New Zealand
Marathi	Indo-European	Inflectional/polysynthetic	Eurasia/India
Movima	Movima	Agglutinative	South America/Bolivia
Nelemwa	Austronesian	Isolating	SE Asia and Oceania/ New Caledonia
Pipil	Uto-Aztecan	Agglutinative	North America/El Salvador
Tatar	Altaic	Agglutinative	Eurasia/Russia
Telugu	Dravidian	Agglutinative	Eurasia/India
Tibetan	Sino-Tibetan	Inflectional/agglutinative	SE Asia and Oceania/ China
Vietnamese	Austro-Asiatic	Isolating	SE Asia and Oceania/ Vietnam
Yoruba	Niger-Congo	Isolating	Africa/Benin, Nigeria
Zulu	Niger-Congo	Agglutinative	Africa/South Africa

Partial postposing reduplication is recorded in the languages shown in Table 3.37.

Table 3.37. *Partial postposing reduplication in the study sample*

Language	Family	Morphological type	Area
Amele	Trans-New Guinea	Polysynthetic/synthetic	Australia-New Guinea/ Madang
Bardi	Australian	Fusional	Australia-New Guinea/ Australia
Dangaléat	Afro-Asiatic	Agglutinative	Africa/Chad

Language	Family	Morphological type	Area
Diola-Fogny	Niger-Congo	Agglutinative	Africa/Gambia, Senegal
Georgian	Kartvelian	Inflectional/agglutinative	Eurasia/Georgia
Hebrew	Afro-Asiatic	Inflectional	Africa/Israel
Kalkatungu	Australian-Aboriginal	Agglutinative	Australia-New Guinea/Australia
Mandarin Chinese	Sino-Tibetan	Isolating/analytic	SE Asia and Oceania/China
Māori	Austronesian	Isolating	SE Asia and Oceania/New Zealand
Nelemwa	Austronesian	Isolating	SE Asia and Oceania/New Caledonia
Tamil	Dravidian	Agglutinative	Eurasia/Tamil Nadu
Telugu	Dravidian	Agglutinative	Eurasia/India
Tibetan	Sino-Tibetan	Inflectional/agglutinative	SE Asia and Oceania/China
Totonac	Totonacan	Agglutinative/polysynthetic	North America/Mexico
Vietnamese	Austro-Asiatic	Isolating	SE Asia and Oceania/Vietnam

The occurrence of both partial preposing and partial postposing reduplication is again similar to what is reported in Bourchier (2008). Infixation is the only type of reduplication for which our data differ considerably from Bourchier's. Infixing reduplication is recorded in the languages shown in Table 3.38.

Table 3.38. *Infixing reduplication in the study sample*

Language	Family	Morphological type	Area
Amele	Trans-New Guinea	Polysynthetic/synthetic	Australia-New Guinea/Madang
Amharic	Afro-Asiatic	Inflectional	Africa/Ethiopia
Hebrew	Afro-Asiatic	Inflectional	Africa/Israel
Ilocano	Austronesian	Agglutinative	SE Asia and Oceania/Philippines
Movima	Movima	Agglutinative	South America/Bolivia

While our data comply with the general resistance of languages to the violation of the integrity of stem (root) morphemes, Bourchier's data diverge markedly, also because infixing reduplication occurs in languages which do not permit infixation proper: 'the prevalence of infixation within reduplication remains an unresolved issue. It is not clear why infixation should be more readily permitted for reduplicated morphemes than for fixed-segment morphemes, especially given that both cause the same disturbance to root integrity and prosody' (Bourchier 2008: 14).

3.2.1.1   Formal characteristics

Roberts (1991) notes that reduplications like those in (314) and (315) have a reduplicated stem:

(314)   Amele   *budu~bada~ec*   <   *buduec*
                        'thud repeatedly in a haphazard manner'

(315)   Amele   *fag~fug~doc*   <   *fagdoc*
                        'stick repeatedly in a haphazard manner'

This indicates the repeated action (iterative aspect), and then a vowel alternation which indicates the haphazard manner of the repeated action. Without vowel alternation in the reduplicated formant, the meaning is 'repeated action', whereas with vowel alternation, the meaning is 'repeated action + irregular motion'. Thus, a process of vowel alternation indicates a grammatical category of 'irregular motion'. The meaning of this 'irregular motion' category will be different for the context of the action expressed by each verb. The form of the alternation is different depending on the operative vowel in the verb stem. According to Roberts, eight possibilities have been observed (see Table 3.39).

Table 3.39. *Vowel alternation in reduplication in Amele*

/u/		/a/
/u/		/i/
/a/		/u/
/i/	>	/u/
/i/		/o/
/i/		/a/
/o/		/i/
/e/		/u/

Some languages, like Amele (Roberts 1991) or Indonesian, make use of both complete and partial reduplication. The following are some examples of complete reduplication in Indonesian and Karao:

(316)   Indonesian   *jalan~jalan*
                    walk~walk
                    'walk around'

(317)   Karao   *Otik-otik   moy   sakbat na   charat say*
                        little.by.little ERG.2SG-ABS carry   GEN sand   so.that

> eg   ka   mebdiy   a   chakos
> NEG ABS.2SG PAS.IRR-tired LNK   right.away
> 'You carry the sand bit by bit so that you will not get tired right away'[58]

In Amele, complete reduplication can be divided into whole-word reduplication (including inflectional morpheme) and whole-stem reduplication. While the former applies to all major word-classes, the latter only applies to verbs. Examples are given in Table 3.40.

Table 3.40. *Whole-word and whole-stem reduplication in Amele by word-class*

	Whole-word reduplication			Whole-stem reduplication	
Nouns (non-possessed)	(318)	Amele	*bagac~bagac* leaf~leaf 'thin'		
Nouns (possessed)	(319)	Amele	*ʔebinag~ʔebinag* sibling~sibling 'brother and sister'		
Pronouns	(320)	Amele	*oso~oso* one~one 'anyone'		
Adjectives	(321)	Amele	*nag~nag* small~small 'very small, many small things'		
Verbs	(322)	Amele	*feʔ~feʔ* see~see 'seeing'	(323) Amele	*budu~<bada>~ena* it.thuds~RDP 'it thuds sporadically'

By contrast, partial reduplication in Amele is primarily leftward from the base form, probably as a compensating device for the absence of prefixation, because regular inflection is by suffixation (Roberts 1991: 120).[59] Roberts

---

[58] According to Brainard (pers. comm.), Karao, like many Northern Philippine languages, has a number of reduplication patterns that occur in both verbs and nouns. In (317), the adjective *otik* 'little' or 'few' can function as a verb of manner when it is completely reduplicated as *otik-otik* 'little by little'.

[59] According to Roberts, partial rightward reduplication is also possible. It involves so-called mirror-image reduplication. A CV string becomes a reduplicated VC string with an epenthetic glottal stop inserted. Mirror-image reduplication occurs with some of the locative pronouns and also with some of the postpositions:

> Amele   *ene-ʔ~en*
>   here~RDP
>   'It is here'

demonstrates that leftward reduplication usually copies the first CV of the base form (324) and (325), but V and VC types also exist (326):

(324)   Amele   *da~dahig*
                          RDP~his.ear
                          'ears of everyone'

(325)   Indonesian   *le~laki*
                               RDP~husband
                               'man'[60]

(326)   Amele   *ab~abale?*
                          RDP~search.with.hands
                          'search repeatedly with hands'

Partial infixing reduplication is also present in Amele:

(327)   Amele   *a~<me>~meg*   <   *ameg*
                          his eyes
                          'the eyes of everyone'   'his eyes'

Example (328) illustrates partial preposing reduplication in Karao:

(328)   Karao   *me~so~sodok*
                          me-RDP~solok
                          STA.IRR-DIM-more.than
                          'be a little more than'

Specific cases can be found concerning reduplication, e.g. reduplication in Nelemwa can also be accompanied by stem modification:

(329)   Nelemwa   *ko~xole*
                            ko~kole
                            RDP~throw.away/empty
                            'scatter, spread, sow'

Reduplication is most frequently used with verbs and nouns, but other word-classes are also possible, mainly adjectives. The word-formation reduplication of adverbs, pronouns and numerals is relatively rare, in descending order. Reduplication is productive in Amele (Roberts, pers. comm.) and in Japanese (Kimenyi 2008). In the latter it is especially so with stem reduplication of words that consist of two syllables. This complies with the

---

[60] In Indonesian partial reduplication is based on the repetition of the initial stem syllable with vowels usually being reduced. Full reduplication is much more productive in word-formation (Mojdl 2006: 73). Reduplication may also occur in compound words (Mojdl 2006: 78):

    Indonesian   *surat-khabar~surat-khabar*
                    letter-news~letter-news
                    'newspaper'

cross-linguistic preference for a disyllabic foot melodic template as suggested in Mutaka and Hyman (1990). All types of words (verbs, nouns, adjectives, numerals, adverbs, pronouns, prepositions) can occur in the reduplicated form. Examples in (330) and (331) illustrate disyllabic structures and examples in (332) and (333) illustrate double reduplication in Japanese in which words with two independent stems reduplicate them both:

(330)   Japanese   ヒリヒリ
                     hiri~hiri
                     'taste hot'

(331)   Japanese   生き生き
                     iki~iki
                     'lively, fresh'

(332)   Japanese   正々堂々
                     sei~sei~dô~dô
                     'play fair and square'

(333)   Japanese   戦々恐々
                     sen~sen~kyô~kyô
                     'with fear and trembling'

As illustrated by Kimenyi, the Rendaku rule, the voicing of the consonant of the first syllable in Japanese compounds, also applies in reduplication:

(334)   Japanese   はるばる
                     haru~baru
                     'all the way'

(335)   Japanese   軽々
                     karu~garu
                     'easily, without any effort'[61]

Some languages, like Pipil, make use of partial reduplication only. Apart from using reduplication for the expression of plurality, it is frequently used with verbs. As stated by Campbell (1985: 80), reduplication in verbs can be of two types:

> both reduplicate the initial consonant(s) and the first vowel of the root, or only the vowel if no consonant occurs. In both cases the vowel is short. They differ in that one has only this form (i.e. CV-) while the other takes an additional *h* (i.e. CVh-). The latter is quite productive ... The former (CV-) is not productive, but many examples of it exist, typically with *-ka*, or *-tsa* verbs ... It means that plural objects or repetition of the action are involved.

---

[61] For a detailed analysis of reduplication in Japanese, cf. Kimenyi (2008).

Relevant examples are:

(336)   Pipil   a. *ki~kinaka*
                     'complain.v'
                  b. *tu~tu:nia*
                     'heat.v'
                  c. *tsu~tsu:na*
                     'play (a musical instrument)'

(337)   Pipil   *ah~ahwa*
                  RDP-bark.v, scold.v
                  'scold.v, bark.v'

(338)   Pipil   *pah~pachua*
                  RDP-hold.down.v
                  'press.v'

In addition, reduplication is also used with the so-called diffusion verbs[62] to express repetition. If the verb is intransitive, it ends in *-ka* and, if it is transitive, it ends in *-tsa* (see Table 3.41).

Table 3.41. *Intransitive and transitive verbs with reduplication in Pipil*

	Diffusion verb		Intransitive		Transitive
(339) Pipil	*kwala:ni* 'get angry'	>	*kwa~kwalaka* 'boil.v'	>	*kwa~kwalatsa* 'boil.v'
(340) Pipil	*tsili:ni* 'ring.v'	>	*ih~tsilika* 'tremble.v'	>	*ih~tsilitsa* 'shake.v, ring.v' (Campbell 1985: 91)

Kwakw'ala has formally a highly differentiated system of complete and partial reduplication, where partial preposing reduplication includes a number of cases (Boas 1947: 220).[63] Hindi can completely reduplicate nouns (341), adjectives (342), participles (343) and adverbs (344) and participles admit partial preposing reduplication (Kachru 2006: 122):

(341)   Hindi   घर ~घर
                  ghər~ ghər
                  house~house
                  'every house'

(342)   Hindi   ताजे ~ताज
                  taze~taze

---

[62] Campbell uses the term *diffusion verbs* to refer to all verbs of sound (including verbs denoting action which produces sounds, such as breaking and tearing).

[63] For a thorough overview, cf. Boas (1947: 220ff.).

fresh~fresh
'each one fresh'

(343)   Hindi   लिख ~लिखकर
likh~likh kər
'having written repeatedly'

(344)   Hindi   पल ~पल
pəl~pəl
'every moment'

Ambiguous cases can also be found concerning the existence or not of reduplication in a given language. According to Schiffman (1996) in Tamil, as in other South Asian languages, there is a kind of reduplication process which consists in taking a lexical item and following it with the same item reduplicated, except that the first consonant and vowel are replaced by the CV sequence. The general meaning of this construction is '(item) and other things like it':

(345)   Tamil   ஐறி' டி'றி
puli~kili
'tigers and other beasts'
(Schiffman 1996)

(346)   Tamil   ஐளு·ஹ்பு டி'ளு·ஹ்பு
paratte~kiratte
'nasty words, aspersions, etc.'
(Schiffman 1996)

Schiffman also gives examples of the distributive function of reduplication aimed at specifying different kinds of things, at linking different things in a certain relationship or at distributing qualities among various members of a set of things. In this case, reduplication is complete (the final vowel of the first constituent and the initial vowel of the second constituent merge):

(347)   Tamil   அவன்க்~அவன்க
avang~avanga
RDP~avanga
'all kinds of different people'
(Schiffman 1996)

(348)   Tamil   அத்~அது
ad~adu
RDP~adu
'each and every thing'
(Schiffman 1996)

Another ambiguous case is that of Dangaléat, where the separation inflection vs derivation is involved. According to Shay (pers. comm.), there is

some evidence of derivational reduplication in verb stems of Dangaléat
with the structure C1VC2C1VC2. These represent rightward reduplication
of the root consonants and insertion of a high vowel, which matches the
final consonant for the feature [+ ROUND]. The newly formed syllable has the
same tone as the original syllable. Reduplicated verb stems show evidence of
derivation from both Dangaléat and Arabic:

(349)   Dangaléat   *bòrbìre*
                        comm[64]~RDP
                        dry-TR~RDP
                        'cool off-INTR'

(350)   Dangaléat   *làwlùwe*
                        lawwa[65]~RDP
                        bend~RDP
                        'roll up'

In Shay's view, such reduplication may once have been inflectional, e.g. to
encode plurality or intensity of an event.

A final case of ambiguity of reduplication involves the distinction between
compounding and reduplication. Thái Ân (pers. comm.) notes that sometimes there is no clear distinction between compounding and reduplication
in Vietnamese. An example of indisputable reduplication is given in (351):

(351)   Vietnamese $ɲɛ^{21}$ $ɲɛ^{31ʔ}$
                        nhè~nhẹ.ADV
                        RDP~light
                        'gently, lightly'
                        (Thái Ân)

Finally, reduplication may be recursive. The literature cites several cases:
Harrison (1973: 426),[66] Moravcsik (1978: 301)[67] and Wiltshire and Marantz
(2000: 559)[68] speak of 'triplication' and Rose (2003: 114) cites examples of

---

[64] Possible source from Dangaléat.

[65] Possible source from Chadian Arabic, an Afro-Asiatic language spoken in Africa.

[66] Triplication in Mokilese, an Austronesian language spoken in South East Asia and Oceania,
here expresses continuative. Reduplication expresses progressive aspect:

Mokilese	*roar*	*roar~roar*	*roar~roar~roar*
	'give a shudder'	'be shuddering'	'continue to shudder'

[67] Triplication in Mokilese here illustrates continuous action:

Mokilese	*rik sakai*	vs	*rik~rik~rik sakai*
	'gather stones'		'continue to gather stones'

[68] These authors illustrate it in reference to Zhang's (1987: 379) example of adjectives whose
semantics is different from reduplication in the Southern Min dialect of Chinese, also
known as *Taiwanese*:

Taiwanese	*ang*	*ang~ang*	*ang~ang~ang*
	'red'	'reddish'	'extremely red'

Tigré, an Afro-Asiatic language spoken in Africa.[69] That these cases are not rare also follows from Moravcsik's (1978: 312) observation of 'instances of multiple reduplication in many languages and possibly in all', even if this claim seems to be rather strong. The existence of recursive reduplication has been expressly denied for several languages (e.g. Ilocano, Karao or Telugu). In Hausa, triplication is not common according to Newman (pers. comm.), although it does occur with ideophones. As far as the sample studied here is concerned, examples of recursive reduplication may be found in Slovak diminutives, as in (248).

As to the distribution of the reduplicated material, as maintained by Wiltshire and Marantz (2000: 560), 'the position of the material in the base that is copied in reduplication may vary ... material copied from base-initial position may appear in prefix, suffix or infix position. Base-final material may be copied by prefixes, suffixes, or infixes as well.' In the case of partial reduplication, the most frequent position of the reduplicated material is at the beginning of a base (Rubino 2005a: 114) (see Table 3.42).

Table 3.42. *Some distributional patterns of reduplicated material*

Stem-final material copied by suffix	(352)	Bardi	*jala~la* see~RDP 'stare'		
	(353)	Māori	*pätai~tai* ask~RDP 'ask frequently'	< *pätai* 'ask'	
	(354)	Nelemwa	*fwa~wa* hole~RDP 'full of holes, tattered'		
Stem-final material copied by infix	(355)	Ilocano	*ag~<tilmo>~tilmón* swallow~<RDP> 'swallow repeatedly'		
Stem-initial material copied by prefix	(356)	Afrikaans	*glim~glimlag* RDP~smile 'smiling tentatively'		
	(357)	Amele	*ab~abale~* RDP~search.v.with.hands 'search repeatedly with hands'		
	(358)	Anejom	*al-alai* RDP~swell.up.v 'fat, thick'		

---

[69] Reduplication here causes increasing attenuation:

Tigré	*dəgm-a* 'tell, relate'	*dəga:~gəm-a* 'tell stories occasionally'	*dəga:~ga:~gəm-a* 'tell stories very occasionally'	*dəga:~ga:~ga:~gəm-a* 'tell stories infrequently'

	(359)	Clallam	*yə́~yə̀čt* RDP~arrow 'bunch of arrows'
	(360)	Datooga	*jakˤ-jak-s* RDP~throw.something.at 'throw (something) at (somebody) repeatedly'
	(361)	Hausa	*sas~sāfe* RDP~early.in.the.morning 'very early in the morning'
	(362)	Ilocano	*sik~sika* RDP~you 'only you'
	(363)	Indonesian	*le~laki* RDP~husband 'man'
	(364)	Māori	*pah-pachua* RDP~pachua RDP~hold.down.v 'press.v'
	(365)	Nelemwa	*bi~bilic* RDP~be.weak/flexible 'be very weak/flexible'
	(366)	Tatar	*jäm~jäšel* RDP~green 'very green' (Wertheim)
	(367)	Telugu	నట్ట నడుము naTTa~naDuma RDP~centre 'absolute centre'
	(368)	Zulu	*iji~gijim-a* RDP~run-V 'run a little'
Stem-initial material copied by suffix	(369)	Vietnamese	*dɛp³¹ʔ dɛ³⁵ʔ* đẹp~đẽ nice/fine~RDP 'nice, fine' (Thái Ân)
Stem-initial material copied by infix	(370)	Amele	*hili~<holo>~doc* 'ripple repeatedly in a haphazard manner'
	(371)	Clallam	*ɬúɬp'* ɬúp~<ɬ> eat.soup 'eating soup'

	(372)	Nelemwa	*ko~<xo>~le* < kole
			throw.away/empty~<RDP>
			'scatter, spread, sow' 'throw away'
Stem-internal material copied by infix	(373)	Clallam	*sq~<aʔ>~áʔxaʔ*
			dog~<RDP>
			'puppy'
	(374)	Ilocano	*ag~<sa>~sao*
			speak~<RDP>
			'speak.CON'
	(375)	Karao	*man~<ba>~bakal*
			fight.v.each.other[70]<RDP>
			'fight each other'[71]
Mirror-image reduplication with stem final material copied as suffix	(376)	Amele	*ene~ʔ -en*
			here~RDP
			'it is here'
Mirror-image reduplication with stem internal material copied as infix	(377)	Tibetan	ষལ་ལེ་བ
			sal-le-ba
			be-bright~<RDP>
			'very bright'

One of the formal features of partial reduplication recorded is that the stem material is copied on the side from which it is taken, i.e. prefixes tend to copy stem-initial material, suffixes stem-final material and infixes stem-internal material. This seems to relate to Marantz's account of reduplication as an affixation process. He argues that the reason why all the diverse morphological processes labelled as *reduplication* are subsumed under this general label 'is the resemblance of the added material to the stem being reduplicated' (Marantz 1982: 436). In his view, reduplication is the affixation of a CV skeleton (a reduplicating morpheme) of an autosegmental tier, e.g. the phonemic melody, from the stem to which the reduplicating morpheme affixes.

Apart from the absolute linear position of the reduplicated material, segmental vowelhood and consonantality are crucial for the formal description of reduplications (Moravcsik 1978: 305, 307). Table 3.43 shows the most frequent structures of reduplicated material in our sample.

Table 3.43. *Some consonant/vowel patterns of reduplication*

CV	(378)	Amele	*ab-abalena*
			'he searches repeatedly with hands'
	(379)	Bardi	*jalala*
			'stare'

---

[70] With two participants.
[71] With more than two participants.

	(380)	Hausa	*bībiyu* 'two each'
	(381)	Marathi	सुस्वागत suswaagata su-su-aagata 'most welcome'
	(382)	Māori	*papai* 'very good'
	(383)	Nelemwa	*duduji* 'be very tired'
	(384)	Pipil	*tutu:nia* 'heat.v'
CVC	(385)	Clallam	*nəč̓ə́cuʔ* 'one after'
	(386)	Romanian	*bun-bunişor* 'top quality'
	(387)	Tatar	*kap-kara* 'very black'
	(388)	Vietnamese	*ba:n³⁵ biək³⁵* bán biếc 'sell.v'[72] (Alves)
CVV	(389)	Māori	*pätaitai* 'ask frequently'
V	(390)	Gã	*jò-jò-ó-I* dance-dance-ITE-PL 'dance in several places or on several occasions'
VC	(391)	Anejom	*al-alai* 'fat, thick'
CVCV	(392)	Zulu	*giji-gijim-a* 'run a little'
CVCCV	(393)	Ilocano	*ag-tilmo-tilmón* 'swallow repeatedly'

A final case concerning formal characteristics is that of echo compounding. According to Kachru (2006: 128), echo compounding is characteristic of South Asian languages. It is based on the principle of copying the first constituent except for the first consonant. In Hindi, the first consonant of the echo constituent is always *v-*. This means that, whatever the initial consonant of the first constituent is, it is changed to *v-* in the echo constituent. The meaning of the echo constituent (which never occurs on its own) is 'and the like':

---

[72] Pejorative.

(394)   Hindi   किताब-विताब
                         kitab-vitab
                         'books and the like'

(395)   Hindi   सुन्दर-वुन्दर
                         sundər-vundər
                         'beautiful and the like'

Similar examples can be found in other languages:

(396)   Indonesian   *sayur-mayur*
                         'various sorts of vegetable'

(397)   Malayalam   *avile oru vaṇṭiim kiṇṭiim onnum kiṭṭilla*
                         there a vehicle-COO such-like-COO anything get-
                         FUT-NEG
                         'You won't get a vehicle and such-like there'[73]

(398)   Telugu   పాలు గీలు
                         paalu-giilu
                         'milk and other things'

3.2.1.2   Semantic characteristics

Reduplication has received considerable attention for its importance in non-European languages. Moravcsik's (1978: 316) review of reduplication in a number of languages finds out that the meanings associated with reduplication strikingly recur across languages. What follows agrees with this statement, but also disagrees with her view that 'there is no *a priori* reason why reduplication ... should serve as the expression of some meanings rather than as that of others' (Moravcsik 1978: 316).

The fact that the most common meanings of reduplicated forms are intensification and iterativity suggests that the role of iconicity, in particular diagrammaticity, is crucial. This is in accordance with the assumptions of Natural Morphology: extended form is accompanied by semantic enlargement, in other words, the reduplication of a particular form is an indicator of a growing quantity of items, actions or quality in general, as in the numeral 'two' in Kalkatungu, where doubling the form doubles the meaning:

(399)   Kalkatungu *lyuati~lyuati*
                         two~two
                         'four'

---

[73] Although the process is less common than in, say, Tamil and in Kannada, a Dravidian language spoken in Eurasia, compounds are sometimes formed by the juxtaposition of a noun root and a partially reduplicated form of the same root. The variation is in the first syllable, in which the base form is usually a consonant-initial. Both consonant and vowel, long or short, are retained. The most usual initial syllable of the echo is *ki-*, but other plosive-vowel sequences are possible. The meaning of an echoed word 'X' is 'X and that sort of thing' (Asher and Kumari 1997: 399).

Thus, while Regier's (1994: 3–4) radial category model identifies repetition as the core semantic concept, the core semantic concept may be specified more generally, in particular, as increased quantity (of various kinds), with a range of manifestations mentioned by Moravcsik (1978), Nomura and Kiyomi (1993)[74] and Regier (1994), among others. However, the same process of reduplication may have different and even contradictory semantic effects in the same language with two different word-classes: in Hausa, many adverbs comply with the core meaning of increased quantity when reduplicated (400), but adjectives generally run counter to this core meaning and reduplication leads to reduced quantity (401):[75]

(400)   Hausa   *maza-maza*
                  fast-fast
                  'very fast'

(401)   Hausa   *fari-fari*   <   *farii*
                  'whitish'   'white'

This is not an isolated case of the violation of the iconicity principle. In fact, the quantity-raising meanings of reduplication, like intensity, iterativity, continuity or augmentativity have their counterparts in the quantity-reducing meanings of approximation, attenuation, diminutiveness, distribution, hypocoristics, etc. Thus, one and the same process can have two opposite effects in terms of iconicity, and this has attracted considerable interest.[76]

Mattes (2006)[77] discusses full reduplication in Bikol, an Austronesian language spoken in South East Asia and Oceania which can produce both augmentative and diminutive meanings of the same form, and presents a different view: these are different realizations of the underlying concept of the change of quantity, with both types of meaning being iconic.

The languages studied here illustrate a wide range of meanings and shades of meaning that can be expressed by reduplication. Among these, the most frequent variants of the basic semantic concept of increased quantity are iterativity (in compliance with Regier 1994) and intensification, i.e. the meanings which correspond to the basic natural iconic function of reduplication (see Table 3.44).

---

[74] Nomura, M. and Kiyomi, S. 1993. 'How to motivate the meanings of verbal reduplication: cognitive and typological perspectives', Handout at Berkeley/UCSD Cognitive Linguistics Workshop. University of California, San Diego, CA.

[75] The process also involves shortening of the final vowel.

[76] Cf. Kiyomi (1995), Abraham (2005), Bakker and Parkval (2005) and Kouwenberg and LaCharité (2005), among others.

[77] Mattes, V. 2006. 'One form – opposite meanings? Diminutive and augmentative interpretation of full reduplication in Bikol', paper presented at the Tenth International Conference on Austronesian Linguistics, 17–20 January 2006, Puerto Princesa City, Palawan, Philippines. URL: www.sil.org/asia/philippines/ical/papers/mattes-Diminutive%20and%20 Augmentative%20Bikol.pdf

Table 3.44. *Semantic diversity in reduplication*

1. Intensification	(402)	Amele	*ʔebit-ʔebit* slow-slow 'very slow' (Roberts 1991: 123)	
	(403)	Amharic	ሰባበረ säbabbärä 'smash'	< ሰበረ säbbärä 'break'
	(404)	Anejom	*ahen-hen* roast-RDP 'be too hot'	
	(405)	Cirecire	*|ham|ham* urinate-urinate 'incontinence'	
	(406)	Georgian	ცივ-ცივ-ი civ-civ-i cold-cold-NOM 'very cold'	
	(407)	Hausa	*sas-sāfe* RDP-early.in.the.morning 'very early in the morning'	
	(408)	Indonesian	*besar-besar* tall-tall 'very tall' (Mojdl 2006: 77)	
	(409)	Kalkatungu	*puyurr-puyurr* hot-hot 'very hot'	
	(410)	Konni	dɪɪ-dɪɪ follow-follow 'really intensively and sincerely follow'	
	(411)	Luganda	*dugu-dugu* knock.v-knock.v 'fight heavily'	
	(412)	Marathi	लहान-लहान lahaana-lahaana small-small 'very small'	
	(413)	Nelemwa	*du-duji* RDP-be.tired 'be very tired'	
	(414)	Romanian	*bun-bunişor* good-goodish 'top quality'	

	(415)	Slovak	*šír-o-šír-y* RDP-LNK-wide-IFL 'extremely vast'	
	(416)	Tatar	*kap-kara* RDP-black 'very black' (Wertheim)	
	(417)	Telugu	ఎద్దపెద్ద pedda-pedda large-large 'very large'	
	(418)	Tibetan	སྒུམ་སྒུམ ldum-ldum round-round 'very round'	
	(419)	Vietnamese	*lɔ²¹ mæːˀ²¹ lɔ²¹ mɔ²¹* lò mà lò mò grope-RDP 'grope.v'[78] (Alves)	
2. Iterativity	(420)	Amele	*li-li-eʔ* 'go repeatedly'	< *leʔ* 'go.v'
2.1. Regular iteravitity[79]	(421)	Clallam	*nəc'-nə́c'uʔ* RDP-one 'one after'	
	(422)	Datooga	*gul-gul* RDP-pound 'knock repeatedly'	
	(423)	Hausa	*tàmbàye-tàmbàye* ask-ask 'repeated questioning'	< *tàmbàya*
	(424)	Ilocano	*ag-tilmotilmón* 'swallow repeatedly' (Rubino 2005b)	< *ag-tilmón* 'swallow.v'
	(425)	Karao	*man-odi-odi*[80] IPF.AG-RDP-return 'go back and forth between two places'	
	(426)	Māori	*pätaitai* ask-RDP 'ask frequently'	

---

[78] Emphatic.

[79] Roberts (1991: 130ff.) describes two types of iterativity for Amele: regular (420) and irregular (430). The latter refers to a repeated action that is irregular in some way, i.e. haphazard,
spasmodic, intermittent, etc. This form involves reduplication of the verb stem but with a
vowel change.

[80] The root is *oli* [ʔoli] 'return.v'.

	(427)	Marathi	लव-लवणे lava-lavaNe RDP-bend.frequently 'moving frequently'	
	(428)	Nelemwa	*taraxe* 'throw several times'	< *taxe* 'throw, give'
	(429)	Pipil	*chah-chalua* RDP-hit,beat 'beat.v' (Campbell 1985: 80)	
2.2. Irregular iteravity	(430)	Amele	*lub-lab* joist-RDP 'one who builds in a haphazard manner'	
	(431)	Amharic	ፈላለገ fälalläga 'search here and there'	< ፈለገ < fälläga 'search.v'
3. Continuity[81, 82]	(432)	Amele	*gaid gaid* always-always 'continuously'	
	(433)	Hausa	*cìye-cìye* eat-eat 'constant eating'	
	(434)	Indonesian	*senyum-senyum* smile-smile 'keep smiling' (Mojdl 2006: 75)	
	(435)	Marathi	करत-करत karata-karata doing-doing 'doing continuously'	
	(436)	Georgian	ხევ-ხუვ-ებ-ი xev-xuv-eb-i gorge-gorge-PL-NOM 'small/unimportant gorges'	

[81] A type of modification of continuous action is graduality, as in this example from Estonian:

    Estonian   *järk-järgu-lt.* ADV
                    stage-stage-ABL
                    'stage by stage, gradually'

[82] Reduplication in Karao expresses continuity productively, i.e. an action occurs over an extended period of time. Brainard (pers. comm.) notes that the verb forms *singsingked* and *mandodotho* signal on-going action, in contrast to non-continuous actions in *singked* (where -*in*- is an allomorph of -*iy*-) and *mandotoak*:

    Karao   *mandotoak*   vs   *mandodothoak*
                man-dotho-ak   man-CV-dotho-ak
                IPF-cook-ABS.1SG   IPF-CON-cook-ABS.1SG
                'I will cook'   'I am cooking'

Whether reduplication expresses a continuous action (or state) or repetition of an action appears to depend on the semantics of the verb root itself.

	(437)	Hausa	*Làadi-idi* Ladi-RDP 'little Ladi'		
	(438)	Karao	*inootoo* RDP-person 'doll'		
	(439)	Mandarin Chinese	車車 chēchē car-car 'little car, car'[83]		
4. Attenuation	(440)	Belorussian	*ximpbl-ximpbl* khitry-khitry cunning-cunning 'very cunning, very clever'		
	(441)	Hausa	*fari-fari* white-white 'whitish'	<	*farī*
	(442)	Zulu	*giji-gijim-a* RDP-run-V 'run a little'		
5. Augmentativeness	(443)	Hausa	*gandameemèe* 'long and strong'	<	*gandamī* (essentially the same meaning)

6. Plurality (for the
  expression of
  plural nouns,
  but also for the
  following nuances
  of meaning)
	(444)	Amele	*oso-oso*
			one-one
			'anyone'		

6.1. Distributive plurality	(445)	Georgian	ს3Ə-ს3Ə-ი sam-sam-I three-three-NOM 'three each'		
	(446)	Hausa	*bībiyu* RDP-two 'two each'		
	(447)	Telugu	'ఇల్లు 'ఇల్లు illu illu 'house-house' 'every house, house by house'		
6.2. Plurality of location and time	(448)	Gã	*jò-jò-ó-I*[84] dance-dance-ITE-PL 'dance in several places or on several occasions'		

---

[83] Addressing a child.
[84] Also classifiable under 2.2. in this table.

6.3. All-inclusive totality	(449)	Amele	*da-dahig* RDP-his.ear 'ears of everyone'	
	(450)	Mandarin Chinese	人人 rénrén person-person 'everybody'	
6.4. All-inclusive totality for location	(451)	Amele	*na-na* in, at-in, at 'in every one, at every place'	
	(452)	Luganda	*kasuru-kasuru* break-break 'break everywhere'	
6.5. Restricted applicability	(453)	Ilocano	*sik-sika* RDP-you 'only you'	
6.6. Indeterminate plurality	(454)	Māori	*papai* RDP-good 'good of several items'	
	(455)	Marathi	काहीबाही kaahiibaahii some-RDP 'something, anything'	
	(456)	Telugu	చిల్ల రగిల్ల ర cillara-gillara change-ECHO 'change and other things'	
6.7. Diversity	(457)	Indonesian	*ikan-ikan* fish-fish 'various kinds of fish'	
6.8. Reciprocity	(458)	Amele	*dodoldode?* approach-RDP 'approach each other' (Roberts 1991: 142)	
	(459)	Ilocano	*rupan-rúpa* RDP-face 'face to face'	< *rúpa* 'face'
6.9. Collective plural	(460)	Clallam	*yə́-yə̀čt* RDP-arrow 'another bunch of arrows'	
7. Similarity	(461)	Amele	*ho ho* pig-pig 'pig-like' (Roberts 1987: 151)	
	(462)	Indonesian	*kaki kaki* leg-leg 'stilts'	

8. Simultaneity	(463)	Amele	*meledo-don*	<	*meledo?*
			'as he examined'		'examine.v'
			(Roberts 1991: 129)		
9. Expressivity or features perceived by the five senses	(464)	Telugu	తళతళ taLa taLa shining-shining 'shining-twinkling'		
10. Causativity	(465)	Cirecire	*muumuu* see-see 'show.v'		
	(466)	Hausa	*fāḍàḍā* 'widen.v'	<	*fāḍī* 'breadth'
11. Transitivity	(467)	Nelemwa	*torop* 'be rotting'	<	*top* 'be rotten'
12. Inchoativity	(468)	Nelemwa	*khexela* 'lose balance'	<	*khela* 'slip.v'
13. Tentativity	(469)	Mandarin Chinese	寫寫看 xiěxiěkàn write-write-see 'try writing'		
14. Action with specified quality	(470)	Totonac	*a'klhtzaj-aja* with.one's.head.raised.up.high 'moving with one's head raised up high'		
15. Stativity	(471)	Cirecire	*kuikui* stick.together-stick.together 'be appended, be stuck together'		
16. Restriction	(472)	Ilocano	*sik-sika* RDP-you 'only you'		
17. Pejorativeness	(473)	Vietnamese	*ba:n³⁵ biək³⁵* bán biếc sell-RDP 'sell.v'[85] (Alves)		
18. Time	(474)	Anejom	*adiat-adiat* be.daylight-be.daylight 'be midday'		

Among the semantic features of reduplication, the basic semantic concept expressed by reduplication in word-formation apparently is the *natural* concept of increased quantity, mainly represented as iterativity and intensification of action. This overview of various categories of meaning and diverse shades of meaning indicates the extreme semantic capacity of reduplication

[85] Pejorative.

as a word-formation process which, outside Indo-European languages, approaches the capacity of affixation processes. In languages like Amele,[86] in which the semantic changes expressed by reduplication may be accompanied by word-class change, the possibility to distinguish between class-changing and class-maintaining reduplication strengthens the analogy to affixation processes.

3.3   Blending

Blending is discussed within this chapter because the underlying principle of its formation is identical to any other type of complex words covered here: blends are based on a combination of stems. Unlike the other stem-based processes, the formation process continues by speaker-friendly form-reduction which often eliminates the morphosemantic transparency of this kind of coinage.

Blending is recorded in the languages shown in Table 3.45 (23.64 per cent of the study sample).

Table 3.45. *Blending in the study sample*

Language	Family	Morphological type	Area
Cirecire	Khoisan	Isolating	Africa/Botswana
English	Indo-European	Isolating	Eurasia/Ireland and UK
Estonian	Uralic	Agglutinative/fusional	Eurasia/Estonia
Finnish	Uralic	Agglutinative	Eurasia/Finland
Georgian	Kartvelian	Inflectional/ agglutinative	Eurasia/Georgia
Greek	Indo-European	Fusional	Eurasia/Greece
Hebrew	Afro-Asiatic	Inflectional	Africa/Israel
Ilocano	Austronesian	Agglutinative	SE Asia and Oceania/ Philippines

---

[86] Reduplicated adjectives in Amele may convey the meaning 'many things with the quality X' (Roberts 1991: 120–1):

    Amele   *ben-ben*
                big-big
                'many big things'

This suggests that, if reduplication of an adjective is not followed by a governing noun, it is class-changing. The reduplicated noun often performs the functions associated to adjectives or adverbs:

    Amele   *baga?-baga?*   < *baga?*
                leaf-leaf
                'leaf-like, thin'   'leaf'
    Amele   *gemo-gemo*
                middle-middle
                'through the middle'
                (Roberts 1991: 3)

Language	Family	Morphological type	Area
Japanese	Japanese	Agglutinative	Eurasia/Japan
Nelemwa	Austronesian	Isolating	SE Asia and Oceania/New Caledonia
Slovak	Indo-European	Inflectional	Eurasia/Slovakia
Spanish	Indo-European	Inflectional	Eurasia/Spain
Vietnamese	Austro-Asiatic	Isolating	SE Asia and Oceania/ Vietnam

As Table 3.45 shows, blending is mainly a feature of Indo-European languages. Each of these languages makes productive use of compounding, which supports the postulate that both compounding and blending are based on the same word-formation principles and that blending is compounding with subsequent form-reduction (Štekauer 2005: 217). In the study sample, blending often co-occurs with compounding and adjectival coordinative compounding (the latter with the exception of Vietnamese).

In general, blending is a peripheral phenomenon. It could be considered as word-formation in the service of stylistics. Examples outside the English-speaking world are mostly restricted to advertisements, product names and related areas. Thus, Japanese has blending as a word-formation process, but it is generally limited to the fanciful naming of new products and, thus, is not as productive as in English. Probably the best-known example, according to Kageyama (pers. comm.), is (475):

(475)   Japanese   ゴジラ   <   ゴジラ＋クジラ
                             gojira   gorira + kujira
                             'godzilla'   'gorilla' + 'whale'

Examples of blends can be given for a number of other languages:

(476)   Afrikaans   *selfoon*
                             sellulêre telefoon
                             cellular-telephone
                             'cell phone'

(477)   French   *photocopillage*
                             photocopy-pillage
                             'illegal photocopying'

(478)   Greek   παντο
                             panto
                             palto-manto
                             coat-light.coat
                             'coat'

(479)   Georgian   კოლმეურნეობა
                      k'olmeurneoba
                      k'olektiur-i-meurneoba
                      collective-LNK-farming
                      'collective farming'

(480)   Hebrew   ערפיח
                      'arpiax
                      'arafel-piax
                      fog-soot
                      'smog'

(481)   Ilocano   *sariugma*
                      sarita-ugma
                      story-ancient
                      'legend'

(482)   Italian   *cantautore*
                      cantante-autore
                      sing-author
                      'singer-songwriter'

(483)   Nelemwa   *ceemode*
                      ceego-mode
                      bite-break
                      'cut with one's teeth'

(484)   Portuguese   *portunhol*
                      português-espanhol
                      'Portuguese-Spanish'

(485)   Romanian   *zdrumica*
                      zdrobi-dumica
                      crush.v-crumble.v
                      'crunch.v'

(486)   Serbian-Croatian   *fiskultura*
                      fizička-kultura
                      physical-culture
                      'physical culture'

(487)   Slovak   *sladucha* (in poetry)
                      sladká-mladucha
                      sweet-bride
                      'sweet bride'

(488)   Swedish   *ekomjölk*
                    ekologiskt-mjölk
                    ecological-milk
                    'ecologically produced milk'

3.4   Summary

The chapter reviews various types of word-formation processes which combine free morphemes, like compounding, incorporation, reduplication and blending. Within these, subtypes are discussed, like adjective + adjective compounds, verbal compounds, noun + noun compounds, exocentric and endocentric compounds, and borderline and/or ambiguous cases. The discussion of verbal compounds focuses on their description as such or as a different word-formation process, according to the interpretations available in the literature, and this discussion leads to the concept of noun incorporation. Formal and semantic effects of compounding and of incorporation are discussed, showing a diversity of types which makes it difficult to find cross-linguistic patterns.

4   Word-formation processes with bound morphemes

> [D]iachronically, the transmutation of a 'blurred' compound into an
> affixal derivative is an almost trivial phenomenon.   (Malkiel 1978: 128)

As with any other word-formation process, the significance of affixation in
natural languages varies substantially. If we disregard the non-existence of
any of the affixation processes in various languages, its distribution may range
from about 400 suffixes in use in West Greenlandic to one genuine prefix in
Estonian and Finnish. Affixes are in principle well-defined elements in linguistics by being labelled as *bound morphemes*. However, this term encompasses a range of phenomena which differ in their functional characteristics,
in their degree of naturalness and in their role in word-formation.

This chapter discusses the status of affixes (4.1) and reviews the role of
suffixation and prefixation (4.1.1), with emphasis on recursiveness (4.1.1.1)
and base modification (4.1.1.2) and then on one-to-many (4.1.2) and many-
to-one relations (4.1.3) within affixation. The chapter then presents minor
types of affixation (4.2), notably infixation (4.2.1), prefixal-suffixal derivation
(4.2.2), circumfixation (4.2.3), and prefixal-infixal and infixal-suffixal derivation (4.2.4).

4.1   Affixation

Morphology sometimes alludes to affixes as well-defined elements
that in fact may vary considerably. A number of examples illustrate the
difficulty in defining the boundaries of derivational affixes with respect to
inflectional affixes or to other structural units.

Thus, Malkiel (1978) refers to German elements, most of which are formally
and semantically paralleled by prepositions and/or adverbs (cf. Table 2.1).
This might suggest that words containing these elements are compounds.
However, the existence of prefixes without any corresponding lexical counterparts like *be-*, *er-*, *ge-* and *ver-* suggests that these words result from
affixation. Malkiel (1978: 127–8) argues that it would be counterintuitive to
separate *be-*, *er-*, *ge-* and *ver-* from the remainder of German prefixes with
which they interact paradigmatically. A similar situation characterizes the
majority of Latin verbal prefixes.

In fact, as pointed out by Kastovsky (2009: 327), affixes often go back to
compound members due to loss of their content. Thus, English *-less* goes
back to Old English *less* meaning 'devoid of, free from', *-ship* to Old English

135

scipe 'form, state' and *-dom* to Old English *dōm* 'evil fate'. Synchronically, this source may be traced in the existence of the so-called semiaffixes (English *-berry*, *-man*, etc., cf. Marchand 1960: 290ff.). These semiaffixes share features of bound morphemes (reduced pronunciation, loss of stress, generalized meaning, high productivity) and features of free morphemes as constituents of compounds, and justify Malkiel's quotation in the chapter's motto. Malkiel mentions cases like German *-wärts* in *rückwärts* 'back' and *vorwärts* 'forward, ahead' and English *-ward* which developed from the word meaning 'turn, bent, slant', a cognate of Latin *vertere*. Evidence of a similar development can be found in Ket, Kott and Yugh: their verbal semiaffixes developed from root morphemes, occurring in a series of compound words which are no longer used as an independent word. This can be illustrated with the Ket semi-suffix *-bet* (Werner 1998: 105ff.):

(1)   Ket   *il'-bet*
                  broken/destroyed-make
                  'break, destroy'

(2)   Ket   *nan'bet*
                  bread-make
                  'bake bread'

Werner also gives examples of semantic bleaching of some common Ket morphemes used in compound nouns through which they have come to resemble derivational affixes. For instance, *-git* 'man' now signifies the young of any animal or tree:

(3)   Ket   *qaj-git*
                  χajgit
                  'baby elk'
                  (Werner 1998: 53)

For Kastovsky (2009: 327), the diachronic shift from a compound constituent to a bound morpheme results in a synchronic cline. Kastovsky does not find the postulation of semiaffixes acceptable, as it 'replaces a two-way by a three-way distinction adding an additional stepping stone on something which for diachronic reasons must be viewed as a cline without providing criteria for delimitation'.

The blurred limits of affixes also manifest themselves in the vague boundary between inflectional and derivational affixes, as in the infinitive suffix in Romance languages (Malkiel 1978: 129), because many infinitives are subject to nominalization. The nominalized infinitives then behave like other nominalizations resulting from suffixation. In Romanian, all the original infinitives were nominalized and subsequently replaced by a new set of infinitives. The same kind of nominalization, e.g. *lesen* 'read.v' vs *das Lesen* 'reading.N' is very productive in German. In general, this is closely related to the role of inflectional paradigms as derivational devices. Thus, the Slovak adjective *domáci* 'domestic' can be converted into the corresponding noun meaning 'landlord' and also into a plural noun meaning 'the home team'. If accounted for as zero-derivation or derivation by zero morpheme (e.g. Marchand 1960; Kastovsky 1969, 1982), then this and other cases of conversion fall within the scope of affixation.

Kwakw'ala provides another borderline case. As explained by Anderson (1985: 26), many suffixes are noun-like, verb-like or adjective-like, i.e. they correspond to nouns, verbs and adjectives in other languages. In addition, there are also suffixes that function as conjunctions. All in all, there are bound elements in Kwakw'ala corresponding to all major word-classes. Kwakw'ala is a good example of the difficulties inherent in the category of affix and in its subcategories, in that an affix can sometimes be analyzed as either a suffix or infix (Anderson 1985: 32): the suffix *-əm*, which indicates that things whose location is specified by a following locative suffix are plural, may also be analyzed as an infix:

(4)   Kwakw'ala   *axaxud*   vs   *axəmaxud*
                          'put down'   'put several down'

Anderson assumes that *-əm-* may be said to be infixed into a stem ending in a locative suffix and placed immediately before that.

This introduction finally presents another ambiguous case which illustrates how complex the issues in question may be. This time, it concerns the decision between the allomorphic vs morphemic status of Slovak prefix(es) *pre-* and *prie-* as in *pre-behnút* 'run.v.PFV' vs *prie-beh* 'course (of events)'. Formally, they differ in quantity, as the former has a short vowel and the latter a diphthong. Furdík (2004: 44) generalizes that in these and other similar cases we should speak about variants at morphematic level rather than at word-formation level, because the diphthongized variant does not result from a word-formation process, unlike the short variant which is an unambiguous case of prefixation from *behat* 'run.v.IPFV'. In the subsequent word-formation step, *prie-* is not treated as a prefix. Instead, it is considered to be a part of the base. Some other examples cited by Furdík are *na-/ná-* (*narazit* 'strike.v' > *náraz* 'stroke'), *pri-/prí-* (*prisúdiť* 'predicate.v' > *prísudok* 'predicate.N'), etc.

While this non-derivational assumption holds for these pairs, this is not quite so in relation to *pre-/prie-* pairs, i.e. the short/long vowel opposition in other than *pre-/prie-* pairs occurs between a motivating verb and the resulting noun. In the *pre-/prie-* pairs this opposition often concerns the relation between two nouns. Consequently, as pointed out by Slančová (pers. comm.), while the prefix *prie-* is a quantitative variant of *pre-*, the quantitative difference may also have a semantic distinctive force, i.e. while *prie-* refers to location, *pre-* indicates action:

(5)   Slovak   *prechod*   *priechod*
                   'transition'   'gangway'

(6)   Slovak   *prepad*   *priepad*
                   'assault, attack'   'spillway'

Unfortunately, this basic semantic specialization does not apply in all cases
and sometimes the meanings may overlap partly or completely:

(7)   Slovak   *predel*   *priedel*
                   'local or temporal limit'

(8)   Slovak   *previs*   *prievis*
                   'overhang'   'sag'

There are also cases when only one of the prefixes forms an actual word:

(9)   Slovak   *prečin*   vs   **priečin*
                   'offence, delinquency'

Thus, while a semantic difference supports the hypothesis of two prefixes, the
inconsistency with which this opposition is applied and the semantic merger
in other cases show that it is very difficult to make an unambiguous judge-
ment about the status of *pre-/prie-* in the Slovak word-formation system.

4.1.1   Suffixation and prefixation

Suffixation is recorded in the languages shown in Table 4.1 (96.36
per cent of the study sample).

Table 4.1. *Suffixation in the study sample*

Language	Family	Morphological type	Area
Amele	Trans-New Guinea	Polysynthetic/synthetic	Australia-New Guinea/ Madang
Amharic	Afro-Asiatic	Inflectional	Africa/Ethiopia
Anejom	Austronesian	Agglutinative	SE Asia and Oceania/ Vanuatu
Bardi	Australian	Fusional	Australia-New Guinea/ Australia
Breton	Indo-European	Fusional	Eurasia/France
Cirecire	Khoisan	Isolating	Africa/Botswana
Clallam	Salishan	Polysynthetic	North America/USA
Dangaléat	Afro-Asiatic	Agglutinative	Africa/Chad
Datooga	Nilo-Saharan	Agglutinative/ fusional	Africa/Tanzania

Language	Family	Morphological type	Area
Diola-Fogny	Niger-Congo	Agglutinative	Africa/Gambia, Senegal
English	Indo-European	Isolating	Eurasia/Ireland and UK
Estonian	Uralic	Agglutinative/fusional	Eurasia/Estonia
Finnish	Uralic	Agglutinative	Eurasia/Finland
Gã	Niger-Congo	Agglutinative	Africa/Ghana
Georgian	Kartvelian	Inflectional/ agglutinative	Eurasia/Georgia
Greek	Indo-European	Fusional	Eurasia/Greece
Hausa	Afro-Asiatic	Fusional	Africa/Niger, Nigeria
Hebrew	Afro-Asiatic	Inflectional	Africa/Israel
Hungarian	Uralic	Agglutinative	Eurasia/Hungary
Ilocano	Austronesian	Agglutinative	SE Asia and Oceania/ Philippines
Indonesian	Austronesian	Agglutinative	SE Asia and Oceania/ Indonesia
Japanese	Japanese	Agglutinative	Eurasia/Japan
Jaqaru	Aymaran	Agglutinative	South America/Peru
Kalkatungu	Australian-Aboriginal	Agglutinative	Australia-New Guinea/ Australia
Karao	Austronesian	Inflectional/ polysynthetic	SE Asia and Oceania/ Philippines
Ket	Yeniseian	Agglutinative	Eurasia/Russia
Konni	Niger-Congo	Agglutinative	Africa/Ghana
Kwakw'ala	Wakashan	Polysynthetic	North America/Canada
Lakhota	Siouan	Synthetic to polysynthetic	North America/USA
Luganda	Niger-Congo	Agglutinative	Africa/Uganda
Luo	Nilo-Saharan	Agglutinative	Africa/Kenya, Tanzania
Maipure	Arawakan	Agglutinative	South America/ Venezuela
Malayalam	Dravidian	Agglutinative	Eurasia/India
Mandarin Chinese	Sino-Tibetan	Isolating/analytic	SE Asia and Oceania/ China
Māori	Austronesian	Isolating	SE Asia and Oceania/ New Zealand
Marathi	Indo-European	Inflectional/ polysynthetic	Eurasia/India
Movima	Movima	Agglutinative	South America/Bolivia
Nelemwa	Austronesian	Isolating	SE Asia and Oceania/ New Caledonia
Pipil	Uto-Aztecan	Agglutinative	North America/El Salvador
Slavey	Na-Dene	Polysynthetic	North America/ Northwest Territories

Language	Family	Morphological type	Area
Slovak	Indo-European	Inflectional	Eurasia/Slovakia
Spanish	Indo-European	Inflectional	Eurasia/Spain
Swahili	Niger-Congo	Agglutinative	Africa/Tanzania
Tamil	Dravidian	Agglutinative	Eurasia/Tamil Nadu
Tatar	Altaic	Agglutinative	Eurasia/Russia
Telugu	Dravidian	Agglutinative	Eurasia/India
Tibetan	Sino-Tibetan	Inflectional/ agglutinative	SE Asia and Oceania/ China
Totonac	Totonacan	Agglutinative/ polysynthetic	North America/Mexico
Tzotzil	Mayan	Agglutinative/ polysynthetic	North America/Mexico
Udihe	Altaic	Agglutinative	Eurasia/Russia
West Greenlandic	Eskimo-Aleut	Polysynthetic	North America/ Greenland
Wichí	Matacoan	Agglutinative	South America/ Argentina and Bolivia
Zulu	Niger-Congo	Agglutinative	Africa/South Africa

Prefixation is recorded in the languages shown in Table 4.2 (70.91 per cent of the study sample).

Table 4.2. *Prefixation in the study sample*

Language	Family	Morphological type	Area
Amharic	Afro-Asiatic	Inflectional	Africa/Ethiopia
Anejom	Austronesian	Agglutinative	SE Asia and Oceania/Vanuatu
Breton	Indo-European	Fusional	Eurasia/France
Clallam	Salishan	Polysynthetic	North America/USA
Datooga	Nilo-Saharan	Agglutinative/ fusional	Africa/Tanzania
English	Indo-European	Isolating	Eurasia/Ireland and UK
Estonian	Uralic	Agglutinative/ fusional	Eurasia/Estonia
Finnish	Uralic	Agglutinative	Eurasia/Finland
Gã	Niger-Congo	Agglutinative	Africa/Ghana
Georgian	Kartvelian	Inflectional/ agglutinative	Eurasia/Georgia
Greek	Indo-European	Fusional	Eurasia/Greece
Hausa	Afro-Asiatic	Fusional	Africa/Niger, Nigeria
Hebrew	Afro-Asiatic	Inflectional	Africa/Israel
Ilocano	Austronesian	Agglutinative	SE Asia and Oceania/ Philippines
Indonesian	Austronesian	Agglutinative	SE Asia and Oceania/Indonesia

Language	Family	Morphological type	Area
Japanese	Japanese	Agglutinative	Eurasia/Japan
Karao	Austronesian	Inflectional/ polysynthetic	SE Asia and Oceania/ Philippines
Ket	Yeniseian	Agglutinative	Eurasia/Russia
Konni	Niger-Congo	Agglutinative	Africa/Ghana
Lakhota	Siouan	Synthetic to polysynthetic	North America/USA
Luganda	Niger-Congo	Agglutinative	Africa/Uganda
Luo	Nilo-Saharan	Agglutinative	Africa/Kenya, Tanzania
Malayalam	Dravidian	Agglutinative	Eurasia/India
Mandarin Chinese	Sino-Tibetan	Isolating/analytic	SE Asia and Oceania/China
Māori	Austronesian	Isolating	SE Asia and Oceania/New Zealand
Marathi	Indo-European	Inflectional/ polysynthetic	Eurasia/India
Nelemwa	Austronesian	Isolating	SE Asia and Oceania/New Caledonia
Pipil	Uto-Aztecan	Agglutinative	North America/El Salvador
Slavey	Na-Dene	Polysynthetic	North America/Northwest Territories
Slovak	Indo-European	Inflectional	Eurasia/Slovakia
Spanish	Indo-European	Inflectional	Eurasia/Spain
Swahili	Niger-Congo	Agglutinative	Africa/Tanzania
Tamil	Dravidian	Agglutinative	Eurasia/Tamil Nadu
Telugu	Dravidian	Agglutinative	Eurasia/India
Totonac	Totonacan	Agglutinative/ polysynthetic	North America/Mexico
Tzotzil	Mayan	Agglutinative/ polysynthetic	North America/Mexico
West Greenlandic	Eskimo-Aleut	Polysynthetic	North America/Greenland
Wichí	Matacoan	Agglutinative	South America/Argentina and Bolivia
Yoruba	Niger-Congo	Isolating	Africa/Benin, Nigeria
Zulu	Niger-Congo	Agglutinative	Africa/South Africa

There are only two languages in the study sample that do not use suffixation for coining new words: Vietnamese, which, as an isolating language *par excellence*, has no affixation at all, and Yoruba, another isolating language, which makes only use of prefixation. By contrast, prefixation is not so widespread, and this deserves further comment. It was pointed out in the opening lines of this chapter that Estonian has only one prefix, *eba-* 'false, pseudo-, quasi-' (Kilgi, pers. comm.),[1] even if certain morphemes are sometimes also considered prefixes, e.g. *mitte* 'non-, un-', *ala* 'under-, sub-' and *üli* 'over-, super-, ultra-, hyper-':

(10)   Estonian   *mitte-soovitav*
                    'inadvisable'

(11)   Estonian   *ala-jaotis*
                    'subdivision'

(12)   Estonian   *üli-agar*
                    'overeager'

In Finnish there is also one prefix (*epä-* for negation),[2] and even this is not considered very productive (Laakso, pers. comm.): it is applied to some adjectives and to even fewer nouns, and the meaning is not completely predictable. These are examples of the limited cross-linguistic frequency of prefixation, which has been reported in the literature to be lower than that of suffixation (E. Sapir 1921: 67; Cutler, Hawkins and Gilligan 1985: 747; Laca 2001).

This observation gives support to the view that the difference between suffixation and prefixation is not merely positional. In this connection, let us recall Marchand's viewpoint (1967) which assigns prefixation and compounding to the word-formation processes of expansion, while suffixation is based on different principles and is a special case of transposition. Marchand's distinction should be much appreciated, even if we cannot agree with all his arguments, in particular with the assumption that suffixes always function as *determinata* (heads), while prefixes are always *determinants* (modifiers). This assumption, later formulated by Williams (1981) as the Right-hand Head Rule, is a rather radical position which was subject to extensive criticism and raised discussion on headedness in terms of the content of the notion of head, its defining characteristics and, what is more important for the present topic, the capacity of prefixes to act as heads.[3]

Štekauer (2001) argues in favour of the capacity of prefixes to function as heads, on a par with suffixes, for formal and semantic reasons:

(a)   like suffixes, prefixes can also be divided into class-changing and class-maintaining; in view of their postulated treatment as heads they may be preferably labelled as *class-changing* and *class-confirming*, and

---

[1] The prefix *eba-* can also function as a stem: some words are formed by adding suffixes, e.g. *eba-rd* 'monster, freak' and *eba-le-ma* 'hesitate.V'. In its capacity to combine with affixes, it resembles the combining forms of English neoclassical compounds.

[2] This is, historically, a present participle of the negation verb *e-*.

[3] Cf. Hudson (1980), Lieber (1981, 1992), Selkirk (1982), Zwicky (1985), Di Sciullo and Williams (1987), Scalise (1988), L. Bauer (1988, 1990), Anderson (1992) and Kastovsky (1995).

(b) while one of the basic features of heads (*determinata*, onomasiological bases) is that they stand for a general conceptual group,
a class or a species, modifiers (*determinants*, onomasiological
marks) restrict their scope (Dokulil 1962). Therefore, in complex
words which contain 'both a word-formation base and affix,
the latter is the head because affixes stand for a more general
category' (Štekauer 2001: 352).

Consequently, although they are different processes, suffixation and prefixation play an equally important role in word-formation because both can
function as heads. Furthermore, even if suffixation is recorded in a higher
percentage in the sample, prefixation also plays a major role both in terms
of the number of languages which use it for coining new words and for its
functional load. This is so in a large number of languages, especially in Slavic
and Romance languages, where a high productivity of prefixing derivation
can be observed:

(13)   Slovak   a. *písať*   'write'
                    b. *do-písať*   'complete writing'
                    c. *na-písať*   'write down'
                    d. *od-písať*   'write back, reply, write off, write down,
                                        depreciate, condemn'
                    e. *o-písať*   'describe, (to take a) copy'
                    f. *pod-písať*   'sign'
                    g. *po-písať*   'write (something) all over'
                    h. *pre-písať*   'rewrite, assign'
                    i. *roz-písať*   'leave a thing half-written, specify, write
                                        down details'
                    j. *s-písať*   'make out (a list of)'
                    k. *u-písať*   'subscribe to, sign on'
                    l. *v-písať*   'write into'
                    m. *vy-písať*   'write up, make notes of (something)'
                    n. *za-písať*   'write down, enter a thing on a list,
                                        enrol, excerpt, advertise, put out for
                                        tender, enlist'[4]

Latin examples are similarly comprehensive:

(14)   Latin   a. *a-scrībō*
                    b. *circum-scrībō*
                    c. *de-scrībō*
                    d. *con-scrībō*

---

[4] There is also the possibility of double prefixation by means of the prefix *po-* combining the
durative and the perfective meanings: *po-do-pisovať* ('ITE-write into'), *po-pre-pisovať* ('ITE-
re-write'), *po-za-pisovať* ('ITE-write down'), *po-vy-pisovať* ('ITE-write out'). In these cases, it
is combined with durative versions of the prefixed 'write'-based words.

    e. *ex-scrībō*
    f. *in-scrībō*
    g. *inter-scrībō*
    h. *prae-scrībō*
    i. *pro-scrībō*
    j. *per-scrībō*
    k. *re-scrībō*
    l. *sub-scrībō*
    m. *trans-scrībō*

In reference to similar examples in Russian, Malkiel (1978: 135) notes that one can observe a 'uniquely close enmeshment of aspect, tense and prefixation within the verbal system'. Example series (13) and (14) demonstrate that the scope of prefixes in the verbal system of these and a number of other languages by far exceeds the limits of aspect, as they can express very subtle shades of meaning. This contributes significantly to the word-formation capacity of these languages.

Prefixes may be selective in their combinability, a phenomenon which is well described for English. The restrictions may be various in nature. In Telugu, for example, prefixation occurs only with words of Sanskrit origin (Pingali, pers. comm.).

4.1.1.1   Recursiveness in affixation

4.1.1.1.1 Recursive suffixation Recursive suffixation is recorded in the languages shown in Table 4.3.

Table 4.3. *Recursive suffixation in the study sample*

Language	Family	Morphological type	Area
Anejom	Austronesian	Agglutinative	SE Asia and Oceania/ Vanuatu
Bardi	Australian	Fusional	Australia-New Guinea/ Australia
Breton	Indo-European	Fusional	Eurasia/France
Clallam	Salishan	Polysynthetic	North America/USA
Datooga	Nilo-Saharan	Agglutinative/ fusional	Africa/Tanzania
Diola-Fogny	Niger-Congo	Agglutinative	Africa/Gambia, Senegal
English	Indo-European	Isolating	Eurasia/Ireland and UK
Estonian	Uralic	Agglutinative/fusional	Eurasia/Estonia
Finnish	Uralic	Agglutinative	Eurasia/Finland
Georgian	Kartvelian	Inflectional/ agglutinative	Eurasia/Georgia

Language	Family	Morphological type	Area
Greek	Indo-European	Fusional	Eurasia/Greece
Hebrew	Afro-Asiatic	Inflectional	Africa/Israel
Hungarian	Uralic	Agglutinative	Eurasia/Hungary
Ilocano	Austronesian	Agglutinative	SE Asia and Oceania/ Philippines
Indonesian	Austronesian	Agglutinative	SE Asia and Oceania/ Indonesia
Japanese	Japanese	Agglutinative	Eurasia/Japan
Jaqaru	Aymaran	Agglutinative	South America/Peru
Kalkatungu	Australian-Aboriginal	Agglutinative	Australia-New Guinea/ Australia
Ket	Yeniseian	Agglutinative	Eurasia/Russia
Kwakw'ala	Wakashan	Polysynthetic	North America/Canada
Luo	Nilo-Saharan	Agglutinative	Africa/Kenya, Tanzania
Maipure	Arawakan	Agglutinative	South America/Venezuela
Malayalam	Dravidian	Agglutinative	Eurasia/India
Mandarin Chinese	Sino-Tibetan	Isolating/analytic	SE Asia and Oceania/ China
Marathi	Indo-European	Inflectional/ polysynthetic	Eurasia/India
Nelemwa	Austronesian	Isolating	SE Asia and Oceania/ New Caledonia
Pipil	Uto-Aztecan	Agglutinative	North America/El Salvador
Slavey	Na-Dene	Polysynthetic	North America/Northwest Territories
Slovak	Indo-European	Inflectional	Eurasia/Slovakia
Spanish	Indo-European	Inflectional	Eurasia/Spain
Swahili	Niger-Congo	Agglutinative	Africa/Tanzania
Tamil	Dravidian	Agglutinative	Eurasia/Tamil Nadu
Tatar	Altaic	Agglutinative	Eurasia/Russia
Telugu	Dravidian	Agglutinative	Eurasia/India
Tibetan	Sino-Tibetan	Inflectional/ agglutinative	SE Asia and Oceania/ China
Totonac	Totonacan	Agglutinative/ polysynthetic	North America/Mexico
Tzotzil	Mayan	Agglutinative/ polysynthetic	North America/Mexico
Udihe	Altaic	Agglutinative	Eurasia/Russia
West Greenlandic	Eskimo-Aleut	Polysynthetic	North America/ Greenland
Wichí	Matacoan	Agglutinative	South America/Argentina and Bolivia
Zulu	Niger-Congo	Agglutinative	Africa/South Africa

Recursiveness varies widely from language to language. Slavic and Germanic languages offer a wealth of examples, Tibetan less so, and Slavey shows constraints, in that recursiveness is restricted to possessed augmentatives and diminutives. In some other languages, recursiveness depends on the standpoint taken. In Gã the only possible case of co-occurrence of two suffixes is the combination of the reduplication and suffixation processes. In particular, verbs that have the iterative suffix -mO may reduplicate to show distributive event, often with the additional suffix -i:

(15)   Gã   *tsO-mO-tsO-mO-i*
                turn-over-turn-over-SFX
                'turn over and over, many things in many places'

The number of permissible suffixes in a word also varies cross-linguistically. Hardman (2000: 51) characterizes Jaqaru in terms of recursiveness as follows: 'the processes of nominalization and verbalization are recursive. It is not uncommon for nouns to be verbalized and then renominalized, or vice versa.' Apart from simpler cases like (16) and (17), there are also much more complex recursive derivations as in (18) and (19) (see Table 4.4).

Table 4.4. *Recursive suffixation in Jaqaru*

N>N>V	(16)	Jaqaru	*jucha-ni-w-t'a*[5] 'abruptly be one who has committed a fault or error, to abruptly be a sinner'
N>V>N	(17)	Jaqaru	*waraja-w-kir-na* 'in where the stars are, there'
N>V>N>V>N	(18)	Jaqaru	*yanh-ish-mashi-Ø-nush-ru-wa* 'for the one who helped us'
N>V>N>V>N>V	(19)	Jaqaru	*Juncx'-shu-ta-y-nush-mashi-w-ta-wa* hot.out>N>V>N-for-mate-V-2P-SS [for being burned (first five morphemes) you are mate (next three morphemes) PK last] 'You are a companion of having been burned together (speaker and addressee)'

Jaqaru is also interesting for the capacity of some of its suffixes to recur on the same verb root:[6]

---

[5] The derivational suffixes are -*ni* and -*w*.

[6] The two that most often recur are -*ishi* mutual/reflexive and -*ya* causative. When -*ishi* occurs twice, it is a lexicalization in the first occurrence, with the mutuality/reflexiveness coming from the second occurrence. The double occurrence of -*ya* results in a causation (Hardman 2000: 88).

(20)   Jaqaru   *yanh-shi-rqay-ishi*
                      yanh-ishi-rqaya-ishi
                      help-MUT-everyone-MUT
                      'help each other'

Fortescue (1980: 261) maintains that there can be up to a dozen affixal morphemes in a West Greenlandic verb form and up to four of the same category. In his view, there are over 400 suffixes in West Greenlandic, ranging from fully productive to fully lexicalized. As in Jaqaru, these can be used recursively to build up complex verbs and nouns, with possible switches back and forth between verbal and nominal base several times within a single word:[7]

(21)   West Greenlandic   *allattu-i-vvi-ssaaliqi-sar-sima-qa-anga*
                                  write.down-APS-LOC.of-lack-FRE-PFV-INT-
                                  1SG.IND
                                  'I was really short of notebooks'

Unlike English, derivational suffixes in West Greenlandic may reverse their relative order, the result of which is a change of meaning, as in the following example (Fortescue 1984: 313):

(22)   West Greenlandic   a.   *Urnik-kusun-niqar-puq*
                                     come.to-want-PAS-3SG.IND
                                     'Somebody wanted to come to him'
                               b.   *Urnin-niqa-rusup-puq*
                                     come.to-PAS-want-3SG.IND
                                     'He wanted somebody to come to him'

The relative freedom of suffixes in Kwakw'ala is also a source of a specific sort of recursiveness, because it permits alternate orders of suffixes corresponding to distinct meanings. Anderson (1985: 33) gives an example of the suffixes *-amas* 'cause' and *-exsd* 'want'. From the verb *ne'nak*[w] 'go home', we can form *ne'nak*[w]*exsd* 'want to go home'. By attaching the suffix *-amas* we obtain *ne'nak*[w]*exsdamas* 'cause to want to go home'. On the other hand, from *q'aq'oλa* 'learn' we can make *q'aq'oλaamas* 'cause to learn, teach' and, from this, *q'aq'oλamadzexsd* 'want to teach' can be formed in turn. In these examples, the same suffixes appear in opposite orders, corresponding to different meanings 'cause to want' vs 'want to cause'. Consequently, new forms of arbitrary complexity can be produced ('want to cause to want to cause to ...').

According to Cowan (1969: 97), it is quite common for a radical stem in Tzotzil to be formed by a root followed by three derivational suffixes.

---

[7]   Cf. Fortescue (1980, 1984) for examples of many of them.

Sometimes, a derivational affix is preceded by a perfective, referential,[8] passive or subjunctive morpheme. Cowan considers these morphemes to be derivational, because they may be followed by other derivational suffixes:

(23)   Tzotzil   *vó-b-il-al*   <   *vó-b-il*
                    'roasted (things)'   'roasted (by someone)'

(24)   Tzotzil   *yáx-em-al*   <   *yáx-em*
                    'wound'   'wounded'

According to Volpe (pers. comm.), recursive suffixation is also very productive in Japanese, in particular, in cases like (25) and (26):

(25)   Japanese   言語学者
                     gengo-gaku-sha   <   gengo-gaku   <   gengo
                     'linguist'   'linguistics'   'language'

(26)   Japanese   社会学者
                     shakai-gaku-sha   <   shakai-gaku   <   shakai
                     'sociologist'   'sociology'   'society'

The dominating word-classes in recursive suffixation are nouns and verbs, but examples of adjectives are also possible. Table 4.5 gives examples of all three cases.

Table 4.5. *Recursive suffixation in nouns, verbs and adjectives*

	Nouns		Verbs		Adjectives
(27) Breton	*kig-er-ez* meat-AG-F 'butcher's wife, female butcher'	(28) Anejom	*ati-i-so-kou* put-TR-down-distant 'put it down over there'	(29) Pipil	*chipak-nah* chipa:wa-k clear-INC-somewhat 'somewhat clear' (Campbell 1985: 63)
(30) Catalan	*port-er-ia* gate-AG-LOC 'porter's lodge'	(31) Clallam	*ʔəxíkʷstəŋ* scrape-body-TR-PAS 'its body is scraped'	(32) Russian	*зл-ост-н(ый)* zlostny evil-N-ADJ(M. SG.NOM) 'angry'

---

[8]   If a transitive clause is both perfective and passive, its verb is referential (i.e. inflected as though there were a referent).

Nouns		Verbs		Adjectives
(33) Datooga	*daam-úu-yán-da* beard-PL-SGT-SG.SPE 'hair or beard'	(34) Georgian	გა-მ-ა-კ'ეთ-ებ-ინ-ებ-დ-ე-ს-ო ga-m-a-k'et-eb-in-eb-d-e-s-o PREVERS-IO1.SG-version-do-TH-CAU-IPF-SBJ-S3.SG-QUO '[If/when] s/he would make me do it, s/he says/said'	(35) Slovak *uči-teľ-k-in* učiť-eľ-ka-in teach-AG-F-POS 'female teacher's'
(36) Hebrew	ילדותיות yald-ut-iy-ut child-hood-ish-ness 'childishness' (Berman)	(37) Luo	*tëëniïtyä* tëënä-ïïtu-yë same-ICP-SOC[9] 'become the same'	
(38) Ilocano	*saka-an-an* foot-NMR-LOC 'foot of mountain'	(39) Malayalam	*kaṟakk-ipp-ikk-*[10] rotate.TR-CAU-CAU 'make X rotate Y' (Asher and Kumari 1997: 279)	
(40) Tatar	*uylavchi* uy-la-v-chï thought-DNL.V-VL.N-AG 'thinker' (Schamiloglu)	(41) Nelemwa	*u-paare-a-r-a* way.of-tell-DET-it-of me (lit. 'way of telling of it of me') '[It's] my way of telling it'	
		(42) Swahili	*fik-ish-i-a* arrive-CAU-APP-IND 'cause to arrive for (somebody)'	

[9] Each other.
[10] From the intransitive stem *kaṟaŋŋ-*.

Nouns	Verbs	Adjectives
(43) Totonac	*li:-ma:-panh-e:-nín* INS-CAU-explode-CAU-nín 'set off rockets or firecrackers'	
(44) Wichí	*n'-t'on-'am-kwe-pj* 1SBJ-shout.V-2OBJ-DIR.ALL-ITE 'I yell at you repeatedly'	
(45) Zulu	*ni-khal-el-a-ni?* you.PL-cry-for-v-what? 'Why are you crying?'	

Like simple suffixation, recursive suffixation can result in a change of word-class. This is fairly common, especially in the direction from verb to noun, as in (46) to (52), but is also possible in the direction from noun to verb (53) and from verb to adjective (54):

(46) Afrikaans   *skei-baar-heid*
                    separate-able-ity
                    'separability'

(47) Diola-Fogny *atɛk-ɔr-a* <   *-tɛk*
                    hit-RCP-AG
                    'boxer'   'hit.v'
                    (D. J. Sapir 1965: 56)

(48) Indonesian   *pakai-an-nya*
                    wear-NMR-DEF
                    'the clothes'

(49) Maipure   *sunua-ta-tí*
                    sit-CAU-NMR
                    'chair'

(50) Marathi   मंगल-मय-ता
                     mangala-maya-taa
                     holy-full.of/with-ABN.MRK
                     'holiness'

(51) Telugu   ప్రేమించడం
                     prem-inc-aDam
                     love-VL.SFX-GRN
                     'the act of loving'

(52) Tibetan   ཐག་ག་པ
                     thag-a-pa
                     weave-NMR-PEF
                     'weaver'

(53) Kalkatungu   *mimi-yan-ati*
                     breast-having-become
                     'getting breasts'

(54) Belorussian   *буд-аў-ніч-ы*
                     budaynichy
                     build-V.SFX-ADJ.SFX-ADJ (M.SG.NOM)
                     'building.ADJ'

4.1.1.1.2 Recursive prefixation Recursive prefixation is recorded in the
languages shown in Table 4.6.

Table 4.6. *Recursive prefixation in the study sample*

Language	Family	Morphological type	Area
Anejom	Austronesian	Agglutinative	SE Asia and Oceania/ Vanuatu
Breton	Indo-European	Fusional	Eurasia/France
Clallam	Salishan	Polysynthetic	North America/USA
English	Indo-European	Isolating	Eurasia/Ireland and UK
Georgian	Kartvelian	Inflectional/ agglutinative	Eurasia/Georgia
Greek	Indo-European	Fusional	Eurasia/Greece
Hebrew	Afro-Asiatic	Inflectional	Africa/Israel
Ilocano	Austronesian	Agglutinative	SE Asia and Oceania/ Philippines
Indonesian	Austronesian	Agglutinative	SE Asia and Oceania/ Indonesia

Language	Family	Morphological type	Area
Ket	Yeniseian	Agglutinative	Eurasia/Russia
Lakhota	Siouan	Synthetic to polysynthetic	North America/USA
Luo	Nilo-Saharan	Agglutinative	Africa/Kenya, Tanzania
Mandarin Chinese	Sino-Tibetan	Isolating/analytic	SE Asia and Oceania/ China
Māori	Austronesian	Isolating	SE Asia and Oceania/ New Zealand
Marathi	Indo-European	Inflectional/ polysynthetic	Eurasia/India
Nelemwa	Austronesian	Isolating	SE Asia and Oceania/ New Caledonia
Pipil	Uto-Aztecan	Agglutinative	North America/El Salvador
Slavey	Na-Dene	Polysynthetic	North America/ Northwest Territories
Slovak	Indo-European	Inflectional	Eurasia/Slovakia
Spanish	Indo-European	Inflectional	Eurasia/Spain
Swahili	Niger-Congo	Agglutinative	Africa/Tanzania
Totonac	Totonacan	Agglutinative/ polysynthetic	North America/ Mexico
Yoruba	Niger-Congo	Isolating	Africa/Benin, Nigeria
Zulu	Niger-Congo	Agglutinative	Africa/South Africa

While the identification of prefixes in terms of both form and meaning is usually easy (but cf. 4.1.1 above), the analysis is not always simple and it may influence the assumption of the (non-)existence of recursive prefixation. A case in point is the combination of prefixes *mem-* and *per-* in Indonesian:

(55)   Indonesian   *memper-kenal-kann*
             TR.ACT-know-TR
             'introduce (somebody)'

Müller (pers. comm.) maintains that, although *memper-* in cases like (55) can be analyzed as consisting of two prefixes (*mem-* and *per-*), it does not follow the usual morphophonemic constraints of the prefix *mem-* (specifically, the [p] following *mem-* should elide but it does not). So, if *memper-* is analyzed as two prefixes, then Indonesian has recursive prefixation, otherwise it does not.

Table 4.7 provides examples for nouns, verbs as well as adjectives, showing that recursive prefixation is bound to the same word-class. While suffixal recursiveness is cross-linguistically most characteristic of nouns, prefixal recursiveness is most typical of verbs.

Table 4.7. *Recursive prefixation in nouns, verbs and adjectives*

Nouns	Verbs	Adjectives
(56) Luo *kaap-kii-rwääk* LOC-NMR-discuss 'council place'	(57) Belorussian *na-na-nica-ць* *panapisac'* a.lot-PFV-write-INF 'write a lot'	(58) Dutch *ver-ont-waardig* PRX-PRX-worthy 'be angry'
(59) Mandarin Chinese 前副總統 qiánfùzǒngtǒng previous-deputy/vice-president 'former vice-president'	(60) Breton *di-gem-poues-a~n*[11] REV-together-weight-INF 'unbalance.v'	(61) Marathi अ-सु-रक्षित *a-su-raksh-ita* NEG-better-protect-ed 'which is not protected'
(62) Swahili *ki-ji-toto* < *m-toto* DIM-INT[12]-child child 'very little child'	(63) Catalan *des-en-caden-ar* un-en-chain-INF 'unleash'	(64) Spanish *anti-pre-histórico* 'anti-pre-historical'
	(65) Greek *αποδιοργανόνω* apo-di-organono undo-REV-organize 'deorganize'	
	(66) Ilocano *n-ag-ka(inn)-awat-an-da* PFV-AV-CMT(RCP)-understand-NMR-3PL 'they understood each other'	
	(67) Italian *ri-s-comporre* 're-de-compose'	

11 *ken-* is a prefix meaning 'together' (cf. Latin *con-*), here lenited by *di-* and assimilated to the place of articulation of the following stop: *ken* > *gem*.

12 The *ji-* intensifier is only used (i.e. is potentiated) by the preceding diminutive or augmentative prefixes.

Nouns	Verbs	Adjectives
	(68) Ket	
	da-u-g-d-o-v-il-tang	
	3F.SBJ-3NTR.OBJ-ABL-	
	ACROSS-TH-	
	INS.APP-PST-drag	
	'She dragged it (using a	
	conveyance)'	
	(69) Pipil	
	n-al-ki:xtia	
	1SG-I-DIR-remove	
	'I remove it'	
	(Campbell 1985: 81)	
	(70) Russian	
	до-пере-ключ-а-ть-ся	
	doperekl'uchat's'a	
	completely-change-switch-	
	TH-INF-RFL	
	'switch over excessively'[13]	
	(71) Slavey	
	te-ka-yi-N-ya[14]	
	water-out-activity-PFV-1,2.	
	go	
	'S/he got out of/went out of	
	water'	
	(72) Slovak	
	po-vy-náša-t'[15]	
	PFV-out/up-carry-INF	
	'carry/take out'	
	(73) Zulu	
	be-si-nga-sa-zu-m-biz-a	
	PST-we-NEG-still-FUT-him/	
	her-call-v	
	'We were no longer going to	
	call him/her'	

[13] To get adverse effect by switching something, e.g. TV programmes at random.
[14] Prefixes: teh 'water', ka 'out of'.
[15] A modified stem of niesť 'carry'.

Recursive prefixation, like simple prefixation, may have class-changing effects:

(74)   Anejom   *awo-nev-edou*
        CAU-QSN-way
        'how to do (something)'

(75)   French   *dés-en-cadrer* (un tableau)
        NEG-in-frame
        'take (a picture) out of its frame'

(76)   Lakhota   *i-wá-nah'u*
        PRX-PRX-hear
        'radio'

(77)   Māori   *kai-whaka-haere*
        AG-CAU-go
        'organizer'

(78)   Romanian *ne-des-facut*
        PRX-PRX-touch
        'intact, untouched'

This analysis takes into consideration that in some polysynthetic languages it is very difficult to speak about word-classes at all:

(79)   Clallam   *nəsxʷč̓łqčšłšáʔ*
        nə-sxʷ-č̓ł-łqčšłšáʔ
        my-CAU-ADV-affect-fifty
        'Fifty of them got me'

(80)   Nelemwa   *Hli pe-fa-k,laxi I hli*
        3DUA.RCP-CAU-be.ashamed.of-3DUA
        'They are making each other mutually ashamed'

Recursive derivational prefixation appears to occur in languages in which there is recursive derivational suffixation, with three exceptions in the study sample: Lakhota, Māori and Yoruba (the last of which does not use suffixation for word-formation processes) show recursive prefixation but not recursive suffixation. Recursive compounding also appears to occur in languages where recursive derivational suffixation occurs and, again, some languages show recursive compounding but not recursive suffixation: Amele and Movima.

4.1.1.2   Base modification in affixation

4.1.1.2.1 Word-formation base modification in suffixation Base modification in suffixation is recorded in the languages shown in Table 4.8.

Table 4.8. *Base modification in suffixation in the study sample*

Language	Family	Morphological type	Area
Bardi	Australian	Fusional	Australia-New Guinea/ Australia
Breton	Indo-European	Fusional	Eurasia/France
Clallam	Salishan	Polysynthetic	North America/USA
Dangaléat	Afro-Asiatic	Agglutinative	Africa/Chad
Datooga	Nilo-Saharan	Agglutinative/ fusional	Africa/Tanzania
English	Indo-European	Isolating	Eurasia/Ireland and UK
Estonian	Uralic	Agglutinative/ fusional	Eurasia/Estonia
Finnish	Uralic	Agglutinative	Eurasia/Finland
Gã	Niger-Congo	Agglutinative	Africa/Ghana
Georgian	Kartvelian	Inflectional/ agglutinative	Eurasia/Georgia
Greek	Indo-European	Fusional	Eurasia/Greece
Hebrew	Afro-Asiatic	Inflectional	Africa/Israel
Hungarian	Uralic	Agglutinative	Eurasia/Hungary
Ilocano	Austronesian	Agglutinative	SE Asia and Oceania/ Philippines
Jaqaru	Aymaran	Agglutinative	South America/Peru
Kwakw'ala	Wakashan	Polysynthetic	North America/Canada
Luo	Nilo-Saharan	Agglutinative	Africa/Kenya, Tanzania
Malayalam	Dravidian	Agglutinative	Eurasia/India
Movima	Movima	Agglutinative	South America/Bolivia
Nelemwa	Austronesian	Isolating	SE Asia and Oceania/ New Caledonia
Pipil	Uto-Aztecan	Agglutinative	North America/El Salvador
Slovak	Indo-European	Inflectional	Eurasia/Slovakia
Spanish	Indo-European	Inflectional	Eurasia/Spain
Tamil	Dravidian	Agglutinative	Eurasia/Tamil Nadu
Tatar	Altaic	Agglutinative	Eurasia/Russia
Tibetan	Sino-Tibetan	Inflectional/ agglutinative	SE Asia and Oceania/China
Totonac	Totonacan	Agglutinative/ polysynthetic	North America/Mexico
Tzotzil	Mayan	Agglutinative/ polysynthetic	North America/Mexico
Udihe	Altaic	Agglutinative	Eurasia/Russia

Language	Family	Morphological type	Area
Wichí	Matacoan	Agglutinative	South America/Argentina and Bolivia
Zulu	Niger-Congo	Agglutinative	Africa/South Africa

As in prefixation, the changes are mostly caused by assimilation, but other types of changes are also possible, as in Bardi, where suffixes with *o* cause vowel harmony, and -*n* initial suffixes cause trill deletion (*rr* + *n* > *n*) (Bowern, pers. comm.). A range of morphophonological stem modifications within the same language is illustrated by Estonian. Most common changes of the stem during the word-formation process of suffixation in Estonian are shown in Table 4.9.

Table 4.9. *Base modification and suffixation in Estonian*

If the suffix begins with a vowel, the stem shortens and ends in a consonant	(81)	Estonian	*kal-ur* kala-ur fish-SFX 'fisher'		
If the suffix begins with the same phoneme as the stem ends with, only one remains[16]	(82)	Estonian	*tühik* tühi-ik empty-NMR 'blank, gap'		
Vowel at the end of the stem may change	(83)	Estonian	*puha-ng* 'blow, blast'	<	*puhu-ma* 'blow.v'
A link may arise between stem and suffix	(84)	Estonian	*liikme-s-kond.*N member-LNK-SFX 'membership, all the members'		
The stem may be in weak grade, even if all the forms of the word are in the strong grade	(85)	Estonian	*pehme-ne-ma.*V soft-SFX-SUP (weak grade) 'soften.v'	<	*pehme.*ADJ soft (strong grade) 'soft'

According to Laakso (pers. comm.), some suffixes in another Finno-Ugric language, Finnish, consist (in the traditional analysis) of vowels that replace the stem-final vowel by regular (morpho-)phonological processes, such as the labial vowel in action derivatives (historically going back to a **w* suffix):

(86)   Finnish   *laul-u*   <   *laula-*
                    'song'   'sing.v'

---

[16] This rule applies regularly with vowels and *s*.

(87)   Finnish   *näk-ö*   <   *näke-*
                   'sight'   'see.v'

Other suffixes may contain satellite vowels which replace the stem-final vowel:

(88)   Finnish   *koivi-kko*
                   koivu-kko
                   birch.tree.COL
                   'birch grove'

(89)   Finnish   *pahe-ne*
                   paha-ne
                   bad-TRN.V
                   'get worse'

A characteristic change in the base due to the change of intransitive verbs to transitive verbs by suffixation in Malayalam is consonant gemination. Asher and Kumari (1997: 275–6) distinguish five types of gemination:[17]

(a)   the result of doubling *k* > *kk*, *ṭ* > *ṭṭ* , *r* > *rr*: *kayaṟ-* 'climb' vs *kayarr-* 'cause to climb',

(b)   a change from double nasal or homorganic nasal + plosive to the corresponding double plosive: *ŋŋ* > *ŋk, mp* > *pp*: *kuump-* 'fold-INTR' vs *kuupp-* 'fold-TR',

(c)   a change from a lateral to a double plosive: *ḷ* > *ṭṭ*, *l* > *rr*: *cuẓal-* 'rotate' vs *cuẓarr-* 'cause to rotate',

(d)   the addition of a double plosive: Ø > *ṭṭ*: *poṭṭ-* 'break-INTR' vs *poṭṭikk-* 'break-TR', and

(e)   the replacement of one double plosive by another: *kk* > *tt*: *nilkk-* 'stop-INTR' vs *nirtt-* 'stop-TR'.

In principle, stem modifications may be divided into vowel modifications (Table 4.10) and consonant modifications (Table 4.11).

Table 4.10. *Vowel modification and suffixation*

Root vowel shortening	(90)	Luo	*körömïït*[18]
			koroom-iit
			fierce-ICP
			'become fierce'
	(91)	Slovak	*vinár*[19]
			víno-ár
			wine-AG
			'vintner'

---

[17] Gemination also accompanies other types of suffixation, e.g. the derivation of agentive names by the suffix *-kaaran* as in *tooṭṭakkaaran* < *tooṭṭam-kaaran* (garden-agent) 'gardener'.

Stem-vowel weakening	(92)	Gã	bɔlɔ bo-lo shout-ITE 'shout several times'
Vowel alternation	(93)	Breton	louzaou-enn[20] weeds.COL-SGT 'weed'
	(94)	Nelemwa	kau-n[21] ka-n year-POS.3SG 'his age'
	(95)	Russian	настра-ива-ть nastraivat' настро-ить nastroit' 'tune.V-IPF'
Vowel deletion	(96)	Georgian	ბერძნ-ულ-ი berdzn-ul-i berdzen-ul-i a.Greek-PST.PTC-NOM 'Greek' (Hillery 1996–2006)
	(97)	Hebrew	פסנתרן psantran psanter-an piano-AG 'pianist'
	(98)	Hungarian	barn-it[22] barna-it brown-CAU 'make brown, tan'
	(99)	Ilocano	itd-an ited-an give-TR 'give to'

[18] Before inceptive suffix.
[19] The shortening of a long stem vowel is characteristic of Slovak, and is connected with the operation of the so-called Rhythmical Law. Cf. also (252).
[20] Stump (pers. comm.) maintains that in Breton -enn causes a stem-final ou to change to aou. Because stress is penultimate, -enn puts the preceding syllable in tonic position, causing the vowel change. Other Breton suffixes may also have this effect.
[21] Vowel alternation here restitutes the etymological vowel in Proto-Oceanic *taqun 'year'.
[22] In Hungarian adjectives end in a vowel if a causative suffix is added.

	(100) Jaqaru[23]	*ut-mashi*
		uta-COM
		house-mate
		'roommate'
	(101) Tzotzil	*k'ïšnax*[24]
		k'ïsin-ax
		warm-INTR
		'become warm'
Vowel insertion	(102) Udihe	*lagban-a-wan-*[25]
		stick-0-CAU
		'glue (something)'
		(Nikolaeva and
		Tolskaya 2001: 301)
Vowel reduction and vowel deletion with loss of stress	(103) Clallam	*ʔəɬn-ístxʷ*
		ʔíɬən-ístxʷ
		eat-CAU
		'feed'

Example (104) from Ilocano shows the influence of suffix in a prefixal-suffixal derivation:

(104)   Ilocano   *pastreken*   <   *pa-serrek-en*
          CAU-enter-TR
          'let in'

In (105), the suffix selects the Latin participle *emiss-* instead of the regular *emesso*:

---

[23] According to Hardman (2000: 9), 'each suffix of the language carries as part of its identity rules governing its combination with other morphemes of the language, subject to alternation for grammatical purposes. That is, some suffixes require the preceding morpheme to drop its vowel ... some require that the preceding vowel be retained.' Specifically, 'the first vowel of all roots is never deleted. Three vowel roots normally lose at least one vowel when entering into derivational or inflectional constructions; where two vowel roots would lose one vowel, the three vowel roots may lose one or two of the vowels' (Hardman 2000: 5).

[24] In Tzotzil, the stem loses its vowel when the intransitivizing suffix -*Vx* is attached to a stative stem (unlike transitive stems which preserve the vowel). When the suffix -*Om* 'act' or 'process' is combined with a transitive stem, the stem loses a vowel:

    Tzotzil   *ʔïkatsnom*
                ʔïkatsin-om
                carry.it.as.a.load-NMR
                'act of carrying loads'
                (Cowan 1969: 106)

[25] Insertion of an epenthetic vowel between the stem and the causative suffix -*wAn-*.

(105)   Italian   *emissione*
'emission'

The formation of diminutives is a frequent source of morphophonological change. Example (106) illustrates diminutive formation accompanied by vowel alternation:

(106)   Tibetan   ཪྟེཝུ
rtevu
rta-vu
'horse-DIM'

A special variant of vowel change due to diminutive formation is Slovak diphthongization:

(107)   Slovak   *žienka*
žen-k-a
'woman-DIM-F.NOM.SG'

The category of diminutiveness brings us at the same time to the area of stem consonant changes, because it is a general phenomenon in Slavic languages, as illustrated in Serbian-Croatian and Slovak, but also in some other languages, like Romanian, and in Zulu, where root-medial and final labial consonants become palatal in the diminutive (also in the locative and the passive):

(108)   Serbian-Croatian   *ruč-ic-a*
ruk-a
hand-DIM-F.NOM.SG
'little hand, handle'

(109)   Slovak   *rúč-k-a*
ruka-DIM-F.NOM.SG
hand-DIM
'little hand'

(110)   Romanian   *cărucior*   <   *căruță*
'perambulator'   'cart/waggon'

(111)   Zulu   *nkony-ana*   <   *n-komo*
'calf'   'cow/bull'

Stem consonant changes are not limited to the category of diminutiveness. Some other cases are shown in Table 4.11.

Table 4.11. *Consonant modification and suffixation*

Change of place of articulation	(112)	Greek	*γράψιμο* grap-simo graf-simo write-NMR 'writing'
Consonant alternation (hardening)	(113)	Kwakw'ala[26]	*dzəlxwsi'stala* dzəlkʷa-si'stala run-around 'run around in circles' (Anderson 1985: 28)
Consonant alternation (softening)[27]	(114)	Catalan	*electricitat* elèctric-itat 'electricity'
	(115)	Pipil	*i:xi-tia* i:sa-tia wake up-TR 'wake (somebody) up' (Campbell 1985: 85)
	(116)	Slovak	*mladík* /d'/ mladý-PAT /d/ young-PAT 'youngster'
Consonant alternation (voicing)	(117)	Serbian-Croatian	*svad-ba* svat-ba guest.at.the.wedding-EVN 'wedding'
	(118)	Tatar	*bigräk* bik-räk much-CMP 'more' (Wertheim)
Tone change	(119)	Dangaléat	*sèwgì* séwg-é wrestle-NMR 'wrestling matches'

---

[26] In Kwakw'ala there are two types of stem-final consonant modification by suffixes: hardening (glottalizing) and softening (voicing) (Boas 1947: 226).

[27] Here illustrated with an example of the so-called softening determined by the quality of the following [i] (114). In (115) it is illustrated with velar softening. In the latter case the vowel reduction following stress shift is phonological.

When the Tzotzil suffix -*ol* 'act of' combines with intransitive roots of the shape CVC plus -*in*, the final *n* changes to *m*:

(120)   Tzotzil   *táximol*
táxin-ol
play-NMR
'game, play'
(Cowan 1969: 107)

The stem-final /n/ may change to /m/ also in Udihe and the causative suffix changes to -*uAn*-:

(121)   Udihe   *lagbam-uan-*
stick-CAU
'glue (something)'
(Nikolaeva and Tolskaya 2001: 301)

With certain verbs (Class II), the stem-final /n/ in Udihe merges with suffix-initial /g/ of the repetitive suffix -*gi*-, which results in -*ŋi*-:

(122)   Udihe   *ilaktan-ŋi-*
ilaktan-gi
appear-ITE
'appear again'
(Nikolaeva and Tolskaya 2001: 317)

As in Nelemwa prefixation and in Nelemwa suffixation, stem modification mostly concerns phonological lenition, in this case with transitive (123) and with possessive suffixes on nouns (traces of proto-stems) (124), while another example illustrates extension of stem due to suffixation (125):

(123)   Nelemwa   *cawi*
cap-I
escape-TR
'escape from (something)'

(124)   Nelemwa   *jixela-ny*
jixet-POS.1SG
rifle-POS.1SG
'my rifle'

(125)   Nelemwa   *haroon*
aroo-n
husband-POS.3SG
'marry.v'

As in English, suffixes in Spanish and Totonac may cause stress shift. In the latter case, the nominalizing suffix shifts the stress leftwards:

(126)   Spanish   *horroroso* /oroɾóso/
                     horror-oso /oróɾ/
                     horror-SFX.ADJ
                     'horrific'

(127)   Totonac   *liné'he'*   <   *li:ne'hé:*
                     li:-ne'hé:-h   li:-ne'hé:
                     INS-fan-NMR
                     'fan'   'fan with (something)'

Finally, Romanian shows a combination of vowel and consonant alternations *ia ~ ie/ t ~ ț*:

(128)   Romanian   *băiat – băiețel – băiețaș – băiețandru – băiețoi*
                      'boy   – 'urchin' – 'a slip of a boy' – 'youngster' –
                      'tomboy, hoyden'

4.1.1.2.2 *Word-formation base modification in prefixation* Base
modification in prefixation is recorded in the languages shown in Table 4.12.

Table 4.12. *Base modification in prefixation in the study sample*

Language	Family	Morphological type	Area
Amele	Trans-New Guinea	Polysynthetic/ synthetic	Australia-New Guinea/ Madang
Anejom	Austronesian	Agglutinative	SE Asia and Oceania/Vanuatu
Bardi	Australian	Fusional	Australia-New Guinea/ Australia
Breton	Indo-European	Fusional	Eurasia/France
Datooga	Nilo-Saharan	Agglutinative/ fusional	Africa/Tanzania
English	Indo-European	Isolating	Eurasia/Ireland and UK
Greek	Indo-European	Fusional	Eurasia/Greece
Hausa	Afro-Asiatic	Fusional	Africa/Niger, Nigeria
Hebrew	Afro-Asiatic	Inflectional	Africa/Israel
Ilocano	Austronesian	Agglutinative	SE Asia and Oceania/ Philippines
Indonesian	Austronesian	Agglutinative	SE Asia and Oceania/ Indonesia
Japanese	Japanese	Agglutinative	Eurasia/Japan
Karao	Austronesian	Inflectional/ polysynthetic	SE Asia and Oceania/ Philippines
Ket	Yeniseian	Agglutinative	Eurasia/Russia
Luo	Nilo-Saharan	Agglutinative	Africa/Kenya, Tanzania

Language	Family	Morphological type	Area
Nelemwa	Austronesian	Isolating	SE Asia and Oceania/ New Caledonia
Pipil	Uto-Aztecan	Agglutinative	North America/El Salvador
Slavey	Na-Dene	Polysynthetic	North America/Northwest Territories
Yoruba	Niger-Congo	Isolating	Africa/Benin, Nigeria
Zulu	Niger-Congo	Agglutinative	Africa/South Africa

While prefixation with base modification is reportedly rare in Catalan, English, Hebrew and Russian, it is frequent in other languages, like Datooga, and occurs systematically in Breton, because it participates in the system of mutations (Stump, pers. comm.):

(129)   Breton   *digoulouma~n*
                          di-koulouma~n
                          'un-tie'

In Afrikaans, the only change in the base is orthographic: capitalization disappears in the names of languages after prefixation:

(130)   Afrikaans   *ver-afrikaans*
                               vr-Afrikaans
                               'make Afrikaans'

According to Carstens (pers. comm.), any other changes in the base are not a result of the prefix with which it combines, but a coincidental occurrence where fossilized ablaut has become associated with the use of a prefix in a particular complex word:

(131)   Afrikaans   *ver-swe-e*   <   *swyg*
                               vr-silent-ATTR
                               'tacit'   'remain silent'

The changes recorded are of diverse nature and seem to be highly language-specific, often even affix-specific. Müller (pers. comm.) remarks that, although some processes may exist and indeed be very productive, they may be so only for a very small number of affixes. Müller illustrates this observation with an example from Indonesian, where morphophonemic alternation of the stem when adding a prefix occurs productively with the various allomorphs of the prefixes *peng-* and *meng-*, but not with any other Indonesian prefixes:

(132)   Indonesian   *mem-egang*
                                  meng-pegang
                                  TR-hold
                                  'take hold of'

In Slavey, the changes bear on the voicing alternations of stem-initial fricatives determined by the immediately preceding prefix. The so-called D-effect
combines a prefix *d-* with a stem-initial fricative or glottal stop.

As noted by Brainard (pers. comm.), Karao displays a set of complex
morphophonological alternations in connection with prefixes and infixes.
The processes are governed by the canonical shape of the affix and the root
and may affect both the affix and the root. If the canonical shapes of the
affix and root are eligible to undergo a particular process, then the process
will automatically apply.[28] Thus, when a prefix ending in *N* attaches to a
root beginning with a CV(C) syllable, *N* assimilates to the same point of
articulation as the root-initial consonant, and the root-initial consonant is
then deleted. When *e-* attaches to a root beginning with a CeCV(C) root, the
prefix changes to *iya-*, *e* is deleted and the root-initial consonant changes to
its syllable-final allomorph (if it is different):

(133)   Karao   *ena-cha*
                    eN-cha-cha
                    AG-help
                    'help.v'

(134)   Karao   *iyalpek*
                    e-depek
                    PAS.real-wet
                    'be wet'

In Bardi, all (C)V- prefixes cause changes in obstruent-initial roots and there
is also a set of complex cluster reduction rules (Bowern, pers. comm.):

(135)   Bardi   *ngaambala*
                    nga-jambala
                    '1SG-foot'[29]

In Zulu, the root *-mb-* 'dig' becomes *-emb-* after a prefix ending in *-a*:

(136)   Zulu   *basemba*
                    ba-sa-mb-a
                    'They are still digging'

The vowel *-a* of the prefix falls away before *e-* and so (as assumed by van der
Spuy, pers. comm.) this situation could be alternatively interpreted as the
root changing a preceding *-a* to *-e*. However, there are only about five roots
in the language that display this phenomenon. Other changes are shown in
Table 4.13.

---

[28] Cf. Brainard (1994).
[29] Cf. *irr-jambala* 'their feet'.

Table 4.13. *Prefixation and base modification*

Assimilation of homorganic nasals	(137)	Ilocano	*mangged* maN-tegged AV-toil 'worker'
Assimilation of manner	(138)	Luo	*chëëpköösäät* cheep-wöös-aat F-mad-NOM 'mad person'
Consonant devoicing[30]	(139)	Datooga	*gítàràbèeṭ < gíd-dàràbèeṭạ* 'personal name of a male'
Consonant voicing (Rendaku rule)[31]	(140)	Japanese	間近 majika ma-chika real-close 'nearby'
Gemination[32]	(141)	Japanese	真っ白 ma-sshiro ma-shiro real-white 'pure white'
Lenition	(142)	Breton	*divamm* di-mamm 'motherless'
	(143)	Nelemwa	*pexoI* pe-ko-l RCP-chase-RCP 'run after each other'
Stress shift[33]	(144)	Greek	*κατακαλόκαιρο* kata-kalókero kata-kalokér(i) over-summer 'high summer'

[30] Caused by prefixation with *git-*.

[31] Often caused by prefixation with *ma-*.

[32] Often caused by prefixation with *ma-*.

[33] For the stress shift due to Class 1 affixation in English, cf. Allen, M. R. 1978. 'Morphological investigations'. Doctoral dissertation, University of Connecticut, Storrs, CT or Siegel (1979).

4.1.2   One-to-many relation in affixation

The title of this section avoids speaking about polysemy/homonymy of affixes, because it is often unclear which of the two is present.[34] In many cases, the borderline is fuzzy. Owing to the absence of clear criteria for the distinction between polysemy and homonymy in general and between polysemy and homonymy of affixes in particular, these cases are considered here as a combination of a single form with several meanings, without examining the degree of semantic relatedness which may lead to an interpretation as polysemy or as homonymy.

The one-to-many relation in prefixation is recorded in the languages shown in Table 4.14.

Table 4.14. *One-to-many relation in prefixation in the study sample*

Language	Family	Morphological type	Area
Breton	Indo-European	Fusional	Eurasia/France
English	Indo-European	Isolating	Eurasia/Ireland and UK
Georgian	Kartvelian	Inflectional/ agglutinative	Eurasia/Georgia
Greek	Indo-European	Fusional	Eurasia/Greece
Hausa	Afro-Asiatic	Fusional	Africa/Niger, Nigeria
Hebrew	Afro-Asiatic	Inflectional	Africa/Israel
Indonesian	Austronesian	Agglutinative	SE Asia and Oceania/ Indonesia
Karao	Austronesian	Inflectional/ polysynthetic	SE Asia and Oceania/ Philippines
Ket	Yeniseian	Agglutinative	Eurasia/Russia
Luo	Nilo-Saharan	Agglutinative	Africa/Kenya, Tanzania
Mandarin Chinese	Sino-Tibetan	Isolating/analytic	SE Asia and Oceania/China
Marathi	Indo-European	Inflectional/ polysynthetic	Eurasia/India
Pipil	Uto-Aztecan	Agglutinative	North America/El Salvador
Slavey	Na-Dene	Polysynthetic	North America/Northwest Territories
Slovak	Indo-European	Inflectional	Eurasia/Slovakia
Spanish	Indo-European	Inflectional	Eurasia/Spain
Swahili	Niger-Congo	Agglutinative	Africa/Tanzania
Wichí	Matacoan	Agglutinative	South America/Argentina and Bolivia

[34] This is also noted by Rice (pers. comm.), who emphasizes that the answer to this question depends on the theoretical framework from which the problem may be approached: 'This depends on analysis. For instance, [in Slavey] *ná-* is analyzed as several morphemes, including continuative and "down". The prefix *d-* is analyzed as an inceptive, as a noun class marker, as a self-benefactive, and as other things, including something with no identifiable meaning.'

The one-to-many relation in suffixation is recorded in the languages shown in Table 4.15.

Table 4.15. *One-to-many relation in suffixation in the study sample*

Language	Family	Morphological type	Area
Breton	Indo-European	Fusional	Eurasia/France
English	Indo-European	Isolating	Eurasia/Ireland and UK
Estonian	Uralic	Agglutinative/fusional	Eurasia/Estonia
Finnish	Uralic	Agglutinative	Eurasia/Finland
Gã	Niger-Congo	Agglutinative	Africa/Ghana
Georgian	Kartvelian	Inflectional/ agglutinative	Eurasia/Georgia
Greek	Indo-European	Fusional	Eurasia/Greece
Hebrew	Afro-Asiatic	Inflectional	Africa/Israel
Hungarian	Uralic	Agglutinative	Eurasia/Hungary
Karao	Austronesian	Inflectional/ polysynthetic	SE Asia and Oceania/ Philippines
Ket	Yeniseian	Agglutinative	Eurasia/Russia
Luo	Nilo-Saharan	Agglutinative	Africa/Kenya, Tanzania
Malayalam	Dravidian	Agglutinative	Eurasia/India
Marathi	Indo-European	Inflectional/ polysynthetic	Eurasia/India
Movima	Movima	Agglutinative	South America/Bolivia
Pipil	Uto-Aztecan	Agglutinative	North America/El Salvador
Slavey	Na-Dene	Polysynthetic	North America/ Northwest Territories
Slovak	Indo-European	Inflectional	Eurasia/Slovakia
Spanish	Indo-European	Inflectional	Eurasia/Spain
Swahili	Niger-Congo	Agglutinative	Africa/Tanzania
Tamil	Dravidian	Agglutinative	Eurasia/Tamil Nadu
Telugu	Dravidian	Agglutinative	Eurasia/India
Tzotzil	Mayan	Agglutinative/ polysynthetic	North America/Mexico
Udihe	Altaic	Agglutinative	Eurasia/Russia
Wichí	Matacoan	Agglutinative	South America/ Argentina and Bolivia
Zulu	Niger-Congo	Agglutinative	Africa/South Africa

As with any other phenomenon, the degree and the extent of the one-to-many relation between form and meaning varies cross-linguistically. In Greek, Ket and Zulu it is rare, in Georgian suffixes tend to show one-to-one correspondence between form and meaning,[35] and in Gã and Nelemwa each prefix and suffix has a single meaning, with the exception of the middle-reciprocal Nelemwa prefix *pe-*, which features significant polysemy/homonymy, as shown in Table 4.16 (Bril 2005: 42), and of the gerundive Gã suffix *-mO*, which can form a gerundive but also derive an iterative/pluractional form of the verb (145).

Table 4.16. *Meanings of Nelemwa* pe- *in relation to the lexical category of the root*

	Reciprocal subjects	Reciprocal objects[36]	Associative (collective dispersive spontaneous)	Other
pe- + intransitive verb	+		+	+
pe- + transitive verb	+	+	+	+
pe- + stative verb	comparison		+	+
pe- + noun	in predicate function	comparison		
	in argument function	+	+	
pe- + pronouns[37]			+	

(145)	Gã	*tsu-mO*	vs	*tsO-mO*
		work-GRN		turn-GRN
		'working.N, sending.N'		'turn over and over'

Various semantic differences/semantic shades of *pe-* (collective (146), reciprocal (147) and spontaneous action (148)) are possible (Bril 2005: 42):

(146)	Nelemwa	*pe-hî*	(*hada*)
		pe-1DUA.ICL	(only)
		'we (two) together only'	

---

[35] However, the so-called thematic suffixes, among which *-eb* is most productive, have no clear single function. They are used with causatives, as a present marker, etc.

[36] This refers to patients which are set in a symmetrical relation by an agent, as in (147).

[37] Independent, deictic or anaphoric pronouns; *pe-* is never prefixed to subject or object personal pronouns.

(147)   Nelemwa   *I   pe-khi   dooviu   mahliili*
                     3SG   pe-hit   iron   those2.ANP
                     'He hit the two metal pieces against each other'

(148)   Nelemwa   *Pe-nukdu   bwa   doo   pwâ-mago*
                     pe-fall   DIR on   earth   fruit-mango
                     'Mangoes are falling [because they are ripe]'

In Mandarin Chinese, the one-to-many relation seems to be restricted to some verbal prefixes which have a basic (149) and an extended meaning (150):

(149)   Mandarin Chinese   死别
                             sībié
                             die/death-part/be.parted
                             'be parted by death'

(150)   Mandarin Chinese   死等
                             sīděng
                             death-wait
                             'wait interminably (to the death)'

This is common in other languages too. Thus, in Hausa the most productive polysemantic/homonymous prefix is *ma-*, which derives agentive (151), instrumental (152) and locative nouns (153):[38]

(151)   Hausa   *maà-ikàc-ī*
                   AG-work-M.SG
                   'worker'

(152)   Hausa   *ma-girbī*
                   'harvesting tool'

(153)   Hausa   *majēmā*
                   'tannery'

The polysemy/homonymy of affixes has been widely discussed in the literature on Indo-European languages, especially in relation to the categories agent, instrument and, partly, location. To these categories, the category patient, defined as a 'bearer of state', should be added. The difference between agent and patient nouns is thus one between action and state, i.e. between the features [+ DYNAMIC] and [– DYNAMIC].

---

[38] Derivation of agent nouns by *ma-* is reportedly productive: according to Newman, one could morphologically create an agent noun from almost any verb. Most nouns of location end in *-ā*. A smaller number end in *-ī*.

The following examples illustrate that the one-to-many relation between the form and the meaning of affixes in relation to the four semantic categories above is not restricted to Indo-European languages. A trivial condition for such a relation is the existence in a language of suffixation and/or prefixation processes. However, it should be noted that a similar kind of overlap can also be found in the relation between agents and patients formed by compounding, as illustrated by Cirecire (154) and Vietnamese (155):

(154)   Cirecire   *cóõ-coo*
                       herbs-coo
                       'doctor'

(155)   Vietnamese   *ŋɯəj²¹ dɯək³¹ʔ fawŋ^{m313} vən³⁵*
                       người được phỏng vấn
                       human-PAS-interview.v
                       'interviewee'
                       (Thái Ân)

In Vietnamese, *được* is used to express passive meaning and functions as a constituent morpheme forming patient nouns. Since, however, its presence is not always necessary, an agent noun may look like a patient noun.

Otherwise, the affixal overlap does not seem to be restricted geographically or genetically. This is an important indication also in terms of what was pointed out by Rainer (2005: 29), in particular, that 'we still don't have even an approximate idea about how frequent our polysemy really is in the languages of the world'. This is largely due to the lack of research and relevant data in this field. Rainer (2005) provides a summary of the approaches to this problem, including a diachronic–synchronic discussion of agentive and instrumental nouns where he refers to several possible sources of the formal identity of agentive, instrumental and locative suffixes, notably reinterpretation and approximation,[39] both based on semantic shift, and instances of non-semantic motivation, in particular ellipsis, homonymization and borrowing. Table 4.17 illustrates the multiplicity and diversity of one-to-many relations in the categories agent, patient and instrument across the languages of our sample.[40]

---

[39] According to Rainer (2005: 23), reinterpretation includes three stages: at first, there are only agentive formations, then some of them acquire an instrumental interpretation due to semantic shift and, finally, the instrumental formations are reinterpreted as an independent word-formation pattern. Approximation skips the second stage.

[40] Cf. also Hausa examples in (151) to (153).

Table 4.17. *One-to-many relations in the semantic categories agent, patient and instrument* [41]

	Agent	Patient	Instrument
(156) Dutch	werk-er / work-AG / 'worker'		(157) Dutch — open-er / open-INS / 'opener'
(158) English	teach-er / teach-AG / 'teacher'		(159) English — drill-er
(160) Finnish	opetta-ja / teach-AG / 'teacher'		(161) Finnish — nito-ja / staple-INS / 'stapler' (Koivisto)[41]
(162) German	Lehr-er / teach-AG / 'teacher'		(163) German — Schläger / beat-INS / 'whisk, egg-beater'
(164) Greek	ελευθερωτής / elefthero-tis / eleftheron(o)-tis / liberate-AG / 'liberator'		(165) Greek — κόπτης / koft-tis / kov(o)-tis / cut-INS / 'cutter'
(166) Hindi	फसरी / fastr-ī / science-AG / 'scientist' (Kachru 2006: 116)		(167) Hindi — रेती / ret-ī / retna-ī / file.V-INS / 'file' (Kachru 2006: 116)
(168) Hungarian	szerel-ő / he.fits-AG / 'technician'	(169) Hungarian — halad-ó / he.advances-PAT / 'advanced student'	(170) Hungarian — ás-ó / he.spades-INS / 'spade'[42]

[41] This apparently goes against Booij's (1986) claim that this kind of polysemy/homonymy does not exist in Finnish.
[42] The suffix variant ó is used for stems with back vowels, and the variant ő for stems with front vowels.

	Agent		Patient		Instrument
(171)	Indonesian	*pe-sawah* AG-paddy.field 'paddy-field peasant'	(172) Indonesian	*pemalas* PAT-lazy 'lazy person'	(173) Indonesian *pemenyapu* INS-sweep.V 'broom'
(174)	Italian	*lavora-tore* work-AG 'worker'			(175) Italian *frullatore* blend-INS 'blender'
(176)	Japanese	言語学者 gengo-gaku-sha language-study-person 'linguist'	(177) Japanese 被害者 higai-sha damage-PAT 'victim'		
(178)	Ket	*súlbets* make.v.a. sled-AG 'sledmaker'			
(179)	Diola-Fogny	*a-teb-a* SG-build-AG 'builder'			(180) Diola- Fogny *ɛ-lib-a* SG-cut-INS 'knife'
(181)	Malayalam	*nuṇa-yan*[43] lie-AG.M 'male liar'	(182) Malayalam *ti-yani-yan*[44] fatness-PAT.M 'fat man'		
(183)	Mandarin Chinese	作者 zuòzhě create-AG 'writer'	(184) Mandarin Chinese 受害者 shòuhàizhě receive/suffer-harm-PAT 'victim'		
(185)	Pipil	*takwi:ka-ni* sing-AG 'singer' (Campbell 1985: 49)	(186) Pipil *miki-ni* die-PAT 'dead person' (Campbell 1985: 49)		

(187) Serbian-Croatian *propoved-nik* preach-AG 'preacher'

(188) Serbian-Croatian *ranje-nik* wound-PAT 'wounded person'

(189) Slovak *hrá-č* play-AG 'player'

(190) Slovak *vlasá-č* hair-PAT 'longhair'

(191) Slovak *počíta-č* compute-INS 'computer'

(192) Spanish *trabaja-dor* work-AG 'worker'

(193) Spanish *despertador* wake-INS (lit. 'waker') 'alarm clock'

(194) Swedish *lärare* teach-AG 'teacher'

(195) Swedish *gräsklippare* grass-mow-INS 'lawnmower'

(196) Udihe *zeu-ŋku* food-AG 'breadwinner'

(197) Udihe *degde-ŋku* raise lift-PAT 'jolly person'

(198) Udihe *akpu-ŋku* sweep-INS 'broom'

(Nikolaeva and Tolskaya 2001: 153)

43 Compare its feminine counterpart:
  Malayalam *muɳa-cci*
       lie-AG.F
       'female liar'

44 Compare its feminine counterpart:
  Malayalam *taʈi-cci*
       fatness-PAT.F
       'fat woman'

The complete series along with location can be observed in (199a) to (199d):

(199)   Tzotzil   a. *j-ʔábtel*
                           AG-work
                           'worker'
                           (Cowan 1969: 109)
                       b. *j-chamel*
                           PAT-sickness
                           'a sick person'
                           (Haviland 1980)
                       c. *kʼáxan-eb*   <   *kʼáxan*
                           harvest.it-INS
                           'harvesting instrument'
                           (Cowan 1969: 105)[45]
                       d. *váy-eb*
                           sleep-LOC
                           'place for sleeping, bed'
                           (Cowan 1969: 105)

It seems from this brief overview that the one-to-two and even one-to-three relations between form and meaning of affixes have few geographic or genetic restrictions. The data also seem to suggest that it is the category agent (rather than patient) which conditions the existence of polysemantic/ homonymous instrumental affixes, as there are no instances in our sample of patient/instrument polysemy/homonymy with no agent in this relation. On the other hand, the patient's absence in the one-to-many relation between agent/instrument is quite common.

The one-to-many relations between form and meaning in word-formation are not limited to the above categories. The following reviews the diversity of one-to-many relations in some languages, first in suffixation and then in prefixation.

In general, the range of combinations of meanings bound to a single suffixal form in Estonian is large. However, according to Kilgi (pers. comm.), there are three groups of suffixes in Estonian:

(a)   suffixes which have only one meaning,
(b)   suffixes that have mostly one meaning but may have more than one, and
(c)   suffixes that have a very general meaning (Table 4.18).

---

[45] The asterisk means that the stem does not occur alone, without an affix.

Table 4.18. *One-to-many relation in Estonian suffixes*

Suffixes with one meaning	-tu	Location	(200)	Estonian	*pilvi-tu*.ADJ 'cloudless'	
	-la	Negation	(201)	Estonian	*kana-la*.N 'hennery'	
Suffixes with more than one meaning	-us	Abstract noun	(202)	Estonian	*pikk-us*.N long-SFX 'length'	
		Action noun	(203)	Estonian	*ärat-us*.N wake-SFX 'waking'	< *ärata-ma*.V to waken-SUP
		Other	(204)	Estonian	*kaupl-us*.N trade-SFX 'shop'	< *kauple-ma*.V to trade-SUP
	-line	Person	(205)	Estonian	*seene-line*.N mushroom.GEN-AG 'mushroomer'	
		Feature	(206)	Estonian	*ruudu-line*.ADJ square.GEN-FEA 'squared, chequered'	
Suffixes with general meaning	-ik		(207)	Estonian	*põlv-ik*.N knee-SFX 'knee-length stocking'	
			(208)	Estonian	*tuul-ik*.N wind-SFX 'windmill'	

Similar tables could be designed for a number of languages: Finnish *-iö* combines the meanings of location (209a) and individual (209b) (Koivisto, pers. comm.):

(209) Finnish a. *keitt-iö*
       cooking-SFX
       'kitchen'
     b. *el-iö*
       live-SFX
       'organism'

Hebrew ן *-on* may express diminutive-derogatory (210a), periodical (210b), collection (210c) or other meanings (210d):

(210) Hebrew a. דובון
       dub-on < dov
       bear-DIM   'bear'
       'small bear'

b. שנתון
shnat-on
shana-on
year-TI
'annual publication'

c. שאלון
she'el-on
she'ela-on
question-COL
'questionnaire'

d. אשפתון
ashpat-on
ashpa-on
garbage-LOC
'dumpster'

Hungarian -gat/-get combines iterativity (211a) and diminutiveness (211b):

(211)   Hungarian   a. *nyit-ogat*
open-ITE
'open repeatedly'

b. *dolgoz-gat*
he.works-DIM
'go on working slowly'

Italian -ino combines the meanings of relational adjective (212a), diminutiveness (212b) and instrument (212c):

(212)   Italian   a. *sal-ino*
salt-REL
'saline'

b. *tavol-ino*
table-DIM
'small table'

c. *spazz-ino*
sweep-INS
'road-sweeper'

Breton -enn has a range of uses: it is usually a singulative suffix (213a), but can also be used to name a countable unit of a substance named by a mass noun (213b), to name a particular object made of a substance (213c) or to name an expanse consisting of a substance named by a mass noun (213d):

(213)   Breton   a. *nezenn*
nits-SFX
'weed'

b. *glavenn*
rain-COU
'raindrop'

c. *direnn*
steel-INS
'dagger'

d. *traezenn*
sand-LOC
'beach'

The Malayalam infinitive suffix -*uka* (and its variants -*a*, -*ka*, -*ika*) can also have a nominalizing function and form verbal nouns, as in (214), where the verbal noun functions as subject of a sentence (Asher and Kumari 1997: 385):

(214)   Malayalam   *vaiki*   *varika*   *nannalla*
          late   come-INF   good-NEG
          'Coming late is not good'

The following examples from Russian are parallel to the notorious case of English -*er*:

(215)   Russian   a. *утр-ен-ник*
                          utrennik
                          morning-LNK-SFX
                          'matinee'

                      b. *дн-ев-ник*
                          dnevnik
                          day-LNK-SFX
                          'diary'

                      c. *началь-ник*
                          nachal'nik
                          begin-AG
                          'chief'

                      d. *ноч-ник*
                          nochnik
                          night-INS
                          'night lamp'

While in Zulu (van der Spuy, pers. comm.) suffixes usually have only one meaning, there are exceptions: -*is*- (causative) means 'make (somebody) do (something)', but it can also mean 'help (somebody) do (something)'; similarly, -*el* 'on behalf of' can also mean 'in the direction of':

(216)   Zulu   *w-a-gijim-el-a e-ndl-ini*
                   'He ran into the house'

Swahili illustrates the homonymy of an agentive (217a) and a negative present tense suffix (217b):

(217)   Swahili   a. *m-wind-i*
                              N.CLASS.PRX.1-hunt-AG
                              'hunter'

                   b. *h-a-wind-i*
                              NEG-3SG.SBJ-hunt-NEG.PRS
                              'S/he does not hunt'

Finally, the following examples of Wichí combine stative (218a) and locative (218b):

(218)   Wichí   a. *o-awanta-hi*
                              3SBJ-to bear-STA
                              'S/he bears'

                   b. *o-yukwaj-hi*
                              3SBJ-bite.V-LOC.in
                              'S/he chews'

Prefixation also provides ample examples of diverse combinations of meanings. The following examples from Karao illustrate this point in relation to the fuzzy nature of the relation between inflection and derivation:

(219)   Karao   a. *pan-dotho/impan-dotho*
                              NMR-cook
                              'act of cooking, time of cooking'

                   b. *pan-chinel-an*   *mo-ak*
                              ITE-depend.on-IPF.PAT   ERG.2SG-ABS.1SG
                              'You can always depend on me'

                   c. *pan-apal*   *taha*
                              IPF.CAU.PAT-jealous   1SG/2SG
                              'I will make you jealous of each other'

                   d. *pan-dotho*   *ka!*
                              IMP-cook   ABS.2SG
                              'Cook!'

Acording to Stump (pers. comm.), the Breton prefix *di-* can be negative (220a), privative (220b) and reversative (220c) and *em-* can express reciprocity (221a) and reflexiveness (221b):

(220)   Breton   a. *di-wir*[46]
                              NEG-true
                              'untrue'

---

[46] *di- + gwir.*

b. *di-vamm*[47]
PRI-mother
'motherless'

c. *digoulouma~n*[48]
REV-tie
'untie'

(221)   Breton   a. *em-gav*[49]
RCP-find/meet
'rendez-vous'

b. *em-laz*
RFL-kill
'suicide.v'

The combination of reciprocity and reflexiveness is quite common cross-linguistically. It also characterizes the Karao verbal prefix *man-/iyan-* (intransitive form) (222a) and (222b) and the Wichí prefix *lhi-*, which indicates co-referentiality between subject and object like a reflexive (223a) and reciprocity, if the plural suffix is added (223b):

(222)   Karao   a. *manbakal*
man-bakal
IPF.AG/PAT-fight
'fight each other'

b. *manna-mes*
man-na-mes
IPF.AG/PAT-bathe
'bathe oneself'

(223)   Wichí   a. *n'-lhi-w'en*
1SBJ-RFL-see
'I see myself'

b. *n'-lhi-w'en-hen*
1SBJ-RCP-see-PL
'We see each other'

The reflexive-reciprocal combination of meanings is also a common feature of derivation in Slavic languages like Czech, Russian or Slovak, and it may be postulated to be one of the most regular types of the derivational one-to-many relation:

---

[47] *di-* + *mamm*.
[48] *di-* + *koulouma~n*.
[49] *em-* + *kav*.

(224)   Slovak   a. *umývať sa*
                    'wash oneself'
                b. *nenávidieť sa*
                    'hate (each other)'

On the other hand, in Marathi, the prefix उप- *upa-* can express various semantic shades of secondariness, as in (225a) and (225b), and the prefix गैर- *gaira-* may express semantic shades of negation, as in (226a) and (226b):

(225)   Marathi   a. उप-आयुक्त
                    upa-ayukta
                    'deputy-commissioner'
                b. उप-नाम
                    upa-naama
                    'second/alternative-name'

(226)   Marathi   a. गैर-हजर
                    gaira-hajara
                    'not present, absent'
                b. गैर-वापर
                    gaira-vaapara
                    'wrong-use'

In Pipil (Campbell 1985: 77ff.), the prefix *ta-* can express 'unspecified object' referring to a (non-human) object of a transitive verb, especially if the focus is on the verb and the object is of little relevance (227a), reduplicated *ta-* (with an additional *h*) is used productively for repetitive action (227b) and also with nouns derived from transitive verbs (227c):

(227)   Pipil   a. *ni-ta-hkwilua*
                I-something-write
                'I write (something)'
              b. *tah-taketsa*
                RDP-talk
                'chat.v'
              c. *ta-chalis*
                ta-chiya
                NMR-look
                'sight'

Finally, the following examples are illustrative of an extremely rich polysemy/homonymy of prefixes in Slavic languages. Slovak *pre-* can express perfectiveness/completion of action (228a), excessiveness (228b) or change/ modification (228c) and the Serbian-Croatian suffix *ne-* may express negation (229a), oppositeness (229b), evil (229c) or inconvenience (229d):[50]

---

[50] All Serbian-Croatian examples are combinations of the prefix *ne-* and a noun.

(228)   Slovak   a. *pre-piť*
                      CPL-drink
                      'drink away'
                   b. *pre-soliť*
                      EXC-salt
                      'oversalt.v'
                   c. *pre-hodnodiť*
                      CHN-evaluate
                      're-evaluate.v'

(229)   Serbian-Croatian   a. *ne-puš-ač*
                                NEG-smoke-AG
                                'non-smoker'
                             b. *ne-red*
                                NEG-order
                                'disorder'
                             c. *ne-delo*
                                NEG-deed
                                'crime'
                             d. *ne-doba*
                                NEG-time
                                'bad time, wrong moment'

4.1.3   Many-to-one relation in affixation

This section examines the opposite relation between form and meaning, in particular, the existence of variants of affixes used in word-formation. A discussion on synonymy of affixes is also included in chapter 6. It is illustrated with numerous examples of both rival affixes and rival word-formation processes which can be used to express various semantic categories. The many-to-one relation in prefixation is recorded in the languages shown in Table 4.19.

Table 4.19. *Many-to-one relation in prefixation in the study sample*

Language	Family	Morphological type	Area
Amharic	Afro-Asiatic	Inflectional	Africa/Ethiopia
Anejom	Austronesian	Agglutinative	SE Asia and Oceania/ Vanuatu
Bardi	Australian	Fusional	Australia-New Guinea/Australia
Breton	Indo-European	Fusional	Eurasia/France
Clallam	Salishan	Polysynthetic	North America/USA

Language	Family	Morphological type	Area
Datooga	Nilo-Saharan	Agglutinative/ fusional	Africa/Tanzania
English	Indo-European	Isolating	Eurasia/Ireland and UK
Georgian	Kartvelian	Inflectional/ agglutinative	Eurasia/Georgia
Greek	Indo-European	Fusional	Eurasia/Greece
Hausa	Afro-Asiatic	Fusional	Africa/Niger, Nigeria
Hebrew	Afro-Asiatic	Inflectional	Africa/Israel
Indonesian	Austronesian	Agglutinative	SE Asia and Oceania/ Indonesia
Japanese	Japanese	Agglutinative	Eurasia/Japan
Karao	Austronesian	Inflectional/ polysynthetic	SE Asia and Oceania/ Philippines
Ket	Yeniseian	Agglutinative	Eurasia/Russia
Konni	Niger-Congo	Agglutinative	Africa/Ghana
Luo	Nilo-Saharan	Agglutinative	Africa/Kenya, Tanzania
Mandarin Chinese	Sino-Tibetan	Isolating/analytic	SE Asia and Oceania/ China
Māori	Austronesian	Isolating	SE Asia and Oceania/ New Zealand
Marathi	Indo-European	Inflectional/ polysynthetic	Eurasia/India
Pipil	Uto-Aztecan	Agglutinative	North America/El Salvador
Slavey	Na-Dene	Polysynthetic	North America/ Northwest Territories
Slovak	Indo-European	Inflectional	Eurasia/Slovakia
Spanish	Indo-European	Inflectional	Eurasia/Spain
Swahili	Niger-Congo	Agglutinative	Africa/Tanzania
Telugu	Dravidian	Agglutinative	Eurasia/India
Totonac	Totonacan	Agglutinative/ polysynthetic	North America/ Mexico
Tzotzil	Mayan	Agglutinative/ polysynthetic	North America/ Mexico
Zulu	Niger-Congo	Agglutinative	Africa/South Africa

The many-to-one relation in suffixation is recorded in the languages shown
in Table 4.20.

Table 4.20. *Many-to-one relation in suffixation in the study sample*

Language	Family	Morphological type	Area
Anejom	Austronesian	Agglutinative	SE Asia and Oceania/ Vanuatu
Bardi	Australian	Fusional	Australia-New Guinea/ Australia
Breton	Indo-European	Fusional	Eurasia/France
Clallam	Salishan	Polysynthetic	North America/USA
Datooga	Nilo-Saharan	Agglutinative/ fusional	Africa/Tanzania
Diola-Fogny	Niger-Congo	Agglutinative	Africa/Gambia, Senegal
English	Indo-European	Isolating	Eurasia/Ireland and UK
Estonian	Uralic	Agglutinative/ fusional	Eurasia/Estonia
Finnish	Uralic	Agglutinative	Eurasia/Finland
Greek	Indo-European	Fusional	Eurasia/Greece
Hausa	Afro-Asiatic	Fusional	Africa/Niger, Nigeria
Hungarian	Uralic	Agglutinative	Eurasia/Hungary
Japanese	Japanese	Agglutinative	Eurasia/Japan
Jaqaru	Aymaran	Agglutinative	South America/Peru
Kalkatungu	Australian- Aboriginal	Agglutinative	Australia-New Guinea/ Australia
Karao	Austronesian	Inflectional/ polysynthetic	SE Asia and Oceania/ Philippines
Ket	Yeniseian	Agglutinative	Eurasia/Russia
Konni	Niger-Congo	Agglutinative	Africa/Ghana
Luganda	Niger-Congo	Agglutinative	Africa/Uganda
Luo	Nilo-Saharan	Agglutinative	Africa/Kenya, Tanzania
Malayalam	Dravidian	Agglutinative	Eurasia/India
Māori	Austronesian	Isolating	SE Asia and Oceania/ New Zealand
Marathi	Indo-European	Inflectional/ polysynthetic	Eurasia/India
Movima	Movima	Agglutinative	South America/Bolivia
Nelemwa	Austronesian	Isolating	SE Asia and Oceania/ New Caledonia
Pipil	Uto-Aztecan	Agglutinative	North America/El Salvador
Slavey	Na-Dene	Polysynthetic	North America/ Northwest Territories
Slovak	Indo-European	Inflectional	Eurasia/Slovakia

Language	Family	Morphological type	Area
Spanish	Indo-European	Inflectional	Eurasia/Spain
Swahili	Niger-Congo	Agglutinative	Africa/Tanzania
Tamil	Dravidian	Agglutinative	Eurasia/Tamil Nadu
Tatar	Altaic	Agglutinative	Eurasia/Russia
Tibetan	Sino-Tibetan	Agglutinative/ inflectional	SE Asia and Oceania/ China
Totonac	Totonacan	Agglutinative/ polysynthetic	North America/ Mexico
Tzotzil	Mayan	Polysynthetic/ agglutinative	North America/ Mexico
Udihe	Altaic	Agglutinative	Eurasia/Russia
West Greenlandic	Eskimo-Aleut	Polysynthetic	North America/ Greenland
Zulu	Niger-Congo	Agglutinative	Africa/South Africa

Two interesting conclusions can be drawn from Table 4.19 and from Table 4.20: one is that the many-to-one relation between form and meaning appears to be more frequent than the opposite relation, and the other is that there is a conspicuous analogy between prefixes and suffixes in both of the examined relations.

4.1.3.1   Suffixation

The most frequent reason for the existence of suffix variants is phonological conditioning (assimilation). Thus, in Estonian a suffix beginning with a vowel cannot be added to a vowel-final stem. Therefore, the stem is often shortened (230) and, if the stem is too short to be shortened, other variants of the suffix are used, such as *-mus, -dus, -vus, -tus* (Kilgi, pers. comm):

(230)   Estonian   *kõrg-us.*N   <   *kõrge.*ADJ
                      high-NMR
                      'height'

Another example of assimilation shows that, in Udihe, with certain verbs (Class II), the stem-final /n/ merges with the suffix-initial /g/ of the repetitive suffix *-gi-*, which results in *-ŋi-* (Nikolaeva and Tolskaya 2001: 301):

(231)   Udihe   *ilaktan-ŋi-*   <   *ilaktan*
                     'appear again'   'appear'

Further examples of this phenomenon are shown in Table 4.21. They illustrate a number of phonologically conditioned forms in Belorussian ((232) and (233)), Estonian ((239) and (240)) and Malayalam ((243) to (246)) or different realizations of suffixes according to what precedes and/or follows them (Luo (236) to (238)):

Table 4.21. *Many-to-one relation in suffixation*

Agentive suffix in Belorussian	-чык -chyk	(232)	Belorussian	газет-чык gazet-chyk newspaper-AG 'journalist'
	-шчык -chyk	(233)	Belorussian	барабан-шчык baraban-shchyk drum-AG 'drummer'
Denominal verb derivation in Hausa	-ta	(234)	Hausa	gubàn-tā[51] poison-CAU 'poison.V'
	-ce	(235)	Hausa	dālib-cē[52] student-FCT 'become a student'
Essive (intransitivizing) suffix in Luo	-iisye	(236)	Luo	mang-ïïsyë dwell-ESS 'be alive'
	-sye	(237)	Luo	kuur-syë call-ESS 'call out'
	-iisyeer	(238)	Luo	päy-ïïsyëër-a make-ESS-INTR 'use.V'
Factitive suffix in Estonian	-ta-	(239)	Estonian	köie-ta-ma.V rope-GEN-FCT-SUP 'provide with a rope'
	-da-	(240)	Estonian	ahel-da-ma.V chain-FCT-SUP 'chain.V'
Causative suffix in Udihe	-wAn- with epenthetic vowel before the suffix	(241)	Udihe	lagban-a-wan- stick-0-CAU 'glue (something)' (Nikolaeva and Tolskaya 2001: 301)
	-uAn- with change of /n/ to /m/	(242)	Udihe	lagbam-uan- stick-CAU 'glue (something)' (Nikolaeva and Tolskaya 2001: 301)

[51] From gubàa.
[52] From āliibī.

Suffix -*al* in Malayalam[53]	(243)	Malayalam	*koṭuk-kal* koṛukkuka-al give-NMR 'giving' (Asher and Kumari 1997: 385)
	(244)	Malayalam	*cey-yal* ceyyuka-al do-NMR 'action' (Asher and Kumari 1997: 385)
	(245)	Malayalam	*vi-ṭal* viṛuka-al leave-NMR 'release' (Asher and Kumari 1997: 385)
	(246)	Malayalam	*paṟac-call-il* paṟayuka-al say-NMR 'saying, rumour' (Asher and Kumari 1997: 385)

Dissimilation is sometimes at play as well. Cowan (1969: 99, 101) shows that the variants of the Tzotzil intransitivizing suffix -*ub* 'developmental' and the transitivizing suffix -*Vn* are controlled by the dissimilation principle: the former suffix appears as -*ib* if the stem contains a back vowel and as -*ub* after other vowels. But when the stem vowel is *o*, the suffix vowel is also *o* (247). The latter suffix occurs with *i* after back vowels of root and with *u* after others (248):

(247)   Tzotzil   a. *p'ix-ub*
                        wise-INTR
                        'become wise'
                     b. *kúš-ib*
                        rust, mould-INTR
                        'rust.v, mould.v'
                     c. *šók-ob*
                        šókol-ub
                        empty, unoccupied-INTR
                        'be unoccupied'

(248)   Tzotzil   *bált'šun*
                     *bált'š cf. bál
                     roll it up-TR
                     'roll it over and over'[54]

[53] Possible realizations are -*al*, -*tal*, -*kkal*, -*ccal* and -*ccil* (Asher and Kumari 1997: 385).
[54] The asterisk means that the stem does not occur alone.

In Jaqaru, variants of suffixes result from systematic vowel-drop in combination with certain other suffixes following them. Hardman (2000: 90) explains that 'all suffixes with two vowels will drop at least one of the vowels in most constructions'. An example with the diminutive suffix *-uña* is given below:

(249)   Jaqaru   *utxitx t"ak-uñ-cha-qa*
                           'It is a little tiny road'

Swahili provides an example of allomorphy due to the opposition of vocalic vs consonantal environment. In Contini-Morava's examples, the variants illustrate post-vocalic allomorphy in the applicative suffix combined with the vowel-harmony principle:

(250)   Swahili   *fik-ish-i-a*
                           arrive-CAU-APP-IND
                           'cause to arrive for (somebody)'

(251)   Swahili   *chuku-li-a*
                           carry-APP-IND
                           'carry for (somebody)'

This brings us to another source of suffix variants, such as vowel harmony, which is typical of agglutinative languages. The following examples come from Hungarian:

(252)   Hungarian   a. *költöz-és*
                              költözni-és
                              remove-NMR
                              'removal'
                         b. *ollóz-ás*
                              ollóz-ás
                              plagiarize-NMR
                              'plagiarism'

(253)   Hungarian   a. *barát-ság*
                              friend-STT
                              'friendship'
                         b. *pék-ség*
                              baker-LOC
                              'bakery'

Pipil illustrates an influence of an affix upon the form of another affix. In particular, the short variant of the adjectival suffix *-a:wa-k*/*-a-k* occurs in combination with the following suffix. From the inchoative verb we get the adjective *chipa:wa-k* 'clear' where *-wa* is an inchoative suffix. If the suffix *-nah* is attached, the long suffix *-a:wak* is reduced to *-ak* (Campbell 1985: 62).

Another source of suffixal variants is the so-called Rhythmical Law. This law imposes a requirement upon Slovak words to avoid two long syllables next to each other. The operation of the law is illustrated for the agentive suffix variants *-ik* (long variant) in (254a) and short *-ik* (short variant) in (254b):

(254)   Slovak   a. *rečn-ík*
                         speak-AG
                         'speaker'
                   b. *básn-ik*
                         poem-AG
                         'poet'

In Zulu, there is a co-existence of a productive variant *-kazi* (phonologically identical with the augmentative) and a rare unproductive variant allomorph *-azi*:

(255)   Zulu   a. *m-vu-kazi*
                         C9-sheep-F
                         'ewe'
                   b. *nkomazi*[55]
                         C9-cow/bull-F
                         'cow'

Finally, Stump (pers. comm.) points out that several Breton suffixes participate in alternations of the form X ~ iX with lexical conditioning, though with some partial phonological regularities:

(256)   Breton   a. *gaou-iad*
                         lie.N-SFX
                         'lying'
                   b. *hegar-ad*
                         affable-SFX
                         'amiable'

(257)   Breton   a. *ober-iant*
                         do-SFX
                         'active'
                   b. *beg-ant*
                         point-SFX
                         'pointed'

There are also unpredictable variants. Cowan (1969: 98ff.) illustrates this possibility with one of eight intransitivizing suffixes used in Tzotzil. This suffix is based on the combination of a V(owel) and *x*, where V is realized unpredictably as *a, e, i, o* or *u*:

---

[55] From *n-komo-azi*.

(258)   Tzotzil   a. *tšáp-ax*
                         roll it up[56]-INTR
                         'be taken care of, have affairs arranged by officials'
                      b. *nát-ex*
                         tall-INTR
                         'grow tall, long'
                      c. *k'óp-ox*
                         language-INTR
                         'talk'

The last example, taken from Dutch, is of similar flavour. At the same time, it demonstrates how complex the relation between variants of a morpheme may be in word-formation. Don (pers. comm.) refers to De Haas and Trommelen (1993: 298), for whom the distribution of '-*lijk* and -*elijk* is not fully complementary and hence also not fully predictable'.[57] De Haas and Trommelen discuss five tendencies which are summarized by Don as follows:

(a)   after a stem-final syllable containing schwa, we get -*lijk*: *open* > *openlijk*, *openelijk 'openly',
(b)   after a stem-final plosive we get -*elijk*: *hoop* > *hopelijk* 'be hoped',
(c)   after a fricative there is preference for -*elijk*: *stof* > *stoffelijk* 'material' (but also forms in -*lijk* are found after fricatives),
(d)   after a stem-final long vowel followed by a nasal or liquid, we find -*lijk*: *natuurlijk* 'natural', and
(e)   after a stem-final diphthong or glide, we usually get -*elijk*: *vrouwelijk* 'female'.

4.1.3.2   Prefixation
          As with suffixal allomorphy, the dominant reason for the existence of prefixal allomorphs is phonological conditioning. In Hausa, *ma-* often assimilates to /mu/ when the vowel in the following syllable is /u/ (259). Some patronymic prefixes in Totonac also have variant forms, as in (260) and (261):

(259)   Hausa   *muhūjī*   <   *mahūjī*
                       'boring tool'

(260)   Totonac   *laka-/laʿha-*
                         'face'

(261)   Totonac   *aʿk-/aʿh-/kuk-/hoh-*
                         'head'

---

[56] As rope.
[57] Translation by Jan Don.

Phonological condition applies also in the transitive active verbal prefix *me-* in Indonesian (Mojdl 2006: 46–8). It exists in five different variants depending on the stem-initial phoneme:

(a)   the variant *mem-* is used before stem-initial *-b-*, *-p-* and *-f-*, as in *mempakai* 'wear',

(b)   the variant *men-* is used before stem-initial *-t-*, *-d-*, *-c-* and *-j-*, as in *mencari* 'look for, find',

(c)   the variant *meng-* is used before stem-initial *-k-*, *-g-*, *-h-* and before a vowel, as in *mengolah* 'cheat.v',

(d)   the variant *meny-* is used before stem-initial *-s-* and *-sy-* (the initial *-s-* and *-sy-* is dropped), as in *menyewa* 'rent.v' (from *sewa* 'rent.N'), and

(e)   the variant *me-* is used before *-m-*, *-n-*, *-ng-*, *-ny-*, *-l-*, *-r-*, *-w-* and *-y-*, as in *melompat* 'jump.v'.

Phonological conditioning occurs in other languages, too (see Table 4.22).

Table 4.22. *Phonologically conditioned prefixes*

Anejom[58]	*er-*	(262)	Anejom	*er-aji* mutual-stand 'stand together'
	eri-	(263)	Anejom	*eri-tas* mutual-talk 'speak as one'
Italian	*il-*	(264)	Italian	*il-limitato* NEG-limited 'unlimited'
	in-	(265)	Italian	*in-utile* NEG-useful 'unuseful'
Pipil	*mu-*	(266)	Pipil	*mu-i:x-pa:ka* RFL-face-wash.V 'wash one's face'
	m-[59]	(267)	Pipil	*m-a:ltia < k-altia* RFL-bathe.V 'bathe oneself'
Romanian[60]	*con-*	(268)	Romanian	*con-viețui* 'co-habit'
	co-	(269)	Romanian	*co-asociat* 'co-partner'

---

[58] The form *eri-* occurs before consonants and the form *er-* occurs before vowels.

[59] In prevocalic position (Campbell 1985: 75–6).

[60] Unlike Anejom and Telugu, Romanian requires that the prefix-final and the stem-intial phonemes be of the same type, i.e. two consonants or two vowels.

Telugu[61]	*a-*	(270)	Telugu	అసత్యం	a-satyam NEG-truth 'lie'
	an-	(271)	Telugu	అనారోగ్యం	an-aaroogyam NEG-health 'ill-health'
Ukrainian	*без-* *bez-*	(272)	Ukrainian	*без-робітт-я*	bezrob'ic'c'ja without-work-IFL 'unemployment'
	безо-[62] *bezo-*	(273)	Ukrainian	*безо-дн-я*	bezodn'ja without-bottom-IFL 'abyss'

The following example of Breton shows a different type of phonological conditioning in which, unlike the prototypical cases of phonological conditioning, there is no complementary distribution of the allomorphs:

(274)   Breton   a. *ken-vreur*
                         together-brother
                         'fellow member'
                    b. *kevlusk*
                         together-movement
                         'commotion'

Stump (pers. comm.) explains that the alternation in the prefix *ken-/kev-* is phonologically conditioned in a rather weak sense: *ken-* can appear with essentially any stem and *kev-* appears with stems beginning with oral sonorant sounds. Similarly, the alternation in the prefix *ad-/as-* is phonologically conditioned in a weak way: *ad-* can appear with essentially any stem and *as-* appears with stems beginning with voiceless obstruents. In neither instance is the distribution complementary: *ken-*, like *kev-*, can precede an oral sonorant and *ad-*, like *as-*, can precede a voiceless obstruent. In this way, as noted by Stump, they are reminiscent of *im-/in-* (with the meaning 'in') in English: *im-* precedes bilabial sounds (*import, immigrate*), while *in-* precedes any sort of sound, including bilabials (*inmate, input*).

This leads to free variants, as exemplified by the Afrikaans prefix *dis-*. The choice between the two variants is reportedly arbitrary:

(275)   Afrikaans *dis-infekteer*
                    des-infekteer
                    'disinfect'

---

[61] The form *a-* occurs before consonants and the form *an-* occurs before vowels.
[62] With an epenthetic vowel between the consonant-final prefix and a consonant-initial stem.

Another important factor is stress. In Clallam, unstressed schwas tend to be deleted (Montler, pers. comm.):

(276)   Clallam   *nsƛ̌éʔ*

         nə-s-ƛ̌eʼʔ

         my-NMR-like

         'I like it'

Another different type of allomorphy, i.e. other than phonologically conditioned, is illustrated by Tzotzil: according to Cowan (1969: 109), the allomorph *ax-* of the prefix *x-* occurs after a pronoun:

(277)   Tzotzil   a. *x-ʔábtel*

            AG-work

            'worker'

           b. *k ax-ʔábtel*

            'my hired help'

The following example from Zulu (van der Spuy, pers. comm.) shows a word-class-conditioned selection of allomorphs. Zulu adjectives and certain adverbial forms can be used as predicates. There, the prefix *sa-* 'still' is combined with verbs (278a) and *se-* with non-verbal predicates (278b):

(278)   Zulu   a. *si-sa-sebenz-a*

           we-still-work-v

           'We are still working'

          b. *si-se-khona*

           we-still-here

           'We are still here'

A completely different condition for the existence of variants of a prefix is mentioned by Hudson (pers. comm.): the use of the causative prefix *a-/as-* in Amharic is determined by the category of transitivity such that *a-* is used for intransitives and *as-* for transitives (however, with many exceptions):

(279)   Amharic   a. አፈላ

            afälla

            a-fla

            CAU-boil

            'He boiled'

           b. አስፈለገ

            as-fällägä

            as-flg

            CAU-seek

            'It made seek (~was necessary)'

The relations between the asymmetric form-meaning prefixal relations and the influence of prefixation on the form of the word-formation base are very diverse (see Table 4.23).

Table 4.23. *Prefixation vs suffixation: discrepancies between one-to-many and many-to-one relations*

	Prefixation		Suffixation	
	One-to-many (polysemy/ homonymy)	Many-to-one (allomorphy)	One-to-many (polysemy/ homonymy)	Many-to-one (allomorphy)
Amharic		+		
Estonian			+	+
Finnish			+	+
Gã			+	
Georgian	+	+	+	
Hausa	+	+		+
Hebrew	+	+	+	
Indonesian	+	+		
Luganda				+
Malayalam			+	+
Mandarin Chinese	+	+		
Movima			+	+
Nelemwa				+
Tamil			+	+
Telugu		+	+	
Zulu		+	+	+

4.1.4   Suffixation, prefixation and word order

Croft and Deligianni (2001) maintain that, cross-linguistically, the VO and OV word orders are found in approximately half of the world's languages and are equally likely.[63] However, our sample is characterized by a dominant position of the VO type. The OV word order is recorded in the languages shown in Table 4.24 (25.45 per cent of the study sample).[64]

[63] Croft, W. and Deligianni, E. 2001. 'Asymmetries in NP word order', paper presented at the International Symposium on Deictic Systems and Quantification in Languages Spoken in Europe and Northern and Central Asia, May 2001, Udmurt State University, Izhevsk, Russia.

[64] Amele is listed along with OV languages but not with SOV languages, and in chapter 7 it is not considered with the rest of the languages which are recorded as SOV in this table.

Table 4.24. *The OV word order in the study sample*

Language	Family	Morphological type	Area
Amele	Trans-New Guinea	Polysynthetic/ synthetic	Australia-New Guinea/Madang
Amharic	Afro-Asiatic	Inflectional	Africa/Ethiopia
Bardi	Australian	Fusional	Australia-New Guinea/Australia
Japanese	Japanese	Agglutinative	Eurasia/Japan
Jaqaru	Aymaran	Agglutinative	South America/Peru
Kalkatungu	Australian-Aboriginal	Agglutinative	Australia-New Guinea/Australia
Ket	Yeniseian	Agglutinative	Eurasia/Russia
Marathi	Indo-European	Inflectional/ polysynthetic	Eurasia/India
Tamil	Dravidian	Agglutinative	Eurasia/Tamil Nadu
Tatar	Altaic	Agglutinative	Eurasia/Russia
Telugu	Dravidian	Agglutinative	Eurasia/India
Tibetan	Sino-Tibetan	Inflectional/ agglutinative	SE Asia and Oceania/ China
Udihe	Altaic	Agglutinative	Eurasia/Russia
West Greenlandic	Eskimo-Aleut	Polysynthetic	North America/ Greenland

The VO word order is recorded in the languages shown in Table 4.25 (52.73 per cent of the study sample).

Table 4.25. *The VO word order in the study sample*

Language	Family	Morphological type	Area
Cirecire	Khoisan	Isolating	Africa/Botswana
Dangaléat	Afro-Asiatic	Agglutinative	Africa/Chad
Diola-Fogny	Niger-Congo	Agglutinative	Africa/Gambia, Senegal
English	Indo-European	Isolating	Eurasia/Ireland and UK
Estonian	Uralic	Agglutinative/fusional	Eurasia/Estonia
Finnish	Uralic	Agglutinative	Eurasia/Finland
Gã	Niger-Congo	Agglutinative	Africa/Ghana
Georgian	Kartvelian	Inflectional/ agglutinative	Eurasia/Georgia
Hausa	Afro-Asiatic	Fusional	Africa/Niger, Nigeria
Hebrew	Afro-Asiatic	Inflectional	Africa/Israel
Hungarian	Uralic	Agglutinative	Eurasia/Hungary

Language	Family	Morphological type	Area
Indonesian	Austronesian	Agglutinative	SE Asia and Oceania/ Indonesia
Konni	Niger-Congo	Agglutinative	Africa/Ghana
Lakhota	Siouan	Synthetic to polysynthetic	North America/USA
Luganda	Niger-Congo	Agglutinative	Africa/Uganda
Luo	Nilo-Saharan	Agglutinative	Africa/Kenya, Tanzania
Maipure	Arawakan	Agglutinative	South America/ Venezuela
Malayalam	Dravidian	Agglutinative	Eurasia/India
Mandarin Chinese	Sino-Tibetan	Isolating/analytic	SE Asia and Oceania/ China
Slavey	Na-Dene	Polysynthetic	North America/ Northwest Territories
Slovak	Indo-European	Inflectional	Eurasia/Slovakia
Spanish	Indo-European	Inflectional	Eurasia/Spain
Swahili	Niger-Congo	Agglutinative	Africa/Tanzania
Totonac	Totonacan	Agglutinative/ polysynthetic	North America/ Mexico
Vietnamese	Austro-Asiatic	Isolating	SE Asia and Oceania/ Vietnam
Wichí	Matacoan	Agglutinative	South America/ Argentina and Bolivia
Yoruba	Niger-Congo	Isolating	Africa/Benin, Nigeria
Zulu	Niger-Congo	Agglutinative	Africa/South Africa

One of the first achievements of extensive typological research in the second half of the twentieth century was an observation that inflectional prefixes are bound to languages with the default VO word order while suffixes occur in both VO and OV languages (cf., among others, Hawkins and Gilligan 1988: 219). Grandi and Montermini (2005: 144) extended this assumption to derivational morphology, suggesting that prefixes may also occur in OV languages 'although they are rarer than in VO languages'. The relation between word-formation processes and word order is analyzed in chapter 7.

4.2   Minor types of affixation

Minor word-formation processes may be labelled as *less natural* or even *unnatural* from the perspective of Natural Morphology. Conversion (5.1.1), derivation by stress (5.1.2) and tone/pitch change (5.1.3) are characterized by the absence of diagrammaticity (constructional iconicity) or even by anti-diagrammaticity, as in the case of subtracting techniques (back-formation, 5.2.1). Some of those processes are viewed in chapter 5, but we also include here those word-formation processes which violate the integrity of morphemes, either stem morphemes (infixation, 4.2.1), or derivational morphemes (like circumfixation, 4.2.3), or which produce new words by adding derivational material at two different points (prefixal-suffixal derivation (4.2.2) and prefixal-infixal derivation and infixal-suffixal derivation (4.2.4). Dressler (1987) predicts that these word-formation processes should be less frequent cross-linguistically than natural word-formation processes like prefixation, suffixation and compounding. Figure 7.1 confirms this in our sample (cf. 7.2).

4.2.1   Infixation

Moravcsik (2000: 546) defines a prototypical infix as an affix which is positioned inside the base such that the preceding and following portions are not meaningful by themselves. Moravcsik also mentions a number of peripheral types of infixation, such as those in which an infix is a free form or, instead of violating the integrity of the base, is inserted between two morphemes of the base. Infixation is recorded in the languages shown in Table 4.26 (25.45 per cent of the study sample).

Table 4.26. *Infixation in the study sample*

Language	Family	Morphological type	Area
Amharic	Afro-Asiatic	Inflectional	Africa/Ethiopia
Clallam	Salishan	Polysynthetic	North America/USA
Dangaléat	Afro-Asiatic	Agglutinative	Africa/Chad
Hebrew	Afro-Asiatic	Inflectional	Africa/Israel
Ilocano	Austronesian	Agglutinative	SE Asia and Oceania/ Philippines
Indonesian	Austronesian	Agglutinative	SE Asia and Oceania/ Indonesia
Karao	Austronesian	Inflectional/polysynthetic	SE Asia and Oceania/ Philippines
Luganda	Niger-Congo	Agglutinative	Africa/Uganda
Mandarin Chinese	Sino-Tibetan	Isolating/analytic	SE Asia and Oceania/ China
Slovak	Indo-European	Inflectional	Eurasia/Slovakia
Spanish	Indo-European	Inflectional	Eurasia/Spain
Tatar	Altaic	Agglutinative	Eurasia/Russia
Totonac	Totonacan	Agglutinative/polysynthetic	North America/ Mexico
Yoruba	Niger-Congo	Isolating	Africa/Benin, Nigeria

Infixation has been described in the literature as chiefly derivational (Ultan 1975: 160; Bybee 1985: 97). This is understandable because derivational infixes reflect 'the closer semantic link between base and derivational affix than what holds between base and inflectional affix' (Moravcsik 2000: 548). In other words, inflectional morphemes serve to express grammatical relations between words, and placing them inside a word-base would mean an obstacle for this function. As usual, the picture is not completely clear in this respect. Thus, if transfixation (root-and-pattern) is viewed as a case of infixation, then infixation is productive in Arabic and Hebrew, where it would also cover inflectional processes.

The importance of laying emphasis on the word-formation nature of the infix follows from its definitions. Thus, Krupa and Genzor (1996) define *infix* in their encyclopedic book on languages of the world as a grammatical or derivational morpheme inserted in a word root. Similarly, the morphematic dictionary of Slovak (Sokolová, Moško, Šimon and Benko 1999: 48) defines infixes as extending morphemes, either grammatical (i.e. thematic submorphemes) or derivational (interfixed submorphemes) which can be attached in two different ways: they extend a grammatical or a derivational morpheme (Buzássyová, pers. comm.):

(280)   Slovak   *diev-č-at-á*   <   *dievča*
                     'girls.PL'   'girl'

(281)   Slovak   *diev-č-at-k-o*   <   *dievča*
                     'little girl'   'girl'

(282)   Slovak   *dv-aj-a*   <   *dva*
                     'two male persons'   'two'

An interesting borderline case is offered by Wichí. According to Nercesian (pers. comm.), there are no infixes in Wichí. However, a root can be interrupted by a suffix and behave like an infix. Such is the case when a suffix, generally indicating direction, is co-lexicalized with root, but if any other suffix (e.g. plural) is added, then it occurs between the root and the co-lexicalized suffix:

(283)   Wichí   a. *ta-taypho*
                     3SBJ-sits.down
                     'S/he sits down'
                  b. *ta-ta...-che...pho*
                     3SBJ-sit down...-PL
                     'They sit down'

An infix, like other affixes, is a bilateral unit with form and meaning. It must be distinguished from interfixes (empty morphs), as the latter 'regularly intervene between stems and derivational suffixes or between two stems in composition, are not associated with any particular semantic or grammatical value, and are very often optional, as for instance, the morph -et- in Spanish *lam-et-ón* or the morph -s- in German *Verfassung-s-treue'* (Laca 2001: 1220–1). Szymanek (2009) shows that interfixes, too, can play an important role in word-formation by being an inherent part of productive word-formation rules (albeit a formal one). This is characteristic of the so-called interfix-suffixing derivation and interfix-paradigmatic derivation. In the former, an interfix and a suffix together function as exponents of the category (Szymanek 2009: 468). Examples can be cited for Polish (284) and also for Czech (285) and Slovak (286):

(284)   Polish   *prac-o-daw-ca*
                  praca-o-dawać-ca
                  job-ITX-give-AG
                  'employer'

(285)   Czech   *zákon-o-dár-ce*
                  law-ITX-give-AG
                  'legislator'

(286)   Slovak   *nosorožec*[65]
                  nose-ITX-horn-PAT
                  'rhinoceros'

Sometimes, as observed by Szymanek (2009: 469) the gender of the compound may differ from that of the head word when used separately. This, in turn, means that the compound belongs to a different inflection class. In that case, the word-formation process is labelled as *interfix-paradigmatic*:

(287)   Polish   *wod-o-głow-ie* [+NTR]
                  woda-o-głowa-F
                  water-ITX-head-IFL
                  'hydrocephalus'

A slightly different example comes from Slovak, where the formation is of the same gender as the head constituent *slov-o* 'word' ([+NEUTER]), but the declensional paradigm changes:

(288)   Slovak   *tvar-o-slov-ie*
                  form-ITX-word-IFL
                  'inflectional morphology'

Finally, the interfix also plays its role of formal indicator of compounding in formations whose second constituent is a converted deverbal noun with a zero marker of the nominative singular. Two of Szymanek's examples (2009: 469) are:

---

[65] Also in Czech.

(289)   Polish   *kork-o-ciag-ø*
         korek-o-ciagnąć
         cork-pull
         'corkscrew'

(290)   Polish   *śrub-o-kręt-ø*
         śruba-o-kręcić'
         screw-twist
         'screwdriver'

In many cases, the converted unit does not exist independently, e.g. **mierz* or **kręt*. There are also analogical formations in Slovak and other Slavic languages:

(291)   Slovak   *ruk-o-pis-ø*[66]   <   *písať*
         ruka-o-pis
         hand-write
         'manuscript, handwriting'

(292)   Slovak   *blesk-o-zvod-ø*[67]
         blesk-o-zvod
         lightning-conductor,lead
         'lightning conductor'

A limited use of infixation in the languages of the world may be explained by the universal preference for morphotactic transparency, in particular, by the preference for continuous (rather than discontinuous) morphemes (Dressler 2005: 273). It is probably for this reason that there are no languages which make use of infixation without employing prefixation or suffixation (Greenberg 1963). From this it follows that, if a language makes use of infixation, it may also be expected to employ prefixation and/or suffixation in word-formation (cf. Plank 2007: 58). Exceptions to this assumption include Yoruba, which uses infixation but not suffixation, and Tatar, which uses infixation but not prefixation.

4.2.1.1   Formal characteristics

It has been shown that infixes invariably appear near one of the edges of a root, a stem or a word (Yu 2003, 2007).[68] Yu calls this the Edge-Bias Effect, and it has been explained diachronically by Plank (2007: 59–60): infixes developed from adfixes primarily by phonological reordering in order to optimize prosodic structures.[69]

---

[66] Also in Czech, where it is derived from *psát* 'write.V'.

[67] In Czech *blesk-o-svod-ø* is derived from *svod*, with the same meaning as in this example.

[68] Yu, A. C. L. 2003. 'The morphology and phonology of infixation'. PhD thesis, Department of Linguistics, University of California, Berkeley, CA.

[69] 'Edge-boundedness, with "edge" defined prosodically, and external occurrence in the case of some edges strongly support the analysis of "infixes" as created by phonological reordering from morphological adfixes' (Plank 2007: 60).

According to Ultan (1975: 164–8), it is primarily the beginning of the base that serves for infixation. This clearly follows from the hierarchy of infix positions identified by Ultan according to frequency.[70]

The limited data on infixation available in the sample do not allow conclusions to be drawn on the formal and semantic patterns of infixing derivation. In principle, the data follow Ultan's (1975: 162–4) and Moravcsik's (2000: 547) observations that infixes seem to prefer to involve at least one consonant, and that the participating consonants tend to be sonorants, i.e. liquids and nasals and glides. The vowels, according to Ultan, are usually short and are mainly high or central.

Ultan (1975: 162–4) also identifies C, CC, CV and VC as the most frequent infix structures, and the data also support this expectation. While our sample provides examples of various formal structures of infixes, the most frequent are structures with a consonant, especially the VC structure with a nasal or liquid (cf. the relevant examples of infixes in Belorussian -im-, Ilocano -um-, Indonesian -el- and Karao -im-), but other types of consonants also occur in this infix structure type, e.g. plosives, as in Spanish (-it-). Other structures include CV with a glide, as in Clallam (-yə) and a plosive, as in Mandarin Chinese (-bù-), VCV (with a fricative consonant), as in Serbian-Croatian (-iva-), single consonant (glottal stop in Clallam and -t- in Tatar), VCVC in Spanish (-isim-) and two (low) vowels, as in Dangaléat (-áa-).

As to word-classes, verbal infixation clearly dominates, but the semantics of verbal infixation ranges over a large number of different categories. This also confirms Moravcsik's assumption (2000: 548) that the meaning of infixes covers 'a broad semantic range'.

4.2.1.2   Semantic characteristics

The range of semantic categories found is shown in Table 4.27.

---

[70] In the following order, from most to least frequent: after the first consonant, after the first consonant cluster, after the first vowel, after the first syllable, after the second consonant, after the vowel of the penultimate syllable, before the final syllable, and before the final consonant. Other options are also possible, e.g. the infix is after the first consonant of the second syllable, as in the following examples:

Spanish	*lej-isim-os*
	far<AUG>SFX.ADR
	'very far'
Spanish	*cerqu-it-a*
	close-<DIM> SFX.ADR
	'so close'

In the second example, there is an orthographical variation: to retain the phoneme /k/ (spelt 'c' before 'a', 'o' or 'u', and 'qu' before 'e' and 'i').

Table 4.27. *Semantic range of infixes*

Augmentativeness	(293)	Spanish	*lej\<ísim\>os* far\<AUG\>SFX.ADR 'very far'
Causativity	(294)	Tatar	*asha\<t\>ïrga* eat\<CAU\>INF 'feed' (Schamiloglu)
Collectivity	(295)	Clallam	*snə́\<yə\>xʷɬ* canoe\<PL\> 'bunch of canoes'
Diminutiveness	(296)	Spanish	*cerqu\<it\>a* close\<DIM\>SFX.ADR 'so close'
Imperfectivity	(297)	Belorussian	*узн\<ім\>ацъ < узняцъ* uzn'imac' uzn'yac' lift\<IPF\>-INF 'lift.v'
Inchoativeness	(298)	Ilocano	*d\<um\>akkel* big\<um\>INC.AV 'grow'
Iterativity	(299)	Dangaléat	*áty\<áa\>pé* átyípé\<áa\>pé hit\<PL\> 'hit (several times)'
	(300)	Serbian- Croatian	*do-pis\<iva\>ti* PRX-write\<ITE\>INF.SFX 'complete writing'
	(301)	Slovak	*do-pis\<ova\>t'* PRX-V.STM\<ITE\>INF.SFX 'complete writing, add in writing'
Negation	(302)	Mandarin Chinese	老不休 lǎobùxiū old\<NEG\>rest 'an old person who doesn't stop being active'
Perfectivity	(303)	Karao	*k\<im\>owa* go/come\<PFV.PAT\> 'come.v/go.v'

4.2.2   Prefixal-suffixal derivation

It has been claimed that 'clear examples of circumfixation are rare or nonexistent' (Carstairs-McCarthy 2006: 86). This view does not separate prefixal-suffixal derivation from circumfixation: 'a circumfix is a combination of a prefix and a suffix that co-occur (at least with bases of specified type) to fulfil a joint function' (Carstairs-McCarthy 2006: 85). One of the few examples accepted as circumfixation in this framework is derivation of verbs meaning 'become X' from adjectival roots:

(304)   Italian   *invecchiare*   <   *vecchio*
                      'age.v'   'old'

An opposite view is that of Hall (2000: 535), who defines circumfix as 'an affix of which one part is bound before, and the other part after, the base'. It is this understanding of circumfixation that was used for this book, such that circumfixation is explained as the case when 'the two parts of circumfix cannot exist independently. They represent a single meaning' (cf. Appendix II). Circumfixation is thus distinguished from prefixal-suffixal derivation,[71] which is based on actual affixes and is defined for our research as follows: 'the two forms represent two different morphemes each of them contributing to the meaning of the word-formation base. Both of them are attached simultaneously, within a single word-formation process' (cf. Appendix II). Prefixal-suffixal derivation is recorded in the languages shown in Table 4.28 (32.73 per cent of the study sample).

Table 4.28. *Prefixal–suffixal derivation in the language sample*

Language	Family	Morphological type	Area
Clallam	Salishan	Polysynthetic	North America/USA
Datooga	Nilo-Saharan	Agglutinative/ fusional	Africa/Tanzania
English	Indo-European	Isolating	Eurasia/Ireland and UK
Georgian	Kartvelian	Inflectional/ agglutinative	Eurasia/Georgia
Hebrew	Afro-Asiatic	Inflectional	Africa/Israel
Ilocano	Austronesian	Agglutinative	SE Asia and Oceania/ Philippines
Indonesian	Austronesian	Agglutinative	SE Asia and Oceania/ Indonesia
Japanese	Japanese	Agglutinative	Eurasia/Japan
Konni	Niger-Congo	Agglutinative	Africa/Ghana

[71] Cases when a single morpheme is realized by two or more affixes are labelled as *synaffixes* by L. Bauer (1988). Certainly, *morpheme* is then necessarily defined as an 'abstract entity, which is realized by morphs' (L. Bauer 1988: 17). Out of a number of examples adduced from various languages, let us mention the derivational morpheme *-istic*, as in *characteristic* or *stylistic*. As stated by Bauer, the two affixes *-ist* and *-ic* should be treated as a single morpheme, borne out by such words as *stylistic*, which in terms of semantics cannot be considered as derived from *stylist*. Synaffixes may have a different structure, including cases with more than one prefix, more than one infix, suffix plus prefix, suffix plus infix, etc.

Language	Family	Morphological type	Area
Lakhota	Siouan	Synthetic to polysynthetic	North America/USA
Luo	Nilo-Saharan	Agglutinative	Africa/Kenya, Tanzania
Marathi	Indo-European	Inflectional/ polysynthetic	Eurasia/India
Nelemwa	Austronesian	Isolating	SE Asia and Oceania/ New Caledonia
Pipil	Uto-Aztecan	Agglutinative	North America/El Salvador
Slovak	Indo-European	Inflectional	Eurasia/Slovakia
Swahili	Niger-Congo	Agglutinative	Africa/Tanzania
Totonac	Totonacan	Agglutinative/ polysynthetic	North America/ Mexico
Zulu	Niger-Congo	Agglutinative	Africa/South Africa

Malkiel (1978: 146) observes that this type of word-formation, sometimes called *parasynthesis*, is very productive with German adjectives in *-lich*. This suffix usually requires one of a long series of prefixes, as exemplified in (305):

(305)　　　German　　a. *ab-kömm-lich*　　'available'
　　　　　　　　　　　　b. *an-geb-lich*　　'alleged'
　　　　　　　　　　　　c. *be-greif-lich*　　'understandable'
　　　　　　　　　　　　d. *ein-träg-lich*　　'profitable'
　　　　　　　　　　　　e. *ent-setz-lich*　　'horrible'
　　　　　　　　　　　　f. *er-sprieß-lich*　　'fruitful'
　　　　　　　　　　　　g. *über-heb-lich*　　'arrogant'
　　　　　　　　　　　　h. *un-säg-lich*　　'ineffable'
　　　　　　　　　　　　i. *unter-schied-lich*　　'distinctive'
　　　　　　　　　　　　j. *ver-läß-lich*　　'dependable'
　　　　　　　　　　　　k. *ver-mein(t)-lich*　　'presumed, presumable'
　　　　　　　　　　　　l. *zer-brech-lich*　　'breakable'

As with other word-formation processes, the boundary between prefixal-suffixal derivation and circumfixation may be fuzzy. A borderline case can be found in Karao, where prefixal-infixal derivation and infixal-suffixal derivation are considered types of circumfixation because, according to Brainard (pers. comm.), both affixes are required and unique meanings cannot be assigned to each affix. Thus, two affixes are combined in Karao, which implies prefixal-infixal, infixal-suffixal type of derivation. Since, however, the two affixes cannot be assigned specific semantic contributions to a new word, the pattern resembles circumfixation.

Indonesian is also unclear in this respect. Mojdl (pers. comm.) notes that the suffix *-an*, which is a part of the confixes *pe- -an*, *per- -an* and *ke- -an*, can

Table 4.29. *Confixes in Indonesian*

	Deadjectival	Denominal	Deverbal
me- -kan	(306) Indonesian *me-man di-kan* CFX-have.a.bath- CFX 'bath (somebody)'		(307) Indonesian *me-ntertawa-kan* CFX-laugh.V-CFX 'mock (somebody)'
me- -i	(308) Indonesian *mem-baik-i* CFX-good-CFX 'repair.V, improve.V'	(309) Indonesian *meng-air-i* CFX-water-CFX 'irrigate (something)'	(310) Indonesian *me-lukis-i* CFX-draw.V-CFX 'draw something'
memper- -kan	(311) Indonesian *memper-jahat-kan* CFX-bad-CFX 'worsen (something)'	(312) Indonesian *memper-suami-kan* CFX-husband-CFX 'marry (somebody)'	
memper- -i		(313) Indonesian *memper-setuju-i* CFX-agree.V-CFX 'approve of (something)'	

also be used independently for productive derivation.[72] Consequently, from the synchronic point of view, the confixes *per- -an* and *ke- -an* are somewhere between the prefixal-suffixal and circumfixal status, because neither *per-* nor *ke-* is used for independent derivation. On the other hand, the verbal confixes *me- -kan, di- -kan, me- -i, di- -i, memper- -kan, diper- -kan, memper- -i, diper- -i, ber- -an, ber- -kan*, etc. are used for prefixal-suffixal derivation covering a diversity of verbal meanings. An outline of this system, including examples, is given in Table 4.29. The confixes form transitive verbs (and sometimes also causatives) from intransitive verbs, nouns and adjectives (Mojdl 2006: 132–40).

Further examples of prefixal-suffixal derivation are given in (314) to (327):

(314)   Afrikaans   *ge-lag-ery*
                     PST-laugh-NMR
                     'laughing.N'

(315)   Belorussian   *пры-бярэж-н-ы*
                       pryb'yarezhny
                       near-bank-ADJ.SFX (M.SG.NOM/ACC)
                       'riverside.ADJ'

(316)   Clallam   *ʔsɬáxʷɬ*   <   *ɬaxʷ*
                   ʔs.STA-go.straight-ɬ.DUR
                   'be straight'

(317)   English   *em-bold-en*
                   make-bold-make
                   (Carstairs-McCarthy)

(318)   Georgian   უ-ნაკლ-ო   უ-ნაკლ-ი-ო
                    u-nak'l-o   u-nak'l-i-o
                    PRX-flaw-SFX
                    'flawless'
                    (Hillery 1996–2006)

(319)   Hebrew   חד-כיוונ
                  xad-kivun-i
                  one-direction-ADJ.SFX
                  'one-way.ADJ'

---

[72] The prefixes *per-* and *ke-* used to be productive in the past, but are no longer used for derivation. The prefix *pe-* is synchronically productive, but its meaning is different from that in the confix *pe- -an*.

(320)   Ilocano   *agallayada*
                           agaC-laya-da
                           smell.like-ginger-3PL
                           'They smell like ginger'

(321)   Japanese   無意識的
                           mu-ishiki-teki
                           non-conscious-ADJ.SFX
                           'unconsciously'

(322)   Lakhota   *wa-kága-pi*
                           PRX-make-SFX
                           'statue'

(323)   Luo   *kii-neet-at*
                           NOM-teach-NOM
                           'teaching'

(324)   Marathi   सु-आगत-अर्ह
                           su-aagata-arha
                           good-come-like
                           'which can be welcomed'

(325)   Pipil   *tatuːkal*
                           PRX-plant.V-NMR
                           'planting'
                           (Campbell 1985: 79)

(326)   Serbian-Croatian *na-prst-ak*
                           PRX-finger-SFX
                           'thimble'

(327)   Swahili   *m-fung-o*
                           NMR-close(VL.STM)-SFX[73]
                           'act of closing, fastening'

4.2.3   Circumfixation

Circumfixation is recorded in the languages shown in Table 4.30 (21.82 per cent of the study sample):

---

[73] This suffix is used to derive deverbal nouns.

Table 4.30. *Circumfixation in the study sample*

Language	Family	Morphological type	Area
Georgian	Kartvelian	Inflectional/ agglutinative	Eurasia/Georgia
Hebrew	Afro-Asiatic	Inflectional	Africa/Israel
Ilocano	Austronesian	Agglutinative	SE Asia and Oceania/ Philippines
Indonesian	Austronesian	Agglutinative	SE Asia and Oceania/Indonesia
Karao	Austronesian	Inflectional/ polysynthetic	SE Asia and Oceania/ Philippines
Maipure	Arawakan	Agglutinative	South America/Venezuela
Nelemwa	Austronesian	Isolating	SE Asia and Oceania/New Caledonia
Slovak	Indo-European	Inflectional	Eurasia/Slovakia
Spanish	Indo-European	Inflectional	Eurasia/Spain
Tamil	Dravidian	Agglutinative	Eurasia/Tamil Nadu
Totonac	Totonacan	Agglutinative/ polysynthetic	North America/Mexico
Wichí	Matacoan	Agglutinative	South America/Argentina and Bolivia

Circumfixation is not a widespread means of word-formation but, as noted by Hall (2000: 540), it occurs in a large number of language families. Brainard (pers. comm.) remarks that, traditionally, Philippinists have ana-lyzed co-occurring discontinuous affixes as circumfixation, because it is not possible to assign independent meanings to each affix consistently. Some lin-guists, however, do not accept this analysis. From this it follows that Karao circumfixations may also be classified as prefixal-suffixal derivation. This reduces the cross-linguistic power of circumfixation as a word-formation process even more and highlights the problems of its delimitation observed by Hall (2000: 542ff.). Some examples of circumfixation are given below:

(328)   Ilocano   *pag-basa-an*
                     LOC-read-LOC
                     'school'

(329)   Karao   *pengedaan*
                   peN-ala-an
                   NMR.IPF-get-__
                   'the place where (something) will be got'[74]

---

[74] As in *Toy pengedaan mo i?* 'Where will you get it?' (Brainard, pers. comm.)

(330)   Maipure   *ma-wana-tení*
                    PRI-body-PRI
                    'one who has no body'[75]
                    (Zamponi 2003: 28)

(331)   Totonac   *xma:le:ni:má:ka'*
                    ix-ma:-le:n-i:-má:-ka'
                    PST-CS-take-CAU-PRG-IDF
                    'S/he was being made to take it'

The evidence gathered here suggests that circumfixation is not bound to a single word-class. While nouns dominate, as exemplified in (328) to (330) and in Table 4.31, circumfixation in Romanian (333), Spanish (335), Totonac (331) is bound to verbs.

Table 4.31. *Nominal and verbal circumfixation*

		Noun			Verb
(332)	Afrikaans	*ge-steen-te*	(333)	Romanian	*în-cruciș-a*
		CRX-stone-CRX			CRX-crosswise-CRX
		'precious stone'			'cross.v'
		(Carstens)			
(334)	Nelemwa	*â-vabuu-n*	(335)	Spanish	*en-jaul-ar*
		CRX-grandchild-CRX			LOC-cage-CRX
		'the grandfather and			'encage.v'
		his grandchild'			
(336)	Slovak	*predmestie*			
		pred-mesto-ie			
		before-town-LOC			
		'suburb'			

Other possible word-classes are ordinal numbers (337):

(337)   Georgian   მე-სამ-ე
                     me-sam-e
                     CRX-three-CRX
                     'third'

4.2.4   Prefixal-infixal and infixal-suffixal derivation

Prefixal-infixal and infixal-suffixal types of derivation are even less natural than prefixal-suffixal derivation, because they violate the principles

---

[75] I.e. 'spirit'.

of naturalness by expressing the word-formation meaning by means of two separate elements and also violate the integrity of the word-formation base. These two word-formation processes are therefore rare. Prefixal–infixal derivation is recorded in the languages shown in Table 4.32 (7.27 per cent of the study sample).

Table 4.32. *Prefixal-infixal derivation in the study sample*

Language	Family	Morphological type	Area
Hebrew	Afro-Asiatic	Inflectional	Africa/Israel
Ilocano	Austronesian	Agglutinative	SE Asia and Oceania/ Philippines
Karao	Austronesian	Inflectional/ polysynthetic	SE Asia and Oceania/ Philippines
Slovak	Indo-European	Inflectional	Eurasia/Slovakia

Infixal-suffixal derivation is recorded in the languages shown in Table 4.33 (10.91 per cent of the study sample).

Table 4.33. *Infixal-suffixal derivation in the study sample*

Language	Family	Morphological type	Area
Hebrew	Afro-Asiatic	Inflectional	Africa/Israel
Ilocano	Austronesian	Agglutinative	SE Asia and Oceania/Philippines
Karao	Austronesian	Inflectional/ polysynthetic	SE Asia and Oceania/ Philippines
Luganda	Niger-Congo	Agglutinative	Africa/Uganda
Mandarin Chinese	Sino-Tibetan	Isolating/analytic	SE Asia and Oceania/China
Slovak	Indo-European	Inflectional	Eurasia/Slovakia

Prefixal-infixal derivation is used in the same group of languages as infixal-suffixal derivation, with the exception of Luganda and Mandarin Chinese. It should be noted that in Hebrew the infixation part of the process corresponds with the use of transfixes, as in (338) and (339):

(338)　Hebrew　מגדל
　　　　　　　　migdal　　< 　root *g-d-l*; pattern *mi- -a-*
　　　　　　　　'tower'

(339)　Hebrew　שלישי
　　　　　　　　šliši　　< 　root *š-l-š*; pattern *- -i-I*
　　　　　　　　'third'

According to Brainard (pers. comm.), prefixal-infixal derivation occurs in Karao in restricted classes of words, e.g. verbs in which the action may be performed reciprocally but the action is not inherently reciprocal. Within this restricted class, prefixal-infixal derivation is frequent:

(340)   Karao   *manchina-cha*
                                      man-cha-cha-in-
                                      RCP.IPF-help-__
                                      'help each other'

Examples from some of the other languages are given in (341) to (343):

(341)   Ilocano   *pinnintasan*
                                      pintas{inn}-an
                                      beauty{RCP}-N
                                      'beauty contest'

(342)   Mandarin Chinese   傻里傻氣
                                      shǎlishǎqì
                                      silly-EMP-silly-air
                                      'goofy, silly'

(343)   Slovak   *pretrvávať*
                                      pre-trv-áv-ať
                                      PRX-last.V-DUR.IFX-INF.SFX
                                      'persist.V'
                                      (Buzássyová)

4.3   Summary

Suffixation is the most frequent affixation process, followed by prefixation. The reason is obvious: these two types of affixation are natural word-formation processes. Both suffixation and prefixation are recursive in a number of languages, with the possibility of the class-change effect. Assimilation stands out as the major type of base modification.

The types of affixation which violate the integrity of morphemes, either stem morphemes (infixation) or derivational morphemes (circumfixation) or which produce new words by addition of affixes at two different points (prefixal-suffixal derivation, prefixal-infixal derivation and infixal-suffixal derivation or root-and-pattern derivation) are comparatively rare and allow for a variety of formal and semantic features, as well as for borderline cases.

5 Word-formation without addition of derivational material and subtractive word-formation

> If we had set out from Māori, rather than from Indo-European languages, I doubt that we'd have come up with such a concept [*as conversion*]! (W. Bauer, pers. comm.).

The previous two chapters in Part II discuss word-formation processes in which derivational material is added to the base and which abide by the constructional iconicity principle, compounding and affixation. This chapter gives an overview of word-formation processes which run counter to the constructional iconicity principle: a new meaning is added which is not supported by any derivational morpheme. For convenience, the chapter groups together processes which may have little in common, e.g. stress shift and stem modification.

This chapter reviews conversion (5.1.1), stress (5.1.2), tone/pitch (5.1.3) and internal stem modification (5.1.4) within the same section. Back-formation, an even less natural process, in which the addition of new meaning is accompanied by the reduction of form, is discussed in 5.2.1.

5.1 Word-formation without addition of derivational material

5.1.1 Conversion

The term *conversion* is connected, in the majority of English-written literature, with the prototypical case of English conversion as a process of forming a new word which belongs to a different word-class without any formal change. From the point of view of constructional iconicity, conversion is not a natural word-formation process: unlike compounding and affixation, the new meaning is not expressed by an additional form (Dressler 2005: 269).

This definition of conversion is, however, tricky for the vagueness of notions like word-class and lack of formal change. As noted by L. Bauer and Valera (2005: 8), 'virtually all of this has been questioned at one point or another and yet the concept of conversion remains in use, very much as the conventional system of word-classes does in languages for which it is theoretically inadequate'.[1] This remark shifts the focus to the issue

---

[1] Filipec and Čermák (1985: 104) take over Dokulil's term *transflexion* (1982) and define conversion in Czech as derivation of new words by the change of inflectional paradigm, and Furdík (2004: 68–9) defines conversion in Slovak as the transition to a different inflectional

of word-classes for cross-linguistic description. A case in point is Māori (W. Bauer, pers. comm.):

> one can make a case for saying that Māori doesn't really have a vocabulary classified into parts of speech, as most bases can be used in both nominal and verbal constituents without change of form, though they change their sense appropriately in the two contexts. This underlies Bruce Biggs's classification of words in Māori (1969) into a small number of classes, one of which he called Universals – i.e., precisely those which are regularly found in both nominal and verbal constituents.

Therefore, while conversion may seem justified from the Indo-European linguistic perspective, it may not be so in other language families. The message of the motto of this chapter is in no way exceptional:[2] it can also be said of other Polynesian languages (W. Bauer 1997: 65)[3] and is apparent from Spencer's (2000: 316) examples of inflected verbs used as nouns in Navajo, a Na-Dene language spoken in North America:

(1)   Navajo   *ha-do*   vs   *ha-k'az*
                    3IPS-warm   3IPS-cold
                    (lit. 'it is warm')   (lit. 'it is cold')
                    'heat'   'coldness'
                    (Spencer 2000: 316)

More importantly, this gives support to the view that lexical entries are neutral as regards word-classes (Farrell 2001). The implication for the theory of conversion is, as pointed out by L. Bauer and Valera (2005: 9), 'that the relationship between nouns and verbs of related form (e.g. [English] *a bridge* and *to bridge*) is no more than a matter of inflection'. This view has found support in the literature (Myers 1984; Josefsson 1997; Giegerich 1999), but it is admittedly rejected more often than not.

---

pattern. Word-class change is not a necessary condition in their view. Consequently, cases like Slovak *sused* 'neighbour.M' >*suseda* 'neighbour.F' or Czech *kmotr* 'godfather' > *kmotra* 'godmother' are also treated as conversion. This is in line with Dokulil's (1968: 230) view that the basic feature of conversion is 'the participation of the word in morphological oppositions' (translation by Salvador Valera). Let us also mention cases of semantic conversion included in the realm of conversion by Stein (1977: 229–35), like English *container* 'magazine, bin' > *container* 'the contents of the magazine, bin'.

2   Cf. the following quotation from Boas (1947: 280) about Kwakw'ala: 'there is no clear cut distinction between noun and verb. Any "verb" preceded by an article is a noun: *yɛxa k!waᵋs* 'the one who sits on the ground'; any noun with predicative endings is a verb: *ᵋne'k°eda bɛgwa'nɛm* 'that one said, it was the man'; *bɛgwa'nɛmeda ᵋne'k a* 'it was the man he said'. The two forms mean the same.'

3   Thus, in Kambera, an Austronesian language spoken in South East Asia and Oceania, a lexeme 'can function either as a verb or as a noun without having an overt morpheme relating these two categories derivationally' (Klamer 1998: 109). Similarly, Taba, an Austronesian language spoken in South East Asia and Oceania, like many other Austronesian languages, has many roots which do not belong to a specific word-class (Bowden 2001: 93).

Conversion is recorded in the languages shown in Table 5.1 (61.82 per cent of the study sample).

Table 5.1. *Conversion in the study sample*

Language	Family	Morphological type	Area
Amele	Trans-New Guinea	Polysynthetic/synthetic	Australia-New Guinea/ Madang
Breton	Indo-European	Fusional	Eurasia/France
Cirecire	Khoisan	Isolating	Africa/Botswana
Clallam	Salishan	Polysynthetic	North America/USA
Dangaléat	Afro-Asiatic	Agglutinative	Africa/Chad
Datooga	Nilo-Saharan	Agglutinative/fusional	Africa/Tanzania
English	Indo-European	Isolating	Eurasia/Ireland and UK
Estonian	Uralic	Agglutinative/fusional	Eurasia/Estonia
Finnish	Uralic	Agglutinative	Eurasia/Finland
Greek	Indo-European	Fusional	Eurasia/Greece
Hausa	Afro-Asiatic	Fusional	Africa/Niger, Nigeria
Hebrew	Afro-Asiatic	Inflectional	Africa/Israel
Hungarian	Uralic	Agglutinative	Eurasia/Hungary
Ilocano	Austronesian	Agglutinative	SE Asia and Oceania/ Philippines
Japanese	Japanese	Agglutinative	Eurasia/Japan
Karao	Austronesian	Inflectional/polysynthetic	SE Asia and Oceania/ Philippines
Ket	Yeniseian	Agglutinative	Eurasia/Russia
Kwakw'ala	Wakashan	Polysynthetic	North America/ Canada
Luo	Nilo-Saharan	Agglutinative	Africa/Kenya, Tanzania
Maipure	Arawakan	Agglutinative	South America/ Venezuela
Māori	Austronesian	Isolating	SE Asia and Oceania/ New Zealand
Marathi	Indo-European	Inflectional/polysynthetic	Eurasia/India
Nelemwa	Austronesian	Isolating	SE Asia and Oceania/ New Caledonia
Slovak	Indo-European	Inflectional	Eurasia/Slovakia
Spanish	Indo-European	Inflectional	Eurasia/Spain
Swahili	Niger-Congo	Agglutinative	Africa/Tanzania
Telugu	Dravidian	Agglutinative	Eurasia/India
Tibetan	Sino-Tibetan	Inflectional/agglutinative	SE Asia and Oceania/ China
Totonac	Totonacan	Agglutinative/polysynthetic	North America/Mexico
Udihe	Altaic	Agglutinative	Eurasia/Russia

Language	Family	Morphological type	Area
Vietnamese	Austro-Asiatic	Isolating	SE Asia and Oceania/ Vietnam
Wichí	Matacoan	Agglutinative	South America/ Argentina and Bolivia
Yoruba	Niger-Congo	Isolating	Africa/Benin, Nigeria
Zulu	Niger-Congo	Agglutinative	Africa/South Africa

Conversion can be found in a number of languages: Serbian-Croatian *dobro* may be an adjective ('good'), a noun ('property') and an adverb ('well'). In Ket it is common for nouns, adjectives and sometimes verbal infinitives to have the same form (cf. (18)), and in Maipure, the same entry may also be a stative verb, an adjective and an adverb (Zamponi 2003: 46) (cf. (20)). Similarly, in Amele *abul-doc* can mean 'struggle.v' as well as 'struggle.N' and *ihan-ec* can mean 'sacrifice.v' as well as 'sacrifice.N'.[4] In Hausa, simple adjectives have the same form as nouns, create feminines and plurals essentially like nouns and use the same genitive linker as nouns; in fact, many words exist in Hausa both as nouns and adjectives (Newman, pers. comm.).

Thái Ân (pers. comm.) explains the high productivity of conversion in Vietnamese by referring to Spencer (2004: 3), who maintains that 'in so-called "isolating languages" it is common for a single word to have the syntax of a noun or a verb indiscriminately, but arguably we are better talking of categorical indeterminacy here rather than mixing'. This must be distinguished from the situation in Jaqaru, where there is a common pro-root which 'functions as a stand-in for all other roots. The pro-root {inchi} may be a pro-noun or a pro-verb or simply a filler. It may carry any or all suffixes of nouns, verbs or sentence suffixes or it may stand alone as a particle' (Hardman 2000: 8).[5]

Probably as a consequence of the different word-class systems that can be found in different languages, individual cases of conversion may feature various degrees of transfer to a new word-class. Nikolaeva and Tolskaya (2001: 166–8) illustrate different degrees of nominalization of verbs in Udihe:

(2)   Udihe   *zima*   <   *zima-*
                  'visit, guests'   'go on a visit'

---

[4] In Amele, 'adverbs are not formally distinguished from nouns and adjectives' (Roberts 1987: 158). Similarly, 'many verbs can function as nouns in their nominalized form ... the nominalized form of the verb is identical to the infinitive form' (Roberts 1987: 325).

[5] This should be distinguished from what happens in Slavey, where many stems can be used as a noun and as a verb, but the verb always has at least one prefix with it (Rice, pers. comm.):

          Slavey   *shoN*   >   *joN* (D + shoN)
                     'old age'   'be old'
          Slavey   *tthiNh*   >   *-tthiNh*
                     'axe.N'   'chop with axe'

(3)   Udihe   *tukä*   <   *tukä*
              'running'   'run.v'

These converted nouns show some verbal properties: they preserve the valency of the corresponding verb and can be modified by an adverbial. The function of converted nouns is to fill the object valency of certain verbs.[6] By contrast, other converted nouns, as (4) and (5), have undergone further nominalization and take all inflections typical of nouns:

(4)   Udihe   *teluŋu*   <   *teluŋu-*
              'story'   'tell'

(5)   Udihe   *etete*   <   *etete-*
              'work.N'   'work.v'
              (Nikolaeva and Tolskaya 2001: 168)

Apart from the prototypical cases of non-homonymous conversion or, rather, conversion as it is understood in Indo-European languages, examples of other subtypes can also be found, e.g. intra-categorial conversion or secondary word-class conversion. In Swahili, the noun *sauti* means 'voice' if accompanied by Class 9 concord and 'thick/harsh voice' if accompanied by Class 5 concord.[7] Examples (6) and (7) illustrate this process in other languages too:

(6)   Belorussian   *пяч-энн-е*   vs   *пяч-энн-е*
                    pyačen'ne   pyačen'ne
                    'baking.ACN'   'cookies'

(7)   Russian   *супруг*   vs   *супруг-а*
                    suprug   supruga
                    '(male) spouse'   '(female) spouse'

Another borderline case can be found in Bardi, where, according to Bowern (pers. comm.), all adjectives and many nouns can be used as coverbs in complex predicates:

(8)   Bardi   *ngaada*   vs   *ngaada-joogooloo-*
                                 -joogooloo- 'break'
              'short'   'break in half'

---

[6]   In this case they take the accusative suffix *-wa*, but they may not inflect for person:

> Udihe   *Sagdi ma:ma ča:la-inji bu-gi-we sita-wa*
>   big grandmother want-3sG give-ITE-ACC child-ACC
>   'The great grandmother agrees to give the child'
>   (Nikolaeva and Tolskaya 2001: 167)

[7]   Normally amplicatives are formed by replacing the noun class prefix with zero but, if the source noun lacks a prefix, its concord can signal amplicative reading (Contini-Morava, pers. comm.).

However, it seems better not to consider these and similar cases of conversion for their dependence on another verb, i.e. they cannot occur independently and, in this respect, they resemble clitics.

All these facts bring the description back to Hockett's (1958: 221) almost forgotten rejection of the traditional concept of word-classes and to the proposal of new categories like AV, NA, VN and NAV, depending on whether the respective lexeme functions both as an adjective and a verb, a noun and an adjective, etc.[8] This book does not pursue this issue and limits itself to providing cross-linguistic evidence which might contribute to answering the question of the correctness or falsity of this direction of consideration.

In our sample, the majority of languages where conversion is recorded allow conversion within the categories adjective, noun, verb and, less markedly, adverb. No records of other word-classes have been cited. It should be emphasized, however, that the following analysis reflects the limited scope of data bound to a single item in our questionnaire examining the existence of a productive word-formation process of conversion.

5.1.1.1   Formal characteristics

Homonymous conversion is perhaps the most canonical view of conversion. It occurs in examples (9) to (27):

(9)	Amele	*ben* 'big'	>	*ben* 'big thing'
(10)	Catalan	*finlandès* 'Finnish'	>	*finlandès* 'Finn'
(11)	Clallam	*swəy'qa* 'man'	>	*swəy'qa* 'be a man'
(12)	Cirecire	*dau* 'ash, burning'	>	*dau* 'burn'
(13)	Dangaléat	*káté* 'go.V'	>	*káté* 'going.N'
(14)	Dutch	*feest* 'party'	>	*feest* 'have a party'
(15)	Hausa	*tsōhō* 'old'	>	*tsōhō* 'elder.N'
(16)	Ilocano	*aso* 'dog'	>	*aso* 'be a dog'

---

[8]   Consider also Halliday's (1966) proposal of the so-called scattering of a lexeme.

(17) Karao   *Emahay*   *daba.*
                 e-maha-i   daba
                 PASS.REAL-DRY-ABS   laundry
                 'The laundry was dry'

(18) Ket   *i'l*   >   *i'l*   >   *i'l*
                 'song'   'sing'   'singing.ADJ'

(19) Luo   *pan*   >   *pan*
                 'curse.N'   'curse.V'

(20) Maipure   *maisuíni*   >   *maisuíni*   >   *maisuíni*
                 'be bad'[9]   'bad.ADJ'   'badly.ADR'
                 (Zamponi 2003: 46)

(21) Mandarin   熟悉   >   熟悉
      Chinese   shóuxī   shóuxī
                 'familiar'   'become familiar with'

(22) Māori   *te pai*   >   *te pai*
                 'goodness'   'DET.good'

(23) Nelemwa   *uya*   >   *uya*
                 'arrive.V'   'arrival'

(24) Romanian   *frumosul*   >   *frumosul*
                 'beautiful'   'beauty'

(25) Serbian-   *mlada*   >   *mlada*
      Croatian   'young'   'bride'

(26) Totonac   *páxni'*   >   *páxni'*
                 'washed'   'pig'

(27) Zulu   *kahle*   >   *kahle*
                 'well'   'fine.ADJ'

As far as the identical form criterion is concerned, this rather general definition lends itself for analytic, non-inflecting languages, but can hardly be applied without modification to inflectional ones. It has been argued, however, that the form of the stem – rather than the form of the word – is important. In the majority of cases, it remains intact. Thus, the situation in Slavic languages shows that, from the formal point of view, this phenomenon is far from being as simple as it might seem when we limit our focus to English. Smirnickij and Achmanova (1952) and Smirnickij (1953, 1954, 1956) point out that conversion in Russian is based on the

---

[9] Stative verb.

change of paradigm. Smirnickij (1953: 24) maintains that conversion in Russian is one of the so-called morphological word-formation processes, where *morphological* is synonymous with *inflectional paradigm*. From this it follows that, while no derivational affix is added, formal changes occur. The paradigm thus fulfils the function of a derivational affix (cf. Dokulil 1968: 218).

Consequently, unlike in English, where in the vast majority of cases conversion entails formal identity, and only a minor group of conversion pairs bear some formal change (*re'cord*.v vs *'record*.N), conversion is not homogeneous cross-linguistically:

(28) Czech   *dobr-ý*.ADJ   >   *dobr-o*.N
                 'good.ADJ'   'good.N'
                 (Dokulil 1968: 221ff.)

(29) Estonian   *julge*.ADJ   >   *julge-ma*.V
                 'brave'   'dare.v'

(30) French   *vol(er)*.V   >   *vol*.N
                 'fly.v'   'flight'

(31) German   *schlafen*.V   >   *Schlaf*.N
                 'sleep.v'   'sleep.N'

(32) Hindi   चमक   >   चमकना
                 cəmək   cɛməkna
                 'shine.N'   'shine.v'
                 (Kachru 2006: 116)

(33) Japanese   泳ぐ   >   泳ぎ
                 oyogu   oyogi
                 'swim.v'   'swimming.N'

(34) Slavey   *shoN*.N   >   *joN*.V
                 (D[10] + shoN)
                 'old age'   'be old'

(35) Spanish   *aceite*.N   >   *aceit-ar*.V
                 'oil.N'   'oil.v'

Another subtype can be illustrated by German *schneiden* 'cut.v' vs *Schnitt* 'cut.N', which shows that one of the stems need not be a citation form.[11] Such cases are not unique cross-linguistically. A relatively frequent source of conversion are participles. This poses serious theoretical problems as to the status of e.g. *-ing* participles/adjectives in English, which, in turn, comes back to the issue of the definition of conversion, especially as participles,

[10] D = D-element.
[11] *Schnitt* is the stem of preterite and past participle.

both present as in (36), (37), and past (38), take part in conversion in a number of languages:

(36) Hebrew   מנהל   vs   מנהל
               menahel   menahel
               nihel-PRS.PTC
               'managed, organized'   'boss, director'

(37) Romanian *tremurândă*   vs   *tremurândă*
               'shaking'   'shaky'

(38) Romanian *Plimbatul de dimineață e sănătos*   <   *plimbatul*
               'The walk in the morning is healthy'   'walked'

In Udihe, resultative participles derived with the suffix *-ktu* are converted to adjectives that can be modified by degree adverbials, like *c'o* 'most' or *belem* 'even more', and can head a comparative adjective phrase (Nikolaeva and Tolskaya 2001: 197):

(39) Udihe   *koŋo-ktu*
               'lean, thin'

(40) Udihe   *soŋo-ktu*
               'crying, whining'

Similarly, passive is used in Karao (41) and past tense forms may be used in Ilocano (42):

(41) Karao   *emahay*   *daba*
               e-maha-i   daba
               PAS.REA-dry-ABS   laundry
               'The laundry was dry'

(42) Ilocano *immay*   vs   *immay*
               'came'   'one who came'

The status of imperative as a converting form in Telugu, as in (43), is ambiguous according to Pingali (pers. comm.):

(43) Telugu   చదువు   vs   చదువు
               caduwu   caduwu
               'read.V'   'education'

For Pingali, verb roots in Telugu are bound forms and they become words with the affixation of at least a suffixal vowel. It is unclear how conversion should be captured as a process, whether the *-u* in derived *caduwu* should be seen as an epenthetic vowel (since words cannot end in consonants) or whether conversion is to be seen as converting the imperative form, which is *caduwu* with the imperative suffix *-u*.

Another formal variant of conversion is one which encompasses the addition of a stem-forming morpheme (theme), as illustrated by the following example from Marathi:

(44)   Marathi   मोठ्याने   मो ा
                  moThyaane   moThaa
                  moth-yaa-ne
                  elder.ADJ-saamaanyarup.SFX-by-ERG[12]
                  'elder.ADJ'   'by elder brother/person'

Czech examples are *zelenat, zelenět, zelenit* 'be green', for which Dokulil (1968: 225) postulates stem-forming grammatical morphemes, i.e. thematic morphemes (*-a-, -e/ě-, -i-*) rather than a derivational suffix.

Conversion may also be accompanied by vowel/consonant alternations, as in Czech and Hindi:

(45)   Czech   *silný*   >   *silně*   [n > ň]
                'strong'   'strongly'
                (Dokulil 1968: 231)

(46)   Hindi   मेला   <   मिलना
                mela   milna
                'fair'   'meet.V'
                (Kachru 2006: 116)[13]

Conversion may also be a part of a combined word-formation process and so, for Slovak, a range of conversion variants can be distinguished (see Table 5.2).[14]

Table 5.2. *Conversion combined with other processes in Slovak*

Transflexion	(47) Slovak	*posypať*	<	*posyp*
		'grit.V'		'grit.N'
Transflexion + consonant alternation	(48) Slovak	*bežať*	<	*beh*
		'run.V'		'run.N' (ž/h)
Transflexion + vowel alternation	(49) Slovak	*nasypať*	<	*násyp*
		'sprinkle'		'bank, dike' (a/á)
Transflexion + consonant +vowel alternation	(50) Slovak	*chodiť*	<	*chôdza*
		'walk.V'		'walk.N' (o/ô, ď/dz)
Prefixal-transflexional derivation	(51) Slovak	*z-havran-ieť*	<	*havran*
		'renounce.V'		'raven'
Prefixal-transflexional derivation + consonant alternation	(52) Slovak	*z-vlč-iť*	<	*vlk*
		'become wild'		'wolf'

[12] The *saamaanyarup* suffix is a stem-forming suffix.
[13] *-na* is an infinitive suffix.
[14] Examples by Horecký and Ološtiak and by Štekauer *et al.* (2001: 74).

Transflexional-reflexive derivation	(53)	Slovak	*líška-ťsa* 'fawn.v'	<	*líška* 'fox'
Transflexional-reflexive derivation + consonant alternation	(54)	Slovak	*opič-iťsa* 'ape.v'	<	*opica* 'ape.N'
Prefixal-transflexional-reflexive derivation	(55)	Slovak	*vy-somár-iť* 'solve a difficult problem'	<	*somár* 'donkey'

The productivity of conversion may differ both cross-linguistically and inside one particular language, if various conversion subtypes are taken into account. In Udihe 'virtually every adjective may receive certain nominal properties within headless noun phrase' (Nikolaeva and Tolskaya 2001: 169). In Hindi, the infinitive suffix *-na* yields an abstract noun and therefore, except for the invariable *cahiye* 'should, ought to', Hindi verbs have infinitive forms which can act as abstract nouns (Kachru 2006: 115). In addition, the root of the verb may be used in Hindi as an abstract noun. By contrast, conversion is reportedly rare in other languages, like Finnish, even if some examples can be found:[15]

(56) Finnish *tihku*   vs   *tihku*
                'drizzle.V'   'drizzle.N'

(57) Finnish *kulu*   vs   *kulu*
                'expend.V'   'expense.N'

In Finnish, Laakso (pers. comm.) notes that there are some cases where the stem-final vowel of a noun coincides with the one-vowel suffix of a verb. In Laakso's view, from a synchronic perspective, these could be classified as cases of conversion because they share the stem *paini-* 'wrestle.v' and *paini* 'wrestling' and both ultimately go back to *paina-* 'press.v'. Laakso notes that there is also a handful of noun–verb ambiguous stems (*tuule-*, NOM.SG.*tuuli* 'wind', *tuule-* 'blow.v (of the wind)'). As there is no clear morphosyntactic boundary between adjectives and nouns, this adjective–noun ambiguity might be considered a kind of conversion.

Given the above-mentioned difficulties concerning the limits of conversion, our cross-linguistic research examines conversion as the formation of new complex words by shift of categorial meaning (following Cetnarowska 1993: 86) in the framework of the conventional system of word-classes, prototypically, without formal change in the stem.[16]

---

[15] Especially one's nationality, country.
[16] Cf. Biese (1941: 6), Pennanen (1975: 221), Lieber (1981: 126, 1992: 159), Kastovsky (1982: 78–9, 1994: 95, 2000: 121), L. Bauer (1983: 32, 2005), Tournier (1985: 49, 169, 197), Vogel (1996: 1), Štekauer (2000: 14–17) or Plank (2010).

5.1.1.2   Semantic characteristics

Conversion offers a wide range of meanings which, despite the scepticism of Clark and Clark (1979), seem to be fairly well predictable for the individual novel converted complex words. Štekauer's (2006) data show that, with the majority of this kind of neologisms, there is usually one, rarely two dominant meanings, much more predictable than the other potential readings of the coinage. Table 5.3 shows a hint of the wide semantic capacity of conversion as a word-formation process.

Table 5.3. *Semantic diversity in conversion*

Agent	(58)	Ilocano	*immay* 'came'	vs	*immay* 'one who came'
	(59)	Greek	κυνηγός kinig-os 'hunter'	vs	κυνηγο kinig-o 'hunt.v'
Instrument	(60)	Italian	*fucile* rifle-Ø-IFL.SFX 'rifle'	vs	*fucilare* 'shoot.v'
	(61)	Maipure	*nau* 'paddle.N' (Zamponi 2003: 44)	vs	*nau* 'paddle.v'
Object of action	(62)	Breton	*had* 'seed'	vs	*hadañ* 'sow'
	(63)	French	*clou*.N 'nail.N'	vs	*clou(er)*.V 'nail.v'
Patient	(64)	Belorussian	малады malady 'young.ADJ'	vs	малады malady 'fiancé'
	(65)	Swedish	*vit* 'white'	vs	*vit* 'white person'
Process	(66)	Afrikaans	*lag* 'laugh.N'	vs	*lag* 'laugh.v'
	(67)	Portuguese	*andar* 'walk.v'	vs	*andar* 'walk.N'
Quality	(68)	Hausa	*farī* 'white'	vs	*farī* 'whiteness'
	(69)	Nelemwa	*coola* 'be strong'	vs	*coola* 'strength'
Result of action	(70)	Slovak	*násyp* 'dyke/levee'	vs	*nasypať* 'grit.v, pour.v'
State	(71)	Nelemwa	*khîlû* 'ill'	vs	*khîlû* 'illness'

5.1.2   Stress

Stress is recorded in the languages shown in Table 5.4 (7.27 per cent of the study sample).

Table 5.4. *Change in stress in the study sample*

Language	Family	Morphological type	Area
English	Indo-European	Isolating	Eurasia/Ireland and UK
Hebrew	Afro-Asiatic	Inflectional	Africa/Israel
Luganda	Niger-Congo	Agglutinative	Africa/Uganda
Vietnamese	Austro-Asiatic	Isolating	SE Asia and Oceania/Vietnam

Even in these languages, stress does not play any significant role in word-formation, or at least its function as an independent word-formation device is questionable. Such is the case of English, where examples of stress as a word-formation process are traditionally associated with conversion:

(72)   English   *'record.*N   vs   *re'cord.*V

(73)   English   *'torment.*N   vs   *tor'ment.*V

However, in these and similar examples of word-class-conditioned stress change, the position of stress results from the main word-formation process (conversion) which shifts stress to the status of a secondary phenomenon. Štekauer (1996: 55–95) argues that stress difference as in (72) and (73) does not result from an independent word-formation process and that such pairs should be treated as a specific subgroup within conversion.

The value of stress as a word-formation device is perhaps better appreciated comparing English and Luganda: while stress shift may be viewed in English as a by-product of certain cases of conversion (disyllabic nouns, verbs and adjectives), conversion does not exist in Luganda and yet stress shift has the same derivational effect:

(74)   Luganda   *k'uruju*   vs   *kur'uju*
                   'farm.v'   'agriculture'

In yet other languages, like Hebrew, the examples are diverse in nature: some noun–verb pairs parallel the above examples of English and therefore raise the same doubts. Hebrew does not seem to make relevant use, if any, of stress as a word-formation device. Semantic unrelatedness occurs in similar examples of Romanian and Ukrainian, where the total absence of any semantic relation argues against the word-formation status of stress:

(75)   Romanian   *tórturi*   vs   *tortúri*
                   'cakes'   'tortures'

(76)   Ukrainian   *мукá*   vs   *мýка*
                        muka   muka
                        'flour'   'suffering'

These are different from the example taken from Ukrainian (77), which is
a case of semantic divergence from one and the same source word, i.e. a
diachronic process rather than one of word-formation:

(77)   Ukrainian   *зáмок*   vs   *замóк*
                        zamok   zamok
                        'castle'   'lock'

This is supported by Slovak and Czech equivalents, both of these pairs
having the same form, i.e. they are homonyms: Slovak *zámok* and Czech
zámek. However, the two meanings (identical to those in Ukrainian) are not
distinguished by stress.

Another borderline case includes examples for Belorussian and Vietnamese,
where stress shift is at the border between inflection and derivation:

(78)   Belorussian   *рассыпáць*   vs   *рассы́паць*
                        rassypac'   rassypac'
                        'spill.PFV'   'spill.IPF'

(79)   Vietnamese $\varepsilon m^{33}\ ut^{35}$ vs $\varepsilon m^{33}\ ut^{35}$
                        em út   em út[17]
                        'younger/-est   'the younger/-est/junior/
                        brother/sister'   inferior/-est brother/sister'

5.1.3   Tone/pitch

Like stress shift, the role of tone/pitch in word-formation seems
comparatively minor, except in tonal languages. Tone/pitch is recorded in the
languages shown in Table 5.5 (12.73 per cent of the study sample).

Table 5.5. *Tone/pitch in the study sample*

Language	Family	Morphological type	Area
Cirecire	Khoisan	Isolating	Africa/Botswana
Dangaléat	Afro-Asiatic	Agglutinative	Africa/Chad
Datooga	Nilo-Saharan	Agglutinative/fusional	Africa/Tanzania
Hausa	Afro-Asiatic	Fusional	Africa/Niger, Nigeria
Konni	Niger-Congo	Agglutinative	Africa/Ghana
Mandarin Chinese	Sino-Tibetan	Isolating/analytic	SE Asia and Oceania/China
Vietnamese	Austro-Asiatic	Isolating	SE Asia and Oceania/Vietnam

---

[17] I.e. both *ém* and *út* are stressed vs only *út* is stressed.

Chebanne (pers. comm.) explains that Cirecire has two fundamental tones, high and low (H and L, respectively), and two derived tones that are super-high (SH) in the context of consecutive HH tones in sentence-final position and super-low (SL) in the context of consecutive LL tones in sentence-final position. Tone has a derivational function in the following examples:

(80)   Cirecire   ‖àô   vs   ‖àó
                   'fly.v'   'eagle'

(81)   Cirecire   tshàúú   vs   tsháúú
                   fourth finger   hand
                   'four'   'palm'

Tonal properties of verbal and nominal derived forms are given in (82) to (84):

(82)   Cirecire   qúì   vs   qùíí
                   'live.v'   'life'

(83)   Cirecire   qá   vs   qáà
                   'drink.v'   'drinking.N'

(84)   Cirecire   úè   vs   úèè
                   'break.v'   'breaking.N'

Tone in Cirecire interacts with other word-formation processes, as illustrated in Table 5.6.

Table 5.6. *Tone and other word-formation processes in Cirecire*

[L HH] derives from [LL#HH]	(85)	Cirecire	djùbéé 'cow'	<	djùù, béé 'home', 'beast'
[H HHH] derives from [HH#LHH]	(86)	Cirecire	djú cúáá 'black person'	<	djúú, cùáá 'black', 'person'
[LLL LL-SL] derives from [LLSL#LLL]	(87)	Cirecire	‖gàètà tsàùù 'five'	<	‖gàètàà tsàùù 'four finger', 'thumb'
[LH-HL] derives from [LL#HH]	(88)	Cirecire	bàšáâ 'old woman'	<	bàà šáá 'old', 'woman'
[LL HHH] derives from [LLL#HHH]	(89)	Cirecire	gùbù ñ‖áá 'north'	<	gùbùù, ñ‖áá 'Kalanga', 'side'
[HH LL] derives from [HHH#LL]	(90)	Cirecire	íó kòxà 'zebra'	<	íóó kòxà 'wild', 'horse'

Tone is an important aspect of Datooga inflection, which also has repercussions in derivational morphology. With respect to tonal behaviour, we have to identify tone-integrative suffixes, i.e. suffixes that impose tone patterns onto the noun as a whole, overriding lexical tone patterns. All the nominal plural suffixes do so. There is also a process of tone conversion by which plurals are derived from singulars: generally speaking, a switch from tone class 2 (H(H)L) to tone class 1 (L(L)H) derives a plural form from singulars in *0* and in *-èe*. Nouns with the primary suffix *0* that display tone conversion are shown in Table 5.7.

Table 5.7. *Tone conversion in Datooga (nouns with primary suffix 0)*

	Singular				Plural	
(91)	Datooga	*díyàay-da* 'animal'	HL	(92)	Datooga	*d yáa -g* 'animals'	LH
(93)	Datooga	*máastèew-da* 'branding iron'	HL	(94)	Datooga	*màastèe-ka* 'branding irons'	LH
(95)	Datooga	*sídáagèe-da* 'awl'	HHL	(96)	Datooga	*sìdàagée -a* 'awls'	LLH

Nouns with the primary suffix *-èe* display tone conversion. Some are shown in Table 92.

Table 5.8. *Tone conversion in Datooga (nouns with primary suffix -èe)*

	Singular				Plural	
(97)	Datooga	*gíij-èe-da* 'mountain'	HL	(98)	Datooga	*gìij-ééŋ-ga* 'mountains'	LH
(99)	Datooga	*máaŋ-èe-da* 'front leg of animal'	HL	(100)	Datooga	*màaŋ-ée-ga* 'front legs of animal'	LH
(101)	Datooga	*gáal-èe-da* 'stomach'	HL	(102)	Datooga	*gàal-ée-ga* 'stomachs'	LH
(103)	Datooga	*nàq-èe-da* 'fat'	LL	(104)	Datooga	*nàq-ée-gạ* 'fats'	LH
(105)	Datooga	*ʃ-èe-da* 'moon, month'	L	(106)	Datooga	*ʃ-èe-ga* 'moons, months'	H
(107)	Datooga	*fúqár-ée-da* 'cleverness, wit'	HHL	(108)	Datooga	*fùqár-ééŋ-ga* 'clevernesses, wits'	LHH
(109)	Datooga	*hìrj-èe-da* 'front side of house'	LL	(110)	Datooga	*hìrj-ééŋ-ga* 'front sides of houses'	LH
(111)	Datooga	*áp-èe-da* 'bottom, buttock'	HL	(112)	Datooga	*àp-ée-ga* 'bottoms, buttocks'	LH

Newman's (pers. comm.) examples for Hausa are verbal nouns derived from stems of a particular grade: monosyllabic H-tone verbs ending in short *i* have verbal nouns that end in a long *-ī* and have a falling tone:

(113)   Hausa   *bî*   <   *bi*
                          'following'   'follow'

In Dangaléat, tone can distinguish gender (114) and in Mandarin Chinese tone is sometimes used as a basis for morphological class (115):

(114)   Dangaléat   *kòkìra*   vs   *kókírá*
                          'hen'   'rooster'

(115)   Mandarin Chinese   釘子   vs   釘釘子[18]
                              dīngzi   dìngdīngzi
                              'nail'   'hammer in a nail'

Interestingly, tone does not function as a word-formation device in Vietnamese, even though it is a tone language[19]. It can only have a meaning-distinctive function in homonymous lexemes, as in (116):

(116)   Vietnamese *mæ:³⁵*   vs   *mæ:³¹ʔ*
                      má (high pitch level)   mạ (low pitch level)
                      'cheek/mother'   'rice/seedling'
                      (Thái Ân)

The same can be found in Konni (117):

(117)   Konni   *kpáá-ŋ*   vs   *kpàá-ŋ*
                     oil-SG   guineafowl-SG
                     'oil'   'guinea fowl'

5.1.4   Word-formation by internal modification

5.1.4.1   Stem vowel alternation

Stem vowel alternation is recorded in the languages shown in Table 5.9 (23.64 per cent of the study sample):

---

[18] In these cases, a first-tone noun becomes fourth tone when used as a verb ('pound in (a nail)').

[19] As emphasized by Alves (pers. comm.), this assumption is true with the exception of Southern Vietnamese third person pronouns derived from family terms. Thus, *o'ng a''y* /sir - that/ 'He (older, respectful)' in official/standard Vietnamese is equivalent to *o'ʔng* (where *ʔ* represents the rising hoi tone) in Southern Vietnamese. This pattern is consistent with other referential terms and some location terms (cf. L. C. Thompson 1967).

Table 5.9. *Stem vowel alternation in the study sample*

Language	Family	Morphological type	Area
Anejom	Austronesian	Agglutinative	SE Asia and Oceania/ Vanuatu
Dangaléat	Afro-Asiatic	Agglutinative	Africa/Chad
Datooga	Nilo-Saharan	Agglutinative/fusional	Africa/Tanzania
English	Indo-European	Isolating	Eurasia/Ireland and UK
Hausa	Afro-Asiatic	Fusional	Africa/Niger, Nigeria
Hebrew	Afro-Asiatic	Inflectional	Africa/Israel
Ket	Yeniseian	Agglutinative	Eurasia/Russia
Luganda	Niger-Congo	Agglutinative	Africa/Uganda
Luo	Nilo-Saharan	Agglutinative	Africa/Kenya, Tanzania
Marathi	Indo-European	Inflectional/polysynthetic	Eurasia/India
Slovak	Indo-European	Inflectional	Eurasia/Slovakia
Tibetan	Sino-Tibetan	Agglutinative/inflectional	SE Asia and Oceania/China
Tzotzil	Mayan	Agglutinative/polysynthetic	North America/Mexico

5.1.4.1.1 Formal characteristics Stem vowel alternation is frequent in Arabic and Hebrew. Vowel alternation is their fundamental word-formation process and is generally labelled *root-and-pattern*. According to Schwarzwald (2001: 23), 'the number of roots [in Hebrew] runs somewhere between 3,000 and 4,500 roots. The number of patterns is limited to approximately 200. A single root may be inserted into many patterns', e.g. *g-d-l* in nouns, verbs and adjectives (see Table 5.10).

Table 5.10. *An example of root-and-pattern in Hebrew: g-d-l*

	Nouns		Adjectives		Verbs
(118) Hebrew	גדולה gdula 'greatness'	(119) Hebrew	גדול gadol 'big'	(120) Hebrew	גדילה gadal 'grew up'
(121) Hebrew	גדילה gdila 'growth'	(122) Hebrew	מגודל megudal 'large (grown up)'	(123) Hebrew	גידל gidel 'raised'
(124) Hebrew	גדלות gadlut 'greatness'	(125) Hebrew	מוגדל mugdal 'enlarged'	(126) Hebrew	הגדיל higdil 'enlarged'
(127) Hebrew	גודל gódel 'size'				

Nouns	Adjectives	Verbs
(128) Hebrew גידול gidul 'growth, tumour'		
(129) Hebrew הגדלה hagdala 'enlargement'		
(130) Hebrew מגדל migdal 'tower'		

At the same time, one and the same pattern can be used for the derivation of many new words (Schwarzwald 2001: 23):

(131)   Hebrew   *CiCaCon*   >   ביטחון
                                       bita<u>x</u>on
                                       'security'

                              >   דיבאון
                                   dika'on
                                   'depression'

                              >   היגיון
                                   higayon
                                   'logic'

                              >   זיכרון
                                   zikaron
                                   'memory'

                              >   חיסרון
                                   xisaron
                                   'fault'

                              >   שיגעון
                                   šiga'on
                                   'insanity'

According to Zwarts (pers. comm.), the derivation in the following examples from Luo consists of merely a floating [+ ATR] feature that autosegmentally attaches itself to the vowels of the verb root. Thus, the derivation process is based on changing a vowel from [– ATR] to [+ ATR]. Remarkably, the resulting agentive noun is in plural:

(132)   Luo   *choor*   >   *chöör*
                    'steal.v'   'thieves'

(133)   Luo   *rum*   >   *rüm*
                'murder.v'   'murderers'

There are also combined types of stem modification, in which a vowel change accompanies the main word-formation process. Vowel modification is often combined with other processes, as with reduplication in Konni and Tibetan, with stem vowel modification in Marathi or with suffixation in Breton and Malayalam (see Table 5.11).

Table 5.11. *Vowel modification in combination with other word-formation processes*

Vowel modification and reduplication	Vowel modification and stem vowel modification	Vowel modification and suffixation
(134) Konni *di-digi-ru* RDP~cook-AG 'cook'	(135) Marathi अनिच्छा anichchhaa an-iichchhaa NEG-wish '(with) no wish'	(136) Breton *louzaouenn*[20] louzou-enn weeds.-COLL- SG.SFX 'weed'
(137) Tibetan ཀན་ཀོན་ rgan-rgon old-old 'very old'		(138) Malayalam *dhairyam* dhiiram-am courageous- NMR 'courage'

5.1.4.1.2   Semantic characteristics The range of functions of vowel modification as a word-formation process is broad and no generalizations seem to be possible. It is used to derive verbal nouns in Dangaléat (139), German (140) and Hausa (141):

(139)   Dangaléat   *ɛyìwì*   vs   *ɛyàawe*
                     'walk.N'   'walk.V'

(140)   German   *Gang*   <   *gehen*
                     'walk.N'   'go.V'

(141)   Hausa   *guugàa*   <   *googèe*
                     'rubbing.N'   'rub.V'

Other semantic changes caused by vowel alternation are shown in Table 5.12.

---

[20] The vowel change combined with suffixation is due to the penultimate position of stress; *-enn* puts the preceding syllable in tonic position, causing the vowel to change (Stump, pers. comm.).

Table 5.12. *Semantic diversity of vowel alternation*

Causative[21]	(142) Datooga	*ruut rit* come.out 'take out'		
Intransitive verbs from roots	(143) Tzotzil	*k'ak'* 'burn.v' (Haviland 1980)	<	*k'Ak* (root)
Transitive from intransitive	(144) Anejom	*etjem* 'dive for (something)'	<	*atjem* 'dive'
Momentary vs. frequentative	(145) Russian	носить nosit' 'carry-ITE'	<	нести nesti 'carry-MOM'
	(146) Slovak	*nosit'* 'carry-ITE'	<	*niest'* 'carry-MOM'

5.1.4.2   Stem consonant alternation

Stem consonant alternation is recorded in the languages shown in Table 5.13 (7.27 per cent of the study sample).

Table 5.13. *Stem consonant alternation in the study sample*

Language	Family	Morphological type	Area
Datooga	Nilo-Saharan	Agglutinative/fusional	Africa/Tanzania
English	Indo-European	Isolating	Eurasia/Ireland and UK
Malayalam	Dravidian	Agglutinative	Eurasia/India
Slovak	Indo-European	Inflectional	Eurasia/Slovakia

This word-formation process seems to play an important role only in Malayalam derivation. However, even this depends on the interpretation, because processes like vowel alternation and consonant alternation in Malayalam can also be interpreted as instances of affixation (Mohanan, pers. comm.):

(147)   Malayalam   *maraccu*   <   *maran~n~u*
                            'covered.TR'   'disappeared'

In English (148) there are cases of denominal verb formation by consonant alternation, but this process is not productive (Carstairs-McCarthy, pers. comm.). Similar examples can be found in Datooga (with change of *q* to *g*) (149) and Slovak (150):

---

[21] English causatives like *lay* vs *lie* or *raise* vs *rise* are considered scarcely productive (Carstairs-McCarthy, pers. comm.). Carstairs-McCarthy notes that it is unhelpful to talk in these cases of constituent morphemes. For many morphologists, there is only one morpheme in these forms.

(148)	English	*wreathe*	<	*wreath*
(149)	Datooga	*gwalgwal-ees* 'steal upon (somebody)'	<	*qwalqwal-aad* 'tiptoe'
(150)	Slovak	*tíš* 'quietness'	<	*tich-ý* 'quiet'

5.2   Subtractive word-formation processes

5.2.1   Back-formation

Back-formation is recorded in the languages shown in Table 5.14 (16.36 per cent of the study sample).

Table 5.14. *Back-formation in the study sample*

Language	Family	Morphological type	Area
Anejom	Austronesian	Agglutinative	SE Asia and Oceania/Vanuatu
English	Indo-European	Isolating	Eurasia/Ireland and UK
Finnish	Uralic	Agglutinative	Eurasia/Finland
Greek	Indo-European	Fusional	Eurasia/Greece
Hebrew	Afro-Asiatic	Inflectional	Africa/Israel
Marathi	Indo-European	Inflectional/polysynthetic	Eurasia/India
Slovak	Indo-European	Inflectional	Eurasia/Slovakia
Spanish	Indo-European	Inflectional	Eurasia/Spain
Tamil	Dravidian	Agglutinative	Eurasia/Tamil Nadu

This process may be regarded as a truly peripheral one. This is especially so as the question may be raised whether back-formation is not relevant only from a diachronic point of view, as assumed by Marchand (1960). From the synchronic point of view, Marchand (1960: 3) proposes the following equation for English back-formation: *peddle : peddler = write : writer*. This means that, synchronically, back-formation is analyzed analogically with suffixation. This makes sense because, logically, the cutting off of an affix postulates the prior attachment of this affix, even if the corresponding word-formation base was not in use before.

It has already been noted that, unlike Marchand, Kiparsky (1982a) explains the process of forming verbs like *air-condition*.v or *spotweld*.v (traditionally explained by back-formation) as compounding, based on the rule $[Y Z]_x$, with X being V. Similarly, Štekauer (1998, 2005) explains this type of example on a par with other word-formation processes, based on the Morpheme-to-Seme-Assignment Principle.

All these approaches, from the synchronic perspective, call into doubt the process of back-formation, and further undermine its status among word-formation processes from both cross-linguistic and language-specific points of view. The scarcity of back-formation does not, however, preclude it from ranging over various categories in some languages, as illustrated by Romanian (see Table 5.15).

Table 5.15. *Back-formation in Romanian*

Denominal nouns	(151) Romanian	*banan* 'banana tree'	<	*banană* 'banana'
Deverbal nouns	(152) Romanian	*înghet* 'frost'	<	*îngheţa* 'freeze.v'
Denominal verbs	(153) Romanian	*aniversa* 'celebrate.v'	<	*aniversare* 'celebration'
Deadjectival verbs	(154) Romanian	*nemuri* 'render immortal'	<	*nemuritor* 'immortal'

In the majority of cases, the direction is from nouns to verbs, which express the action contained in the meaning of the motivating noun. This applies to several languages:

(155)   German   *seiltanzen*   <   *Seiltänzer*
                   'ropewalk.v'   'ropewalker'

(156)   Italian   *gest-ire*   <   *gestione*
                    'manage.v'   'management'

(157)   Spanish   *televis-ar*   <   *televisión*
                    'televise.v'   'television'

(158)   Swedish   *nöjessegla*   <   *nöjessegling*
                    'sail for pleasure'   'sailing for pleasure'

Sometimes the back-formation process does not reach beyond the boundaries of a particular word-class, as in the following examples from Serbian-Croatian and Slovak:

(159)   Serbian-Croatian   *bratimiti*   <   *pobratimiti*
                            'fraternize.IPF'   'fraternize.PFV'[22]

(160)   Slovak   *ekonóm*   <   *ekonómia*
                   'economist'   'economics'

Aside from denominal verbs like (161), Finnish provides examples of an opposite direction, i.e. from verb to noun (162):

(161)   Finnish   *hiekkapuhaltaa*   <   *hiekkapuhallus*
                    'sandblast.v'   'sand-blasting'
                    (Laakso)

---

[22] This example illustrates a rare case of prefix elimination.

(162)   Finnish   *riehaantu-*   >   *rieha*
                    'to go wild'   'happening/being
                                            boisterous' (Koivisto)

Clearly, back-formation is a typical European (plus all types of Englishes) matter, covering Germanic, Romance and Slavic. Back-formation in Finno-Ugric languages is non-existent or very rare. According to Kilgi (pers. comm.), there are some examples of back-formation in the history of Estonian, but it is not a productive word-formation process nowadays (cf. however (163) and (164)) and in Finnish it depends on the account of relatively rare compound verbs traditionally explained either as calques (165) or back-formations (166) (Laakso, pers. comm.):

(163)   Estonian   *eelis*.N   <   *eelistama*.V
                    'advantage'   'prefer.V'

(164)   Estonian   *ravi*.N   <   *ravitsema*.V
                    'medical treatment'   'nurse.V'

(165)   Finnish   *alle-kirjoittaa*
                    under-write
                    '(under)sign'

(166)   Finnish   *hiekkapuhaltaa*   <   *hiekkapuhallus*
                    'sandblast.V'   'sand-blasting'

There are few exceptions to the Eurocentric nature of back-formation in our sample. An example is taken from Marathi:

(167)   Marathi   कर   करणे
                    kara   karaNe
                    'hand'   'do.V'

5.3   Summary

This chapter reviews word-formation processes which do not involve the addition of derivational material, or which involve subtraction. The former type refers to conversion, stress, pitch/tone and stem alternation. Of these, conversion best exemplifies how the description of certain linguistic concepts is, probably unavoidably, based on the theoretical framework developed for Indo-European languages. As a result, it relies on concepts which otherwise would naturally not be used. By contrast, stress and, more clearly, pitch/tone, are rather foreign to this tradition. Back-formation is presented as the only subtractive word-formation process considered in this book. Its theoretical implications are briefly discussed and it is illustrated in some languages.

6 An onomasiological description

> Typologists must realize that they cannot base their comparisons on formal categories, and need to resort to semantic-pragmatic or phonetic substance as a foundation of their classification and generalizations. (Haspelmath 2007: 128)

This chapter deals with the ways in which the most common semantic categories are expressed in word-formation. This approach has been almost totally ignored in Western twentieth-century linguistics, mainly due to the influence of the form-centred Bloomfieldean structuralism whose position was later taken over by the generative mainstream in linguistics. However, it is an approach that requires at least as much attention as the form-based one. This follows from the semiotic and cognitive foundations of word-formation, i.e. from the formation of new linguistic signs. This approach, it should be noted, complies with insistence by Greenberg (1966: 74), Croft (2003) and Haspelmath (2007: 126), among others, on the crucial role of semantics in typological research.

This chapter reviews the possible realizations of semantic categories by groups: the nominal (6.2), evaluative (6.3), verbal (6.4) and word-class changing categories (6.5). Each of these subsections devotes a part to one semantic category.

6.1 Introduction

The purpose of the onomasiological method is to find out how cognitively grounded categories are linguistically represented through the individual word-formation processes. The selection of a particular word-formation process and of a particular word-formation rule within the process is not pre-determined by strictly prescribed rules of the particular language. There is always space for a creative approach to the linguistic realization of a cognitively captured and processed object that should be named in a language. This is the fundamental idea underlying our concept of creativity within productivity constraints (Štekauer 2005; Štekauer, Chapman, Tomaščíková and Franko 2005).

The selection of a particular naming strategy is always an interplay between on the one hand the limits imposed on the naming process by language through the available productive rules and constraints on productivity and on the other individual naming preferences and knowledge of language determined by factors like education, profession, age or family language background. The overall naming situation in a language is thus a result of all the individual acts of naming implemented by individual language users in a particular environment. It is for this reason that an onomasiological approach lays emphasis on the cognitive and extra-linguistic factors affecting the process of naming and it is for this reason too that a formal description of word-formation processes must be complemented with an onomasiological one.

One may raise the question of why, then, so much attention has been devoted to typology in the form-oriented first part of this volume. There are several reasons. First, the form-centred approach has a very long tradition, including the terminology and procedures used. It greatly contributes to the progress in understanding word-formation processes, rules, the internal structure, the relations in complex words and, in fact, all the major issues of word-formation theory. Any new approach inevitably faces numerous difficulties of acceptance, which sometimes may result in its falling into oblivion. Second, there are very few comprehensive descriptions of word-formation systems (such as Dokulil (1962, 1997) for the Czech language, Horecký, Buzássyová and Bosák (1989) for Slovak and Rainer (1993) for Spanish) which might serve as a basis for contrastive typological research from the onomasiological perspective. We believe that the semasiological (form-centred) and the onomasiological (cognitive, meaning-centred) approaches are mutually complementary.

There are two important limitations on the onomasiological part of this book. First, it has no pretence to cover all semantic categories, largely for the procedure used for data collection: the response tolerance of the informants had to be taken into consideration to ensure a sufficient return rate of questionnaires. Existing grammatical descriptions could not be used either: if the description of word-formation in the great majority of languages is rather poor, the onomasiological viewpoint, i.e. the way of expressing various semantic categories by formal word-formation processes, approaches zero. Unlike other aspects of cross-linguistic research, this *is* a *tabula rasa*. On the other hand, there is no agreement on the number of semantic/conceptual categories and, thus, there is not a universally accepted list of them. The categories included in the questionnaire were selected based on some Indo-European languages. This methodological bias seemed unavoidable. To avoid gaps in this selection, the questionnaire invited informants to adduce any other important semantic/conceptual categories in their respective languages. A long list of examples of these categories indicates a cross-linguistic multiplicity and diversity of these categories and the unequal role played by these categories in various languages of the world. Second, this book does not cover all the possible ways of expressing the selected categories in individual languages. This would exceed the scope of any similar work. In fact, it may be regarded as a highly desired long-term goal requiring extensive cooperation. Nonetheless, the examples given illustrate the individual semantic/conceptual categories and indicate the prevailing tendencies in their expression in individual languages as they represent typical ways of declaring the respective categories, as well as tendencies across languages.

The onomasiological analysis is based on semantic categories which may reflect essential categories of life in human communities. Life is based on activity (conceptual category of action) as a centre of gravity of human existence. This justifies to some extent the selection of the categories agent (as a 'person performing some activity'), patient (as a 'person who is the bearer of state'[1]), instrument (as actions are typically performed by means of instruments) and location (each action takes place at some place). On the other hand, nature depends on the existence of male and female beings, and language reflects this duality by gender. Quantities and emotions intersect in the field of evaluative morphology, specifically in the formation of augmentatives and diminutives. We should therefore ask whether and how this interplay is reflected by word-formation. The inclusion in the questionnaire of the category of action nouns is self-explanatory in light of the central position of activity and action in life. The same applies to all the consequences of human activity: is activity oriented at somebody/something and what is its consequence? This justifies the action-related categories of causativity, intransitivity and transitivity on the one hand, and of the categories of iterativity and intensity of action on the other. Finally, the category of abstract nouns reflects what is characteristic of human beings: the cognitive processes of abstraction and generalization proper to naming acts, but highly demanding in terms of abstract qualities.

Therefore, four groups of semantic categories were analyzed overall. The first group covers the basic nominal categories: agent, patient, instrumental and locative. They commonly share the same formal means and raise extensive synchronic and diachronic debate on the reasons for and the nature of polysemy/homonymy of affixes representing these categories. A small fraction of nouns related to the formal expression of the male vs female opposition in human languages, as a reflection of the paternal principles of the organization of human society worldwide, is also examined here in terms of feminines and masculines.

The second group comprises augmentative and diminutive. This is a relevant group in view of the postulates for some languages of the existence of a third subdiscipline of morphology, i.e. evaluative morphology (cf. Scalise 1984). Unlike the group of nominal categories, these are not bound to any one word-class. Rather, in some languages they (especially diminutives) range not only over major word-classes of nouns, verbs, adjectives and adverbs, but also numerals, interjections, etc.

The third group concerns verbs and is subdivided into three subgroups: causative; intransitive and transitive; and frequentative and intensive. The second subgroup, intransitive and transitive, is included here despite having

---

[1] The category state is one of three variants of the general category action – state, action proper and process.

typically inflectional characteristics, in particular, the relation it expresses to other words in a sentence structure. In other words, the intransitive vs transitive opposition consists in whether a verb does or does not require internal arguments. There are several reasons for including these categories in the discussion of word-formation processes: valence is sometimes considered to be derivational (Bybee 1985: 83)[2], their opposition is based on an additional word-formation meaning, specifically directedness of action, they lack the systematic (automatic) nature of inflectional categories, and, last but not least, transitiveness is derivationally very closely related to causativity. The latter has been well-known in typological research (cf. Comrie 1985). The final two semantic categories, the iterativity and the intensity of action, were selected to represent the borderline category of aspect or, more properly, Aktionsart.

The fourth group focuses on cross-linguistically fairly productive semantic categories, each of which is based on word-class change.

6.2   Nominal categories

6.2.1   Agents

Agent noun formation is recorded in the languages shown in Table 6.1 (89.09 per cent of the study sample).

Table 6.1. *The category agent in the study sample*

Language	Family	Morphological type	Area
Amharic	Afro-Asiatic	Inflectional	Africa/Ethiopia
Bardi	Australian	Fusional	Australia-New Guinea/ Australia
Breton	Indo-European	Fusional	Eurasia/France
Cirecire	Khoisan	Isolating	Africa/Botswana
Datooga	Nilo-Saharan	Agglutinative/fusional	Africa/Tanzania
Diola-Fogny	Niger-Congo	Agglutinative	Africa/Gambia, Senegal
English	Indo-European	Isolating	Eurasia/Ireland and UK
Estonian	Uralic	Agglutinative/fusional	Eurasia/Estonia
Finnish	Uralic	Agglutinative	Eurasia/Finland
Gã	Niger-Congo	Agglutinative	Africa/Ghana
Georgian	Kartvelian	Inflectional/agglutinative	Eurasia/Georgia
Greek	Indo-European	Fusional	Eurasia/Greece
Hausa	Afro-Asiatic	Fusional	Africa/Niger, Nigeria
Hebrew	Afro-Asiatic	Inflectional	Africa/Israel

---

[2] 'Valence-changing categories produce large meaning changes in verbs, since an event can be changed substantially if the number of participants and the nature of their roles change. Thus *kill* differs from *die*, and *send* differs from *go* in the events being described. So it is not surprising that in the cross-linguistic survey, valence was found to be frequently mentioned as a *derivational* category for verbs' (Bybee 1985: 83).

Language	Family	Morphological type	Area
Hungarian	Uralic	Agglutinative	Eurasia/Hungary
Ilocano	Austronesian	Agglutinative	SE Asia and Oceania/ Philippines
Indonesian	Austronesian	Agglutinative	SE Asia and Oceania/ Indonesia
Japanese	Japanese	Agglutinative	Eurasia/Japan
Jaqaru	Aymaran	Agglutinative	South America/Peru
Kalkatungu	Australian- Aboriginal	Agglutinative	Australia-New Guinea/ Australia
Karao	Austronesian	Inflectional/ polysynthetic	SE Asia and Oceania/ Philippines
Ket	Yeniseian	Agglutinative	Eurasia/Russia
Konni	Niger-Congo	Agglutinative	Africa/Ghana
Kwakw'ala	Wakashan	Polysynthetic	North America/Canada
Lakhota	Siouan	Synthetic to polysynthetic	North America/USA
Luo	Nilo-Saharan	Agglutinative	Africa/Kenya, Tanzania
Maipure	Arawakan	Agglutinative	South America/Venezuela
Malayalam	Dravidian	Agglutinative	Eurasia/India
Mandarin Chinese	Sino-Tibetan	Isolating/analytic	SE Asia and Oceania/China
Māori	Austronesian	Isolating	SE Asia and Oceania/ New Zealand
Movima	Movima	Agglutinative	South America/Bolivia
Nelemwa	Austronesian	Isolating	SE Asia and Oceania/ New Caledonia
Pipil	Uto-Aztecan	Agglutinative	North America/El Salvador
Slavey	Na-Dene	Polysynthetic	North America/Northwest Territories
Slovak	Indo-European	Inflectional	Eurasia/Slovakia
Spanish	Indo-European	Inflectional	Eurasia/Spain
Swahili	Niger-Congo	Agglutinative	Africa/Tanzania
Tamil	Dravidian	Agglutinative	Eurasia/Tamil Nadu
Tatar	Altaic	Agglutinative	Eurasia/Russia
Telugu	Dravidian	Agglutinative	Eurasia/India
Tibetan	Sino-Tibetan	Inflectional/agglutinative	SE Asia and Oceania/China
Totonac	Totonacan	Agglutinative/polysynthetic	North America/Mexico
Tzotzil	Mayan	Agglutinative/polysynthetic	North America/Mexico
Udihe	Altaic	Agglutinative	Eurasia/Russia
Vietnamese	Austro-Asiatic	Isolating	SE Asia and Oceania/ Vietnam
West Greenlandic	Eskimo-Aleut	Polysynthetic	North America/Greenland
Wichí	Matacoan	Agglutinative	South America/Argentina and Bolivia
Yoruba	Niger-Congo	Isolating	Africa/Benin, Nigeria
Zulu	Niger-Congo	Agglutinative	Africa/South Africa

Table 6.2 shows the diversity of word-formation processes used for agent formation.

Table 6.2. *Word-formation processes for the category agent*

Circumfixation	(1) Georgian	მე-პურ-ე me-p'ur-e CRX-bread-CRX 'baker'		
Compounding	(2) Cirecire	*cóõ-coo* herbs-person 'doctor'		
	(3) Hausa	*abōkin-cìnikī* friend.of-business 'customer'		
	(4) Vietnamese	*dawk$^{p31?}$ zæ:^{313}* đôc giả read-human 'reader' (Thái Ân)		
Conversion	(5) Luo	*wäl* 'translators'	<	*wal* 'translate.v'
	(6) Slavey[3]	*dagohwhe* 'dancer'	<	*dagohwhe* 'S/he dances'
Prefixal-suffixal derivation	(7) Swahili	*m-wind-aji*[4] N.CLASS.PRX1-hunt-AG 'hunter'		
Prefixation	(8) Hausa	*ma-àikàc-ī* AG-*aikà-tā*-M.SG 'worker'	<	*aikìi* work.N
	(9) Lakhota	*wa-khu `wa* AG-to.hunt.v 'hunter'		
	(10) Māori	*kai-kōrero* AG-speak 'speaker'		
	(11) Nelemwa	*aa-hobwak* AG.NOM-to.guard.v 'guard'		
	(12) Tzotzil	*x-ʼélek* AG-act.of.stealing 'thief' (Cowan 1969: 109)		

---

[3] Here, conversion creates plural nouns. It works through changing the vowel to [+ ATR].

[4] The agent is usually followed by object noun.

Root-and-pattern	(13) Amharic	ሰባሪ säbbari 'breaker'	<	s-b-r + CäCaCi
	(14) Hebrew	רואי banay 'builder'	<	b-n-y + CaCaC
Suffixation	(15) Hausa	àrau àrā-au borrow-AG 'person prone to borrowing'		

Each of the processes above has peculiarities in one or the other language. Thus, Afrikaans relies on a wide range of options (including allomorphs) for the expression of agentive nouns. This is characteristic of many languages (even if not noticeably so) and is, therefore, a good example for the overview of the expression of the category agent (see Table 6.3).

Table 6.3. *Suffix range for derivation of the category agent in Afrikaans*

-ariër	(16) Afrikaans	*parlementariër* 'parliamentary'
-aris	(17) Afrikaans	*argivaris* 'archivist'
-ator	(18) Afrikaans	*kommentator* 'commentator'
-ees	(19) Afrikaans	*Kanadees* 'Canadian'
-eet	(20) Afrikaans	*kategeet* 'catechist'
-ein	(21) Afrikaans	*republikein* 'republican'
-enaar	(22) Afrikaans	*dorpenaar* 'inhabitant of a town'
-enier	(23) Afrikaans	*valkenier* 'falconer'
-enis	(24) Afrikaans	*harpenis* 'harpist'
-ent	(25) Afrikaans	*assistent* 'assistant'
-er	(26) Afrikaans	*werker* 'worker'
-erd	(27) Afrikaans	*lomperd* 'clumsy person'
-erik	(28) Afrikaans	*dommerik* 'stupid person'

-eur	(29)	Afrikaans	*krediteur* 'creditor'
-eut	(30)	Afrikaans	*terapeut* 'therapist'
-iën	(31)	Afrikaans	*elekrisiën* 'electrician'
-ier	(32)	Afrikaans	*winkelier* 'shopkeeper'
-iger	(33)	Afrikaans	*reisiger* 'traveller'
-is	(34)	Afrikaans	*harpis* 'harpist'
-ling/-eling	(35)	Afrikaans	*volgeling* 'follower'
-naar	(36)	Afrikaans	*minnaar* 'lover'
-or	(37)	Afrikaans	*lector* 'lecturer'
-urg	(38)	Afrikaans	*dramaturg* 'dramatist'
-yn	(39)	Afrikaans	*Algeryn* 'Algerian'

Hausa (Neuman, pers. comm.) is a highly productive agent-forming language and does not restrict the formation of agents to a single word-formation process. Reportedly, derivation of agent nouns by the prefix *-ma*, as in (8), is common and, in principle, an agent noun could be created morphologically from almost any verb.[5]

Compounding may be of several types. Hausa illustrates a relatively rare case of agent formation by compounding, in particular, by means of

---

[5]   Hausa agents are (usually) built on verbs. Many of these verbs are built on simple nouns by means of the suffix *-ta*, as in the following example:

> Hausa   *màntau*
> mântā-au
> forget-AG
> 'very forgetful person'

Many agent nouns in Hausa feature a combination of the suffix *-ta* and the prefix *ma-*. Newman (pers. comm.) explains that this is not really a combination of prefix + suffix, rather it is an instance of potentiation. This is comparable to English *unsuccessful*, i.e. *success* + *ful* gives *successful*, and then the prefix *un-* is attached.

In a small number of cases, such as *mazinàacii*, the verb **zinaata* does not actually occur as such, and must be viewed as a derivational step:

> Hausa   *mazìnàacī*   <   *zìnā*
> 'adulterer'   'adultery'

compounds whose left-hand constituent is *dan* 'person of' or *àbōkin* 'friend', followed by the linking element -*n*- and a constituent denoting particular profession, activity or place of origin:

(40)   Hausa   *dan-ƙwàayā*
                 person.of-drug
                 'drug user'

(41)   Hausa   *dan-sìyāsàa*
                 person.of-politics
                 'politician'

Exocentric compounds of the *redskin* and of the *garde-manger* type are also possible, although the former are rarer (see Table 6.4).

Table 6.4. *Compounding of the* redskin *and* garde-manger *types for the category agent*

Redskin compounds		*Garde-manger* compounds
(42) Zulu *ndabezinhle* news-good 'bringer of good news'	(43) Italian	*porta-lettere* carries letters 'postman/woman, mailman/woman'
	(44) Georgian	ცხვარიჭამია cxvar + i-č'am-ia sheep + GEN-eat-SFX 'one (person/animal) that eats sheep'
	(45) Mandarin Chinese	司機 sījī operate-machine 'driver' (Chung 1994: 18)
	(46) Spanish	*cuidacoches* guard cars 'car warden'

Prefixation is used for the category agent in languages in which it is the major word-formation process, like Yoruba (47), but also in other languages, like Ilocano (48), in particular with the prefix *maNCV*-, and Karao (49), where an active verbal prefix cross-references the agent:

(47)   Yoruba   *ọ-dẹ*
                       AG-hunt.V
                       'hunter'

(48)   Ilocano   *mannaniw*
                    maNCV-daniw
                    AG-poem
                    'poet'

(49)   Karao   *mengemag*
                  meN-amag
                  IPF.AG-do/make
                  'the one who does/makes'

Cahill (pers. comm.) points out that a special kind of prefixal-suffixal derivation exists in Konni, where the CV prefix reduplicates the initial consonant
and the vowel is [i~ɪ]. The suffix is either [-tU] or [-rU]:

(50)   Konni   *gbɪ-gbarɪ-tʊ*
                  AG.RDP-watch-AG
                  'watcher'

(51)   Konni   *di-digi-rú*
                  AG-RDP-cook-AG
                  'cook.N'

Cahill also notes that a few common agent nouns omit the prefix part:

(52)   Konni   *kpàà-rʊ*
                  kpaa-rʊ
                  plant.V-AG
                  'farmer'

(53)   Konni   *wàsÌ-rʊ*   <   *wasi*
                  wasi- rʊ
                  greet.V-AG
                  'greeter'   'greet.V'

Suffixation in Zulu is based on attaching the suffix *-i* to a verb root and
placing the resulting stem in class 1/2 by using the prefix *m-* or *ba-* respectively (van der Spuy, pers. comm.). This implies a sort of prefixal-suffixal
derivation:

(54)   Zulu   *m-lim-i*
                 C1-plough-AG
                 'farmer'

Not all agent nouns are derived from uninflected stems. Thus, in Ket 'man'
is added to verbal infinitives (55) and in Tibetan the suffixes *-pa* and *-po* are
added to the present stem of verbs (56):

(55)   Ket   *assano-ket*
                'hunting-man'

(56)   Tibetan   གཅོད་པོ
        gcod-po
        'cutter'

Suffixes may also be selective in terms of the etymology of the base, as in Swedish, where different suffixes combine with elements of specific origins (see Table 6.5).

Table 6.5. *Swedish suffixes and specific bases for the category agent*

Native stems + *-are*			Latin/French stems + *-or/-ör/-ator/-atör* and *-ant/-ent*	
(57) Swedish	*lär-are* 'teacher'	(58)	Swedish	*don-ator* 'donor'
		(59)	Swedish	*prenumer-ant* 'subscriber'
		(60)	Swedish	*produc-ent* 'producer'

Similarly, the formation of agent nouns is usually not limited to a combination of an affix with just one category of word-formation base. They usually can be combined with bases of various word-classes. A case in point is Hindi, where the word-formation base can be a noun, a verb, an adjective and an adverb (Kachru 2006: 116–17):

(61)   Hindi   कुम्हार
        kumhar
        kumbʰ-ar
        pot-AG
        'potter'

(62)   Hindi   खा-ऊ
        kha-ū
        eat-AG
        'glutton'

But it is not only at the language level that agent nouns can be formed from various word-classes. The same applies to individual agentive affixes which can be used with word-formation bases of various word-classes, as in Indonesian (examples (63) and (64)), where the prefixes *pe-* and *juru-* can be attached to both nouns and verbs (Mojdl 2006: 176–7), or in Udihe (examples (65) and (66)), where the suffix *-ŋku, -ŋkA* attaches either to verbs or nouns:

(63)   Indonesian   a. *pe-kedai*
                          AG-shop
                          'shop-keeper'

          b. *pe-mendengar*
              AG-listen
              'listener'

(64)   Indonesian   a. *juru-bahasa*
                            AG-language
                            'translators, interpreter'
                        b. *juru-kira*
                            AG-count
                            'accountant'

(65)   Udihe   *kaŋma-ŋku*
                            practise.evil/magic.V-AG
                            'evil sorcerer'
                            (Nikolaeva and Tolskaya 2001: 153)

(66)   Udihe   *zeu-ŋku*
                            food-AG
                            'breadwinner'
                            (Nikolaeva and Tolskaya 2001: 153)

In other words, not all agentive suffixes comply with Aronoff's (1976: 48) Unitary Base Hypothesis.

6.2.2   Patients

Patient noun formation is recorded in the languages shown in Table 6.6 (61.82 per cent of the study sample).

Table 6.6. *The category patient in the study sample*

Language	Family	Morphological type	Area
Anejom	Austronesian	Agglutinative	SE Asia and Oceania/ Vanuatu
Breton	Indo-European	Fusional	Eurasia/France
Cirecire	Khoisan	Isolating	Africa/Botswana
English	Indo-European	Isolating	Eurasia/Ireland and UK
Estonian	Uralic	Agglutinative/fusional	Eurasia/Estonia
Finnish	Uralic	Agglutinative	Eurasia/Finland
Georgian	Kartvelian	Inflectional/agglutinative	Eurasia/Georgia
Hebrew	Afro-Asiatic	Inflectional	Africa/Israel
Hungarian	Uralic	Agglutinative	Eurasia/Hungary
Ilocano	Austronesian	Agglutinative	SE Asia and Oceania/ Philippines
Indonesian	Austronesian	Agglutinative	SE Asia and Oceania/ Indonesia

Language	Family	Morphological type	Area
Japanese	Japanese	Agglutinative	Eurasia/Japan
Jaqaru	Aymaran	Agglutinative	South America/Peru
Karao	Austronesian	Inflectional/polysynthetic	SE Asia and Oceania/ Philippines
Ket	Yeniseian	Agglutinative	Eurasia/Russia
Konni	Niger-Congo	Agglutinative	Africa/Ghana
Kwakw'ala	Wakashan	Polysynthetic	North America/Canada
Lakhota	Siouan	Synthetic to polysynthetic	North America/USA
Luo	Nilo-Saharan	Agglutinative	Africa/Kenya, Tanzania
Malayalam	Dravidian	Agglutinative	Eurasia/India
Mandarin Chinese	Sino-Tibetan	Isolating/analytic	SE Asia and Oceania/ China
Māori	Austronesian	Isolating	SE Asia and Oceania/ New Zealand
Movima	Movima	Agglutinative	South America/Bolivia
Pipil	Uto-Aztecan	Agglutinative	North America/El Salvador
Slavey	Na-Dene	Polysynthetic	North America/ Northwest Territories
Slovak	Indo-European	Inflectional	Eurasia/Slovakia
Spanish	Indo-European	Inflectional	Eurasia/Spain
Swahili	Niger-Congo	Agglutinative	Africa/Tanzania
Tibetan	Sino-Tibetan	Inflectional/agglutinative	SE Asia and Oceania/ China
Totonac	Totonacan	Agglutinative/ polysynthetic	North America/Mexico
Udihe	Altaic	Agglutinative	Eurasia/Russia
Vietnamese	Austro-Asiatic	Isolating	SE Asia and Oceania/ Vietnam
West Greenlandic	Eskimo-Aleut	Polysynthetic	North America/ Greenland
Zulu	Niger-Congo	Agglutinative	Africa/South Africa

Table 6.7. shows the diversity of word-formation processes used for patient formation.

Table 6.7. *Word-formation processes for the category patient*

Compounding	(67)	Cirecire	*dáú-coo* burn-person 'fire victim'
	(68)	Vietnamese	*ŋɯəj²¹ dɯək³¹ˀ fawŋᵐ³¹³ vən³⁵* ngưòi đưọc phỏng vấn

			human-PAT-interview.V
			'interviewee'[6]
			(Thái Ân)
Conversion	(69)	Afrikaans	*veroordeel-de*
			'convicted'
	(70)	Dutch	*geslagen-e*
			'the one who is beaten'
	(71)	Finnish	*koulute-ttava*
			'the one being educated'
			(Koivisto)
	(72)	Slovak	*poškodený*
			'injured person (legislation)'
	(73)	Spanish	*empleado*
			(lit. 'employed')
			'employee'
	(74)	Swedish	(*en*) *anställd*
			(lit. 'employed')
			'(an) employee'
Infixation	(75)	Ilocano	*d<in>usa*
			punish.TR<PAT>
			'punished one'
Prefixal–suffixal derivation	(76)	Swahili	*ki-lim-o*
			N.CLASS.PRX.7-cultivate-NMR
			'product of cultivation'
Prefixation	(77)	Anejom	*nupu-tooga*
			person.of-foreign
			'foreigner'
	(78)	Indonesian	*pe-malas*
			PAT-lazy
			'lazy person'
			(Mojdl 2006: 145)
	(79)	Karao	*me-kan*
			PAS.IRR.PAT-eat
			'food'
	(80)	Tzotzil	*j-chamel*
			PAT-sickness
			'sick person'
			(Haviland 1980)
Root-and-pattern	(81)	Hebrew	מבוהל
			mevohal
			'scared'
Suffixation	(82)	Jaqaru	*uta-ni*
			house-PAT

---

[6] The form *được* is used to express passive meaning (it also functions as a constituent morpheme of patient nouns but not necessarily). Since *được* does not always exist, an agent noun may look like a patient noun.

'house-owner'
(Hardman 2000: 43)

(83)   Luo   *rat-an*
                    tie.V-PAT
                    'prisoner'

(84)   Slovak   *zbabel-ec*
                    zbabelý-ec
                    cowardly-PAT
                    'coward'

(85)   Zulu   *si-thand-w-a*
                    C7-love-PAS-a
                    'beloved'

Since patients are bearers of state, their important sources are exocentric compounds:

(86)   Afrikaans   *maan-haar*
                            mane-hair
                            'lion with mane'

(87)   Bardi   *oowa-baawa*
                            little-child
                            'toddler'

(88)   Belorussian   *бледн-а-твар-ы*
                            blednatvary
                            pale-LNK-face-M.SG.NOM
                            'paleface'

(89)   Catalan   *pit-roig*
                            breast-red
                            'robin'

(90)   Georgian   რვა-ფეხ-ა
                            rva-pex-a
                            eight-foot-NMR
                            'octopus'

(91)   Hindi   दुधमुँह
                            dudhmũha
                            one who has milk in his mouth
                            'infant'
                            (Kachru 2006: 119)

(92)   Maipure   *cuyalúta kanía nikú*
                            book-be-inside
                            'bookcase'

(93)   Mandarin Chinese   忍冬
                             rěndōng
                             endure-winter
                             'honeysuckle'[7]
                             (Chung 1994: 22)

(94)   Māori   *ihupuku*
                             nose-swollen
                             'sea elephant'

(95)   Marathi   पिकले पान
                             pikale paana
                             matured-leaf
                             'a person likely to die due to age'

(96)   Romanian   *pierde-vară*
                             loses-summer
                             'dawdler'

(97)   Serbian-Croatian   *ne-zna-bog*
                             not-knows-god
                             'non-believer'

(98)   Swedish   *dumhuvud*
                             stupid-head
                             'fool'

(99)   Telugu   సువర్ణ రేఖ
                             suvarna rekha
                             golden line
                             'a sort of mango'

(100)   Tibetan   དྲི་བཟང
                             dri-bzang
                             good-smell
                             'saffron'

A relatively common source of patient nouns in Indo-European languages is conversion of the past participle (passive adjectives) as in (69) to (74). The past participle is not the only inflected word-formation base: in Tibetan, the suffix -*pa* or the suffix -*bya* is added to the future stem of a verb:

(101)   Tibetan   དགག་བྱ
                             dgag-bya
                             'negandum'

---

[7]   A plant that can withstand low temperatures.

Finally, as with agent nouns, some languages make it possible to attach an affix to more than one word-class. Thus, the Udihe suffix *-ŋku, -ŋkA* can be attached either to a verb or a noun:

(102)   Udihe   *boxoli-ŋku*
                    humpack-PAT
                    'humpbacked'
                    (Nikolaeva and Tolskaya 2001: 153)

6.2.3   Instrumentals

Instrumental noun formation is recorded in the languages shown in Table 6.8 (63.64 per cent of the study sample).

Table 6.8. *The category instrumental in the study sample*

Language	Family	Morphological type	Area
Amharic	Afro-Asiatic	Inflectional	Africa/Ethiopia
Anejom	Austronesian	Agglutinative	SE Asia and Oceania/ Vanuatu
Breton	Indo-European	Fusional	Eurasia/France
Cirecire	Khoisan	Isolating	Africa/Botswana
Clallam	Salishan	Polysynthetic	North America/USA
Datooga	Nilo-Saharan	Agglutinative/ fusional	Africa/Tanzania
Diola-Fogny	Niger-Congo	Agglutinative	Africa/Gambia, Senegal
English	Indo-European	Isolating	Eurasia/Ireland and UK
Finnish	Uralic	Agglutinative	Eurasia/Finland
Greek	Indo-European	Fusional	Eurasia/Greece
Hausa	Afro-Asiatic	Fusional	Africa/Niger, Nigeria
Hebrew	Afro-Asiatic	Inflectional	Africa/Israel
Hungarian	Uralic	Agglutinative	Eurasia/Hungary
Ilocano	Austronesian	Agglutinative	SE Asia and Oceania/ Philippines
Indonesian	Austronesian	Agglutinative	SE Asia and Oceania/ Indonesia
Japanese	Japanese	Agglutinative	Eurasia/Japan
Jaqaru	Aymaran	Agglutinative	South America/Peru
Konni	Niger-Congo	Agglutinative	Africa/Ghana
Kwakw'ala	Wakashan	Polysynthetic	North America/Canada
Lakhota	Siouan	Synthetic to polysynthetic	North America/USA
Luo	Nilo-Saharan	Agglutinative	Africa/Kenya, Tanzania
Maipure	Arawakan	Agglutinative	South America/Venezuela
Movima	Movima	Agglutinative	South America/Bolivia

Language	Family	Morphological type	Area
Nelemwa	Austronesian	Isolating	SE Asia and Oceania/ New Caledonia
Slavey	Na-Dene	Polysynthetic	North America/Northwest Territories
Slovak	Indo-European	Inflectional	Eurasia/Slovakia
Spanish	Indo-European	Inflectional	Eurasia/Spain
Swahili	Niger-Congo	Agglutinative	Africa/Tanzania
Totonac	Totonacan	Agglutinative/ polysynthetic	North America/Mexico
Tzotzil	Mayan	Polysynthetic/ agglutinative	North America/Mexico
Udihe	Altaic	Agglutinative	Eurasia/Russia
Vietnamese	Austro-Asiatic	Isolating	SE Asia and Oceania/ Vietnam
West Greenlandic	Eskimo-Aleut	Polysynthetic	North America/Greenland
Yoruba	Niger-Congo	Isolating	Africa/Benin, Nigeria
Zulu	Niger-Congo	Agglutinative	Africa/South Africa

Table 6.9 shows the diversity of word-formation processes used for instrumental formation.

Table 6.9. *Word-formation processes for the category instrumental*

Compounding	(103)	Cirecire	*dji-bee* tool-cut 'axe'
	(104)	Russian	*посудомойка* posudomoyka dish-LNK-washer 'dishwasher'
	(105)	Vietnamese	*kaːjᶟ⁵ kənᶟᶟ* cái cân INS-weigh.V 'balance' (Thái Ân)
Conversion	(106)	Hindi	बेल-ना bel-na[8] roll-INF 'roller'

---

[8]   The infinitive of some verbs is used as an instrumental noun (Kachru 2006: 117).

Prefixal-suffixal derivation	(107)	Swahili	*ki-zib-o* N.CLASS.PRX.7-plug-NMR 'plug, stopper'
	(108)	Totonac	*li:swilú:n* li:-swilú:-n INS-drill-NMR 'drill'
Prefixation	(109)	Anejom	*inta-ahrei* INS-sweep.V 'broom'
	(110)	Clallam	*sxʷtələháy* sxʷ-talə-hay PRX-money-container 'purse'
	(111)	Hausa	*ma-girbī* INS-harvest 'harvesting tool'[9]
	(112)	Ilocano	*panait* paN-dait INS-sew 'thread'
	(113)	Indonesian	*pe-menyapu* INS-sweep.V 'broom' (Mojdl 2006: 176)
	(114)	Lakhota	*i-cháphe* PRX-stab.V 'dagger'
	(115)	Nelemwa	*baa-tiiwo* INS-write.V 'pen'
Root-and-pattern	(116)	Amharic	**መስበሪያ** mäsbär-iya[10] break.V-INS 'breaker, breaking instrument'
	(117)	Hebrew	מגהץ maghec 'iron'

---

[9] The prefix *ma-* is attached to deverbal nouns. All instrumental nouns end in -*ī*, which marks masculine singular (Newman pers. comm.).

[10] In Amharic, root-and-pattern plays its role in the formation of instrumental nouns indirectly: instrumental nouns are formed by adding suffixes to the infinitive. However, infinitive formation varies according to root type, which are about fifteen in number. This example refers to the *sbr* root.

Suffixation	(118)	Diola-Fogny	ɛ-lib-a
			SG-lib-INS
			'knife'
	(119)	Japanese	飛行機
			hikō-ki
			flying-machine
			'airplane'
	(120)	Maipure	*nawa niku-tí*
			see.inside.V-NOM
			'object inside of which
			one sees'
			(Zamponi 2003: 28)

As with agent and patient nouns, exocentric compounds are an important source of instrumental nouns in some languages. Examples are given in (121) to (123) below:

(121)   Catalan   *eixuga-mà*
                         dry.3SG.PRS.IND-hand
                         'towel'

(122)   Nelemwa   *bwaa nok*
                         head-fish
                         'piece of wood to measure the size of the mesh'

(123)   Portuguese   *guarda-roupa*
                         keeps-clothings
                         'a piece of furniture used to keep the clothes'

Almost all affix-based instrumental nouns are attached to a verbal base. An exception is the Clallam causal prefix *sxʷ-*, which in (110) above attaches to a noun + noun compound. The Tzotzil suffix *-Ob* sometimes attaches to stems which never occur independently (Cowan 1969: 105):

(124)   Tzotzil   *k'áxan-eb*
                         *k'áxan (cf. k'áx 'harvest it')-INS
                         'harvesting instrument'

6.2.4   Locatives

Locative noun formation is recorded in the languages shown in Table 6.10 (69.09 per cent of the study sample).

Table 6.10. *The category locative in the study sample*

Language	Family	Morphological type	Area
Amele	Trans-New Guinea	Polysynthetic/ synthetic	Australia-New Guinea/ Madang
Amharic	Afro-Asiatic	Inflectional	Africa/Ethiopia
Breton	Indo-European	Fusional	Eurasia/France
Cirecire	Khoisan	Isolating	Africa/Botswana
Dangaléat	Afro-Asiatic	Agglutinative	Africa/Chad
English	Indo-European	Isolating	Eurasia/Ireland and UK
Estonian	Uralic	Agglutinative/fusional	Eurasia/Estonia
Finnish	Uralic	Agglutinative	Eurasia/Finland
Georgian	Kartvelian	Inflectional/ agglutinative	Eurasia/Georgia
Greek	Indo-European	Fusional	Eurasia/Greece
Hausa	Afro-Asiatic	Fusional	Africa/Niger, Nigeria
Hebrew	Afro-Asiatic	Inflectional	Africa/Israel
Hungarian	Uralic	Agglutinative	Eurasia/Hungary
Ilocano	Austronesian	Agglutinative	SE Asia and Oceania/ Philippines
Indonesian	Austronesian	Agglutinative	SE Asia and Oceania/ Indonesia
Japanese	Japanese	Agglutinative	Eurasia/Japan
Jaqaru	Aymaran	Agglutinative	South America/Peru
Karao	Austronesian	Inflectional/ polysynthetic	SE Asia and Oceania/ Philippines
Konni	Niger-Congo	Agglutinative	Africa/Ghana
Kwakw'ala	Wakashan	Polysynthetic	North America/Canada
Lakhota	Siouan	Synthetic to polysynthetic	North America/USA
Luo	Nilo-Saharan	Agglutinative	Africa/Kenya, Tanzania
Maipure	Arawakan	Agglutinative	South America/Venezuela
Malayalam	Dravidian	Agglutinative	Eurasia/India
Nelemwa	Austronesian	Isolating	SE Asia and Oceania/New Caledonia
Pipil	Uto-Aztecan	Agglutinative	North America/El Salvador
Slavey	Na-Dene	Polysynthetic	North America/ Northwest Territories
Slovak	Indo-European	Inflectional	Eurasia/Slovakia
Spanish	Indo-European	Inflectional	Eurasia/Spain
Swahili	Niger-Congo	Agglutinative	Africa/Tanzania
Tibetan	Sino-Tibetan	Inflectional/ agglutinative	SE Asia and Oceania/ China

Language	Family	Morphological type	Area
Totonac	Totonacan	Agglutinative/polysynthetic	North America/Mexico
Tzotzil	Mayan	Polysynthetic/agglutinative	North America/Mexico
Udihe	Altaic	Agglutinative	Eurasia/Russia
Vietnamese	Austro-Asiatic	Isolating	SE Asia and Oceania/Vietnam
West Greenlandic	Eskimo-Aleut	Polysynthetic	North America/Greenland
Wichí	Matacoan	Agglutinative	South America/Argentina and Bolivia
Zulu	Niger-Congo	Agglutinative	Africa/South Africa

Table 6.11 shows the diversity of word-formation processes used for locative formation.

Table 6.11. *Word-formation processes for the category locative*

Circumfixation	(125)	Georgian	სა-სტუმრ-ო sa-st'umr-o sa-st'umari-o LOC-guest-LOC 'hotel, guest-room'
	(126)	Ilocano	*pag-basa-an* LOC-read-LOC 'school'
	(127)	Indonesian	*per-certak-an* LOC-print.v-LOC 'printing house' (Mojdl 2006: 153)
Compounding	(128)	Cirecire	*debee tshaa* salt-water 'place of salty water'
	(129)	Hungarian	*sör-gyár* beer-factory 'brewery'
	(130)	Japanese	裁判所 saiban-sho trial-place 'courthouse'
	(131)	Malayalam	*cital-puṟṟə* 'ant-hill'
	(132)	Serbian-Croatian	*brod-o-gradilište* 'shipyard'

	(133)	Swedish	*gå-gata* walk-street 'pedestrian zone'		
	(134)	Wichí	*peluta-w'et* ball-place 'pitch'		
Conversion	(135)	Belorussian	*сталовая*_N stalovaya 'dining room'		*сталовая*_{ADJ} stalovaya 'table.ADJ'
Prefixation	(136)	Hausa	*ma-kiyāy-ā*[11] NMR-graze-LOC 'pasture, grazing land'		
	(137)	Lakhota	*o-thí* LOC-dwell.V 'dwelling'		
	(138)	Luo	*kaatäriit* 'nest'	<	*täriit*[12] 'bird'
	(139)	Nelemwa	*hna-fooyet* LOC-cook.V 'kitchen'		
	(140)	Totonac	*ka: he'lhú:n* ka:-he'lhú:-n LOC-scree-PL 'place of loose rocks'		
	(141)	Zulu	*eThekwini*[13] e-theku-ini LOC-Durban-SFX 'at the bay'[14]		
Root-and- pattern	(142)	Amharic	ማቆሚያ m-aqom-iya[15] LOC-stop.V.TR-LOC 'stopping place'		

[11] Deverbal noun with prefix *ma-*. According to Newman (pers. comm.), most nouns of location end in *-ā*, and a smaller number end in *-ī*.

[12] The actual prefix is *kaap-*.

[13] The prefix *e- ~ o-* is reportedly extremely productive; it is usually (but not always) accompanied by the suffix *-ini ~ -eni*. Another prefix is *kwa-*, which attaches to a person's name or a word designating a person:

> Zulu   *KwaZulu*
> LOC-Zulu
> 'land of the Zulus'

[14] The Zulu name for *Durban*.

[15] As with instrumentals, the role of root-and-pattern is indirect in Amharic: to form infinitives from which locatives are formed by prefixal-suffixal derivation:

> Amharic   *m-adärdär-iya*
> LOC-arrange.V-LOC
> 'shelf'

	(143)	Hebrew	מסעדה mis'ada 'restaurant'		
Suffixation	(144)	Pipil	*a:ka-tal* reed-SFX 'canebrake, place of reeds' (Campbell 1985: 46–8)		
	(145)	Tibetan	སྐྱེས་ས skyes-sa birth-LOC 'birthplace'		
	(146)	West Greenlandic	*katirsur-vik* gather-LOC 'place of (people) gathering, gather'	<	*katirsur-*

Examples of exocentric locative compounds come from French and Vietnamese:

(147)   French   *garde-manger*
                       keep-food
                       'pantry'

(148)   Vietnamese   *tiəm³¹ ? baɲ³⁵*
                       tiệm bánh
                       shop-cake
                       'bakery'
                       (Thái Ân)

6.2.5   Gender in animate beings

Feminine noun formation is recorded in the languages shown in Table 6.12 (43.64 per cent of the study sample).

Table 6.12. *The category feminine in the study sample*

Language	Family	Morphological type	Area
Amharic	Afro-Asiatic	Inflectional	Africa/Ethiopia
Breton	Indo-European	Fusional	Eurasia/France
Dangaléat	Afro-Asiatic	Agglutinative	Africa/Chad
Datooga	Nilo-Saharan	Agglutinative/ fusional	Africa/Tanzania
English	Indo-European	Isolating	Eurasia/Ireland and UK
Estonian	Uralic	Agglutinative/fusional	Eurasia/Estonia
Finnish	Uralic	Agglutinative	Eurasia/Finland

Language	Family	Morphological type	Area
Greek	Indo-European	Fusional	Eurasia/Greece
Hausa	Afro-Asiatic	Fusional	Africa/Niger, Nigeria
Hebrew	Afro-Asiatic	Inflectional	Africa/Israel
Hungarian	Uralic	Agglutinative	Eurasia/Hungary
Indonesian	Austronesian	Agglutinative	SE Asia and Oceania/ Indonesia
Ket	Yeniseian	Agglutinative	Eurasia/Russia
Luo	Nilo-Saharan	Agglutinative	Africa/Kenya, Tanzania
Malayalam	Dravidian	Agglutinative	Eurasia/India
Mandarin Chinese	Sino-Tibetan	Isolating/analytic	SE Asia and Oceania/ China
Marathi	Indo-European	Inflectional/ polysynthetic	Eurasia/India
Slovak	Indo-European	Inflectional	Eurasia/Slovakia
Spanish	Indo-European	Inflectional	Eurasia/Spain
Tamil	Dravidian	Agglutinative	Eurasia/Tamil Nadu
Telugu	Dravidian	Agglutinative	Eurasia/India
Tibetan	Sino-Tibetan	Inflectional/ agglutinative	SE Asia and Oceania/ China
Vietnamese	Austro-Asiatic	Isolating	SE Asia and Oceania/ Vietnam
Zulu	Niger-Congo	Agglutinative	Africa/South Africa

Table 6.13 shows the diversity of word-formation processes used for feminine formation.

Table 6.13. *Word-formation processes for the category gender (feminine)*

Compounding	(149)	Finnish	*nais lääkäri* 'woman-physician'
	(150)	Hungarian	*doktor-nő* 'doctor-woman'
Prefixation	(151)	Luo	*cheep-yoos-a* F-old-NOM 'woman'
Suffixation	(152)	Amharic	ልጅቱ ləğ-itu child,boy-F 'girl'
	(153)	Slovak	*učiteľ-ka* teacher.M-F 'female teacher'

| | (154) | Tibetan | ཝ་མོ་
wa-mo
fox-F
'vixen' | | ཝ
wa
'fox' |
| Tone-lowering | (155) | Dangaléat | *kànya*
'female dog' | < | *kányá*
'male dog' |

Prefixation is used for feminines only in Datooga, where *uḍą̀*- derives personal names for feminines from any noun, and in Luo. In addition to those of Table 6.13, examples of compounding come from Vietnamese (159) and also from Ket, which forms female names by adding *am* 'mother' to a noun that by default is used to denote masculine gender or generic gender. Finally, in Mandarin Chinese 女 *nü3* 'female' is combined with a noun, but usually just one morpheme-syllable is taken from a default masculine disyllabic compound to make it feminine.

Masculine noun formation is recorded in the languages shown in Table 6.14 (21.82 per cent of the study sample).

Table 6.14. *The category masculine in the study sample*

Language	Family	Morphological type	Area
Breton	Indo-European	Fusional	Eurasia/France
Datooga	Nilo-Saharan	Agglutinative/ fusional	Africa/Tanzania
Finnish	Uralic	Agglutinative	Eurasia/Finland
Hebrew	Afro-Asiatic	Inflectional	Africa/Israel
Luo	Nilo-Saharan	Agglutinative	Africa/Kenya, Tanzania
Malayalam	Dravidian	Agglutinative	Eurasia/India
Mandarin Chinese	Sino-Tibetan	Isolating/analytic	SE Asia and Oceania/ China
Marathi	Indo-European	Inflectional/ polysynthetic	Eurasia/India
Slovak	Indo-European	Inflectional	Eurasia/Slovakia
Spanish	Indo-European	Inflectional	Eurasia/Spain
Telugu	Dravidian	Agglutinative	Eurasia/India
Vietnamese	Austro-Asiatic	Isolating	SE Asia and Oceania/ Vietnam

Table 6.15 shows the diversity of word-formation processes used for masculine formation:

Table 6.15. *Word-formation processes for the category gender (masculine)*

Back-formation	(156)	Hebrew	אלמן alman 'widower'	<	אלמנה almana 'widow'
Compounding	(157)	Finnish	*mies kätilö* 'man-midwife' (Laakso)		
	(158)	Mandarin Chinese	男護士[16] nánhùshì male-protect-person. trained.in.a.certain. field 'male nurse'		
	(159)	Vietnamese a.	*kaː³³ siː³⁵ʔ* ca sĩ 'NTR-singer'		
		b.	*nɯ³⁵ʔ kaː³³ siː³⁵ʔ* nữ ca sĩ 'female singer'		
		c.	*naːm³³ kaː³³ siː³⁵ʔ* nam ca sĩ 'male singer' (Thái Ân)		
Prefixation	(160)	Luo	*kip-seemseem-yaan* M-slander-SG 'slanderer'		
Suffixation	(161)	Malayalam	*veelakkaaran* 'male worker'	vs	*veelakkaari* 'female worker'
	(162)	Telugu	స్థావకుడు something.aapak- uDu[17] 'man who has established (something)'		
	(163)	Slovak	*vdovec* 'widower'	<	*vdova* 'widow'

[16] In Mandarin Chinese 男 *nan2* 'male' is combined with nouns.

[17] Telugu may also use the suffix *-waaDu*:

     Telugu   *peeda-waaDu*   <   *peeda*
                      'poor man'   'poor'

Pingali (pers. comm.) points out that agent nouns in Telugu are usually realized as masculine or feminine (barring the suffix *-ari*, which is gender neutral). Hence there is some overlap between the masculine/feminine suffixes and agentive suffixes.

Malayalam makes use of specific suffixes for male vs female persons: masculine *-kaaran* vs feminine *-kaari* (Asher and Kumari 1997: 383–4), as in (164), or masculine suffix *-an* vs feminine *-cci*, *-i*, *-ti* (*-cci* being the most productive) attached to an abstract noun (165):

(164)   Malayalam   *kaavalkkaaran*   vs   *kaavalkkaari*
                    '(male) watchman'   '(female) watchman'

(165)   Malayalam   *kaḷḷ-an*   vs   *kaḷḷ-i*
                    kaḷḷam-an
                    theft-M
                    'thief'

Hindi chooses from two strategies to form male nouns from female nouns: the choice is conditioned phonologically. According to Kachru (2006: 47), if an inherently feminine noun ends in *-ī*, the masculine counterpart is formed by replacing *-ī* with *-a*; if the noun ends in a consonant, the masculine counterpart is formed by adding the derivational suffix *-a*:

(166)   Hindi   बकरा   <   बकरी
                bəkra   bəkrī
                'goat.M'   'goat.F'

(167)   Hindi   भाईया   <   भाई
                bheɽa   bheɽ
                'ram'   'sheep'

6.3   Evaluative categories

6.3.1   Augmentatives and diminutives

Augmentative formation is recorded in the languages shown in Table 6.16 (34.55 per cent of the study sample).

Table 6.16. *The category augmentative in the study sample*

Language	Family	Morphological type	Area
Breton	Indo-European	Fusional	Eurasia/France
Cirecire	Khoisan	Isolating	Africa/Botswana
Diola-Fogny	Niger-Congo	Agglutinative	Africa/Gambia, Senegal
Finnish	Uralic	Agglutinative	Eurasia/Finland
Greek	Indo-European	Fusional	Eurasia/Greece
Hausa	Afro-Asiatic	Fusional	Africa/Niger, Nigeria
Hebrew	Afro-Asiatic	Inflectional	Africa/Israel
Ilocano	Austronesian	Agglutinative	SE Asia and Oceania/ Philippines

Language	Family	Morphological type	Area
Japanese	Japanese	Agglutinative	Eurasia/Japan
Karao	Austronesian	Inflectional/ polysynthetic	SE Asia and Oceania/ Philippines
Kwakw'ala	Wakashan	Polysynthetic	North America/Canada
Lakhota	Siouan	Synthetic to polysynthetic	North America/USA
Slavey	Na-Dene	Polysynthetic	North America/Northwest Territories
Slovak	Indo-European	Inflectional	Eurasia/Slovakia
Spanish	Indo-European	Inflectional	Eurasia/Spain
Swahili	Niger-Congo	Agglutinative	Africa/Tanzania
West Greenlandic	Eskimo-Aleut	Polysynthetic	North America/Greenland
Wichí	Matacoan	Agglutinative	South America/Argentina and Bolivia
Zulu	Niger-Congo	Agglutinative	Africa/South Africa

Table 6.17 shows the diversity of word-formation processes used for augmentative formation.

Table 6.17. *Word-formation processes for the category augmentative*

Prefixal-suffixal derivation	(168)	Ilocano	*nag-dakkel-en* AUG-big-AUG 'how big!'
Prefixation	(169)	Breton	*gour-lano* AUG-tide 'high tide'
	(170)	Diola-Fogny	*bu-ko* AUG-head 'big head' (D. J. Sapir 1965: 66)
	(171)	Dutch	*reuze-probleem* AUG-problem 'giant problem' (Bakema and Geeraerts 2000: 1046)
	(172)	Japanese	超国家主義 chō-kokka-shugi ultra-nation-ism 'ultranationalism'
Reduplication	(173)	Cirecire	*ba-ba-shaa* old-old-female 'very old woman'

	(174)	Karao	*man-panga-panga* IPF-PL-branch 'grow lots of branches'
Suffixation	(175)	Greek	*ποδάρα* pod-ara foot-AUG 'big foot'
	(176)	Kwakw'ala	*gˑōʹxu-dzēᵉ* < *-dzē* 'large house' 'large' (Boas 1947: 345)
	(177)	Slovak	*chlap-isko* man-AUG 'big man/beefy fellow'
	(178)	West Greenlandic	*qimmi-rujussuaq* qimmiq-rujussuaq dog-AUG 'enormous dog'

Diminutive formation is recorded in the languages shown in Table 6.18 (67.27 per cent of the study sample).

Table 6.18. *The category diminutive in the study sample*

Language	Family	Morphological type	Area
Anejom	Austronesian	Agglutinative	SE Asia and Oceania/ Vanuatu
Breton	Indo-European	Fusional	Eurasia/France
Cirecire	Khoisan	Isolating	Africa/Botswana
Clallam	Salishan	Polysynthetic	North America/USA
Dangaléat	Afro-Asiatic	Agglutinative	Africa/Chad
Diola-Fogny	Niger-Congo	Agglutinative	Africa/Gambia, Senegal
English	Indo-European	Isolating	Eurasia/Ireland and UK
Estonian	Uralic	Agglutinative/fusional	Eurasia/Estonia
Finnish	Uralic	Agglutinative	Eurasia/Finland
Georgian	Kartvelian	Inflectional/ agglutinative	Eurasia/Georgia
Greek	Indo-European	Fusional	Eurasia/Greece
Hebrew	Afro-Asiatic	Inflectional	Africa/Israel
Hungarian	Uralic	Agglutinative	Eurasia/Hungary
Indonesian	Austronesian	Agglutinative	SE Asia and Oceania/ Indonesia
Japanese	Japanese	Agglutinative	Eurasia/Japan
Jaqaru	Aymaran	Agglutinative	South America/Peru

Language	Family	Morphological type	Area
Karao	Austronesian	Inflectional/ polysynthetic	SE Asia and Oceania/ Philippines
Ket	Yeniseian	Agglutinative	Eurasia/Russia
Konni	Niger-Congo	Agglutinative	Africa/Ghana
Kwakw'ala	Wakashan	Polysynthetic	North America/Canada
Lakhota	Siouan	Synthetic to polysynthetic	North America/USA
Maipure	Arawakan	Agglutinative	South America/ Venezuela
Malayalam	Dravidian	Agglutinative	Eurasia/India
Mandarin Chinese	Sino-Tibetan	Isolating/analytic	SE Asia and Oceania/ China
Marathi	Indo-European	Inflectional/ polysynthetic	Eurasia/India
Pipil	Uto-Aztecan	Agglutinative	North America/El Salvador
Slavey	Na-Dene	Polysynthetic	North America/ Northwest Territories
Slovak	Indo-European	Inflectional	Eurasia/Slovakia
Spanish	Indo-European	Inflectional	Eurasia/Spain
Swahili	Niger-Congo	Agglutinative	Africa/Tanzania
Tatar	Altaic	Agglutinative	Eurasia/Russia
Tibetan	Sino-Tibetan	Inflectional/ agglutinative	SE Asia and Oceania/ China
Tzotzil	Mayan	Agglutinative/ polysynthetic	North America/Mexico
Udihe	Altaic	Agglutinative	Eurasia/Russia
West Greenlandic	Eskimo-Aleut	Polysynthetic	North America/ Greenland
Wichí	Matacoan	Agglutinative	South America/Argentina and Bolivia
Zulu	Niger-Congo	Agglutinative	Africa/South Africa

Table 6.19 shows the diversity of word-formation processes used for diminutive formation.

Table 6.19. *Word-formation processes for the category diminutive*

Compounding	(179)	Indonesian	*anak ayam* child-chicken/fowl 'chicken' (Mojdl 2006: 81)

Prefixation	(180) Malayalam	*aaṭṭinkuṭṭi* aatə-kuɻ̣ṭi goat-young 'kid'
	(181) Anejom	*nalve-eañ* nalve-neañ DIM-coconut 'kind of coconut with small fruit'
	(182) Japanese	小川 ogawa o-kawa DIM-river 'small river, stream'
	(183) Swahili	*kitoto* ki-mtoto DIM-child 'small child, infant'[18]
Reduplication	(184) Clallam	*sqaʔ<áʔ>χaʔ* sqáχaʔ <RDP> dog-DIM 'puppy'
	(185) Karao	*ba-badiy* ba-baliy RDP-house 'toy house'
	(186) Kwakw'ala	*t!a-´t!edzɛm* tla-t!ē´sɛm RDP-stone 'small stone, stone' (Boas 1947: 220)
Suffixation	(187) Tibetan	རྟེའུ rtevu[19] rta-vu horse-DIM 'colt'
	(188) Udihe	*ñukte-zig'a*[20] hair-DIM 'one hair'

[18] The choice of a diminutive prefix depends on inflectional characteristics of the base. A noun class prefix is replaced with *ki-* (Class 7) or *vi-* (plural, Class 8).

[19] In Tibetan, suffixation is accompanied by vowel alternation, in particular with raising the root vowel.

[20] In Udihe, the diminutive suffix *-zig'a*, combined with mass nouns, denotes singularity (Nikolaeva and Tolskaya 2001: 150). This is a counter-iconic formation (addition of form leads to reduction of quantity).

The data gathered do not allow us to provide any examples of infixation[21] or submorphemic formation in which 'phonemes are modified in a systematic way to express diminution' (Bakema and Geeraerts 2000: 1045).[22]

6.3.1.1 Formal characteristics

Bakema and Geeraerts (2000: 1046) maintain that:

> augmentatives are less widespread than diminutives. The two categories are related by an implicational universal: the existence of augmentatives in a language implies the presence of diminutives, but the reverse does not hold. If a language has both categories, diminutives are more frequent and can be formed in more ways than augmentatives.

Our sample gives support to this assumption, and we find two special cases: in Hausa, suffixation is used (even if the productivity is low) to derive a few augmentative adjectives from abstract bases (Newman, pers. comm.), as in (189). In Ilocano, augmentatives are formed from statives only, not from nominals, by prefixal-suffixal derivation (*nag- -en*, *nain- -an*), as exemplified in (190):

(189)   Hausa   *gamɗasheesheè*
                  gàmɟasaà-SFX
                  break.off.a.large.chunk-AUG
                  'huge and muscular'

(190)   Ilocano   *nag-dakkel-en*
                    AUG-big-AUG
                    'how big!'

An interesting thing happens in Swedish. Olofsson (pers. comm.) maintains that the adjective *stor* 'big/great/large' can be used with a prefix-like function and so can *små* 'small' (used in plural). There are many lexicalized combinations formed in present-day Swedish, like *stordator* 'mainframe computer', *stormarknad* 'hypermarket', etc. Furthermore, as pointed out by Olofsson, both *små-* and *stor-* can be used with verbs, too: *småle* 'smile a little', *storgråta* 'weep, cry profusely'. This reflects a close relation between the category of augmentativeness and intensity. The same holds (more with *små-* than with *stor-*) for adjectives and their derived adverbs, but there are fewer examples: *smårolig* 'fairly funny', *storbelåten* 'very pleased'.

---

[21] According to Brainard (pers. comm.), reduplication in Karao is sometimes accompanied by infixation.

[22] These authors provide an example from Basque:

Basque   *txerri*   <   *zerri*
          'small pig'   'pig'

6.3.2   Phonetic iconicity

According to Universal #1926 (formerly #1932) of the Konstanz Archive (Plank and Filimonova 2000), there is an iconic tendency in augmentatives and diminutives: augmentatives tend to contain high back vowels, whereas diminutives tend to contain high front vowels. This expectation is not confirmed by our data. Table 6.20 shows examples of diminutives whose affixes comply and do not comply with Universal #1926:[23]

Table 6.20. *Diminutive affixes and Universal #1926 of the Konstanz Archive (Plank and Filimonova 2000)*

	Compliant			Non-compliant	
(191)	Afrikaans	*mens-ie* 'small person'	(192)	Belorussian	дам-ок damok house-DIM 'little house'
(193)	Breton	*bag-ig* boat-DIM 'little boat'	(194)	Greek	σπιακι spit-aki house-DIM 'little house'
(195)	Diola-Fogny	*fuɲil < -ɲil* 'child'[24] (D. J. Sapir 1965: 63)	(196)	Lakhota	*chicá-la* child-DIM 'little child'
(197)	Estonian	*lambi-ke.*N lamp-GEN-SFX 'little lamp'	(198)	Tatar	*bala-kay* child-DIM 'little child' (Schamiloglu)

---

[23] One of several affixes which are not compliant with Universal #1926 in Karao is the suffix *-an* used with a restricted class of transitive verbs:

Karao	*Otihan* *idotho*	*toy*	*afoy say*	*nat mekset*	*i*	*towa*
	otik-an i-dotho	to-i	afoy say	nat me-keset	i	to-wa
	lessen-IPF.PAT IPF.PAT-cook	ERG.3SG	fire so.that	not PAS.IPF-burn	ABS	ERG.3SG-CON

'She will turn down that flame a little so that it won't burn what she is cooking.'

Another anti-iconic example comes from Portuguese:

Portuguese   *caracol-inho ([u])*
caracol ([ó])-inho
snail-DIM
'little snail'

[24] Change of noun class to the 10/11 pair.

	Compliant			Non-compliant	
(199)	Italian	*tavolino* 'small table'	(200)	Ukrainian	*caд-очок* sadočok 'small orchard'
(201)	Ket	*bɛskit* 'little hare' (Werner 1998: 53)	(202)	Wichí	*atsinha-fwaj* woman-DIM 'little woman'
(203)	Konni	*nuu-biŋ* 'small arm'	(204)	Zulu	*sitshana < si-tsha-ana <si-tsha* 'little dish', 'dish'
(205)	Maipure	*tiniokí-isi* woman-DIM 'small woman'			
(206)	Pipil	*mistun-tsín* cat-DIM 'kitten' (Campbell 1985: 50)			
(207)	Serbian-Croatian	*ručica* < *ruka* 'little hand' 'hand'			
(208)	Swahili	*kitoto* < *mtoto* 'small child' 'child'			

Besides the above, there are special cases like Hungarian, where the principle of vowel harmony influences the character of diminutive suffixes *-cska/-cske*, *-ka/-ke*, which, therefore, occur in two variants, with front vowel and with back vowel (209):

(209)	Hungarian	*tető-cske* 'small roof'

Finally, there are several languages in which both affixes with front vowels and affixes with back vowels are employed. In Slovak, where diminutives are unified by the /k/-type suffixes (i.e. velar consonant) and where the form of the suffix depends on gender, we can find, among others, the *-ík/-ik* affix, as in *stolík* 'small table' from *stôl* 'table', *-ček/-tek* as in *stromček* 'small tree' from *strom* 'tree', but also *-ka* as in *knižka* 'small book' from *kniha* 'book', and *-ko* as in *okienko* 'small window' from *okno* 'window' (Furdík 2004: 90). Similar instances can be found in Finnish and West Greenlandic:

(210)	Finnish	*kirja-nen*[25] 'small book' (Koivisto)

---

[25] Other similar Finnish affixes are *-ykkä* and *-käinen*, as in *lehd-ykkä ~ lehdy-käinen* 'leaflet', *-eli* as in *hauv-eli* 'dog-AFF', but also *-onen* as in *laps-onen* 'small child', and even *-u* as in *nen-u* 'nose-AFF'.

(211)   West Greenlandic   *qimmi-iraq*   <   *qimmiq-iraq*[26]
                                'puppy'   'dog' + 'small, not fully
                                                         grown'

Universal #1926 assumes that augmentatives are formed by high back vowels. Romanian offers examples of both use of a back vowel in augmentatives (212a) and use of both types of vowels (212b). In Ilocano, augmentatives are based on prefixal-suffixal derivation, which may include both types of vowel, as in (213), but also back vowels only (*nain- -an*):

(212)   Romanian   a.   *grăs-an*
                                  'fat man'
                            b.   *lăd-oaie*
                                  'big chest/big trunk'

(213)   Ilocano   *nagdakkelen*   <   *dakkel*
                            'how big!'   'big'

Other languages whose augmentative affixes do not conform with the prediction include Belorussian (214), Hausa (215), Kwakw'ala (216), Russian (217) and Serbian-Croatian (218):

(214)   Belorussian   збан-ішч-а
                            zbanišča
                            jug-AUG-GND
                            'very big jug'

(215)   Hausa   *gamɗashēshèe*   <   *gàmɗasàa*
                            'huge and muscular'   'break off a large
                                                      chunk'

(216)   Kwakw'ala   *g̓ō'xudzēɛ*   <   *-dzē*
                            'large house'   'large'
                            (Boas 1947: 345)

(217)   Russian   *столище*
                            stol'-ishche
                            table-AUG
                            'big table'

(218)   Serbian-Croatian *ručerda*   <   *ruka*
                            'big hand'   'hand'

---

[26] Another similar West Greenlandic affix is *-nnguaq* 'little, dear', as in *miirannguaq* 'little child' formed by *miiraq-nnguaq*.

In principle, our observations correspond with Ultan (1978), who, based on an analysis of 136 languages,[27] concluded that, while front and high vowels prevail as diminutive markers, we can hardly speak of a language universal. What seems to be more relevant is an areal approach to the problem of augmentative/diminutive symbolism, as also assumed by Nichols (1971) with regard to a systematic diminutive consonant symbolism in the languages of western North America.[28] L. Bauer (1996) examined evaluative morphology in fifty languages. His detailed analysis of a language sample from various perspectives[29] concludes that 'phonetic iconicity is not a very strong factor in the development of augmentative and diminutive markers cross-linguistically' (L. Bauer 1996: 197).

6.3.3 Word-classes

L. Bauer (1997: 540) proposes a hierarchy of base types for augmentivization and diminutivization (first noun, second adjective and verb, third adverb, numeral, pronoun and interjection and, finally, determinative). This should be read as follows: 'for a word-class to be used as the base in evaluative morphology in a particular language, word-classes from each step above that must also be so used in that language' (L. Bauer 1997: 540). From this it follows that diminutive formation from adverbs is conditioned by the existence in that language of diminutives formed from adjectives or verbs.

While the great majority of augmentatives and diminutives maintain the word-class of the motivating words, as pointed out, among others, by Merlini Barbaresi (2003: 439), there are infrequent cases of class-changing formations, as in Hausa (219) and Japanese (220):

(219)   Hausa   *gabjeejeè*
                                 gabzaà-RDP
                                 heap.up.a.lot.of.something-DIM
                                 'bulky'

---

[27] The sample of languages contained a high number of Amerindian languages (forty-eight) and also Dravidian languages (eleven).

[28] In particular, the diminutivization is expressed by 'hardening or strengthening shifts. In general the point of articulation is unchanged in these shifts, and a more forceful manner of articulation signals the diminutive. A hierarchy of hardness from lenis to fortis to ejective stop or affricate, from continuant to non-continuant, or from any obstruent or sonorant to its glottalized counterpart, is associated with increasing diminutiveness' (Nichols 1971: 828–9).

[29] Including the predictions of Mayerthaler (1988) and Dressler and Karpf (1995), among others, concerning the role of consonants such that palatal consonants are said to be characteristic of diminutives and velar consonants of augmentatives.

(220)   Japanese   赤ちゃん
                         aka-chan[30]
                         red-DIM
                         'a baby'

6.3.3.1   Semantic characteristics

The vast majority of examples express the meaning of smallness.
However, the range of meanings of diminutives is large (cf. Jurafsky 1993).
Examples with Hindi suffixes -iya, -ṛa/-ṛī illustrate three different dimensions
of evaluative morphology (see Table 6.21).

Table 6.21. *Three dimensions of evaluative morphology in Hindi*

Smallness	Affectionate	Pejorative
(221) Hindi बच्चा-बच्ची	(222) Hindi बीवीयाँ	(223) Hindi कुट्टी
bəchṛa/bəchṛī	biṭiya	kuttī
bəcchªa-ṛa/-ṛī	beṭī-iya	kutta-ī
calf-DIM	daughter-DIM	dog-DIM
'small calf'	'little daughter'	'little bitch'
(Kachru 2006:	(Kachru 2006:	(Kachru 2006:
117)	46)	46)

Other possible nuances are hypocoristics, as in section 3.2.1. The attenuative
meaning is connected in Udihe with the semelfactive, which is built by means
of the suffix -ndA-:

(224)   Udihe   *eme-nde-*
                      come-DIM
                      'come for a short time'
                      (Nikolaeva and Tolskaya 2001: 311)

The attenuative meaning can also be expressed in Udihe by the deintensify-
ing suffix -lA: in the case of colour terms, this is implemented by truncation
within which the suffix -lA replaces the suffix -ligi (the bare stem never occurs
independently, Nikolaeva and Tolskaya 2001: 186):

(225)   Udihe   *pa-la*   <   *pa-ligi*
                      'blackish'   'black'

Other adjectives with attenuative meaning are derived by -lA suffixation:

(226)   Udihe   *saza-la*
                      foolish-DIM
                      'a little foolish'

---

[30] The form *chan* is a corruption of the polite affix *san* 'Mr/Ms', and is used for the young and
intimates (Volpe, pers. comm.).

6.4   Verbal categories

6.4.1   Causatives

Causative verb formation is recorded in the languages shown in Table 6.22 (76.36 per cent of the study sample).

Table 6.22. *The category causative in the study sample*

Language	Family	Morphological type	Area
Amele	Trans-New Guinea	Polysynthetic/ synthetic	Australia-New Guinea/ Madang
Amharic	Afro-Asiatic	Inflectional	Africa/Ethiopia
Anejom	Austronesian	Agglutinative	SE Asia and Oceania/ Vanuatu
Cirecire	Khoisan	Isolating	Africa/Botswana
Clallam	Salishan	Polysynthetic	North America/USA
Dangaléat	Afro-Asiatic	Agglutinative	Africa/Chad
Datooga	Nilo-Saharan	Agglutinative/ fusional	Africa/Tanzania
Diola-Fogny	Niger-Congo	Agglutinative	Africa/Gambia, Senegal
English	Indo-European	Isolating	Eurasia/Ireland and UK
Estonian	Uralic	Agglutinative/ fusional	Eurasia/Estonia
Finnish	Uralic	Agglutinative	Eurasia/Finland
Georgian	Kartvelian	Inflectional/ agglutinative	Eurasia/Georgia
Hebrew	Afro-Asiatic	Inflectional	Africa/Israel
Hungarian	Uralic	Agglutinative	Eurasia/Hungary
Ilocano	Austronesian	Agglutinative	SE Asia and Oceania/ Philippines
Indonesian	Austronesian	Agglutinative	SE Asia and Oceania/ Indonesia
Japanese	Japanese	Agglutinative	Eurasia/Japan
Jaqaru	Aymaran	Agglutinative	South America/Peru
Kalkatungu	Australian-Aboriginal	Agglutinative	Australia-New Guinea/ Australia
Karao	Austronesian	Inflectional/ polysynthetic	SE Asia and Oceania/ Philippines
Ket	Yeniseian	Agglutinative	Eurasia/Russia
Kwakw'ala	Wakashan	Polysynthetic	North America/ Canada
Lakhota	Siouan	Synthetic to polysynthetic	North America/USA
Luo	Nilo-Saharan	Agglutinative	Africa/Kenya, Tanzania

Language	Family	Morphological type	Area
Maipure	Arawakan	Agglutinative	South America/Venezuela
Malayalam	Dravidian	Agglutinative	Eurasia/India
Mandarin Chinese	Sino-Tibetan	Isolating/analytic	SE Asia and Oceania/ China
Māori	Austronesian	Isolating	SE Asia and Oceania/ New Zealand
Marathi	Indo-European	Inflectional/ polysynthetic	Eurasia/India
Nelemwa	Austronesian	Isolating	SE Asia and Oceania/ New Caledonia
Pipil	Uto-Aztecan	Agglutinative	North America/El Salvador
Slovak	Indo-European	Inflectional	Eurasia/Slovakia
Spanish	Indo-European	Inflectional	Eurasia/Spain
Swahili	Niger-Congo	Agglutinative	Africa/Tanzania
Tamil	Dravidian	Agglutinative	Eurasia/Tamil Nadu
Tatar	Altaic	Agglutinative	Eurasia/Russia
Telugu	Dravidian	Agglutinative	Eurasia/India
Totonac	Totonacan	Agglutinative/ polysynthetic	North America/Mexico
Tzotzil	Mayan	Polysynthetic/ agglutinative	North America/Mexico
Udihe	Altaic	Agglutinative	Eurasia/Russia
West Greenlandic	Eskimo-Aleut	Polysynthetic	North America/ Greenland
Zulu	Niger-Congo	Agglutinative	Africa/South Africa

Table 6.23 shows the diversity of word-formation processes used for causative formation.

Table 6.23. *Word-formation processes for the category causative*

Circumfixation	(227) Indonesian	*memper-jahat-kan*	<	*jahat*[31]
		CAU-bad-CAU		'bad'
		'worsen (something)'		
		(Mojdl 2006: 137)		

---

[31] Indonesian uses two confixes for this purpose: *memper- -kan* and *memper- -i* as below:

    Indonesian *mempersetujui*   < *setuju*
                'approve of (something)' 'agree.v'
                (Mojdl 2006: 140)

	(228) Totonac	ma:chipí:	
		ma:-chipá-i:	
		CAU-hold-CAU	
		'make (somebody) hold (something)'	
Incorporation	(229) Catalan	camatrencar	
		leg-break-INF	
		'cause (something) to break its leg'	
Infixation	(230) Marathi	कर्<अव्>अणे	
		kar<av>ane[32]	
		do<CAU>	
		'get done'	
Lengthening	(231) Luo[33]	anyiiny	< anyiny
		'sweeten.v'	< 'sweet'
Prefixal–suffixal derivation	(232) Nelemwa	fa-xere-lî	< khere[34]
		CAU-be.forbidden-TR.SFX	
		'forbid.v'	
Prefixation	(233) Anejom	awor-upni[35]	
		CAU-good	
		'make good, repair'	
	(234) Georgian	მო-ქმედ-ებ-ს vs ა-მო-ქმედ-ებ-ს	
		mo-kmed-eb-s	a-mo-kmed-eb-s
		function-TH-S3.SG	a-function-TH-S3.SG
		'It functions'	'S/he/it makes it'
	(235) Russian[36]	о-астливи-ть	
		oshchastlivit'	
		CAU-happy-INF	
		'make happy'	
	(236) Serbian-Croatian	pri-morati	
		CAU-want/need/must	
		'enforce'	
	(237) Totonac	ma'ha-chu:yá:	
		CAU-be.crazy	
		'drive somebody crazy'	
Root-and-pattern	(238) Hebrew[37]	המית	< מת
		hemit	met
		'kill.v'	'die'
Stem modification	(239) Datooga	ruut	< rit
		'take out'	'come out'

[32] Infix-based causative formation in Marathi is characterized by infixation of the consonant + vowel sequence -va-. Ability verbs have the same form: karavaNe 'get done (able to do/ possible to do)'.

[33] Lengthening of the last syllable of the verb or adjective in Luo.

[34] Nelemwa uses the prefix pa-FCT, or fa-CAU + v + TR.SFX.

[35] The prefix is awo-. Its variant awor- is used before a vowel.

[36] A number of different prefixes like po-, o-, ras-/raz-, u-.

[37] Causatives in Hebrew are formed especially by the pattern hif'il.

Suffixation	(240) Udihe	*etete-wen-*		
		work.V-CAU		
		'cause to work'		
	(241) Udihe	*sele-wen-*	<	*sele-*
		wake.up-CAU		
		'wake (somebody) up'		'wake up'
	(242) Udihe	*diga-wan-*	<	*diga-*
		eat-CAU		
		'cause to eat, feed'		
		(Nikolaeva and Tolskaya 2001: 302)		

Table 6.23 should be complemented with Table 6.24, which shows formation of causatives by various types of incorporation in Amele (Roberts 1987: 309–12) and Cirecire.

Table 6.24. *Incorporation for the category causative*

Noun incorporation		Adjective incorporation		Verb incorporation	
(243) Amele	*sibt q-oc*	(244) Amele	*cecela m-ec*	(245) Amele	*qatan-I q-oc*
	chin-hit		long-put		split-hit
	'yawn'		'become long'		'tear.v'
(246) Cirecire	*tsa'axo*			(247) Cirecire	‖*um-axo*
	oil-make				greet-make
	'cook'				'welcome'

In many cases, causatives are formed by turning intransitive verbs into transitive verbs, as in the following examples from Ilocano and Māori:

(248)   Ilocano   *pa-paurayen*   <   *pa-uray-en*
         CAU-wait-TR
         'have (somebody) wait'

(249)   Māori   *whaka-roa*
         CAU-long
         'lengthen'

Causatives may also be formed from transitive verbs. In Ket, this is limited to a class of verbs with inanimate class objects, in which case the original object is preposed to the verbal infinitive form in P7 (Vajda 2004: 71):

(250)   Ket   *danánbètqajit*
         da[8]-nán/bet[7]-q[5]-a[4]-(j)-t[0]
         3F.SBJ[8]-bread/make[7]-CAU[5]-3M.OBJ[4]-(MS)-MOM.TR[0]
         'She causes him to start baking bread'

In Malayalam, according to Asher and Kumari (1997: 272ff.), the causative verb is usually the last stage of the intransitive-transitive-causative chain.

The causative verb is formed by suffixes -(*i*)*kk*-, -(*i*)*ppikk*- (and their phonologically conditioned variants), which are attached to a transitive verb. The
latter of them, -(*i*)*ppikk*-, is regarded as a sequence of two causative suffixes,
-(*i*)*kk*- + -(*i*)*pp*-:

(251)   Malayalam   *ceyy-ikk-uka*
                      do-CAU-INF
                      'cause to do'

(252)   Malayalam   *kaa-ṭṭuka*   <   *kaaṇ-*
                      see-CAU   see
                      'show.v'   'see'

(253)   Malayalam   *cirri-ppikkuka* <   *cirikk-*
                      laugh-CAU   laugh
                      'cause to laugh'   'laugh'

An example of the above-mentioned chain is given below:

(254)   Malayalam   *tinnuka*   *tiirruka*   *tiirrikkuka*   *tiirrippikkuka*
                      'eat'   'feed'   'make X   'make X
                                               feed Y'   feed Y'
                      (Asher and Kumari 1997: 278)

It follows from this example that forms with -(*i*)*kk*- and -(*i*)*ppikk*-, respectively, need not differ in their meaning.

   In several languages both transitive and intransitive verbs can be used as
bases for causatives, sometimes imposing different resources for the derivation, sometimes not. Thus, Amharic uses the prefix *a*- for intransitives (255a)
and *as*- for transitives (255b) (even if there are many exceptions in this
language), Ket uses the single-consonant morpheme *q* called *determiner* to
derive causatives from both intransitive and transitive verbs (256) and Pipil
uses the suffix -*tia* (-*ltia*) for both transitive (257a) and intransitive (257b)
stems (Campbell 1985: 85):

(255)   Amharic   a.   *a-fälla*   <   *fla*
                          CAU-boil   boil
                          'He boiled'

                    b.   *as-fällägä*   <   *flg*
                          CAU-seek   seek
                          'It made seek (~was necessary)'

(256)   Ket   *daúsqajit*
                          3F.SBJ[8]-warm[7]-CAU[5]-3M.OBJ[4]-MOM.TR[0]
                          'She warms him up'

(257)   Pipil   a.   *ilwitia*   <   *ilwia*
                          say-CAU   say
                          'show.v'

b.   *miktia*   <   *miki*
      die-CAU   die
      'kill.v'   'die'

The combinability in terms of the transitive/intransitive nature of the under-lying verb can also be observed in Udihe, where the suffix *-wAn-* can attach to virtually every verb (Nikolaeva and Tolskaya 2001: 287):

(258)   Udihe   *etete-wen-*
                  work-CAU
                  'cause to work'

(259)   Udihe   *sele-wen-*   <   *sele-*
                  wake.up-CAU   'wake up'
                  'wake (somebody) up'

(260)   Udihe   *diga-wan-*
                  eat-CAU
                  'cause to eat, feed'
                  (Nikolaeva and Tolskaya 2001: 302)

This feature of Udihe is not unique. Comrie (1985: 332) refers to Turkish 'where virtually any verb (including a causative verb) can form a causative'.

As for the word-class of the base, verbs dominate with only some excep-tions, among others in Amele, Luo and Slovak, where verbs as well as adjectives can serve as bases for causative formations:

(261)   Slovak   *čistiť*   <   *čistý*
                   'clean.v'   'clean.ADJ'

6.4.2   Transitivity

As with other semantic categories, this word-formation process may be very idiosyncratic. Thus, Finnish does not have general categories like transitive and intransitive. Instead it has numerous, more or less pro-ductive, verbal derivation suffixes for different Aktionsarten (Laakso, pers. comm.):

(262)   Finnish   *pako-tta-*
                    'make do, force'

(263)   Finnish   *hidas-ta-*
                    'slow.v'

It was noted in section 6.4.1 that transitive verbs sometimes serve to derive causative verbs and that they function in some languages as a link in the intransitive-transitive-causative chain. Let us illustrate this with an example from Pipil (264), where the suffix *-tia* (*-ltia*) can be added to intransitive verbs (Campbell 1985), and from Udihe (265), where causative derivation from intransitive verbs by means of the suffix *-wAn* leads to transitivization (Nikolaeva and Tolskaya 2001: 302):

(264)   Pipil   *machtia*
                    mati-tia
                    know-TR
                    'teach.v'

(265)   Udihe   *zegde-wen-*
                    burn-CAU
                    'set fire to'

The opposite is also possible: Tzotzil can form intransitives from transitives by means of the suffixes *-van* 'characteristic mode', *-Vn* and *-av*:

(266)   Tzotzil   *lútš-van*   <   *lútš*
                      gore.it.TR-INTR
                      'gore characteristically'   'gore it'
                      (Cowan 1969: 97)

(267)   Tzotzil   *núp-un*   <   *núp*
                      meet.her.TR-INTR
                      'be married'   'meet her'
                      (Cowan 1969: 100)

In Japanese, transitive verbs are changed into intransitive verbs by substituting an intransitive suffix for a transitive suffix. Still, Kageyama (pers. comm.) points out that there are many idiosyncratic lexical pairings and that this process is not productive in Japanese:

(268)   Japanese （ロケットを）打ち上げる   vs （ロケットが）打ち上がる
                    (roketto-o) uti-ageru   (roketto-ga) uti-agaru
                    (rocket-ACC) shoot-send.up (rocket-NOM) shoot-go. up
                    'send up (rockets)'   '(rocket) go up/be
                                                  launched'

Transitive verb formation is recorded in the languages shown in Table 6.25 (49.09 per cent of the study sample).

Table 6.25. *The category transitive in the study sample*

Language	Family	Morphological type	Area
Amharic	Afro-Asiatic	Inflectional	Africa/Ethiopia
Anejom	Austronesian	Agglutinative	SE Asia and Oceania/Vanuatu
Clallam	Salishan	Polysynthetic	North America/USA
English	Indo-European	Isolating	Eurasia/Ireland and UK

Language	Family	Morphological type	Area
Estonian	Uralic	Agglutinative/fusional	Eurasia/Estonia
Finnish	Uralic	Agglutinative	Eurasia/Finland
Georgian	Kartvelian	Inflectional/agglutinative	Eurasia/Georgia
Greek	Indo-European	Fusional	Eurasia/Greece
Hebrew	Afro-Asiatic	Inflectional	Africa/Israel
Ilocano	Austronesian	Agglutinative	SE Asia and Oceania/ Philippines
Indonesian	Austronesian	Agglutinative	SE Asia and Oceania/ Indonesia
Kalkatungu	Australian- Aboriginal	Agglutinative	Australia-New Guinea/ Australia
Karao	Austronesian	Inflectional/polysynthetic	SE Asia and Oceania/ Philippines
Ket	Yeniseian	Agglutinative	Eurasia/Russia
Kwakw'ala	Wakashan	Polysynthetic	North America/Canada
Lakhota	Siouan	Synthetic to polysynthetic	North America/USA
Luo	Nilo-Saharan	Agglutinative	Africa/Kenya, Tanzania
Malayalam	Dravidian	Agglutinative	Eurasia/India
Nelemwa	Austronesian	Isolating	SE Asia and Oceania/ New Caledonia
Pipil	Uto-Aztecan	Agglutinative	North America/El Salvador
Slovak	Indo-European	Inflectional	Eurasia/Slovakia
Spanish	Indo-European	Inflectional	Eurasia/Spain
Telugu	Dravidian	Agglutinative	Eurasia/India
Totonac	Totonacan	Agglutinative/polysynthetic	North America/Mexico
Tzotzil	Mayan	Agglutinative/polysynthetic	North America/Mexico
Udihe	Altaic	Agglutinative	Eurasia/Russia
Zulu	Niger-Congo	Agglutinative	Africa/South Africa

Table 6.26 shows the diversity of word-formation processes used for transitivity formation.

Table 6.26. *Word-formation processes for the category transitive*

Circumfixation	(269) Karao	*Kiyakan* kakan-iy-ate-PFV.PAT 'They ate the rice'	*chiy* cha-i ERG.3PL-ABS	*inepoy* inepoy cooked.rice
	(270) Lakhota	*yu-bláska* PRX-flat 'flatten.v'		
	(271) Serbian- Croatian	*iz-leći* TR-lie.down 'hatch.v'		

	(272) Slovak	*vy-sediet'* TR-sit 'hatch.v'		
Prefixal–suffixal derivation	(273) Nelemwa	*fa-xere-lî* CAU-be. forbidden-TR.SFX 'forbid.v'	<	*khere*
Root-and-pattern	(274) Hebrew	לימד limed 'teach.v'		
Stem modification[38]	(275) Marathi	मारणे maaraNe 'kill.v'	<	मरणे maaraNe 'die'
Suffixation	(276) Zulu	*-fik-el-*[39] arrive-APP 'arrive for (somebody)'		

The formation of transitives allows for a number of possibilities in the languages considered here. According to Bowern (pers. comm.), there are about thirty verbs (out of 250) in Bardi which alternate in transitivity. They use a transitive prefix *n- ~ a-*, but they are not productively derived. Many verbs are derived with the use of a light verb *-joo-* 'say'.[40] In Māori, many transitive

---

[38] Stem modification is a part of a more complex process in Malayalam. According to Asher and Kumari (1997: 272ff.), transitive verbs are derived from intransitive verbs by modification of the stem, by changes of consonants and by adding a suffix. This means that the stems of all transitive verbs derived from intransitive verbs end in a double consonant (it may also include a change of a double nasal or a nasal plus a homorganic consonant into a double plosive). Phonetically, it is a long voiceless stop:

Malayalam	*muṟukk-*	<	*muṟuk-*
	'tighten.v'		'become tight'
Malayalam	*uṟakk-*	<	*uṟaŋŋ-*
	'put to sleep'		'sleep.v'

[39] Zulu transitives are formed by the causative suffix *-is-* or the applicative suffix *-el-*. The meaning of the latter is 'do on behalf of':

Zulu *-m-el-*
stand-APP
'represent.v'

[40] *Light verb* is accounted for by Baker and Fasola (2009: 605) as 'a verb that has a very general "bleached" meaning, contributing aspectual information or argument structure properties to the construction it appears in, but little or no encyclopedic meaning'. Mapudungun, an Araucanian language spoken in South America, also provides examples of verb + verb compounds with light verbs, such as *pütre-n-tüku-n* (burn-INF-put-inf, 'set on fire'), *rütre-wül-n* (push-give-INF, 'give a push'), and *kintu-wül-n* (look-give-INF, 'give a look') (Baker and Fasola 2009: 605).

verbs are derived by the prefix *whaka-* (W. Bauer 1997: 44–5).[41] Examples of a transitive formed by this prefix from an action intransitive is given in (277) and from a state intransitive in (278):

(277)   Māori   *whaka-haere*
                  TR-move
                  'run (something)'

(278)   Māori   *whaka-mārama*
                  TR-clear
                  'explain, make clear'

In some languages, word-formation-based transitivization can rely on several word-formation processes. The basic device for the formation of transitive verbs in Indonesian is prefixation by *me-* (with its five phonologically conditioned allomorphs), attached to verbs (279), nouns (280) and adjectives (281) (Mojdl 2006: 48), but a number of confixes are also used (282) (Mojdl 2006: 126ff.):[42]

(279)   Indonesian   *me-makan*
                        TR.PRX-eat
                        'eat (something)'

(280)   Indonesian   *me-lombong*
                        TR.PRX-mine.N
                        'mine.v'

(281)   Indonesian   *me-tinggi*
                        TR.PRX-high
                        'increase.v'

(282)   Indonesian   *me-mandi-kan*
                        TR-have.a.bath.V-TR
                        'bath (somebody)'

Datooga generates transitive verbs by paradigmatic formation, i.e. conversion of a verb from Class 1 to Class 2 (283), by stem modification (284) and by suffixation (285):

---

[41] 'Many transitive verbs created in this way [by the prefix *whaka-*] have come to be associated with one specific transitive sense, which may obscure the relationship, but it is nevertheless true that, if a new intransitive verb is created in Māori, a transitive *whaka-* form can be created from it with a meaning which is predictable at the time of the creation' (W. Bauer 1997: 44–5).

[42] Other confixes are *memper- -an*, *memper- -i* and *me- -i*, the last of which can also be used with verbs, nouns and adjectives:

Indonesian	*me-lukis-i*	*me-ngair-i*	*mem-baik-i*	<	*baik*
	TR-draw-TR	TR-water-TR	TR-good-TR		
	'draw a thing'	'irrigate (something)'	'repair/improve'		'good'

(283)   Datooga   *noos*   <   *noos*
                       (Class 2)   (Class 1)
                       'stick.v'   'be stuck'

(284)   Datooga   *ruut*   <   *rit*
                       'take out'   'come out'

(285)   Datooga   *ɲaṛ-j*
                       be.broken-TR
                       'break.v'

According to Brainard (pers. comm.), Karao makes very productive use of suffixes (*-en, -an*), prefixes (*i-*) and circumfixes (*i- -an*). Nelemwa may form transitives by suffixation (286) and by prefixal-suffixal derivation (cf. (273)):

(286)   Nelemwa   *aw-îlî*[43]
                       laugh.V-TR
                       'laugh at (something)'

Finally, Totonac forms transitives by prefixation (287) and suffixation (288):

(287)   Totonac   *li:-a'hlhche'hxlá:*
                       INS-trip
                       'trip on (something)'

(288)   Totonac   *pa'hlh-ní*
                       burst-BEN
                       'burst (something for somebody)'

As regards word-classes, transitive verbs are derived not only from verbal bases: the examples of Indonesian in (279) to (282) show that nouns and adjectives may also serve as bases for this purpose. This is confirmed, for instance, by the data of Kalkatungu, where the suffix *-puni* is attached to nominal stems (289), and of Kwakw'ala, which may attach suffixes both to intransitive verbs and to adjectives, as in (290) and (291):

(289)   Kalkatungu   *yarrka-puni*
                       far-make
                       'put at a distance'

(290)   Kwakw'ala   *kw'əmdədzud*   <   *kw'əmta*
                       suck-TR   suck
                       'suck on'   'suck.v'

(291)   Kwakw'ala   *'amx-a*
                       watertight-CAU
                       'make watertight'
                       (Boas 1947: 241)

---

[43] From *ap* 'laugh'.

6.4.3   Intransitivity

Intransitive verb formation is recorded in the languages shown in Table 6.27 (40 per cent in the study sample):

Table 6.27. *The category intransitive in the study sample*

Language	Family	Morphological type	Area
Anejom	Austronesian	Agglutinative	SE Asia and Oceania/ Vanuatu
Clallam	Salishan	Polysynthetic	North America/USA
Datooga	Nilo-Saharan	Agglutinative/ fusional	Africa/Tanzania
Estonian	Uralic	Agglutinative/fusional	Eurasia/Estonia
Finnish	Uralic	Agglutinative	Eurasia/Finland
Georgian	Kartvelian	Inflectional/ agglutinative	Eurasia/Georgia
Hebrew	Afro-Asiatic	Inflectional	Africa/Israel
Ilocano	Austronesian	Agglutinative	SE Asia and Oceania/ Philippines
Kalkatungu	Australian- Aboriginal	Agglutinative	Australia-New Guinea/ Australia
Karao	Austronesian	Infectional/ polysynthetic	SE Asia and Oceania/ Philippines
Ket	Yeniseian	Agglutinative	Eurasia/Russia
Lakhota	Siouan	Synthetic to polysynthetic	North America/USA
Luo	Nilo-Saharan	Agglutinative	Africa/Kenya, Tanzania
Pipil	Uto-Aztecan	Agglutinative	North America/El Salvador
Slovak	Indo-European	Inflectional	Eurasia/Slovakia
Spanish	Indo-European	Inflectional	Eurasia/Spain
Swahili	Niger-Congo	Agglutinative	Africa/Tanzania
Totonac	Totonacan	Agglutinative/ polysynthetic	North America/Mexico
Tzotzil	Mayan	Agglutinative/ polysynthetic	North America/Mexico
Udihe	Altaic	Agglutinative	Eurasia/Russia
West Greenlandic	Eskimo-Aleut	Polysynthetic	North America/Greenland
Zulu	Niger-Congo	Agglutinative	Africa/South Africa

Table 6.28 shows the diversity of word-formation processes used for intransitive formation:

Table 6.28. *Word-formation processes for the category intransitive*

Conversion	(292) Breton	*labouseta* < *laboused* 'hunt for birds' 'birds'
Infixation	(293) Ilocano	*t<um>akder* 'stand up'
Prefixation	(294) Karao	*onjo-kow i nga-nga nem engkay* IPF.PAT-sleep ABS child TI soon 'The baby will sleep soon'
	(295) Lakhota	*wa-'óphethu* INTR-buy 'go shopping'
	(296) Serbian-Croatian	*pri-stupiti* DIR-to.step.V 'adjoin.V, accede.V'
Reduplication	(297) Anejom	*ahen-hen* roast-INTR 'be too hot'
Reflexivization[44]	(298) Russian	*разбить-ся* razbit'-s'a 'break.V.RFL'
Root-and-pattern	(299) Hebrew	הלך halax 'go.V'
Suffixation	(300) Datooga	*jeeŋ-ʃ*[45] skin.TR-INTR 'do skinning'
	(301) Ilocano	*ag-lati* INTR-rust 'rust.V'

How complex the derivation of intransitive verbs can be is illustrated in Table 6.29 by Tzotzil and its eight different intransitivizing suffixes (Cowan 1969: 98–100), each of them combining with a specific type of roots and/or stems.

Table 6.29. *Intransitivizing suffixes in Tzotzil*

-van 'characteristic mode'	(302) Tzotzil	*lútš-van* gore.it-INTR 'gore characteristically'

---

[44] Reflexivization by the so-called reflexive pronoun, as *ся -s'a* in Russian, is possible in Slavic languages.

[45] Accompanied by final C alternation.

-V(owel)x	(303) Tzotzil	*tákix* < *tákin* 'dry.v' 'dry.ADJ'
-ub 'developmental'	(304) Tzotzil	*mé²el-ub* < *mé²el'* old.(of.women)-INTR 'become old (of women)'
-Cun 'characteristic motion or sound'[46]	(305) Tzotzil	*mék-mun* mékan-mun lame-INTR 'walk with a limp'
-et 'characteristic state or sound'	(306) Tzotzil	*k'íš-et* k'ïšin-et warm-INTR 'characteristic state or sound'
i 'characteristic stance'	(307) Tzotzil	*nák-i* nákal seated/at.home-INTR 'sit down, live in a place'
-Vn[47]	(308) Tzotzil	*núp-un* meet.her.INTR 'be married'
-av	(309) Tzotzil	*xál-av* weave.it-INTR 'weave.v'

As regards word-classes, intransitive verbs, like transitive ones, are mostly derived from verbal bases. Nominal bases are frequently used as in the case of conversion in Breton (cf. (292)) or suffixation in Kalkatungu (Blake, pers. comm.), where the suffix *-(th)ati* is attached to a nominal stem (310), and Udihe (312), where the suffix *-mA-* forms intransitive verbs with the proto-typical meaning 'catch, hunt for' and the basic noun functions as instrument, and Ukrainian (311):

(310)   Kalkatungu   *thail-ati*
                             hard-INTR
                             'grow hard'

(311)   Ukrainian   *учитeл-ювати*
                             uchitel'uvati
                             teacher-NTR
                             'act as teacher'

---

[46] Where C is a reduplication of the initial consonant of the root.
[47] Where V can be realized as *a*, *i*, or *u*.

(312)   Udihe   *dukta-ma-*
                                  ski-INTR
                                  'ski.v'
                                  (Nikolaeva and Tolskaya 2001: 291)

Affixation to adjectives is also possible in Tzotzil (cf. Table 6.29) and in Slovak (313):

(313)   Slovak   *star-nút'*
                                  starý-INTR
                                  old-INTR
                                  'grow older'

6.4.4   Iterativity and/or intensification

Iterativity and/or intensification verb formation is recorded in the languages shown in Table 6.30 (78.18 per cent of the study sample).

Table 6.30. *The category for iterativity and/or intensification in the study sample*

Language	Family	Morphological type	Area
Amele	Trans-New Guinea	Polysynthetic/ synthetic	Australia-New Guinea/Madang
Amharic	Afro-Asiatic	Inflectional	Africa/Ethiopia
Anejom	Austronesian	Agglutinative	SE Asia and Oceania/ Vanuatu
Bardi	Australian	Fusional	Australia-New Guinea/Australia
Breton	Indo-European	Fusional	Eurasia/France
Cirecire	Khoisan	Isolating	Africa/Botswana
Clallam	Salishan	Polysynthetic	North America/USA
Dangaléat	Afro-Asiatic	Agglutinative	Africa/Chad
Datooga	Nilo-Saharan	Agglutinative/ fusional	Africa/Tanzania
Estonian	Uralic	Agglutinative/ fusional	Eurasia/Estonia
Finnish	Uralic	Agglutinative	Eurasia/Finland
Gã	Niger-Congo	Agglutinative	Africa/Ghana
Georgian	Kartvelian	Inflectional/ agglutinative	Eurasia/Georgia
Greek	Indo-European	Fusional	Eurasia/Greece
Hausa	Afro-Asiatic	Fusional	Africa/Niger, Nigeria
Hebrew	Afro-Asiatic	Inflectional	Africa/Israel
Hungarian	Uralic	Agglutinative	Eurasia/Hungary
Ilocano	Austronesian	Agglutinative	SE Asia and Oceania/ Philippines

Language	Family	Morphological type	Area
Jaqaru	Aymaran	Agglutinative	South America/Peru
Kalkatungu	Australian-Aboriginal	Agglutinative	Australia-New Guinea/Australia
Karao	Austronesian	Inflectional/polysynthetic	SE Asia and Oceania/Philippines
Ket	Yeniseian	Agglutinative	Eurasia/Russia
Konni	Niger-Congo	Agglutinative	Africa/Ghana
Kwakw'ala	Wakashan	Polysynthetic	North America/Canada
Lakhota	Siouan	Synthetic to polysynthetic	North America/USA
Luganda	Niger-Congo	Agglutinative	Africa/Uganda
Mandarin Chinese	Sino-Tibetan	Isolating/analytic	SE Asia and Oceania/China
Māori	Austronesian	Isolating	SE Asia and Oceania/New Zealand
Marathi	Indo-European	Inflectional/polysynthetic	Eurasia/India
Nelemwa	Austronesian	Isolating	SE Asia and Oceania/New Caledonia
Pipil	Uto-Aztecan	Agglutinative	North America/El Salvador
Slavey	Na-Dene	Polysynthetic	North America/Northwest Territories
Slovak	Indo-European	Inflectional	Eurasia/Slovakia
Spanish	Indo-European	Inflectional	Eurasia/Spain
Swahili	Niger-Congo	Agglutinative	Africa/Tanzania
Tamil	Dravidian	Agglutinative	Eurasia/Tamil Nadu
Tatar	Altaic	Agglutinative	Eurasia/Russia
Tibetan	Sino-Tibetan	Inflectional/agglutinative	SE Asia and Oceania/China
Totonac	Totonacan	Agglutinative/polysynthetic	North America/Mexico
Tzotzil	Mayan	Agglutinative/polysynthetic	North America/Mexico
Udihe	Altaic	Agglutinative	Eurasia/Russia
West Greenlandic	Eskimo-Aleut	Polysynthetic	North America/Greenland
Zulu	Niger-Congo	Agglutinative	Africa/South Africa

Table 6.31 shows the diversity of word-formation processes used for iterativity and/or intensification formation:

Table 6.31. *Word-formation processes for the category iterativity and/or intensification*

Prefixation	(314) Breton	*das-kemer* FRE-take 'take intermittently'
	(315) Ilocano	*man-agsugál* ITE-gamble 'always gambling'
	(316) Mandarin Chinese	長住 vs 住 chángzhù zhù long-live 'reside.v' 'reside (semi-)permanently' (Chung 2006: 51)
Reduplication	(317) Pipil	*tah-ta-ketsa* RDP-talk 'chat.v' (Campbell 1985: 78)
Suffixation	(318) Catalan	*allarg-ass-ar*[48] lengthen-INT.INF 'lengthen'
	(319) Jaqaru	*ill-q"-k.ima* see-ITE-1>2 'I will see you again' (Hardman 2000: 59–60)
	(320) Tatar	*jaz-gala-*[49] write-FRE 'write from time to time' (Wertheim)
	(321) Tibetan	ས་ལ་ཨེ sal-e[50] salba-e to.clean.v/to.make.clear.v-INT 'very clear, very clean'
	(322) Tzotzil	*k'élilan* < *k!él* 'repeatedly look at it' 'look at it' (Cowan 1969: 108)
	(323) Wichí	*n'-yahin-pej* 1SBJ-look-ITE 'I look many times'
	(324) West Greenlandic	*anurli-qa-aq* blow(-wind)-very-3s.IND 'It's blowing really hard'[51]

[48] Affix *-ass-*.

[49] Suffix *-kala/-kälä/-gala/-gälä*.

[50] Suffix *-e* accompanied by the loss of clusters in verb stem.

[51] The most productive iterative suffix is *-sar/-tar* and the most productive intensifying suffix is *-qi-*. Its indicative form is *qaaq*.

(325) Zulu   *khal-isis-*
                    cry-INT
                    'cry very loud'

As emphasized by Vajda (pers. comm.), there are numerous ways of expressing frequentative meaning in Ket and other Yeniseian languages. Werner (1998) cites ten different ways. Two of them, taken from Yugh, a Yeniseian language spoken in Eurasia, are given below: replacement of root morphemes in the zero position (326) and replacement of stem (327):[52]

(326)   Yugh   *dɛj-č-ad-di²*   <   *dɛj-č-ed-it*
                'He sends me (always)'   'He sends me'

                14 7 5 2 0   -1   14 7 5 2 0

(327)   Yugh   *di-t-a-d-daq-ŋ*   <   *di-t-a-d-daχ*
                'I fall (again and again)'   'I fall'

The suffix *-ɛla* in Kwakw'ala shows how specific a frequentative meaning can be (328). Similarly, in Udihe, the intensifying suffix *-wAlA* strengthens a qualitative feature (329), while the suffix *-ndima* marks a high degree of a feature or marks the absolute degree of comparison used without an overtly expressed standard of comparison (330):

(328)   Kwakw'ala   *ō'xLosdē's-ɛla*
                    'carry on back up the beach, one person, but an action requiring many steps'
                    (Boas 1947: 306)

(329)   Udihe   *Uligdig'a-wala tege-we   teti-je!*
                    nice-ADJ   gown-ACC dress-IMP.2SG
                    'Put on a very nice gown'
                    (Nikolaeva and Tolskaya 2001: 187)

(330)   Udihe   *Ei   ule: pei-ni   sagdi-ndima*
                    This meat piece-3SG big-ADJ
                    'This piece of meat is bigger (than the other)'
                    (Nikolaeva and Tolskaya 2001: 188)

Regarding word-classes, the following example from Ilocano shows that iterativity is not exclusively bound to the category of verbs, as it can also feature in nouns:

(331)   Ilocano   *mannakigubát*   <   *makigubát*
                    'warrior, habitual fighter in wars' 'join a battle'

---

[52] Position –1 is assumed by the derivational elements *-n-* or *-ŋ*.

6.5 Word-class changing categories

6.5.1 Action nouns

Formation of action nouns is recorded in the languages shown in Table 6.32 (76.36 per cent of the study sample).

Table 6.32. *Formation of action nouns in the study sample*

Language	Family	Morphological type	Area
Amele	Trans-New Guinea	Polysynthetic/ synthetic	Australia-New Guinea/ Madang
Anejom	Austronesian	Agglutinative	SE Asia and Oceania/Vanuatu
Bardi	Australian	Fusional	Australia-New Guinea/ Australia
Breton	Indo-European	Fusional	Eurasia/France
Cirecire	Khoisan	Isolating	Africa/Botswana
Datooga	Nilo-Saharan	Agglutinative/ fusional	Africa/Tanzania
English	Indo-European	Isolating	Eurasia/Ireland and UK
Estonian	Uralic	Agglutinative/ fusional	Eurasia/Estonia
Finnish	Uralic	Agglutinative	Eurasia/Finland
Gã	Niger-Congo	Agglutinative	Africa/Ghana
Georgian	Kartvelian	Inflectional/ agglutinative	Eurasia/Georgia
Greek	Indo-European	Fusional	Eurasia/Greece
Hausa	Afro-Asiatic	Fusional	Africa/Niger, Nigeria
Hebrew	Afro-Asiatic	Inflectional	Africa/Israel
Hungarian	Uralic	Agglutinative	Eurasia/Hungary
Ilocano	Austronesian	Agglutinative	SE Asia and Oceania/ Philippines
Indonesian	Austronesian	Agglutinative	SE Asia and Oceania/ Indonesia
Jaqaru	Aymaran	Agglutinative	South America/Peru
Karao	Austronesian	Inflectional/ polysynthetic	SE Asia and Oceania/ Philippines
Ket	Yeniseian	Agglutinative	Eurasia/Russia
Konni	Niger-Congo	Agglutinative	Africa/Ghana
Lakhota	Siouan	Synthetic to polysynthetic	North America/USA
Luo	Nilo-Saharan	Agglutinative	Africa/Kenya, Tanzania
Malayalam	Dravidian	Agglutinative	Eurasia/India
Mandarin Chinese	Sino-Tibetan	Isolating/analytic	SE Asia and Oceania/China
Māori	Austronesian	Isolating	SE Asia and Oceania/ New Zealand

Language	Family	Morphological type	Area
Marathi	Indo-European	Inflectional/ polysynthetic	Eurasia/India
Movima	Movima	Agglutinative	South America/Bolivia
Nelemwa	Austronesian	Isolating	SE Asia and Oceania/New Caledonia
Pipil	Uto-Aztecan	Agglutinative	North America/El Salvador
Slavey	Na-Dene	Polysynthetic	North America/Northwest Territories
Slovak	Indo-European	Inflectional	Eurasia/Slovakia
Spanish	Indo-European	Inflectional	Eurasia/Spain
Swahili	Niger-Congo	Agglutinative	Africa/Tanzania
Tatar	Altaic	Agglutinative	Eurasia/Russia
Telugu	Dravidian	Agglutinative	Eurasia/India
Tibetan	Sino-Tibetan	Inflectional/ agglutinative	SE Asia and Oceania/China
Tzotzil	Mayan	Polysynthetic/ agglutinative	North America/Mexico
Vietnamese	Austro-Asiatic	Isolating	SE Asia and Oceania/Vietnam
West Greenlandic	Eskimo-Aleut	Polysynthetic	North America/Greenland
Yoruba	Niger-Congo	Isolating	Africa/Benin, Nigeria
Zulu	Niger-Congo	Agglutinative	Africa/South Africa

Table 6.33 shows the diversity of word-formation processes used to form action nouns.

Table 6.33. *Word-formation processes for action nouns*

Back-formation	(332) Marathi	मार maara 'blow.N'	<	मारणे maaraNe[53] 'hit.v'
Compounding	(333) Mandarin Chinese	動作 [54] dòngzuò move-do 'action'		
	(334) Vietnamese	*le³⁵ʔ kuəj³⁵* lễ cưới ceremony-marry 'wedding ceremony' (Thái Ân)		

---

[53] In Marathi, action nominals are formed from verbs by dropping *Ne*.
[54] This is an example of a rare case of verb + verb compounding.

Confixation	(335) Indonesian	*penulisan* pe-tulis-an ANX-write-ANX 'writing' (Mojdl 2006: 152)
Conversion	(336) Dutch	*loop* 'walk'
	(337) Ket	*an'iŋ* 'play.N' < 'play.V' (Werner 1998: 26)
Prefixal-suffixal derivation	(338) Swahili	*u-tamb-o*[55] ANX-prance-ANX 'prancing'
Prefixation	(339) Pipil	*tape:wil*[56] ta-pe:wia ANX-hunt.V 'game, hunt' (Campbell 1985: 79)
	(340) Ilocano	*pan-ag-taray* NMR-AV-run 'running'
	(341) Karao	*pan-biyag* IPF.NMR-live 'way of living'
Root-and-pattern	(342) Hebrew	שמירה šmira 'guarding'
Suffixation	(Cf. Table 6.34. *Suffixes for action nouns in Finnish and Tzotzil*)	

In Estonian, it is possible to form action nouns from all the verbs using the suffix *-mine* or *-us* (Kilgi, pers. comm.):

(343) Estonian *hooli-mine*.N   <   *hooli-ma*.V
                  care-SFX   care-SUP
                  'care.N'   'care.V'

(344) Estonian *lang-us*.N   <   *lange-ma*.V
                  fall-SFX   fall-SUP
                  'fall.N'   'fall.V'

---

[55] The prefix *u-* (N.CLASS.PRX.4) or *m-* (N.CLASS.PRX.3) is attached to a verb stem together with the suffix *-o*:

      Swahili *m-chang-o*
           ANX-collect-ANX
           'collecting'

[56] The prefix *ta-* attaches to nouns derived from transitive verbs by a suffix.

The formation of action nouns need not be restricted to a single suffix or a single word-formation process. Finnish and Tzotzil may use several suffixes (see Table 6.34).

Table 6.34. *Suffixes for action nouns in Finnish and Tzotzil*

(345)	Finnish	*pese-minen* 'washing'	*pes-u*	(346)	Tzotzil	*k!úšubin-el* pity.him/take.care. of.him-ANX 'act of pitying him'
(347)	Finnish	*opet-us* 'teaching, tuition'		(348)	Tzotzil	*tsé²ex* tsé²in-²ex laugh-ANX 'laughter'
(349)	Finnish	*lyö-nti* 'hit(ting)'		(350)	Tzotzil	*²katsn-om* ²katsin-om carry.it.as.a.load-ANX 'act of carrying loads'
(351)	Finnish	*kärsi-mys* 'suffering'		(352)	Tzotzil	*²átim-ol* ²átin-ol bathe-ANX 'bathing' (Cowan 1969: 105–7)

Similarly, more than one word-formation process is used, among others, in Datooga ((353) and (354)) and Telugu ((355) and (356)): Datooga makes use of suffixation, in which case Class 1 verbs derive their action nouns by adding the primary nominal suffixes zero, *-oo*, *-id* or *-ee* preceding the secondary nominal suffix *-da* (353). Class 2 verbs take the prefix *gii-* in addition to the same nominalizing suffixes (354). Telugu uses suffixes *-pu*, *-ta*, *-uDu*, *-aDam* (355) and conversion (356) (see Table 6.35).

Table 6.35. *Word-formation processes for action nouns in Datooga and Telugu*

	Suffixation		Prefixation and suffixation		Conversion
(353)	Datooga	*dées-ìtà* build-ANX 'building'	(354) Datooga	γI I √γυα αλ √δα NMR-teach- SG.SPE 'teaching, lesson'	(355) Telugu *idÀà* < *idÀà* tiTTu tiTTu 'scolding'
(356)	Telugu	*GGţμÀê* uuDc-pu sweep-ANX 'sweeping'			

Suffixal homonymy/polysemy is present in this semantic category. Thus, in present-day Swedish the suffix *-ande/-ende* is homonymous with the suffix for the present participle:

(357)   Swedish   *lärande*
                    'learning'[57]

(358)   Swedish   *beteende*
                    'behaviour'

As to word-classes, while the vast majority of action nouns are derived from verbs, the examples from Indonesian (Table 6.36) illustrate that other word-classes may serve this purpose, too (Mojdl 2006: 152–5):[58]

Table 6.36. *Formation of action nouns by confixation in Indonesian*

From verbs		From adjectives		From nouns	
(359) Indonesian		(360) Indonesian		(361) Indonesian	
pem-baca-an <	*baca*	*pe-manas-an* < *panas*		*per-sekolah-an* < *sekolah*	
ANX-read-ANX		pe-panas`-an		ANX-school-ANX	
'reading'	'read.v'	ANX-hot-ANX		'education'	'school'
		'heating'	'hot'		

6.5.2   Abstract nouns

Formation of abstract nouns is recorded in the languages shown in Table 6.37 (70.91 per cent of the study sample).

Table 6.37. *Formation of abstract nouns in the study sample*

Language	Family	Morphological type	Area
Amharic	Afro-Asiatic	Inflectional	Africa/Ethiopia
Amele	Trans-New Guinea	Polysynthetic/synthetic	Australia-New Guinea/ Madang
Breton	Indo-European	Fusional	Eurasia/France
Cirecire	Khoisan	Isolating	Africa/Botswana
Dangaléat	Afro-Asiatic	Agglutinative	Africa/Chad
Datooga	Nilo-Saharan	Agglutinative/fusional	Africa/Tanzania
Diola-Fogny	Niger-Congo	Agglutinative	Africa/Gambia, Senegal
English	Indo-European	Isolating	Eurasia/Ireland and UK
Estonian	Uralic	Agglutinative/fusional	Eurasia/Estonia
Finnish	Uralic	Agglutinative	Eurasia/Finland

[57] In the sense of 'acquisition of knowledge'.
[58] The most productive confixes include *pe- -an, per- -an* and *ke- -an*. Words derived by these confixes can function in sentences as Adjectives, Verbs and Nouns (Mojdl: pers. comm.)

Language	Family	Morphological type	Area
Gã	Niger-Congo	Agglutinative	Africa/Ghana
Georgian	Kartvelian	Inflectional/agglutinative	Eurasia/Georgia
Greek	Indo-European	Fusional	Eurasia/Greece
Hausa	Afro-Asiatic	Fusional	Africa/Niger, Nigeria
Hebrew	Afro-Asiatic	Inflectional	Africa/Israel
Hungarian	Uralic	Agglutinative	Eurasia/Hungary
Ilocano	Austronesian	Agglutinative	SE Asia and Oceania/ Philippines
Indonesian	Austronesian	Agglutinative	SE Asia and Oceania/ Indonesia
Japanese	Japanese	Agglutinative	Eurasia/Japan
Karao	Austronesian	Inflectional/polysynthetic	SE Asia and Oceania/ Philippines
Ket	Yeniseian	Agglutinative	Eurasia/Russia
Lakhota	Siouan	Synthetic to polysynthetic	North America/USA
Luo	Nilo-Saharan	Agglutinative	Africa/Kenya, Tanzania
Malayalam	Dravidian	Agglutinative	Eurasia/India
Mandarin Chinese	Sino-Tibetan	Isolating/analytic	SE Asia and Oceania/ China
Māori	Austronesian	Isolating	SE Asia and Oceania/ New Zealand
Marathi	Indo-European	Inflectional/polysynthetic	Eurasia/India
Nelemwa	Austronesian	Isolating	SE Asia and Oceania/ New Caledonia
Slavey	Na-Dene	Polysynthetic	North America/ Northwest Territories
Slovak	Indo-European	Inflectional	Eurasia/Slovakia
Spanish	Indo-European	Inflectional	Eurasia/Spain
Swahili	Niger-Congo	Agglutinative	Africa/Tanzania
Tatar	Altaic	Agglutinative	Eurasia/Russia
Telugu	Dravidian	Agglutinative	Eurasia/India
Tibetan	Sino-Tibetan	Inflectional/agglutinative	SE Asia and Oceania/ China
Totonac	Totonacan	Agglutinative/polysynthetic	North America/Mexico
Tzotzil	Mayan	Agglutinative/polysynthetic	North America/Mexico
Vietnamese	Austro-Asiatic	Isolating	SE Asia and Oceania/ Vietnam
West Greenlandic	Eskimo-Aleut	Polysynthetic	North America/ Greenland
Zulu	Niger-Congo	Agglutinative	Africa/South Africa

Table 6.38 shows the diversity of word-formation processes used for the formation of abstract nouns.

Table 6.38. *Word-formation processes for the formation of abstract nouns*

Confixation	(362) Indonesian	*ke-cepat-an* NMR-fast/quick-NMR 'speed' (Mojdl 2006: 157)		
Compounding	(363) Vietnamese	*noj³⁵⁷ buən²¹* *nỗi buồn* NEG-sad 'sadness' (Thái Ân)		
Conversion	(364) Dutch	*de dood* 'death'		
Noun class prefix replacement	(365) Swahili	*utoto* 'childhood'	<	*mtoto* 'child'
Prefixation[59]	(366) Ilocano	*kinasipnget* 'darkness'	<	*sipnget* 'dark'
	(367) Karao	*kathoo* ka-too NMR-person 'personhood'		
	(368) Lakhota	*wó-waste* NMR-good 'goodness'		
	(369) Totonac	*li:há'lha'* li:-há'lha' GRC+big 'size'		
Root-and-pattern	(370) Zulu	*bu-hle* NMR-good,beautiful 'goodness, beauty'		
Suffixation	(Cf. Table 6.39)			

Deverbal abstract nouns appear to be a widespread word-formation pattern. In some languages, like Amele (371), Nelemwa (372),[60] Udihe (373) and Yoruba (374), it is an exclusive source of abstract nouns:

(371)   Amele   *tanaw-ec*
                    'peace'

---

[59] Prefixation on a nominal base in (367) and on adjectival bases in the rest of examples in this table.

[60] Nelemwa makes use of stative verbs, which are combined with the nominalizing prefix *u-:*

Nelemwa   *u-kari   o   orop*
          NMR-yellow   of   dress
          'the yellow of the dress'

(372)   Nelemwa   *u-pwââdagax-o*   *dagak*
                    NMR-be.beautiful   mask
                    'the beauty of the mask'

(373)   Udihe   *bude-ŋku*
                    die-NMR
                    'death'
                    (Nikolaeva and Tolskaya 2001: 152)

(374)   Yoruba   *ì-ṣẹ́*
                    NMR-break.V
                    'poverty'

In other languages, the verbal source is frequent, like in Hindi (375). Specifically, in Hindi, conversion from verbal roots is also a frequent process of abstract nouns. According to Kachru (2006: 115), 'the infinitive suffix *-na* combined with the root of the verb yields an abstract noun, e.g. *cəlna* "to move, movement" ... Therefore, all verbs, except the invariable *cahiye* "should, ought to", have infinitive forms in Hindi which function as abstract nouns.' In addition, the root of the verb in Hindi is sometimes used as an abstract noun and, if applicable, the root vowel undergoes the rules of morphophonemic alternations. An example from Lakhota is given in (376):

(375)   Hindi   चमक   <   चमकना
                    cəmək   cəməkna
                    'shine.N'   'shine.V'

(376)   Lakhota   *wo-wayazañ*
                    NMR-be.sick
                    'sickness'

In addition to conversion, Hindi abstract nouns may be derived using suffixes:

(377)   Hindi   घुमाव
                    gʰum-av
                    gʰūmna-av
                    turn.V-NMR
                    'twist.N'

(378)   Hindi   करनी
                    kər-nī
                    kərna
                    do.V-NMR
                    'deed'

None of these languages forms abstract nouns on all three word-classes. Lakhota can also derive them from adjectives by prefixation; and so can

Tzotzil, from adjectives by suffixation. Still, there are languages, like Dangaléat (Shay, pers. comm.), which admit all three word-classes as a source of abstract nouns.

Some of the languages studied, like Tzotzil (379), use one suffix, while others, like Hausa, use several different suffixes, as exemplified in (380)–(382):

(379) Tzotzil   *cham-el*
                   die.v/get.sick.v-NMR
                   'sickness'
                   (Cowan 1969: 105)

(380) Hausa   *ādal-cìi*
                   just/honest (person)-NMR
                   'fairness, justice'

(381) Hausa   *kutur-tàa*
                   leper-NMR
                   'leprosy'

(382) Hausa   *dàngàntakàa*
                   kin/relatives-NMR
                   'relationship'

Suffixation for this purpose may use nouns as a base, but also adjectives and personal pronouns (see Table 6.39).

Table 6.39. *Suffixation on nominal, adjectival and pronominal bases for the category abstract noun*

Nominal base		Adjectival base		Pronominal base	
(383) Diola-Fogny	*ba-pal-ay* N.Cl.13-friend-NMR 'friendship'	(384) Datooga	*éeʃ-in-dà* white-NMR 'whiteness'	(385) Tibetan	བདག་ཉིད bdag-nyid I/me-NMR 'selfhood'
(386) Māori	*rangatira-tanga* chief-NMR 'chiefhood'	(387) Estonian	*suur-us* big-NMR 'bigness'		
(388) Marathi	मूल-पणा muula-paNaa child-NMR 'behaviour as a child'	(389) Hungarian	*akaratos-ság* wilful-NMR 'wilfulness'		

Nominal base	Adjectival base		Pronominal base
(390) Romanian *rob-ie* slave-NMR 'slavery'	(391) Japanese	大きさ ōki-sa ōkii-sa big-NMR 'size'	
(392) Swedish *broder-skap* brother-NMR 'brotherhood'	(393) Luo	*kärtïït-yä* cold-NMR 'coldness'	
	(394) Tatar	*akïl-lïk* smart-NMR 'intelligence' (Wertheim)	
	(395) Telugu	ఎరుపు eru-pu erra-pu red-NMR 'redness, red colour'	

In some languages more than one word-formation process is used. In Gã, for instance, abstract nouns from nouns are formed by the suffix -*mɔ* or by vowel length (Kropp Dakubu, pers. comm.). In Hindi both suffixation (396) and prefixation (397) from other nouns[61] can be found:

(396)   Hindi   बेहपना
    bəhna-pa
    'sisterhood'

(397)   Hindi   अन-होनी
    ən-honī
    'impossible event'

In fact, Hindi makes use of a number of other prefixes, mostly of Sanskrit origin. Kachru (2006: 114) maintains that 'in general, prefixation is not the preferred process in Hindi; most of the prefixes are restricted to borrowed items. However, some of them are currently being utilized heavily in the creation of technical terms in the official register used in administration'.

---

[61] Mainly Sanskrit loan words, though some of the processes have been extended to Hindi according to Kachru (2006). Most of the prefixes are also of Sanskrit origin. In addition to *ə-*, *ən* 'not without' in (397), the following can also be cited: *ənu-* 'after' as in *ənu-krəmən* 'sequence', *əbʰi-* 'toward, intensity' as in *əbʰi-prerən* 'motivation', *a-* 'to, toward, up to' as in *a-gəmən* 'arrival', *ku-* 'bad, deficient' as in *ku-kərm* 'evil deed', *du-* 'two' as in *du-vidʰa* 'double-mindedness, uncertainty' or *ni-* 'inner' as in *ni-rīkʃən* 'inspection' (Kachru 2006: 112–13).

Similarly, Georgian makes use of suffixation (398) and circumfixation (399) and Mandarin Chinese makes use of derivation by the suffix 性 (*xing4*) 'character, -ness' to an adjective (400) or conversion (401):

(398)   Georgian   ახალგაზრდ-ობა
                                    axalgazrd-oba
                                    young-NMR
                                    'youth or the property of being young'

(399)   Georgian   სი-ლამაზ-ე
                                    si-lamaz-e
                                    NMR-pretty-NMR
                                    'beauty'

(400)   Mandarin Chinese   公平性
                                    gōngpíngxìng
                                    public-even-ness
                                    'fairness'

(401)   Mandarin Chinese   他的美   <   美
                                    tā de měi   měi
                                    'her beauty'   'beautiful'

6.6   Summary

Some semantic categories are represented across most of the sample studied (agents, causative verbs, frequentative and intensive verbs, action nouns). In two oppositions, masculine vs feminine and augmentative vs diminutive, the values are dissimilar. The hierarchy of the categories of intransitivity, transitivity and causativity in terms of the use of word-formation strategies is explained as a relatively common sequence from intransitive to transitive and then to causative verbs.

Grandi and Montermini (2005: 144) maintain that 'in a single language a derivational category tends not to be expressed both by prefixes and suffixes' and that 'a derivational category can be cross-linguistically expressed both by prefixes and suffixes'. The tables at the beginning of each section that present the diversity of word-formation processes for the semantic categories considered here provide an overview of the cross-linguistic multiplicity of word-formation processes in general.

7   Results and discussion

Typology will only be as good as the language particular descriptions it can draw on.   (Plank 2007: 47)

This chapter presents the analysis carried out on the sample studied. The approach is therefore one of data analysis and interpretation of results, specifically relating independent variables to types of word-formation processes and semantic roles. The aim is to identify preferences or associations between three independent variables and word-formation processes in general, as well as between types within word-formation processes (e.g. different types of compounding). Statistical analyses are used for associations, but these associations are not followed by a specific motivation for the association or by ensuing predictions based on these associations when such a motivation or prediction would be a matter of speculation rather than of clear linguistic facts.

This chapter describes the approach to data analysis (7.1), with emphasis on the method used (7.1.1), and the results obtained with that method (7.2).

7.1   Introduction

It has been argued that typological research should have a predictive value (Anderson 1985: 10):

The discovery that language X differs from language Y in respect of property p is only of typological interest if something follows from it: that is, if p is always associated with some apparently distinct property p', such that the discovery that X has p will allow us to predict that it will also have p'.

Although this chapter presents results about the occurrence of linguistic properties and associations between them, no predictions are made about the occurrence of linguistic properties in languages or in language families for two reasons:

(a)   the purpose of the book is not to provide predictions, but to offer a general overview of word-formation across languages which may pave the way for precisely that kind of predictive contributions and

(b)   the data and the findings that these data lead to do not always lend themselves to regularities or predictions. This may be because the picture they give requires further research (for example, for associations which are difficult to understand), but it may also be because the findings reflect associations or facts which may just not be interpretable: what the data reflect can be interpreted in a number of ways and it is difficult to decide, based on this initial cross-linguistic study, which of the possible interpretations is right.

7.1.1   Method

The data are classified as two sets: one for twenty word-formation processes[1] and the other for specific types within some of those processes, specifically for suffixation, compounding, prefixation and reduplication.[2] The first set of data – i.e. word-formation processes – is analyzed by evaluation of the fit of data and by Multiple Correspondence Analysis (MCA, StatSoft 2001) (see below). The second set of data – i.e. the types of word-formation processes – is analyzed only with MCA, as the results obtained with this analysis alone are clear enough.

The twenty word-formation processes of the first set of data were measured against three independent variables:

(a)   language family,
(b)   morphological type, and
(c)   word order.

Language genus was not considered for the low sample size throughout all the language families. Each independent variable comprised a number of types. Not all types were considered for their low sample size. Table 7.1 shows the types studied within each independent variable.

---

[1] Prefixation, suffixation, infixation, circumfixation, prefixation and suffixation, prefixation and infixation, infixation and suffixation, root-and-pattern, vowel alternation, prefixation and vowel alternation, suffixation and vowel alternation, consonant alternation, compounding, incorporation, reduplication, conversion, back-formation, blending, stress, and tone/pitch.

[2] The types considered in compounding are: recursive, adjective + adjective, verb, noun + noun, stem-link, with phonological modification, copulative, copulative compound nouns, copulative compound adjective, exocentric, exocentric of the *redskin* type, and exocentric of the *garde-manger* type. The types for reduplication are: complete, partial, preposing, postposing and infixing. The types for prefixation and for suffixation are: recursive, polysemous, affixation with variants, and affixation with base modification.

Table 7.1. *Types of languages and their sample size within the independent variables*

Language family	Sample size	Morphological type	Sample size	Word order	Sample size
Niger-Congo	7	Agglutinative	22	SVO	28
Indo-European	6	Agglutinative mixed[3]	8	SOV	13
Austronesian	6	Fusional	4	VSO	5
Afro-Asiatic	4	Inflectional	4	VOS	4
Dravidian	3	Isolating	7		
Uralic	3	Polysynthetic	4		

For the occurrence or not of types of processes and/or semantic categories in relation to languages, the questionnaire's dichotomous data (*yes* vs *no*) were converted to numerical values for computation in accordance with the answers given by the informants as follows: 1s (if the process or category in question was marked as *yes* in the questionnaire) vs 0s (if the process or category was marked as *no* in the questionnaire). Uncertain answers by the informants were marked as *?* and these computed as 0 in the counts. The productivity measurements originally requested from the informants were not used for productivity assessment because each informant's perception of productivity may have been widely subjective, even on the 1-to-5 Likert scale used. These data were therefore converted to 1 (occurrence) when a given degree of productivity was reported, and 0 otherwise. This resulted in a table of dichotomous data which were then used, e.g. for computation of the frequency of occurrence of each of the independent variables (language family, morphological type and word order).

Two different statistical approaches were followed. One is based on the evaluation of the fit of data (frequency of occurrence or not) to an arbitrary set of expected frequencies by means of the chi square test (Zar 1984). For each class of each independent variable with a high enough sample size (lowest threshold being three, as shown in Table 7.1), the frequency of occurrence or not of each word-formation process was tested against frequencies expected at random (50 per cent). For example, out of six Austronesian languages, the observed frequency of occurrence of prefixation was six. This was tested against an expected random frequency of occurrence (or not) of three. This yields a chi square value whose p (0.014) establishes the significance of the association between the two variables (here, the occurrence or not of the process and the

---

[3] Types were pooled based on their proximity in the variable *Morphological* for a bigger sample size. The type *agglutinative mixed* encompasses agglutinative-fusional (two languages), agglutinative-inflectional (two languages), agglutinative-suffixal (two languages) and agglutinative-polysynthetic (two languages).

language family). In this example, prefixation occurs more frequently than expected in Austronesian languages. This approach has two limitations:

(a)   it is sensitive to low sample size; the low sample size disallows detection of significances throughout the whole dataset but, where they appear, they do so as the result of a strong pattern, as they appear even with a low sample size, and

(b)   because a number of hypotheses are tested with the same dataset, a correction must be used for apparently significant results which are not: the Bonferroni correction is applied to avoid significant results which are due to chance. Out of the twenty processes studied and their corresponding tests, one may reportedly appear to be significant when in fact it is not. The Bonferroni correction here lowers the significance threshold from 0.05 to 0.0025. This may give a false negative in some cases of the dataset. Therefore, more findings may exist than are reported, but those which are reported here are clear. The results in section 7.2 give data with and without the Bonferroni correction (Sokal and Rohlf 1995).

The other statistical approach is the MCA. This is a descriptive/exploratory technique designed to analyze the structure of categorical variables included in multi-way tables containing some measure of correspondence between the rows and columns. This technique represents the similarities between the row and column points in a table in a manner that retains all or almost all of the information about the differences between the rows and the columns. In other words, it produces a simplified (low-dimensional) representation of the information in a large frequency table. The distances of the points in a low-dimensional space (e.g. a two-dimensional display) are informative in that, for instance, row points that are close to each other are similar with regard to the pattern of relative frequencies across the columns. It is important to remark that, in such plots, one can only interpret the distances between row points and the distances between column points, but not the distances between row points and column points. However, it is appropriate to make general statements about the nature of the dimensions, based on which side of the origin particular points fall. Thus, it can be concluded that an axis separates some row category from the other row categories and that such categories differ in the relative frequency of a second variable (e.g. column). An additional goal of MCA is to find theoretical interpretations (i.e. meaning) for the extracted dimensions but, in general, the meaning of the gradients shown by the dimensions used here needs further study.

The procedure used was as follows: an MCA was first run with all the processes and language families and the amount of variance (i.e. inertia) explained and the quality of representation of each row point (i.e. language family) and of each column point (i.e. process) in the coordinate system defined by the dimensions extracted was explored. A low quality means that the current number of dimensions does not represent well the respective row (or column). The rows with low quality were then discarded and an MCA was run again after checking that such a procedure increased the percentage of variance explained. No processes with low-quality values were discarded, because the processes considered here are the essential processes in a study of word-formation, whereas the languages studied are just languages which may be present or not in a study sample and are, therefore, not essential by themselves. Nonetheless, after excluding the languages with low quality, the quality of the processes increased. The languages for which no data were applicable have been deleted from the dataset. This discards some language families in some types of processes while keeping as much information as possible. Which languages are discarded for which types of processes is explained in the description of the results of the MCA analysis for each particular process in section 7.1.1.

Both approaches allow a complementary overview of tendencies across the word-formation processes and the independent variables. Moreover, the results derived from the MCA analysis are also used to assess the tendencies obtained from the chi analysis. All the statistical analyses were performed with the STATISTICA software package (StatSoft 2001).

Finally, we calculate the frequency of occurrence of the semantic roles described in the last chapter among the twenty word-formation processes, using our fifty-five-language sample, based on the same conversion of the questionnaire's dichotomous data (*yes* vs *no*) described for the previous analyses to 1s and 0s respectively. Uncertain answers by the informants were computed as 0 in the counts (absence). For each semantic role, we convert the frequencies of languages which use each word-formation process into percentages referred to the total number of languages that occur in each semantic role. For example, for the semantic role patient, thirty-four languages use some type of the word-formation process studied. Of these thirty-four languages, 70.59 per cent (twenty-four out of thirty-four languages) use suffixation, 8.82 per cent (three languages) use prefixation and so on. For each semantic role, we select the word-formation processes with the three highest percentages.

7.2   Results and discussion

The first approach analyzes the first dataset, i.e. general word-formation processes without specification of their types, by evaluation of the fit of frequency of occurrence of each language family in each word-formation process.

Figure 7.1 and Figure 7.2 present an overview of the occurrence of word-formation processes in the study sample.

Table 7.2 presents significant associations between occurrence or not of word-formation processes vs the independent variables (language family, morphological type and word order) and gives the p values of the observed

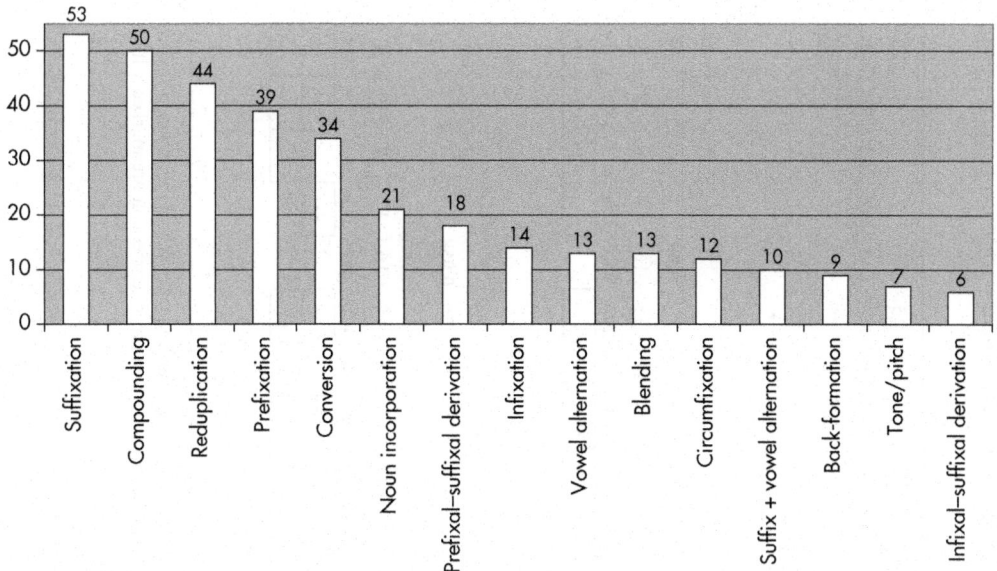

Figure 7.1. *Cross-linguistic use of word-formation processes in the study sample (absolute values with respect to fifty-five languages)*

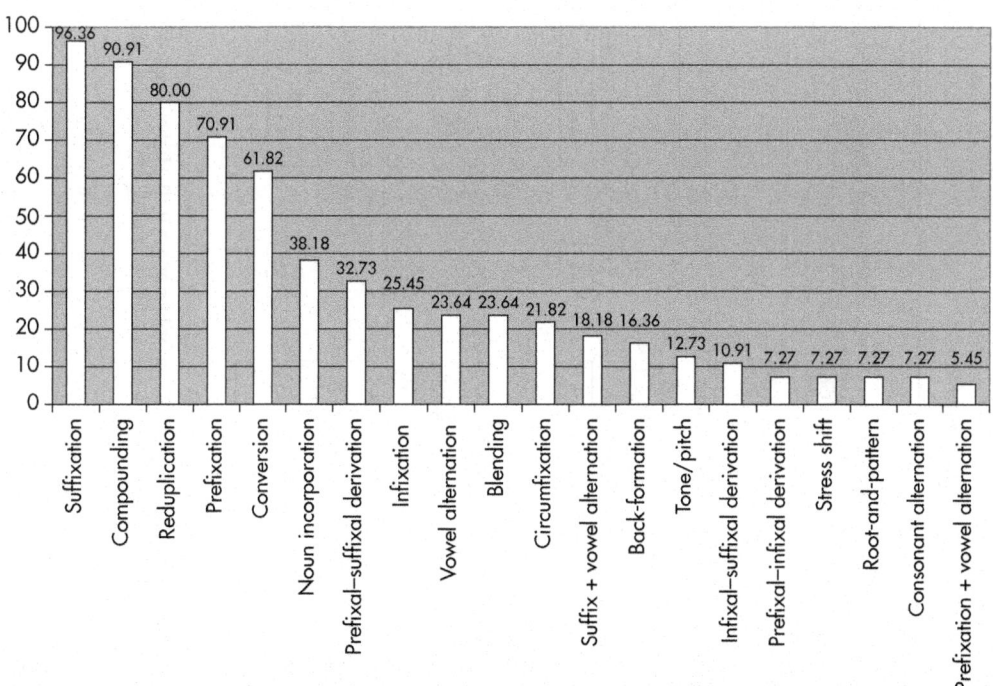

Figure 7.2. *Cross-linguistic use of word-formation processes (percentages)*

Table 7.2. *Significance of the chi square tests for the fit of the frequency of occurrence for each independent variable and each word-formation process (numbered 1 to 20)*

	n	1 PRX	2 SFX	3 IFX	4 CRX	5 PRX-SFX	6 PRX-IFX	7 IFX-SFX	8 RAP	9 VAL	10 PRX+VAL	11 SFX+VAL	12 CAL	13 CPN	14 NIN	15 RDP	16 CNV	17 BFR	18 BLN	19 STR	20 TOP
Language family																					
Niger-Congo	7	**0.058**	**0.058**		**		**	0.058	**	0.058	0.058		**	**0.058**		**		**	**	0.058	0.058
Indo-European	6	*	*	*										*			*			*	*
Austronesian	6		*						*		*		*			*				*	*
Afro-Asiatic	4	*	*	*	*											*					
Dravidian	3	**0.08**	**0.08**	0.08	0.08	0.08	0.08	0.08	0.08	0.08	0.08			**0.08**					0.08	0.08	0.08
Uralic	3		**0.08**	0.08	0.08	0.08	0.08	0.08	0.08	0.08		0.08	0.08	**0.08**			0.08			0.08	0.08
Inflectional type																					
Agglutinative	23	**	***	**	**	***	***	***	***	**	***	***	***	***		***		***	***	***	***
Aggl. mixed	8	*	*	*	*	*	*		*	*	*	*	*	*				*		*	
Fusional	4		*	*		*				0.052			*	*						*	
Inflectional	4	*		*	*						*			*							*
Isolating	7		**0.058**				**	0.058	**	0.058	**			**		**	**0.058**				
Polysynthetic	4		*							*		*	**						*		
Word order																					
SVO	28	**	***	0.058	*	***	***	***	***	**	***	*	***	***		**		***	0.058	***	**
SOV	13		***	**	**	**	***	***	**	0.052	**	**	***	**		***		**	**	***	***
VSO	5		*	**		**								*			*				*
VOS	4	*	*							*			*	*	*	*		*	*		*

Notes: Blank cells stand for non-significant values at p > 0.10. Higher frequency than expected at random is in bold face. Lower frequency than expected is in shaded font. Shown are non-corrected p values. * < 0.05; ** < 0.01; *** < 0.001. The values with statistical significance after the Bonferroni correction are marked with a square.

frequency per word-formation process. The table shows both uncorrected values, which have the value of tendencies, and Bonferroni-corrected values (squared cells), which are fully statistically significant associations.

The following major conclusions can be drawn from these results:

(a) in general, four word-formation processes occur consistently more frequently than expected: prefixation, suffixation, compounding and reduplication. They occur regardless of the internal classifications used (by language family, morphological type or word order), even if only suffixation does so for all the types within the independent variables. Two more processes occur more frequently than expected, but they differ from the former processes in one or other respect: conversion occurs more frequently than expected in each of the independent variables, but it does so markedly less consistently than the former four processes. Incorporation occurs more frequently than expected, but only by one of the independent variables (word order). Incorporation also differs from the former four processes in that it occurs less frequently than expected by morphological type. Prefixation, suffixation, compounding and reduplication are therefore different from conversion and substantially different from incorporation;

(b) all the remaining word-formation processes occur less frequently than expected, regardless of the internal classifications used (by language family, morphological type or word order) with the exception of incorporation, which occurs more frequently than expected by word order, as noted above;

(c) after the Bonferroni correction, all the processes that occur more frequently than expected still do so where sample size is large enough (morphological type and word order). These processes are prefixation, suffixation, compounding and reduplication. Prefixation differs from the rest in that it does not reach statistical significance by morphological type. Conversion and incorporation cease to be significant after the Bonferroni correction, thus confirming that they belong in a different group from prefixation, suffixation, compounding and reduplication; and

(d) similarly, after the Bonferroni correction, all the processes showing significantly low frequency of occurrence still do so where the sample size allows (morphological type and word order), except for infixation, prefixation-suffixation and vowel alternation, which no longer reach statistical significance. Of these, vowel alternation remains significant by morphological type.

Differences in sample size can also bias the results, in that the occurrence of processes in language types (be it family, morphological type or word-order type) with a large sample size may be due to an actual significant association or precisely to the large sample size. Similarly, the non-occurrence of processes in language types with a small sample size may be due to an actual significant association or precisely to the small sample size (the sample is too small to detect the real frequency of the occurrence of a process). Therefore, and to be on the safe side, conclusions are drawn here only from high frequencies in categories with small samples and from low frequencies in categories with large samples. This is a safeguard against the bias that different sample sizes can introduce. For this purpose, the variables (language family, inflectional type and word order) have been divided into a higher sample size set and a lower sample size set, as presented in Table 7.3.

Table 7.3. *Categories within independent variables divided into two sets by sample size*

	Higher sample size set		Lower sample size set	
Language family	Niger-Congo	7	Afro-Asiatic	4
	Indo-European	6	Dravidian	3
	Austronesian	6	Uralic	3
Morphological type	Agglutinative	23	Agglutinative mixed	8
			Fusional	4
			Inflectional	4
			Isolating	7
			Polysynthetic	4
Word order	SVO	28	VSO	5
	SOV	13	VOS	4

Thus, limiting the presentation of results to those which have been confirmed by the Bonferroni correction, associations between the independent variables and the word-formation processes can be found (Table 7.4 and Table 7.5). No statistical claims can be made regarding language family for the low n of families of each type present in the sample, therefore there is not a table of correspondences for language families and word-formation processes.

Table 7.4. *Statistically significant associations between word-formation processes and morphological types. Higher frequency than expected of word-formation processes with high sample size are presented for information purpose (shaded font)*

Morphological type	More frequent than expected	Less frequent than expected
Agglutinative	Suffixation	Circumfixation
	Compounding	Prefixation-infixation
	Reduplication	Infixation-suffixation
		Root-and-pattern
		Vowel alternation
		Prefixation and vowel alternation

Morphological type	More frequent than expected	Less frequent than expected
		Suffixation and vowel alternation
		Consonant alternation
		Back-formation
		Blending
		Stress
		Tone/Pitch

Table 7.5. *Statistically significant associations between word-formation processes and word order. Higher frequency than expected of word-formation processes with high sample size are presented for information purposes (shaded font)*

Word order	More frequent than expected	Less frequent than expected
SVO	Prefixation	Prefixation-infixation
	Suffixation	Infixation-suffixation
	Compounding	Root-and-pattern
		Prefixation and vowel alternation
		Consonant alternation
		Back-formation
		Stress
		Tone/pitch
SOV	Suffixation	Circumfixation
	Compounding	Prefixation-infixation
	Reduplication	Infixation-suffixation
		Prefixation and vowel alternation
		Suffixation and vowel alternation
		Consonant alternation
		Blending
		Stress
		Tone/pitch
VSO	Suffixation	

Application of an MCA analysis to the same dataset (i.e. the second approach described in section 7.1.1) provides additional results. As mentioned above, this analysis produces a simplified representation of the information according to the distance between the points in a two-dimensional display, so that the row points (e.g. languages) that are close to each other are similar with regard to the pattern of relative frequencies across the columns (e.g. processes). For example, Figure 7.3 shows the distances among languages with regard to the pattern of relative frequencies across the processes, with the languages which have similar occurrence/non-occurrence of word-formation processes being closer.

A first analysis with all languages explains a low percentage of variance (15.7 per cent) and shows that a few languages, namely Afro-Asiatic, Austro-Asiatic and Indo-European, have a high quality, i.e., they are well discriminated by the dimensions extracted. This makes sense, since a general classification on the basis of global processes can have less discriminatory power than classifications on more specific processes (e.g. prefixation, suffixation, etc.), as can be seen in the analyses below. Figure 7.3 shows that the three language families mentioned above are the most dissimilar to the rest, whereas the rest are more similar, even if several groups of languages with similar preferences can be distinguished (e.g. Altaic, Australian, Movima and Trans-New Guinean, or Niger-Congo, Nilo-Saharan and Sino-Tibetan).

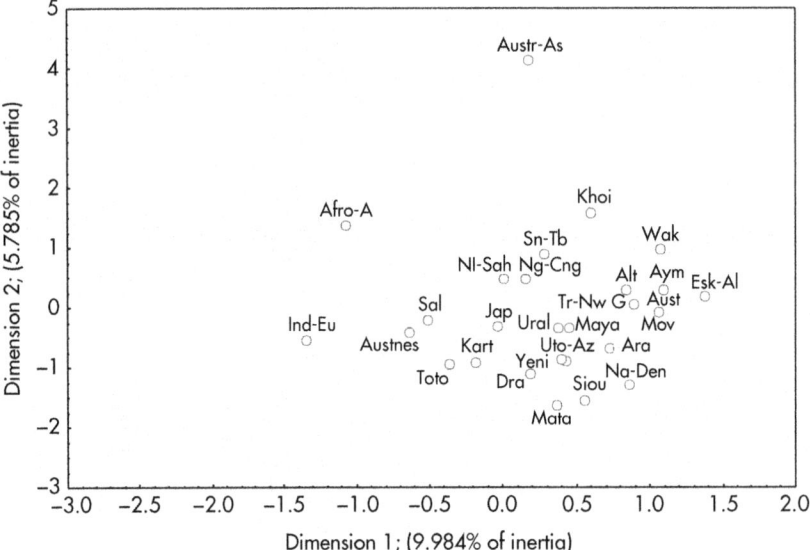

Figure 7.3. *Language families by word-formation process occurrence or not*

Figure 7.4 shows similitudes between processes. In this case, the presence of a process is associated with the presence of the rest of the processes, and the same applies for their absence. This is shown in the figure in the form of .1s and .0s occurring together. As a result, two groups can be observed:

(a)   a loose group for the presence of processes, and
(b)   a more compact one for the absence of processes.

Subgroups can therefore be found mainly within the presences: for example, the presence of infixation-suffixation (represented as 7.1) is associated with the presence of root-and-pattern (represented as 8.1), and the absence of compounding (represented as 13.0) is associated with the absence of prefixation (represented as 1.0). In fact, prefixation (represented as 1.) and tone/

pitch (represented as 20.) are an exception, in that their presence (1.1 and 20.1 respectively) are closer to the absence (.0s) of most other processes.

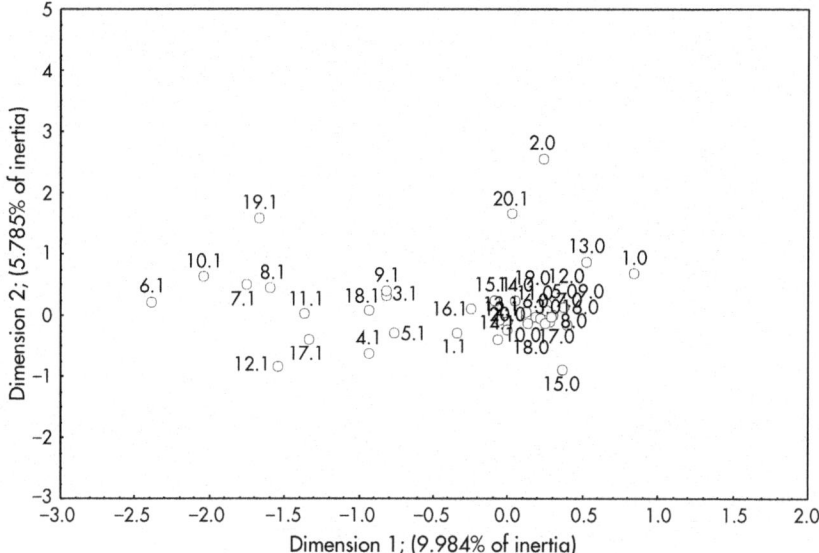

Figure 7.4. *Presence (represented as .1) and absence (represented as .0) of word-formation processes in the study sample. The word-formation processes are represented by their numbers as in Table 7.2*

Figuring out the association between language families and processes is possible by comparing Figure 7.3 and Figure 7.4. However, since the variance explained is low, we preferred to discard those languages with low-quality values (< 0.008). Only the language families Afro-Asiatic, Austro-Asiatic and Indo-European (quality values > 0.23) and all the processes were included in the analysis. With this subset, the variance explained rises to 46.8 per cent. Figure 7.5 suggests an association between the Austro-Asiatic language family and the absence of suffixation (represented as 2.0). It also suggests that the Indo-European family is associated with the absence of tone/pitch (represented as 20.0) and the presence of prefixation (represented as 1.1) and suffixation (represented as 2.1), as can also be seen in Table 7.2. Afro-Asiatic is associated at least with the presence of suffixation (represented as 2.1) and reduplication (represented as 15.1), thus confirming the results expressed in Table 7.2 that could not be confirmed after the Bonferroni correction due to low sample size.

The classifications (i.e. word-formation processes) used for the above associations may seem too broad and, thus, the discrimination ability may be low, with the result that only three language families (Afro-Asiatic, Austro-Asiatic and Indo-European) show distinct patterns. Finer distinctions can be made only when classifications are more precise, as can be seen below, where the processes are divided into types, e.g. types of compounding.

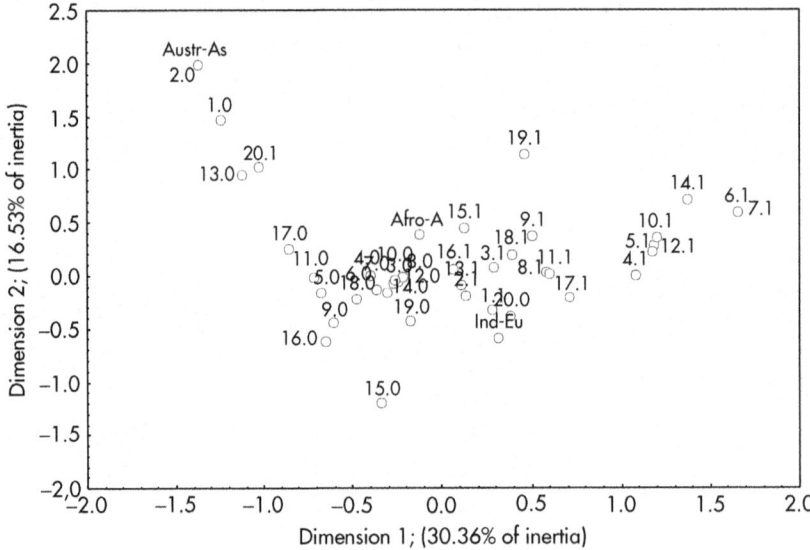

Figure 7.5. *Associations between language families and word-formation processes. Presence is represented as .1 and absence is represented as .0. The word-formation processes are represented by their numbers as in Table 7.2*

The analysis of the second set of data referred to at the beginning of section 7.1.1 can be broken down into four groups, one for each of the word-formation processes considered: prefixation, suffixation, compounding and reduplication.

The first group, prefixation, discarded some languages for which questionnaire data did not apply. Whereas this suppressed completely some language families (Altaic, Austro-Asiatic, Aymaran, Eskimo-Aleut, Khoisan, Movima, Trans-New Guinea and Wakashan), some other families were still represented even though they lost some cases. All the types of prefixation were included. The language families with high-quality values (> 0.10) are Afro-Asiatic, Australian, Dravidian, Indo-European, Japanese, Kartvelian, Sino-Tibetan and Uralic. The quality value for the rest was ≤ 0.09. The variance explained is 48.8 per cent.

Figure 7.6 shows that types of prefixation form a gradient where associations of language families can be established for example, Sino-Tibetan with Kartvelian and Indo-European at one end of the gradient, Dravidian with Uralic at the other, and Australian with Japanese in between.

Regarding processes, presence and absence seem to arrange themselves on the left- and right-hand sides of the chart respectively, i.e. they show a consistent pattern except for absence of prefixation with base modification, which occurs in between the groups of presences and absences at either end of the chart.

Regarding language family and types of prefixation, the major associations seem to occur between the Afro-Asiatic, Australian and Japanese language families and presence of prefixation with base modification; between Indo-European and presence of polysemic prefixation, recursive prefixation and prefixation variants; and between Dravidian and Uralic and absence of polysemic prefixation, of recursive prefixation and of prefixation variants.

The second group, suffixation, discarded one language family (Austro-Asiatic) for which questionnaire data did not apply. All the processes were included. The language families with high-quality values (> 0.10) are Afro-Asiatic, Australian, Indo-European, Kartvelian, Khoisan, Matacoan, Siouan, Trans-New Guinea and Uralic. The quality value for the rest was ≤ 0.09. This subset explains 43.3 per cent of the variance.

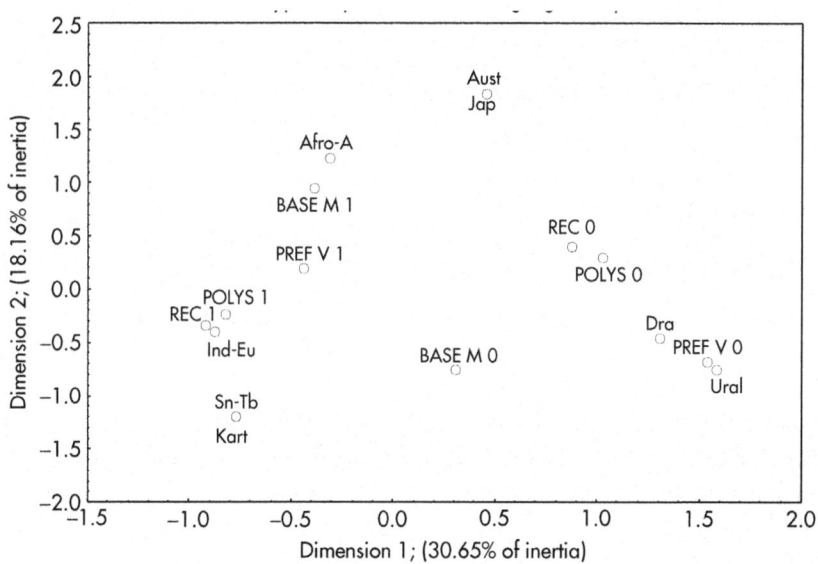

Figure 7.6. *Associations between language families and types of prefixation. Presence is represented as .1 and absence is represented as .0 (the chart discards language families as described in the text)*

Figure 7.7 shows that types of suffixation establish a gradient where most of the language families place themselves at one or the other end of the gradient. Thus, an association can be noticed between Khoisan, Siouan. Trans-New Guinea and Afro-Asiatic, on the one hand, and between Indo-European, Uralic, Kartvelian and Matacoan, on the other. Subgroups can be identified at each end, too: Siouan, Khoisan and Trans-New Guinea are comparatively closer together. So, at the other end, are Kartvelian and Matacoan on the one hand, and Uralic and Indo-European on the other. The family Australian appears to be different from all the others. Dimension

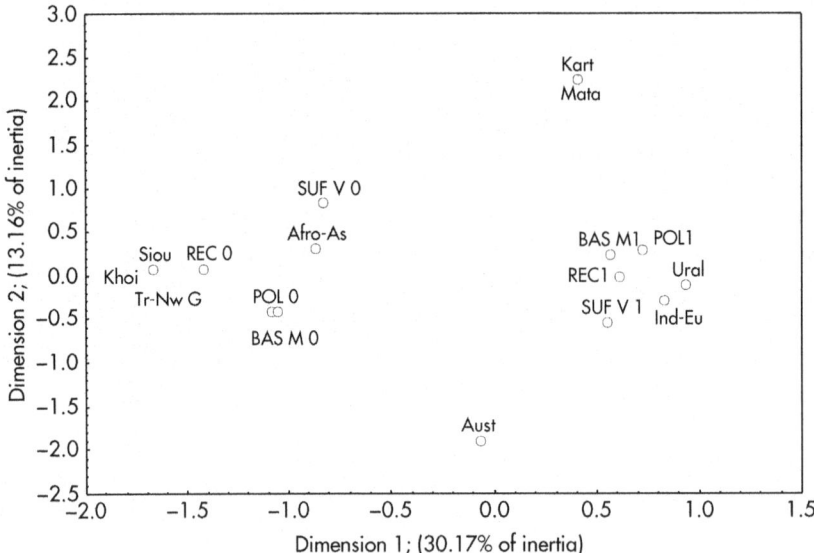

Figure 7.7. *Associations between language families and types of suffixation.*
Presence is represented as .1 and absence is represented as .0 (the chart
discards language families as described in the text)

2 adds in the separation of languages established above according to
Dimension 1, in that it separates Kartvelian and Matacoan from Australian
as two groups.

Regarding processes, presence and absence seem to arrange themselves
parallel on the right- and left-hand sides of the chart respectively, i.e., they
show a consistent pattern, in that presences are associated with presences
and absences with absences.

Regarding language family and types of suffixation, the language families Khoisan, Siouan and Trans-New Guinea are associated with absence
of recursiveness, polysemy and base modification. Afro-Asiatic shows the
same pattern, although some of its languages deviate in showing the presence of some of these types of suffixation. Uralic and Indo-European
have presence of polysemy, base modification, recursiveness and suffix
variants. Kartvelian and Matacoan also seem to be related to the presence of
polysemy, base modification and recursiveness, but less markedly than Uralic
and Indo-European.

The third group, compounding, discards the languages for which questionnaire data on compounding do not apply. This excludes nine languages,
although only four language families (Eskimo-Aleut, Salishan, Uto-Aztecan
and Wakashan) are no longer represented as a result of this. The first
analysis with the languages of the sample explains 20.3 per cent of the
variance. Only languages with a high-quality index (> 0.11) were retained:
Altaic, Indo-European, Niger-Congo, Sino-Tibetan and Totonacan. The

remaining ones had quality values below 0.07. All types of compounding were included. The analysis done with this subset explains more than 51 per cent of the variance.

Figure 7.8 shows associations between language families, associations between presence of types with the presence of other types and the absence of types with the absence of types, and associations between language families and types of compounding.

Language families have fairly distinct patterns of presence/absence, as can be seen from their separation along the axis for Dimension 1. Thus, Dimension 1 discriminates two groups:

(a)   Sino-Tibetan appears to be associated with Indo-European as regards the presence of most types of compounding, and

(b)   Totonacan appears to be associated with Altaic and Niger-Congo as regards the absence of most types of compounding.

Regarding processes, the picture is less clear but, in general, presences appear to be associated with presences and absences with absences. Thus, for example, the presence of recursive compounding is associated with the presence of adjective + adjective compounding, and the absence of adjective + adjective compounding is associated with the absence of copulative compounding. Some exceptions can be noted: presences of some processes are associated with absences, like the presence of verbal compounding and the absence of phonological change.

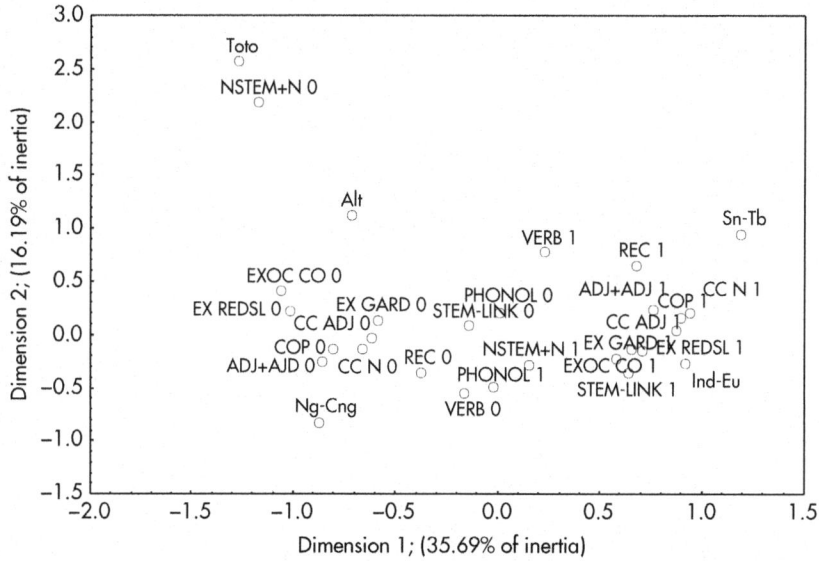

Figure 7.8. *Associations between language families and types of compounding. Presence is represented as .1 and absence is represented as .0 (the chart discards language families as described in the text)*

Finally, concerning the association between language families and processes, the separation of languages into two groups is paralleled by the separation between absence and presence of types of compounding. The clearest association seems to occur between the language family Totonacan and the absence of noun stem + noun stem compounding, both high along Dimension 2.

For the last group, reduplication, all languages were initially taken into consideration and language families with high-quality values (> 0.10) were then selected, namely Afro-Asiatic, Austronesian, Movima, Niger-Congo, Trans-New Guinea and Uralic. The quality value for the remaining languages was < 0.07. The variance explained with this subset was 46.8 per cent, which is considerably higher than the 15.06 per cent of the variance explained when all the languages were taken into consideration. All the types of reduplication were included.

Regarding language families, Figure 7.9 shows that reduplication discriminates well among the language families selected, as all of them are well apart from each other. As in compounding, Dimension 1 establishes a gradient between language families which show presence of all types of reduplication (Trans-New Guinea), absence of all types of reduplication (Uralic), and languages with varying degrees of presence/absence in between (Austronesian, Afro-Asiatic, Movima and Niger-Congo).

Presence and absence of processes seem to arrange themselves parallel on the left- and right-hand sides of the chart respectively, i.e., they show a consistent pattern.

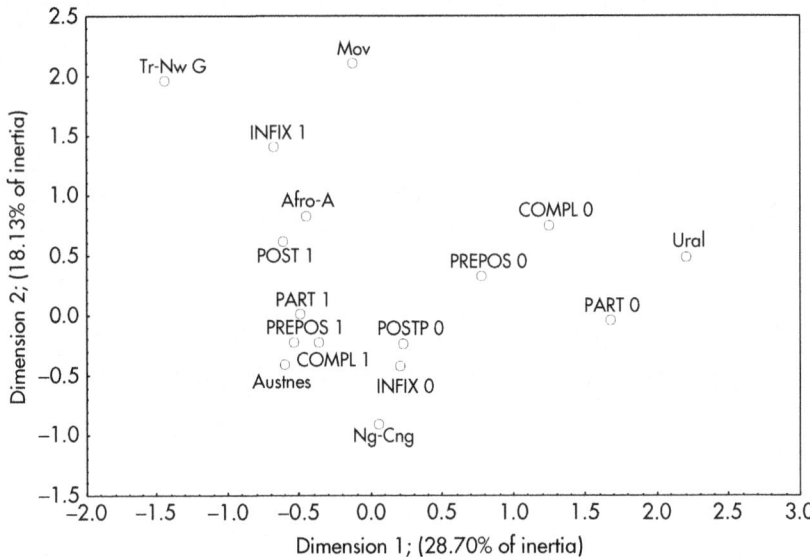

Figure 7.9. *Associations between language families and types of reduplication. Presence is represented as .1 and absence is represented as .0 (the chart discards language families as described in the text)*

Finally, concerning language family and types, the clearest association seems to be that between presence of infixation and the language families Trans-New Guinea and Movima, both high on Dimension 2. High frequency of preposing reduplication, partial reduplication and complete reduplication are also associated with the Austronesian language family, both on Dimension 1 and 2.

It can be observed from the figures above that a limited number of language families appear in the general processes and that types of those word-formation processes open the range to new language families. This is an added value of exploring not only the presence/absence of certain language families in word-formation processes in general, but also in types of certain word-formation processes (here prefixation, suffixation, compounding and reduplication). The results of this approach can be summarized in Table 7.6, which lists language families with high-quality values in relation to word-formation processes and with types of word-formation processes.

This table reveals that the pattern of presence/absence of processes in the Afro-Asiatic and Indo-European language families is distinct in word-formation processes in general, and also in the types of three out of four word-formation processes (Afro-Asiatic has a high quality in prefixation, suffixation and reduplication, and Indo-European has a high quality in prefixation, suffixation and compounding). By contrast, for Austro-Asiatic only the pattern of presence/absence of general word-formation processes, not of types of word-formation processes, is distinct enough to be well represented.

The distinctiveness of presence/absence in some language families holds in several types of word-formation processes (e.g. Uralic in types of reduplication, prefixation and suffixation), while in other language families it holds only in one word-formation process (e.g. Altaic and Totonacan in compounding, Austronesian and Movima in reduplication, Dravidian and Japanese in prefixation, and Khoisan, Matacoan and Siouan in suffixation). Whether this is due to the peculiarity of each language family or to the sample size within each language family requires further research. The low sample size of six out of the nine language families (one language per family) makes their representation appear more peculiar than it probably is. A more accurate description of these families is only possible with a higher sample size. Still, Dravidian (studied in terms of three languages) and, especially, Austronesian (studied in terms of six languages) are genuinely peculiar as regards their presence/absence in types of prefixation and types of reduplication respectively. The Dravidian languages show virtually total absence of prefixation types and the Austronesian languages show presence of complete, partial and preposing reduplication.

It can also be concluded that prefixation and suffixation are the processes that yield distinctive patterns of presence/absence of word-formation processes for more language families (eight and nine language families respectively).

Table 7.6. *Language families with respect to word-formation processes and to types of prefixation, suffixation, compounding and reduplication*

Word-formation processes	Types of prefixation	Types of suffixation	Types of compounds	Types of reduplication
Afro-Asiatic	Afro-Asiatic	Afro-Asiatic		Afro-Asiatic
			Altaic	
	Australian	Australian		
Austro-Asiatic				
				Austronesian
	Dravidian			
Indo-European	Indo-European	Indo-European	Indo-European	
	Japanese			
	Kartvelian	Kartvelian		
		Khoisan		
		Matacoan		
				Movima
			Niger-Congo	Niger-Congo
	Sino-Tibetan		Sino-Tibetan	
		Siouan		
			Totonacan	
		Trans-New Guinea		Trans-New Guinea
	Uralic	Uralic		Uralic

If we compare the results obtained from the two statistical approaches mentioned in 7.1.1 and presented above, we find that some results obtained from the chi square analysis are confirmed by the results obtained from the MCA analysis.

Concerning word-formation processes in general, the two approaches confirm that the Indo-European family is associated with the presence of prefixation, suffixation and compounding, and with the absence of tone/pitch, and also that the Afro-Asiatic family is associated with the presence of suffixation and reduplication.

Concerning types of the four word-formation processes studied, specifically compounding, the two approaches confirm that the Indo-European family seems to be associated with the presence of certain types of compounds. By contrast, the two approaches differ in respect of the association between the Niger-Congo and types of compounding: while the chi square approach gives a significant value for compounding in Niger-Congo languages in Table 7.2 (although not significant after the Bonferroni correction), the Niger-Congo family seems to be associated in Figure 7.8 with the absence of most types of compounding. This suggests that compounding in Niger-Congo languages is mainly of the type noun stem + noun stem, which is the most frequent type of compounding recorded in the languages sampled for this family.

The two approaches confirm the high frequency level of reduplication of Afro-Asiatic, Austronesian and Niger-Congo languages. MCA analysis shows that this high frequency is due mainly to the presence of preposing, complete and partial reduplication. The two approaches also confirm that the Indo-European family is associated with presence of prefixation, specifically, according to the MCA analysis, of polysemic and recursive prefixation. Finally, the two approaches also confirm that the language families Indo-European and Uralic have a high frequency of presence of suffixation.

Overall, both approaches agree in a considerable number of tendencies. These tendencies, detected by a conservative use of the chi square analysis and confirmed by MCA analysis, can therefore be considered reliable.

Onomasiologically, Figure 7.10 and Figure 7.11 show the semantic categories considered in chapter 6, with respect to the number of languages in the study sample in which the individual semantic categories listed above have word-formation relevance.

The expression of semantic categories shows a clear pattern as regards the use by each word-formation process (see Table 7.7). Table 7.7 and Figure

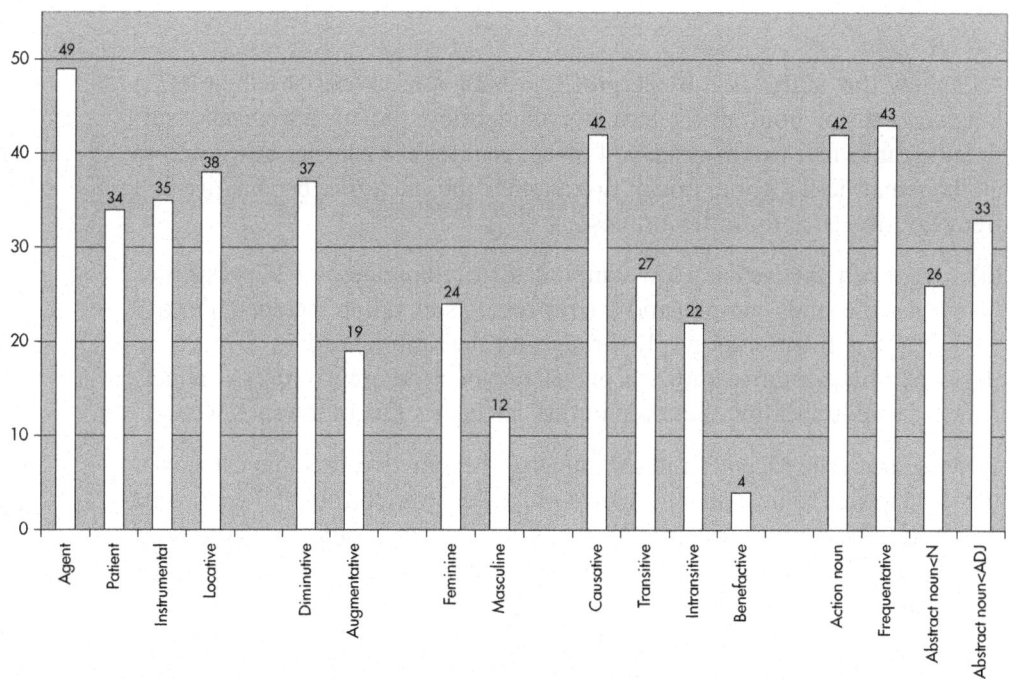

Figure 7.10. *Word-formation relevance of semantic categories in the study sample (absolute values with respect to fifty-five languages)*

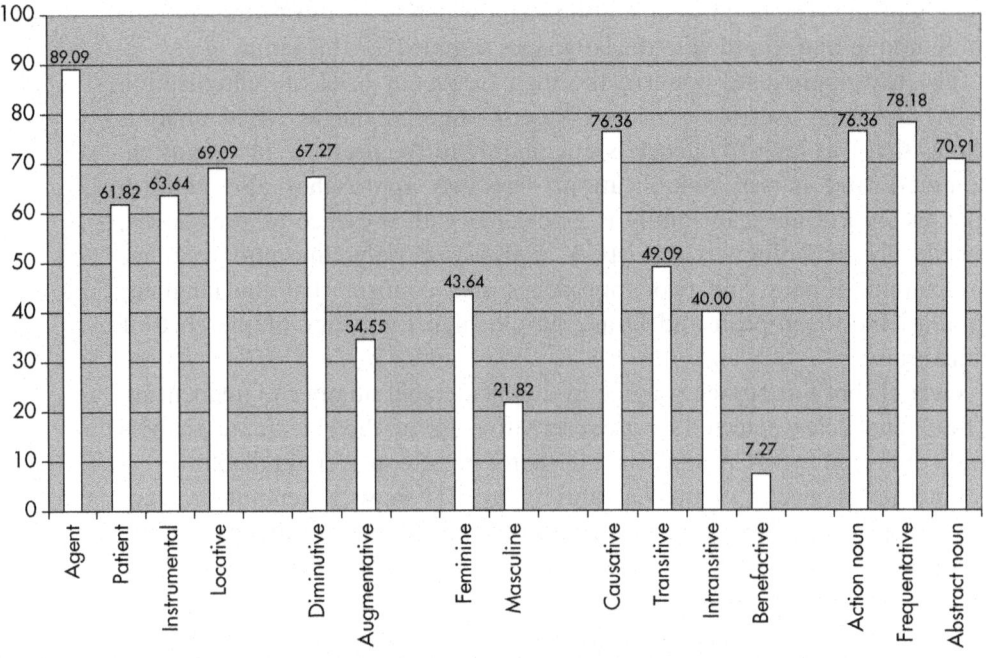

Figure 7.11. *Word-formation relevance of semantic categories (percentages)*

7.12 show that suffixation is the process which is used most by the sample languages throughout all the semantic categories studied. Specifically, suffixation ranks first within a range of 50 per cent to 70.5 per cent of use across all the semantic categories except two, namely the categories benefactive and frequentative, each for different reasons:

(a)   benefactive has a low sample size (four languages, 7.27 per cent of the study sample) and the processes, suffixation included, distribute themselves evenly throughout the sample, and

(b)   frequentative shows a prevalence of a different process, namely reduplication, but even in this category suffixation ranks second.

Leaving aside the exception in the category benefactive, in some categories the third lowest value is shared by two processes, even if Table 7.7 represents only one. These processes are compounding and prefixation-suffixation in agentive, instrumental, causative and action nouns, and compounding and conversion in patient.

Table 7.7. *Percentage of occurrence of semantic categories with respect to word-formation processes in the languages sampled. Only the three word-formation processes which occur most frequently for each semantic category are presented. Blank cells stand for low frequency of occurrence or for absence of languages which express these semantic roles by these word-formation processes.*

	AG	PAT	INS	LOC	DIM	AUG	F	M	CAU	TR	INTR	BEN	ACN	FRE	ABN<N	ABN<A
Suffixation	58.93	70.59	58.33	53.66	69.23	55.00	68.00	50.00	60.00	67.86	68.18	25.00	57.78	28.57	67.86	63.89
Prefixation	14.29	8.82	19.44	14.63		10.00	8.00	16.67	15.56	10.71	18.18	25.00	13.33	14.29	10.71	19.44
Compounding	8.93	5.88	8.33	14.63	5.13		16.00	25.00	4.44				4.44			
Conversion		5.88										25.00			14.29	5.56
Prefixation + suffixation	8.93		8.33						4.44	7.14			4.44			
Reduplication					17.95	15.00					4.55			48.98		

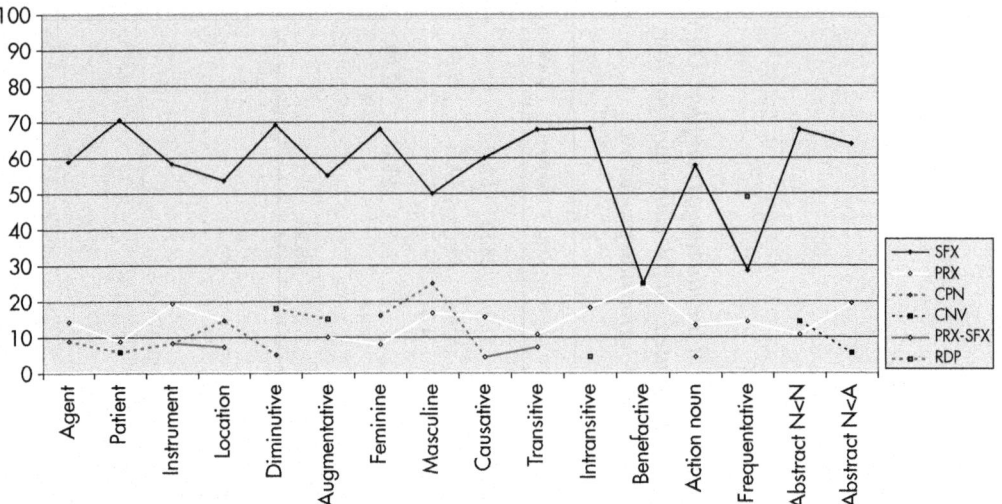

Figure 7.12. *Percentage of occurrence of semantic categories with respect to the most frequently used word-formation processes in the languages sampled*

7.3   Summary

Certain statistical associations can be established between word-formation processes and semantic categories as two separate datasets with respect to three independent variables: language family, morphological type and word order. Suffixation, compounding and, to a lesser extent, reduplication and prefixation, are the word-formation processes that play a major role in word-formation. Finer distinctions and specific associations can be established with respect to the independent variables but, in general, the picture given by the language sample is clearly in the direction of concatenative word-formation and constructional iconicity. Suffixation is the process which is most frequently used throughout all the semantic categories studied.

Epilogue

At the beginning of this volume we identified as the most important, central objective of this book the search for cross-linguistic associations between word-formation processes and/or the individual parameters of word-formation processes. A number of associations were identified, but the picture obtained is not very optimistic for those who may have expected a solid system of regular distribution of word-formation processes depending on genetic and/or morphological characteristics of languages.

Word-formation is an inherent feature of every language. This is both trivial and crucial. A language can only exist if it is able to give names to new objects invented, discovered, designed, encountered, obtained, produced, etc. by the members of a particular speech community. Exclusive use of borrowings and/or descriptive/analytic devices may be viewed as a symptom of a serious disease in a language, as has been confirmed for Bardi where, according to Bowern (pers. comm.), there is not much in the way of productive word-formation. This might be partly because of language death (there are only twenty-five speakers), but a lack of productive derivational morphology has also been noted for some other Australian Aboriginal languages.

There is no language without concatenating word-formation. This has confirmed one of the fundamental postulates of Natural Morphology concerning constructional iconicity as a most natural way of forming new words. This is also in accordance with the fundamental principles of Marchandean and Dokulilean approaches to word-formation, according to which an object is first conceptually processed as a member of a larger class of similar objects and, subsequently, is distinguished from them by highlighting one of its most characteristic features.

Suffixation and compounding, in this order, prevail, and reduplication and prefixation are frequent in the languages studied. Prefixal-infixal derivation, stem consonant alternation and stress shift are rare. Agent formation prevails over other semantic categories, e.g. patient. Diminutives prevail over augmentatives and feminines over masculines. Certain associations can be found between the above and the independent variables like language family, morphological type or word order, but individual word-formation processes and their features depend more on their genetic rather than morphological characteristics.

Languages may be divided into derivationally rich and derivationally poor. Derivationally rich languages make productive use not only of the major but also of the minor word-formation processes. Typical derivationally rich languages are, e.g. Clallam, English, Hebrew, Ilocano, Indonesian, Karao, Konni, Nelemwa, Marathi, Slovak and Totonac. Derivationally poor languages are those whose word-formation capacity is restricted to a minimum (Bardi, Cirecire) and those which make use of a limited number of word-formation processes, like Kalkatungu, Kwakw'ala, Lakhota, Tatar, Tzotzil and West Greenlandic. From this list it follows that at the poor end of the scale there are mostly agglutinative and polysynthetic languages, the latter exclusively from North America. The rich pole of the scale is fairly heterogeneous. These two groups of languages represent opposite ends on the word-formation richness scale. The other languages can be classified between them in terms of the number of processes used and of their productivity. From the point of view of various morphological classifications of languages, it is understandable, as there are no pure types and, thus, one cannot expect that word-formation features of these languages will be homogeneous.

A sample of fifty-five languages lends itself well to the identification of cross-linguistic default values, but it is not possible to draw any generalizations for families represented by a minimum number of languages. Why certain processes or categories prevail, as has been presented here, is hard to interpret. It may well be that there is not just one explanation, and an interplay of factors gives rise to the use of the same resource in a number of respects. From the perspective of this book, it is our belief that future effort should be guided in three major directions:

(a)   an increase in the total number of languages sampled in order to confirm or improve the precision of the findings of this book,

(b)   a search for associations between word-formation processes inside selected language families and/or genera represented by a sufficient number of languages, and

(c)   as the questionnaire used covered only selected areas of word-formation, an extended   scope of the word-formation characteristics covered.

A fascinating feature of any cross-linguistic research is that it makes it possible to reveal the wonderful diversity of individual phenomena. This has been shown, as we believe, in the examples cited in the volume. This diversity ranges over individual languages, families and morphological types. This diversity is a source/reason?/explanation? of the existence of fuzzy boundaries between the individual word-formation processes and also between inflectional morphology and syntax and derivation. In spite of this, the diversity constitutes the unity of the individual phenomena and processes through their most frequent cases that tower over all the less frequent manifestations.

This book draws generalizations based on empirical data, points out associations in word-formation processes cross-linguistically, demonstrates the multifarious manifestations of broadly defined word-formation categories in the languages of the world and illustrates the observations with examples. The aim was to instigate even more extensive and more comprehensive research in this intriguing area of language universals and typology, a task which is insurmountable for one or two linguists. By implication, since it was just the first, tentative probe, many more interesting findings remain to be discovered.

Appendix I. The distribution of word-formation processes in the study sample

	PRX	SFX	IFX	CRX	PRX-SFX	PRX-IFX	IFX-SFX	RAP	VAL	PRX+VAL	SFX+VAL	CAL	CPN	NIN	RDP	CNV	BFR	BLN	STR	TOP
Amele		+										+	+	+	+					
Amharic	+	+	+					+				+		+						
Anejom	+	+					+					+	+	+		+				
Bardi		+										+		+						
Breton	+	+									+	+			+					
Cirecire		+										+		+	+		+		+	
Clallam	+	+	+		+		+					+	+	+	+					
Dangaléat		+	+						+			+		+					+	
Datooga	+	+			+				+			+		+					+	
Diola-Fogny		+												+						
English	+	+		+					+	+		+	+	+	+	+	+	+	+	
Estonian	+	+										+	+	+	+	+				
Finnish	+	+										+		+	+	+				
Gã	+	+										+		+						
Georgian	+	+		+	+							+		+				+		
Greek	+	+										+			+	+	+			
Hausa	+	+							+		+	+		+	+					+
Hebrew	+	+	+	+	+	+	+	+	+	+	+	+	+	+	+	+	+	+		
Hungarian		+										+		+						
Ilocano	+	+	+	+	+	+	+					+		+	+	+				
Indonesian	+	+	+	+	+							+		+						
Japanese	+	+			+							+		+		+				
Jaqaru		+										+		+						
Kalkatungu		+										+		+						
Karao	+	+	+	+		+	+							+	+					
Ket	+	+							+			+	+	+						
Konni	+	+								+	+	+	+	+					+	
Kwakw'ala		+												+	+					
Lakhota	+	+			+							+	+							
Luganda	+	+	+				+		+		+	+		+					+	
Luo	+	+			+				+			+		+	+					
Maipure		+		+								+		+						
Malayalam	+	+								+	+	+								

330

	PRX	SFX	IFX	CRX	PRX-SFX	PRX-IFX	IFX-SFX	RAP	VAL	PRX+ VAL	SFX+ VAL	CAL	CPN	NIN	RDP	CNV	BFR	BLN	STR	TOP
Mandarin Chinese	+	+	+				+						+	+	+					+
Māori	+	+											+	+	+					
Marathi	+	+		+				+	+	+			+	+	+	+				
Movima		+											+	+	+					
Nelemwa	+	+		+	+					+	+		+	+	+	+		+		
Pipil	+	+		+									+	+	+					
Slavey	+	+											+	+						
Slovak	+	+	+	+	+	+	+		+	+	+		+	+	+			+	+	
Spanish	+	+	+	+									+			+		+	+	
Swahili	+	+		+									+	+	+					
Tamil	+	+	+										+	+	+		+			
Tatar		+	+										+	+						
Telugu	+	+											+	+	+	+				
Tibetan		+							+				+	+	+					
Totonac	+	+	+	+	+								+	+	+	+				
Tzotzil	+	+							+				+	+	+					
Udihe		+											+	+	+	+				
Vietnamese													+	+	+			+	+	+
West Greenlandic		+																		
Wichí	+	+		+									+	+		+				
Yoruba	+		+										+	+	+	+				
Zulu	+	+		+									+	+	+					

Appendix II. The questionnaire

Language: Language family:

                                                       Geographic area:

                                                       Morphological Type:

Author (completed by):

Date:

Part I

(1)   **Are words in your language formed productively by the following WF processes?**[1]

WF process	YES/NO	Example	Literal translation of constituent morphemes	English equivalent
A. Prefixation				
B. Suffixation				
C. Infixation				
D. Circumfixation[2]				
E. Prefixal-suffixal derivation[3]				
F. Prefixal-infixal derivation				
G. Infixal-suffixal derivation				

[1] A productive word-formation process is one which is synchronically used for the formation of new words.
[2] The two parts of circumfix cannot exist independently. They represent a single meaning.
[3] The two forms represent two different morphemes each of them contributing to the meaning of the WF base. Both of them are attached simultaneously, within a single WF process.

WF process	YES/NO	Example	Literal translation of constituent morphemes	English equivalent
H. Root-and-pattern derivation (transfixation)				
I. Stem vowel alternation				
J. Prefixation accompanied by vowel alternation				
K. Suffixation accompanied by vowel alternation				
L. Consonant alternation				
M. Compounding				
N. Incorporation[4]				
O. Reduplication				
P. Conversion[5]				
Q. Back-formation/ subtraction				
R. Blending				
S. Clipping				
T. Other productive WF processes				

(2)   **Please estimate the productivity of each of the above-mentioned WF processes in your language using a five-degree scale, where '5' means 'high productivity'[6] and '1' indicates 'low productivity'.[7]**

WF process	Productivity rating
A. Prefixation	
B. Suffixation	
C. Infixation	
D. Circumfixation	
E. Prefixal-suffixal derivation	
F. Prefixal-infixal derivation	
G. Infixal-suffixal derivation	
H. Root-and-pattern derivation (transfixation)	

---

[4] A verb-forming process, whereby a nominal stem is fused with a verbal stem to yield a larger, derived verbal stem.

[5] Including cases of change of class without adding any explicit morpheme, with inflectional paradigm functioning analogically to zero derivational morpheme.

[6] This evaluation should reflect other competing WF processes. Thus, a WF process can get the rating '5' if there is no competing WF process that restricts its applicability.

[7] Please do not use '0' because it means that a WF process is not productively used. We are only interested in productive WF processes.

WF process	Productivity rating
I. Stem vowel alternation	
J. Prefixation accompanied by vowel alternation	
K. Suffixation accompanied by vowel alternation	
L. Consonant alternation	
M. Compounding	
N. Incorporation	
O. Reduplication	
P. Conversion	
Q. Back-formation/subtraction	
R. Blending	
S. Clipping	

(3)   Please answer the following questions:

WF process	YES/NO	Example	Literal translation	English equivalent
A. Prefixation				
(a) Is more than one derivational prefix possible in a word?				
(b) In general, does each derivational prefix form have just one meaning? If no, give some examples of prefixes with more than one meaning.				
(c) Are there variants of derivational prefixes?				
(d) Do derivational prefixes ever cause changes in the base?				
B. Suffixation				
(a) Is more than one derivational suffix possible in a word?				

	WF process	YES/NO	Example	Literal translation	English equivalent
(b)	In general, does each derivational suffix form have just one meaning? If no, give some examples of derivational suffixes with more than one meaning.				
(c)	Are there variants of derivational suffixes?				
(d)	Are there any derivational suffixes that cause changes in the base?				
C.	**Compounding**				
(a)	Is compounding recursive?				
(b)	Are there adjectival (Adjective + Adjective) compounds?				
(c)	Does the language make productive use of verbal compounds?				
(d)	Does the language make productive use of noun (Noun + Noun) compounds? Which of the following are found?				
(d1)	Stem + Stem[8] compounds				
(d2)	Stem + Link + Stem compounds (the link being specific to compounding)				
(d3)	At least one Stem is phonologically modified[9]				
(e)	If the language makes productive use of compounds both with and without a linking element, which type is more productive?				

[8] Stem is defined here as that part of a word which remains after removing all inflectional morphemes. Stem corresponds, in principle, to a WF base.

[9] Cf. Japanese *rendaku*, or Danish compounds with missing *stød*, or compounds with specific tones in modifying positions, etc.

	WF process	YES/NO	Example	Literal translation	English equivalent
(f)	Are there any copulative compounds?[10] Which, if any, of the following are found?				
(f1)	Substantival				
(f2)	Adjectival				
(g)	Are there any exocentric compounds?[11] Which, if any, of the following are found?				
(g1)	words like *redskin*[12]				
(g2)	words like French *garde-manger*[13]				
D.	**Reduplication**				
(a)	Complete reduplication				
(b)	Partial reduplication				
(b1)	Preposing reduplication				
(b2)	Postposing reduplication				
(b3)	Infixing reduplication				
(c)	What meanings can reduplication encode productively?				
E.	**Does stress have a word-forming capacity?**[14]				
F.	**Does pitch level have a word-forming capacity?**				

---

[10] E.g. *producer-director*, *blue-green*. These are sometimes referred to as *dvandvas*. The compound is formed by two elements of equal status, and the compound as a whole is often not a hyponym of either element.

[11] The head of compound is not explicitly expressed; it lies outside the compound.

[12] A type of potato with a red skin – the unexpressed *denotatum* has a red skin.

[13] *Garde-manger* 'keep food' = 'pantry', where a verb and its object are used to denote an entity which carries out this action.

[14] E.g. *record* ['rekəd]$_N$ vs *record* [ri'kɔːd]$_V$.

Part II

Please answer the questions. **If a particular category is not formed in your language by WF processes, simply state 'NO'.**

	Question	Give examples	Estimate the productivity by means of a five-degree scale
1.	The most productive way(s) of forming agent nouns?		
2.	The most productive way(s) of forming patient nouns?		
3.	The most productive way(s) of forming instrumental nouns?		
4.	The most productive way(s) of forming locative nouns?		
5.	The most productive way(s) of forming diminutives?		
6.	The most productive way(s) of forming augmentatives?		
7.	The most productive way(s) of forming feminine nouns from masculine nouns?		
8.	The most productive way(s) of forming masculine nouns from feminine nouns?		
9.	The most productive way(s) of forming causative verbs?		
10.	The most productive way(s) of forming transitive verbs?		
11.	The most productive way(s) of forming intransitive verbs?		
12.	Does your language have a way of forming parts of speech other than noun, verb, adjective or adverb?		

	Question	Give examples	Estimate the productivity by means of a five-degree scale
13.	The most productive way(s) of forming benefactive nouns?		
14.	The most productive way(s) of forming action nominals[15]		
15.	The most productive way(s) of forming frequentative or intensive markers on verbs?		
16.	The most productive way(s) of forming abstract nouns from nouns?		
17.	The most productive way(s) of forming abstract nouns from adjectives?		
18.	Any other important categories in your language?		
19.	Do any of these categories overlap, i.e. is the same morpheme or process ever used to form more than one of these categories?		

---

[15] Abstract nouns derived from verbs, e.g. *engagement*.N from *engage*.V.

Part III

Additional comments completing the picture of PRODUCTIVE word-formation PROCESSES in your language:

References

Aarts, B., Denison, D., Keizer, E. and Popova, G. (eds.) 2004. *Fuzzy Grammar. A Reader*. Oxford University Press.

Abraham, W. 2005. 'Intensity and diminution triggered by reduplicating morphology: Janus-faced iconicity', in Hurch, B. (ed.) *Studies on Reduplication*. Berlin and New York: Mouton de Gruyter, 547–68.

Adams, V. 1973. *An Introduction to Modern English Word Formation*. London: Longman.

2001. *Complex Words in English*. Harlow: Longman.

Agrell, S. 1908. *Aspektänderung und Aktionsartbildung beim polnischen Zeitworte: ein Beitrag zum Studium der indogermanischen Präverbia und ihrer Bedeutungsfunktionen*. Lund: Håkan Ohlssons Buchdruckerei.

Aikhenvald, A. Y. 2007. 'Typological distinctions in word-formation', in Shopen, T. (ed.), 1–65.

Anderson, S. R. 1982. 'Where's morphology?', *Linguistic Inquiry* 13: 571–612.

1985. 'Typological distinctions in word formation', in Shopen, T. (ed.), 4–56.

1992. *A-morphous Morphology*. Cambridge: Cambridge University Press.

Aronoff, M. 1976. *Word Formation in Generative Grammar*. Cambridge, MA: MIT Press.

Asher, R. E. and Kumari, T. C. 1997. *Malayalam*. London and New York: Routledge.

Baerman, M. and Corbett, G. G. 2007. 'Linguistic typology: morphology', *Linguistic Typology* 1: 115–18.

Bakema, P. and Geeraerts, D. 2000. 'Diminution and augmentation', in Booij, G. E., Lehmann, Ch. and Mugdan, J. (eds.) *Morphologie/Morphology. Ein internationales Handbuch zur Flexion und Wortbildung/An International Handbook on Inflection and Word Formation. Vol. I.* Berlin: Walter de Gruyter, 1045–52.

Baker, M. 1985. 'The mirror principle and morphosyntactic explanation', *Linguistic Inquiry* 16: 373–416.

1988. 'Morphology and syntax: an interlocking independence', in Everaert, M., Evers, A., Huybregts, R. and Trommelen, M. (eds.) *Morphology and Modularity: in Honor of Henk Schultink*. Dordrecht: Foris, 9–32.

Baker, M. and Fasola, C. A. 2009. 'Compounding in Mapudungun', in Lieber, R. and Štekauer, P. (eds.), 594–608.

Bakker, D. and Parkvall, M. 2005. 'Reduplication in pidgins and creoles', in Hurch, B. (ed.) *Studies on Reduplication*. Berlin and New York: Mouton de Gruyter, 511–32.

Barz, I. 2005. 'Die Wortbildung', in *Duden. Die Grammatik*. Seventh edition. Mannheim: Dudenverlag, 641–772.

Bauer, L. 1983. *English Word-formation*. Cambridge: Cambridge University Press.

1988. 'A descriptive gap in morphology', *Yearbook of Morphology 1988*: 17–27.

1990. 'Be-heading the word', *Journal of Linguistics* 26: 1–31.

1996. 'No phonetic iconicity in evaluative morphology', *Studia Linguistica* 50/2: 189–206.

1997. 'Evaluative morphology: in search of universals', *Studies in Language* 21/3: 533–75.

1998. 'When is a sequence of two nouns a compound in English?', *English Language and Linguistics* 2/1: 65–86.

2000. 'What you can do with derivational morphology', in Bendjaballah, S., Dressler, W. U., Pfeiffer, O. E. and Voeikova, M. D. (eds.) *Morphology. Selected Papers from the 9th Morphology Meeting. Vienna, 24–28 February 2000.* Amsterdam and Philadelphia: John Benjamins, 37–48.

2001. *Morphological Productivity.* Cambridge: Cambridge University Press.

2005. 'Conversion and the notion of lexical category', in Bauer, L. and Valera, S. (eds.), *Approaches to Conversion/Zero-Derivation.* Munster: Waxmann, 19–30.

2006. 'Compound', in Brown, K. (ed.) *Encyclopedia of Language and Linguistics.* Second edition. Oxford: Elsevier, 718–26.

2008. 'Dvandva', *Word Structure* 1: 1–20.

2009a. 'IE, Germanic: Danish', in Lieber, R. and Štekauer, P. (eds.), 400–16.

2009b. 'Typology of compounds', in Lieber, R. and Štekauer, P. (eds.), 343–56.

Bauer, L. and Renouf, A. 2001. 'A corpus-based study of compounding in English', *Journal of English Linguistics* 29: 101–23.

Bauer, L. and Valera, S. 2005. 'Conversion or zero-derivation: an introduction', in Bauer, L. and Valera, S. (eds.) *Approaches to Conversion/Zero-Derivation.* Munster: Waxmann, 7–17.

Bauer, W. 1997. *The Reed Reference Grammar of Māori.* Auckland: Reed.

Beard, R. E. 1981. *The Indo-European Lexicon: a Full Synchronic Theory.* Amsterdam: North-Holland.

1982. 'The plural as a lexical derivation', *Glossa. An International Journal of Linguistics* 16/2: 133–48.

1995. *Lexeme-Morpheme Base Morphology. A General Theory of Inflection and Word Formation.* Albany, NY: State University of New York Press.

Beck, D. 2004. *Upper Necaxa Totonac.* Munich: Lincom Europa.

Becker, T. 1992. 'Compounding in German', *Rivista di Linguistica* 4: 5–36.

Belimov, E. I. 1991. *Ketskij sintaksis: situacija, propozicija, predloženie.* Novosibirsk: Izdatel'stvo Novosibirskogo Universiteta.

Bickel, B. 2007. 'Typology in the 21st century: major current developments', *Linguistic Typology* 11/1: 239–51.

Biese, Y. M. 1941. 'Origin and development of conversions in English', *Annales Academiae Scientiarum Fennicae* B 45/2: 1–495.

Biggs, B. 1969. *Let's Learn Māori: a Guide to the Study of the Māori Language.* Wellington: A. H. & A. W. Reed.

Bloomfield. L. 1933. *Language.* New York: Henry Holt.

Boas, F. 1911. 'Introduction', in Boas, F. (ed.) *Handbook of American Indian Languages 1.* Washington: Government Printing Office, 5–83.

1947. 'Kwakiutl grammar with a glossary of the suffixes', in Boas Yampolsky, H. and Harris, Z. S. (eds.) *Transactions of the American Philosophical Society* 37/3: 201–377.

Boogaart, R. 2000. 'Aspect and Aktionsart', in Booij, G. E., Lehmann, Ch. and Mugdan, J. (eds.) *Morphologie/Morphology. Ein internationales Handbuch zur Flexion und Wortbildung/An International Handbook on Inflection and Word Formation. Vol. I.* Berlin: Walter de Gruyter, 1165–80.

Booij, G. E. 1986. 'Form and meaning in morphology: the case of Dutch "agent nouns"', *Linguistics* 24: 503–17.

1994. 'Against split morphology', *Yearbook of Morphology 1993*: 27–49.

1995. 'The phonology–morphology interface', *GLOT International* 1/5: 3–7.

2006. 'Inflection and derivation', in Brown, K. (ed.) *Encyclopedia of Language and Linguistics*. Second edition. Oxford: Elsevier, 654–61.

2009. 'Phrasal names: a constructionist analysis', *Word Structure* 2: 219–240.

Bowden, J. 2001. *Taba: Description of a South Halmahera Language*. Canberra, ACT: Pacific Linguistics, Australian National University.

Brainard, S. 1994. *The Phonology of Karao, The Philippines*. Canberra, ACT: Pacific Linguistics, Australian National University.

Bril, I. 2004. 'Coordination strategies and inclusory constructions in New Caledonian and other Oceanic languages', in Haspelmath, M. (ed.) *Coordinating Constructions*. Amsterdam: John Benjamins, 499–534.

2005. 'Semantic and functional diversification of reciprocal and middle prefixes in New Caledonian and other Austronesian languages', *Linguistic Typology* 9/1: 25–76.

Brown, L. and Dryer, M. S. (unpublished manuscript). 'Diminutive as an inflectional category in Walman', available at http://linguistics.buffalo.edu/people/faculty/dryer/dryer/BrownDryerWalmanDimin.pdf (last accessed 3 September 2011).

Bybee, J. L. 1985. *Morphology. A Study of the Relation between Meaning and Form*. Amsterdam and Philadelphia: John Benjamins.

Campbell, L. 1985. *The Pipil Language of El Salvador*. Berlin, New York and Amsterdam: Mouton.

Carstairs-McCarthy, A. 2006. 'Affixation', in Brown, K. (ed.), *Encyclopedia of Language and Linguistics*. Second edition. Oxford: Elsevier, 83–8.

Ceccagno, A. and Basciano, B. 2009. 'Compounding in Chinese', in Lieber, R. and Štekauer, P. (eds.), 478–90.

Cetnarowska, B. 1993. *The Syntax, Semantics and Derivation of Bare Nominalisations in English*. Katowice: Wydawnictwo Uniwersytetu Polskiego.

Cherchi, M. 1999. *Georgian*. Munich: Lincom Europa.

Chung, K. S. 1994. 'Verb + noun function-describing compounds', Revised version of paper originally published in *Bulletin of the College of Liberal Arts, National Taiwan University*, 41: 181–221. URL: http://homepage.ntu.edu.tw/~karchung/pubs/vncomp_rev.pdf (last accessed 15 July 2010).

2006. *Mandarin Compound Verbs*. Taipei: Crane.

Clark, E. V. and Clark, H. H. 1979. 'When nouns surface as verbs', *Language* 55/4: 767–811.

Comrie, B. 1985. 'Causative verb formation and other verb-deriving morphology', in Shopen, T. (ed.), 309–48.

1989. *Language Universals and Linguistic Typology*. University of Chicago Press.

Comrie, B. and Thompson, S. A. 1985. 'Lexical nominalization', in Shopen, T. (ed.), 349–98.

Cowan, M. M. 1969. *Tzotzil Grammar*. Norman, OK: Summer School of Linguistics of the University of Oklahoma.

Croft, W. 2001. *Radical Construction Grammar*. Oxford: Oxford University Press.

2003. *Typology and Universals*. Second edition. Cambridge: Cambridge University Press.

Cruse, A. D. 1986. *Lexical Semantics*. Cambridge University Press.

Cutler, A., Hawkins, J. A. and Gilligan, G. 1985. 'The suffixing preference: a processing explanation', *Linguistics* 23: 723–58.

Daniel, M. 2007. 'Representative sampling and typological explanation: a phenomenological lament', *Linguistic Typology* 11/1: 69–78.

de Haas, W. and Trommelen, M. 1993. *Morfologisch handboek van het Nederlands: een overzicht van de woordvorming*. The Hague: SDU.

de Reuse, W. J. 1994. 'Noun incorporation in Lakota (Siouan)', *International Journal of American Linguistics* 60/3: 199–260.

Di Sciullo, A.-M. and Williams, E. 1987. *On the Definition of Word*. Cambridge, MA: MIT Press.

Dixon, R. M. W. and Aikhenvald, A. Y. (eds.) 2002. *Word. A Cross-Linguistic Typology*. Cambridge University Press.

Dokulil, M. 1962. *Tvoření slov v češtině 1. Teorie odvozování slov.* Prague: Nakladatelství Československé Akademie Věd.

  1968. 'Zur Frage der Konversion und verwandter Wortbildungsvorgänge und -beziehungen', in Isačenko A. V. (ed.) *Travaux Linguistiques de Prague* 3. Prague: Academia, 215–39.

  1982. 'K otázce slovnědruhových převodů a přechodů, zvl. transpozice', *Slovo a slovesnost* 43: 257–71.

  1997. 'The Prague School's theoretical and methodological contribution to "word-formation" (derivology)', in Panevová, J. and Skoumalová, Z. (eds.) *Obsah – výraz – význam. Miloši Dokulilovi k 85. narozeninám.* Prague: Filozofická Fakulta Univerzity Karlovy, 179–210.

Don, J. 2009. 'Compounding in Dutch', in Lieber, R. and Štekauer, P. (eds.), 370–85.

Donalies, E. 2004. 'Hochzeitstorte, laskaparasol, elmas küpe, cow's milk, casa de campo, cigarette-filtre, ricasdueñas... Was ist eigentlich ein Kompositum?', *Deutsche Sprache* 1/03: 76–93.

Dressler, W. U. 1968. *Studien zur Verbalen Pluralität. Iterativum, Distributivum, Durativum, Intensivum in der allgemeinen Grammatik, im Lateinischen und Hethitischen.* Vienna: Hermann Böhlaus.

  1981. 'On word formation in natural morphology', *Wiener Linguistische Gazette* 26: 3–33.

  1982. 'Zur semiotischen Begründung einer natürlichen Wortbildungslehre', *Klagenfurter Beiträge zur Sprachwissenschaft* 8: 72–87.

  1985. 'On the predictiveness of natural morphology', *Linguistics* 21: 321–37.

  1987. 'Word-formation as a part of natural morphology', in Dressler *et al.* (eds.), 99–126.

  1988. 'Preferences *vs.* strict universals in morphology', in Hammond, M. and Noonan, M. (eds.) *Theoretical Morphology: Approaches in Modern Linguistics.* San Diego, CA: Academic Press, 143–54.

  1989. 'Prototypical differences between inflection and derivation', *Zeitschrift für Sprachwissenschaft und Kommunikationsforschung* 42: 3–10.

  1997. 'Universals, typology and modularity in natural morphology', in Hickey, R. and Puppel, S. (eds.) *Language History and Linguistic Modellings.* Berlin: Mouton de Gruyter, 1399–423.

  2000. 'Extragrammatical vs. marginal morphology', in Doleschal, U. and Thornton, A. (eds.) *Extragrammatical and Marginal Morphology.* Munich: Lincom Europa, 1–10.

  2005. 'Word-formation in natural morphology', in Štekauer, P. and Lieber, R. (eds.) *Handbook of Word-formation.* Springer: Dordrecht, 267–84.

Dressler, W. U. and Karpf, A. 1995. 'The theoretical relevance of pre- and proto-morphology in language acquisition', *Yearbook of Morphology 1994*: 99–122.

Dressler, W. U., Mayerthaler, W., Panagl, O. and Wurzel, W. U. (eds.) 1987. *Leitmotifs in Natural Morphology.* Amsterdam and Philadelphia: John Benjamins.

Dryer, M. S. 1997. 'Are grammatical relations universal?', in Bybee, J. L., Haiman, J. and Thompson, S. A. (eds.) *Essays on Language Function and Language Type.* Amsterdam: John Benjamins, 115–43.

Fabb, N. 1998. 'Compounding', in Spencer, A. and Zwicky, A. M. (eds.) *Handbook of Morphology.* Oxford and Malden, MA: Basil Blackwell, 66–83.

Farrell, P. 2001. 'Functional shift as category underspecification', *English Language and Linguistics* 5/1: 109–30.

Fernández-Domínguez, J. 2009. *Productivity in English Word-formation. An Approach to N+N Compounding*. Bern: Peter Lang.

Filipec, J. and Čermák, F. 1985. *Česká lexikologie*. Prague: Academia.

Fortescue, M. 1980 'Affix-ordering in West Greenlandic derivational processes', *International Journal of American Linguistics* 46/4: 259–78.

1984. *West Greenlandic*. London, Sydney and Dover: Croom Helm.

Furdík, J. 2004. *Slovenská slovotvorba*. Prešov: Náuka.

Gaeta, L. 2005. 'Word-formation and typology: which language universals?', in Booij, G. E., Guevara, E., Ralli, A., Sgroi, S. and Scalise, S. (eds.) *Morphology and Linguistic Typology. On-line Proceedings of the Fourth Mediterranean Morphology Meeting (MMM4) Catania, 21–23 September 2003*. University of Bologna, 157–70.

Gerdts, D. B. 1998. 'Incorporation', in Spencer, A. and Zwicky, A. M. (eds.), *The Handbook of Morphology*. Oxford and Malden, MA: Basil Blackwell, 84–99.

Giegerich, H. J. 1999. *Lexical Strata in English*. Cambridge: Cambridge University Press.

2004. 'Compound or phrase? English noun-plus-noun constructions and the stress criterion', *English Language and Linguistics* 8: 1–24.

2009. 'The English compound stress myth', *Word Structure* 2: 1–17.

Glinert, L. 1989. *The Grammar of Modern Hebrew*. Cambridge: Cambridge University Press.

Grandi, N. and Montermini, F. 2005. 'Prefix-suffix neutrality in evaluative morphology', in Booij, G. E., Guevara, E., Ralli, A., Sgroi, S. and Scalise, S. (eds.) *Morphology and Linguistic Typology. On-line Proceedings of the Fourth Mediterranean Morphology Meeting (MMM4) Catania, 21–23 September 2003*. University of Bologna, 143–56.

Greenberg, J. H. 1963. 'Some universals of grammar with particular reference to the order of meaningful elements', in Greenberg, J. H. (ed.) *Universals of Language*. Cambridge, MA: MIT Press, 58–90.

1966. 'Some universals of grammar with particular reference to the order of meaningful elements', in Greenberg, J. H. (ed.) *Universals of Language*. Second edition. Cambridge, MA: MIT Press, 73–113.

(ed.) 1978. *Universals of Human Language. Vol. III. Word Structure*. Stanford University Press.

Guerssel, M. 1983. 'A lexical approach to word formation in English', *Linguistic Analysis* 12: 183–243.

Hall, C. J. 2000. 'Prefixation, suffixation and circumfixation', in Booij, G. E., Lehmann, Ch. and Mugdan, J. (eds.) *Morphologie/Morphology. Ein internationales Handbuch zur Flexion und Wortbildung/An International Handbook on Inflection and Word Formation. Vol. I*. Berlin: Walter de Gruyter, 535–45.

Halle, M. 1973. 'Prolegomena to a theory of word formation', *Linguistic Inquiry* 4/1: 3–16.

Halliday, M. A. K. 1966. 'Lexis as a linguistic level', in Bazell, C. E., Catford, J. C., Halliday, M. A. K. and Robins, R. H. (eds.) *In Memory of J. R. Firth*. London: Longman, 148–62.

Hardman, M. J. 2000. *Jaqaru*. Munich: Lincom Europa.

Harrison, S. P. 1973. 'Reduplication in Micronesian languages', *Oceanic Linguistics* 12: 407–54.

Haspelmath, M. 1996. 'Word-class changing inflection and morphological theory', *Yearbook of Morphology 1995*: 43–66.

2007. 'Pre-established categories don't exist: consequences for language description and typology', *Linguistic Typology* 11: 119–32.

Haspelmath, M., Dryer, M. S., Gil, D. and Comrie, B. (eds.) 2005. *The World Atlas of Language Structures*. Oxford University Press.

Haviland, J. B. 1980. *Sk'op Sotz'leb: the Tzotzil of Zinacantán. An On-line Tzotzil Grammar*. URL: www.zapata.org/Tzotzil/ (last accessed 15 July 2010).

Hawkins, J. A. 1988. 'Explaining language universals', in Hawkins, J. A. (ed.) *Explaining Language Universals*. Oxford: Basil Blackwell, 3–28.

Hawkins, J. A. and Gilligan, G. 1988. 'Prefixing and suffixing universals in relation to basic word order', in Hawkins, J. A. and Holmback, H. K. (eds.) *Papers in Universal Grammar: Generative and Typological Approaches. Lingua Special Issue 74*, 219–59.

Hillery, P. J. 1996–2006. *The Georgian Language. An Outline Grammatical Summary*. URL: http://www.armazi.demon.co.uk/georgian/ (last accessed 15 July 2010).

Himmelmann, N. P. 2005. 'The Austronesian languages of Asia and Madagascar: typological characteristics', in Adelaar, K. A. and Himmelmann, N. P. (eds.) *The Austronesian Languages of Asia and Madagascar*. London and New York: Routledge, 110–81.

Hockett, C. F. 1958. *A Course in Modern Linguistics*. New York: Macmillan.

Hohenhaus, P. 2004. 'Identical constituent compounding – a corpus-based study', *Folia Linguistica* 38/3–4: 297–332.

Horecký, J., Buzássyová, K. and Bosák, J. 1989. *Dynamika slovnej zásoby súčasnej slovenčiny*. Bratislava: Veda.

Hudson, R. A. 1980. 'Constituency and dependency', *Linguistics* 18: 179–98.

Inkelas, S. 2006. 'Reduplication', in Brown, K. (ed.) *Encyclopedia of Language and Linguistics*. Second edition. Oxford: Elsevier, 417–19.

Inkelas, S. and Zoll, C. 2005. *Reduplication: Doubling in Morphology*. Cambridge: Cambridge University Press.

Jackendoff, R. S. 2009. 'Compounding in the parallel architecture and conceptual semantics', in Lieber, R. and Štekauer, P. (eds.), 105–28.

Josefsson, G. 1997. *On the Principles of Word Formation in Swedish*. Lund University Press.

Julien, M. 2006. 'Word', in Brown, K. (ed.) *Encyclopedia of Language and Linguistics*. Second edition. Oxford: Elsevier, 617–24.

Jurafsky, D. 1993. 'Universals in the semantics of the diminutive', in Guenter, J. S., Kaiser, B. A. and Zoll, C. (eds.) *Proceedings of the 19th Annual Meeting of the Berkeley Linguistics Society: Parasession on Semantic Typology and Semantic Universals*. Berkeley Linguistics Society, 423–36.

Kachru, Y. 2006. *Hindi*. Amsterdam and Philadelphia: John Benjamins.

Kageyama, T. 1982. 'Word formation in Japanese', *Lingua* 57: 215–58.

  2009. 'Isolate: Japanese', in Lieber, R. and Štekauer, P. (eds.), 512–26.

Kastovsky, D. 1969. 'Wortbildung und Nullmorphem', *Linguistische Berichte* 2: 1–13.

  1982. *Wortbildung und Semantik*. Düsseldorf: Pädagogischer Verlag-Schwann-Bagel.

  1986. 'Diachronic word-formation in a functional perspective', in Kastovsky, D. and Szwedek, A. (eds.) *Linguistics across Historical and Geographical Boundaries. In Honour of Jacek Fisiak on the Occasion of his Fiftieth Birthday*. Berlin: Mouton de Gruyter, 409–21.

  1994. 'Verbal derivation in English: a historical survey or Much Ado About Nothing', in Britton, D. (ed.) *English Historical Linguistics 1994. Papers from the 8th International Conference on English Historical Linguistics (8. ICEHL, Edinburgh, 19–23 September 1994)*. Amsterdam and Philadelphia: John Benjamins, 93–117.

  1995. 'Wortbildung', in Ahrens, R., Bald, W.-D. and Hüllen, W. (eds.) *Handbuch Englisch als Fremdsprache*. Berlin: Erich Schmidt Verlag, 104–9.

  2000. 'Words and word-formation: morphology in OED', in Mugglestone, L. (ed.) *Lexicography and the OED. Pioneers in the Untrodden Forest*. New York: Oxford University Press, 110–25.

  2009. 'Diachronic perspectives', in Lieber, R. and Štekauer, P. (eds.), 323–42.

Katamba, F. 1993. *Morphology*. London: Macmillan.

Kavka, S. 2003. 'English compounds (revisited) as idiomatic expressions and continua', *Linguistica Praguensia* 13/1: 13–33.

2009. 'Compounding and idiomatology', in Lieber, R. and Štekauer, P. (eds.), 19–33.

Kimenyi, A. 2008. 'The Bantu–Japanese connection: iconicity of reduplication in Japanese and Kinyarwanda'. URL: www.kimenyi.com/reduplication-in-japanese.php (last accessed 15 July 2010).

Kiparsky, P. 1982a. 'Lexical morphology and phonology', in Yang, I. S. (ed.) *Linguistics in the Morning Calm. Selected Papers from SICOL-1981*. Seoul: Hanshin, 3–91.

1982b. 'From cyclic phonology to lexical phonology', in van der Hulst, H. and Smith, N. (eds.) *The Structure of Phonological Representations, Part I*. Dordrecht: Foris, 131–75.

Kiyomi, S. 1995. 'A new approach to reduplication: a semantic study of noun and verb reduplication in the Malayo-Polynesian languages', *Linguistics* 33: 1145–67.

Klamer, M. 1998. *A Grammar of Kambera*. Berlin and New York: Mouton de Gruyter.

Kouwenberg, S. and LaCharité, D. 2005. 'Less is more: evidence from diminutive reduplication in Caribbean Creole languages', in Hurch, B. (ed.) *Studies on Reduplication*. Berlin and New York: Mouton de Gruyter, 533–46.

Kroeber, A. L. 1910. 'Noun incorporation in American languages', in Heger, F. (ed.) *Verhandlungen des XVI. Internationalen Amerikanisten-Kongress*. Vienna and Leipzig: A. Hartleben, 569–76.

Krupa, V. and Genzor, J. 1996. *Jazyky sveta v priestore a čase*. Bratislava: Veda.

Kryk-Kastovsky, B. 2000. 'Diminutives: an interface of word-formation, semantics and pragmatics', in Dalton-Puffer, C. and Ritt, N. (eds.) *Words: Structure, Meaning, Function. A Festschrift for Dieter Kastovsky*. Berlin: Mouton de Gruyter, 165–74.

Laca, B. 2001. 'Derivation', in Haspelmath, M., König, E., Oesterreicher, W. and Raible, W. (eds.) *Language Typology and Language Universals*. Berlin and New York: Walter de Gruyter, 1214–27.

Lazard, G. 1992. 'Y a-t-il des catégories interlangagières?', in Anschütz, S. (ed.) *Texte, Sätze, Wörter, und Moneme: Festschrift für Klaus Heger*. Heidelberg: Heidelberger Orient-Verlag, 427–34.

Lees, R. B. 1960. *The Grammar of English Nominalizations*. Bloomington, IN: Indiana University Press.

1970. 'Problems in the grammatical analysis of English nominal compounds', in Bierwisch, M. and Heidolph, K. E. (eds.) *Progress in Linguistics*. The Hague: Mouton, 174–86.

Levi, J. N. 1978. *The Syntax and Semantics of Complex Nominals*. New York Academic Press.

Leza, I. J. L. 2001. 'Incorporation', in Haspelmath, M., König, E., Oesterreicher, W. and Raible, W. (eds.) *Language Typology and Language Universals*. Berlin and New York: Walter de Gruyter, 714–25.

Libben, G. 2006. 'Why study compound processing? An overview of the issues', in Libben, G. and Jarema, G. (eds.) *The Representation and Processing of Compound Words*. Oxford University Press, 1–22.

Lieber, R. 1981. *On the Organization of the Lexicon*. PhD thesis, MIT, Bloomington, IN, Indiana University Linguistics Club. [Published 1990 in the series Outstanding Dissertations in Linguistics. New York: Garland].

1992. *Deconstructing Morphology. Word Formation in Syntactic Theory*. University of Chicago Press.

2004. *Morphology and Lexical Semantics*. Cambridge: Cambridge University Press.

Lieber, R. and Štekauer, P. (eds.) 2009. *Oxford Handbook of Compounding*. Oxford University Press.

Lüdtke, J. 1996. 'Gemeinromanische Tendenzen IV. Wortbildungslehre', in Holtus, G., Metzeltin, M. and Schmitt, Ch. (eds.) *Lexikon der Romanistischen Linguistik (LRL), Bd. II,1: Lateinisch und Romanisch. Historisch-Vergleichende Grammatik der romanischen Sprachen.* Tübingen: Niemeyer, 235–72.

Macaulay, M. 1996. *A Grammar of Chalcatongo Mixtec.* Berkeley and London: University of California Press.

Malkiel, Y. 1978. 'Derivational categories', in Greenberg, J. H. (ed.), 127–49.

Malouf, R. 1999. 'West Greenlandic noun incorporation in a monohierarchical theory of grammar', in Webelhuth, G., Kathol, K. and Koenig, J.-P. (ed.) *Lexical and Constructional Aspects of Linguistic Explanation.* Stanford, CA: Center for the Study of Language and Information Publications, 47–62.

Marantz, A. 1982. 'Re reduplication', *Linguistic Inquiry* 13/3: 435–82.

Marchand, H. 1960. *The Categories and Types of Present-day English Word-formation.* Wiesbaden: Otto Harrassowitz.

   1965a. 'The analysis of verbal nexus substantives', *Indogermanische Forschungen* 70: 57–71.

   1965b. 'On the analysis of substantive compounds and suffixal derivatives not containing a verbal element', *Indogermanische Forschungen* 70: 117–45.

   1967. 'Expansion, transposition and derivation', *La Linguistique* 1: 13–26.

   1969. *The Categories and Types of Present-day English Word-formation.* Second revised edition. Munich: Carl H. Beck.

   1974. *Studies in Syntax and Word-formation.* Edited by D. Kastovsky. Internationale Bibliothek für Algemeine Linguistik, Bd. 18. Munich: Wilhelm Fink.

Mardirussian, G. 1975. 'Noun incorporation in Universal Grammar', in Grossman, R. E., San, L. J. and Vance T. J. (eds.) *Papers from the 11th Annual Regional Meeting of the Chicago Linguistic Society.* Chicago Linguistic Society, 383–9.

Maslova, E. 2000. 'A dynamic approach to the verification of distributional universals', *Linguistic Typology* 4: 307–33.

Mathesius, V. 1975. *A Functional Analysis of Present Day English on a General Linguistic Basis.* The Hague: Mouton.

Mau, T. 2002. *Form und Funktion sprachlicher Wiederholungen.* Frankfurt am Main and Oxford: Peter Lang.

Mayerthaler, W. 1988. *Morphological Naturalness.* Ann Arbor, MI: Karoma.

McCarthy, J. J. and Prince, A. 1994. 'Prosodic morphology', in Goldsmith, J. (ed.) *A Handbook of Phonological Theory.* Oxford: Basil Blackwell, 318–66.

Merlini Barbaresi, L. 2003. 'Diminutives', in Frawley, W. F. (ed.) *International Encyclopedia of Linguistics.* Second edition. Oxford: Oxford University Press, 438–9.

Mithun, M. 1984. 'The evolution of noun incorporation', *Language* 60: 847–94.

   1986. 'On the nature of noun incorporation', *Language* 62: 32–7.

   2009. 'Compounding in Mohawk', in Lieber, R. and Štekauer, P. (eds.), 564–83.

Mohanan, K. P. 1986. *The Theory of Lexical Phonology.* Dordrecht: Reidel.

Mojdl, L. 2006. *Malajština.* Prague: Academia.

Montler, T. 1989. 'Infixation, reduplication and metathesis in the Saanich actual aspect', *Southwest Journal of Linguistics* 9: 92–107.

Moravcsik, E. A. 1978. 'Reduplicative constructions', in Greenberg, J. H. (ed.), 297–334.

   2000. 'Infixation', in Booij, G. E., Lehmann, Ch. and Mugdan, J. (eds.) *Morphologie/Morphology. Ein internationales Handbuch zur Flexion und Wortbildung/An International Handbook on Inflection and Word Formation. Vol. I.* Berlin: Walter de Gruyter, 545–52.

2007. 'What is universal about typology?', *Linguistic Typology* 11/1: 27–42.

Mukai, M. 2008. 'Recursive compounds', *Word Structure* 1: 178–98.

Mutaka, N. and Hyman, L. 1990. 'Syllables and morpheme integrity in Kinande reduplication', *Phonology* 7: 73–119.

Myers, S. 1984. 'Zero-derivation and inflection', *MIT Working Papers in Linguistics* 7: 53–69.

Neef, M. 2009. 'Compounding in German', in Lieber, R. and Štekauer, P. (eds.), 386–99.

Newman, P. 2000. *The Hausa Language: an Encyclopedic Reference Grammar*. New Haven and London: Yale University Press.

Newmeyer, F. J. 2007. 'Linguistic typology requires crosslinguistic formal categories', *Linguistic Typology* 11/1: 133–57.

Nichols, J. 1971. 'Diminutive consonant symbolism in Western North America', *Language* 47: 826–48.

Nichols, L. 2007. 'Methodology and the empirical base of typology', *Linguistic Typology* 11: 259–64.

Nikolaeva, I. and Tolskaya, M. 2001. *A Grammar of Udihe*. Berlin and New York: Mouton de Gruyter.

Pennanen, E. V. 1966. *Contributions to the Study of Back-formation in English*. Tampere: Acta Academiae Socialis.

1975. 'What happens in back-formation?', in Hovdhaugen, E. (ed.) *Papers from the Second Scandinavian Conference of Linguistics, Lysebu, April 19–20, 1975*. University of Oslo, 216–29.

Perlmutter, D. M. 1988. 'The split morphology hypothesis: evidence from Yiddish', in Hammond, M. and Noonan, M. (eds.) *Theoretical Morphology: Approaches in Modern Linguistics*. San Diego, CA: Academic Press, 79–100.

Plank, F. 1994. 'Inflection and derivation', in Asher, R. E. (ed.) *The Encyclopaedia of Language and Linguistics, Vol. 3*. Oxford: Pergamon, 1671–8.

2007. 'Extent and limits of linguistic diversity as the remit of typology – but through constraints on WHAT is diversity limited?', *Linguistic Typology* 11/1: 43–68.

2010. 'Variable direction in zero-derivation and the unity of polysemous lexical items', *Word Structure* 3: 82–97.

Plank, F. and Filimonova, E. 2000. *The Universals Archive*. URL: http://typo.uni-konstanz.de/archive/intro/ (last accessed: 15 July 2010).

Pořízka, V. 1972. *Hindština – Hindī Language Course*. Prague: Státní Pedagogickeé Nakladatelství.

Rainer, F. 1993. *Spanische Wortbildungslehre*. Tübingen: Niemeyer.

2005. 'Typology, diachrony and universals of semantic change in word formation: a Romanist's look at the polysemy of agent nouns', in Booij, G. E., Guevara, E., Ralli, A., Sgroi, S. and Scalise, S. (eds.) *Morphology and Linguistic Typology. On-line Proceedings of the Fourth Mediterranean Morphology Meeting (MMM4) Catania, 21–23 September 2003*. University of Bologna, 21–34.

Ralli, A. 2009. 'Modern Greek V V dvandva compounds: a linguistic innovation in the history of the Indo-European languages', *Word Structure* 2: 48–68.

Regier, T. 1994. *A Preliminary Study of the Semantics of Reduplication*. Report TR-94-019. Berkeley, CA: International Computer Science Institute.

Rice, K. 2009. 'Compounds in Slavey', in Lieber, R. and Štekauer, P. (eds.), 542–63.

Rijkhoff, J. and Bakker, D. 1998. 'Language sampling', *Linguistic Typology* 2: 263–314.

Roberts, J. R. 1987. *Amele*. London, New York and Sydney: Croom Helm.

1991. 'Reduplication in Amele', in Dutton, T. (ed.) *Papers in Papuan Linguistics 1*. Canberra: Department of Linguistics, Australian National University, 115–46.

Roeper, T. and Siegel, M. E. A. 1978. 'A lexical transformation for verbal compounds', *Linguistic Inquiry* 9: 199–260.

Rose, S. 2003. 'Triple take: Tigre and the case of internal reduplication', *San Diego Linguistic Papers* 1: 109–28.

Rosen, S. T. 1989. 'Two types of noun incorporation: a lexical analysis', *Language* 65: 294–317.

Rubino, C. 2005a. 'Reduplication', in Haspelmath *et al.* (eds.), 114–15.

2005b. 'Iloko', in Adelaar, K. A. and Himmelmann, N. P. (eds.) *The Austronesian Languages of Asia and Madagascar*. London: Curzon Press, 326–49.

2005c. 'Reduplication: form, function and distribution', in Hurch, B. (ed.) *Studies on Reduplication*. Berlin and New York: Mouton de Gruyter, 11–30.

Sadock, J. M. 1980. 'Noun incorporation in Greenlandic: a case of syntactic word-formation', *Language* 57: 300–19.

1985. 'Autolexical syntax: a theory of noun incorporation and similar phenomena', *Natural Language and Linguistic Theory* 3: 379–441.

1986. 'Some notes on noun incorporation', *Language* 62: 19–31.

2006. 'Incorporation', in Brown, K. (ed.) *Encyclopedia of Language and Linguistics*. Second edition. Oxford: Elsevier, 584–7.

Sánchez-Mendes, L. and Müller, A. 2007. 'The meaning of pluractionality in Karitiana', in Deal, A. R. (ed.) *UMOP 35: Proceedings of the 4th Conference on the Semantics of Under-Represented Languages in the Americas*. Amherst, MA: Graduate Linguistics Students Association, 247–57.

Sapir, D. J. 1965. *A Grammar of Diola-Fogny. A Language Spoken in the Basse-Casamance Region of Senegal*. Cambridge University Press.

Sapir, E. 1921. *Language. An Introduction to the Study of Speech*. New York: Harcourt, Brace & World.

Scalise, S. 1984. *Generative Morphology*. Dordrecht: Foris.

1988. 'Inflection and derivation', *Linguistics* 26: 561–81.

Scalise, S. and Bisetto, A. 2009. 'The classification of compounds', in Lieber, R. and Štekauer, P. (eds.), 34–53.

Schäfer, M. 2009. 'A+N constructions in Mandarin and the "compound vs. phrase" debate', *Word Structure* 2: 272–93.

Schiffman, H. F. 1996. *A Grammar of Spoken Tamil*. URL: http://ccat.sas.upenn.edu/plc/tamil-web/book.html (last accessed: 15 July 2010).

Schlegel, F. 1808. *Über die Sprache und Weisheit der Indier. Ein Beitrag zur Begründung der Alterthumskunde*. Heidelberg: Mohr und Zimmer.

Schwarzwald, O. 2001. *Modern Hebrew*. Munich: Lincom Europa.

Selkirk, E. O. 1982. *The Syntax of Words*. Cambridge, MA: MIT Press.

Shopen, T. (ed.) 1985. *Language Typology and Syntactic Description. Vol. III. Grammatical Categories and the Lexicon*. Cambridge: Cambridge University Press.

(ed.) 2007. *Language Typology and Syntactic Description. Vol. III. Grammatical Categories and the Lexicon*. Second edition. Cambridge: Cambridge University Press.

Siegel, D. 1979. *Topics in English Morphology*. New York: Garland.

Smirnickij, A. I. 1953. 'Tak nazyvajemaja konversija i čeredovanije zvukov v anglijskom jazyke', *Inostrannyje Jazyky v Škole* 5: 21–31.

1954. 'Po povodu konversii v anglijskom jazyke', *Inostrannyje Jazyky v Škole* 3: 12–24.

1956. *Lexikologija anglijskogo jazyka*. Moscow.

Smirnickij, A. I. and Achmanova, O. S. 1952. 'Obrazovanija tipa *stone wall, speech sound* v anglijskom jazyke', *Doklady i Soobščenija AN SSSR* 2: 97–116.

Sokal, R. R. and Rohlf, F. J. 1995. *Biometry: the Principles and Practice of Statistics in Biological Research*. Third edition. New York: W. H. Freeman.

Sokolová, M., Moško, G., Šimon, F. and Benko, V. 1999. *Morfematický slovník slovenčiny*. Prešov: Náuka.

Song, J. J. 2007. 'What or where can we do better? Some personal reflections on (the tenth anniversary of) linguistic typology', *Linguistic Typology* 11/1: 5–22.

Spencer, A. 1995. 'Incorporation in Chukchi', *Language* 64: 663–82.

2000. 'Morphology and syntax', in Booij, G. E., Lehmann, Ch. and Mugdan, J. (eds.) *Morphologie/Morphology. Ein internationales Handbuch zur Flexion und Wortbildung/An International Handbook on Inflection and Word Formation. Vol. I.* Berlin: Walter de Gruyter, 312–35.

2004. 'Towards a typology of "mixed categories"', in Orgun, C. O. and Sells, P. (eds.) *Morphology and the Web of Grammar. Essays in Memory of Steven G. Lapointe.* Stanford, CA: Center for the Study of Language and Information Publications, 1–46.

2005. 'Word-formation and syntax', in Štekauer, P. and Lieber, R. (eds.) *Handbook of Word-formation.* Springer: Dordrecht, 73–97.

Stassen, L. 1985. *Comparison and Universal Grammar.* Oxford: Basil Blackwell.

StatSoft, Inc. 2001. *STATISTICA for Windows.* Tulsa, OK: StatSoft, Inc.

Stein, G. 1977. 'The place of word-formation in linguistic description', in Brekle, H. E. and Kastovsky, D. (eds.) *Perspektiven der Wortbildungsforschung. Beiträge zum Wuppertaler Wortbildungskolloquium vom 9.–10. Juli 1976. Anläßlich des 70. Geburtstages von Hans Marchand am 1. Oktober 1977.* Bonn: Bouvier, 219–35.

Štekauer, P. 1996. *A Theory of Conversion in English.* Frankfurt am Main: Peter Lang.

1998. *An Onomasiological Theory of English Word-formation.* Amsterdam and Philadelphia: John Benjamins.

2000. *English Word-formation. A History of Research (1960–1995).* Tübingen: Gunter Narr.

2001. 'Beheading the word? Please, stop the execution', *Folia Linguistica* 34/3–4: 333–55.

2005. 'Onomasiological approach to word-formation', in Štekauer, P. and Lieber, R. (eds.) *Handbook of Word-formation.* Springer: Dordrecht, 207–32.

2006. 'On the meaning predictability of novel context-free converted naming units', *Linguistics* 44/3: 489–539.

2009. 'Meaning predictability of novel context-free compounds', in Lieber, R. and Štekauer, P. (eds.), 272–97.

Štekauer, P., Chapman, D., Tomaščíková, S. and Franko, Š. 2005. 'Word-formation as creativity within productivity constraints. Sociolinguistic evidence', *Onomasiology Online* 6: 1–55.

Štekauer, P., Franko, Š., Slančová, D., Liptáková, L. and Sutherland-Smith, J. 2001. 'A comparative research into the transfer of animal names to human beings', *VIEWS* 10/2: 69–75.

Strauss, S. L. 1982. *Lexicalist Phonology of English and German.* Dordrecht: Foris.

Stump, G. T. 1993. 'How peculiar is evaluative morphology?', *Journal of Linguistics* 29: 1–36.

2005. 'Word-formation and inflectional morphology', in Štekauer, P. and Lieber, R. (eds.) *Handbook of Word-formation.* Springer: Dordrecht, 49–71.

Szymanek, B. 2005. 'The latest trends in English word-formation', in Štekauer, P. and Lieber, R. (eds.) *Handbook of Word-formation.* Springer: Dordrecht, 429–48.

2009. 'Polish', in Lieber, R. and Štekauer, P. (eds.), 464–77.

Ten Hacken, P. 2000. 'Derivation and compounding', in Booij, G. E., Lehmann, Ch. and Mugdan, J. (eds.) *Morphologie/Morphology. Ein internationales Handbuch zur Flexion und Wortbildung/An International Handbook on Inflection and Word Formation. Vol. I.* Berlin: Walter de Gruyter, 349–60.

Thompson, C. 1996. 'The Na-Dene middle voice: an impersonal source of the D-Element', *International Journal of American Linguistics* 62/4: 351–78.

Thompson, L. C. 1967. *A Vietnamese Grammar.* Seattle, WA: University of Washington Press.

Tournier, J. 1985. *Introduction descriptive à la lexicogénétique de l'anglais contemporain.* Paris and Genève: Champion-Slatkine.

Ultan, R. 1975. 'Infixes and their origins', in Seiler, H. (ed.) *Linguistic Workshop III.* Munich: Wilhelm Fink, 157–205.

　1978. 'Size-sound symbolism', in Greenberg, J. (ed.) *Universals of Human Language Vol. II.* Stanford University Press, 525–68.

Urbanczyk, S. C. 2001. *Patterns of Reduplication in Lushootseed.* New York and London: Garland.

Vajda, E. 2004. *Ket.* Munich: Lincom Europa.

van Goethem, K. 2009. 'Choosing between A+N compounds and lexicalized A+N phrases: the position of French in comparison to Germanic languages', *Word Structure 2/2*: 241–53.

van Marle, J. 1995. 'The unity of morphology: on the interwovenness of the derivational and inflectional dimension of the word', *Yearbook of Morphology 1995*: 67–82.

Vogel, P. M. 1996. *Wortarten und Wortartenwechsel. Zu Konversion und verwandten Erscheinungen im Deutschen und in anderen Sprachen.* Berlin: Walter de Gruyter.

Wälchli, B. 2005. *Co-compounds and Natural Coordination.* Oxford: Oxford University Press.

Wegener, H. 2003. 'Entstehung und Funktion der Fugenelemente im Deutschen, oder: Warum wir keine *Autosbahn haben', *Linguistische Berichte* 196: 425–57.

Werner, H. 1998. *Probleme der Wortbildung in den Jenissej-Sprachen.* Munich: Lincom Europa.

　2004. *Die Diathese in den Jenissef-Sprachen aus typologischer Sicht.* Harrassowitz: Wiesbaden.

Whaley, L. J. 1997. *Introduction to Typology: the Unity and Diversity of Language.* Thousand Oaks and London: Sage Publications.

Wierzbicka, A. 1991. *Cross-cultural Pragmatics: the Semantics of Human Interaction.* Berlin and New York: Mouton de Gruyter.

Williams, E. 1981. 'On the notions "lexically related" and "head of a word"', *Linguistic Inquiry* 12/2: 245–74.

Wiltshire, C. and Marantz, A. 2000. 'Reduplication', in Booij, G. E., Lehmann, Ch. and Mugdan, J. (eds.) *Morphologie/Morphology. Ein internationales Handbuch zur Flexion und Wortbildung/An International Handbook on Inflection and Word Formation. Vol. I.* Berlin: Walter de Gruyter, 557–67.

Yu, A. C. L. 2007. *A Natural History of Infixation.* Oxford: Oxford University Press.

Yuan, L., Zhang, S. and Chen, H. (eds.) 2002. *The Contemporary Chinese Dictionary* (Chinese–English edition). Beijing: Foreign Language Teaching and Research Press.

Zamponi, R. 2003. *Maipure.* Munich: Lincom Europa.

　2009. 'Compounding in Maipure-Yavitero', in Lieber, R. and Štekauer, P. (eds.), 584–93.

Zar, J. H. 1984. *Biostatistical Analysis.* New Jersey, NJ: Prentice-Hall.

Zhang, Z.-S. 1987. 'Reduplication as a type of operation', in Bosh, A., Need, B. and Schiller, E. (eds.) *Papers from the 23rd Annual Regional Meeting of the Chicago Linguistic Society.* Chicago Linguistic Society, 376–88.

Zwicky, A. M. 1977. *On Clitics.* Bloomington, IN: Indiana University Linguistics Club.

　1985. 'Heads', *Journal of Linguistics* 21: 1–29.

Author index

Language index

(Language family in small capitals)

Afrikaans xiii, xv, 11n, 56, 59, 79, 92, 94, 119,
132, 150, 165, 193, 207, 210, 224, 243–4,
250–1, 270
AFRO-ASIATIC 12–13, 51–3, 58, 62, 73, 78, 80, 82,
88–9, 94, 99, 101–2, 107–11, 118n, 119, 131,
138–40, 145, 151, 156, 164, 168–9, 183–5,
196, 198, 204, 209, 211, 215, 225–6, 230,
234, 240, 248, 253, 257, 260–2, 264, 266,
275, 281–2, 286, 289, 293, 297–8, 306, 310,
312, 314–18, 320–3
ALTAIC 14, 52–4, 58, 63, 74, 83, 88–9, 102,
108–10, 140, 145, 156, 169, 186, 196, 198,
215, 241, 249, 254, 258, 267, 276, 282, 286,
290, 294, 298, 314, 316, 319, 321–2
Amele xi, xv, 12, 34, 51, 53–4, 58–62, 73, 76,
82, 91, 93, 101, 107–12, 113n, 114, 119–21,
125–31, 126n, 131n, 138, 155, 164, 195n,
196, 215–16, 216n, 218, 257, 275, 278, 280,
289, 293, 299, 330
Amharic xv, 12, 51, 58, 60, 73, 82, 101, 107–8,
111, 125, 127, 138, 140, 183, 194–6, 198,
240, 243, 253, 255, 255n, 257, 259n, 260–1,
275, 279, 281, 289, 297, 330
Anejom xv, 12, 51, 57n, 58, 62, 66, 73, 75, 79, 88,
99–101, 107–9, 119, 122, 125, 130, 138, 140,
144, 148, 151, 155, 164, 183, 185, 192, 192n,
230, 233–4, 248, 250, 253, 255, 266, 268,
275, 277, 281, 286–7, 289, 293, 330
Arabic 118, 199, 230
    Chadian 118n
ARAUCANIAN 283n
ARAWAKAN 11, 13, 52, 73, 80, 83, 139, 145, 197,
209, 215, 241, 253, 257, 267, 276
ARIKEM 32
AUSTRALIAN 13, 51, 73, 79, 88, 101, 107–8, 110,
138, 144, 156, 164, 183, 185, 196, 240, 289,
293, 314, 316–18, 322
AUSTRALIAN-ABORIGINAL 11, 13, 52, 102, 107,
109, 111, 139, 145, 185, 196, 241, 275, 282,
286, 290, 327
AUSTRO-ASIATIC 14, 53–4, 58, 74, 102, 108–11,
132, 197, 216, 225–6, 241, 249, 254, 258,
261–2, 294, 298, 314–17, 321–2

AUSTRONESIAN 3, 12–14, 51–3, 58, 62–3, 73,
78–80, 83, 88–9, 99, 101–3, 107–11, 118n,
124, 124n, 132, 138–41, 144–5, 151–2,
156, 164–5, 168–9, 183–5, 197–8, 204–5,
209, 211, 214n, 215, 230, 234, 241, 248–9,
253–4, 257, 261, 264–7, 275–6, 281–2, 286,
289–90, 293–4, 298, 306–7, 310, 312,
320–3
AYMARAN 13, 52, 73, 80, 82, 94, 99, 102, 107,
139, 145, 156, 185, 196, 241, 249, 253, 257,
267, 275, 290, 293, 316

Bardi xv, 11, 13, 51, 73, 79, 88, 92, 101, 107–8,
110, 119, 121, 138, 144, 156–7, 164, 166,
183, 185, 196, 217, 240, 251, 283, 289, 293,
327–8, 330
Basque 269n
BASQUE 269n
Belorussian xv, 11n, 54, 79, 92, 100, 128, 151,
186–7, 202–3, 207, 217, 224, 226, 251, 259,
270, 272
Bikol 124, 124n
Breton x, xv, 13, 32–4, 51, 53, 73, 76, 79, 82, 86,
88, 93, 97, 99–101, 138, 140, 144, 148, 151,
153, 156, 159, 159n, 164–5, 167–9, 178,
180–1, 183, 185, 190, 193, 215, 224, 232,
240, 248, 253, 257, 260, 262, 264–6, 270,
287–9, 291, 293, 297, 330
Bulgarian 31
Burmese 85, 86

Catalan xv, 11n, 61, 72, 84, 92, 148, 153, 162,
165, 218, 251, 256, 277, 291
Chinese, Mandarin x–i, xvi–xvii, 11, 13, 39,
52–3, 56, 57n, 58, 62–3, 67–8, 73, 80, 83–5,
88–9, 92, 94, 96, 102, 105, 107, 109–11,
128–30, 139, 141, 145, 152–3, 168, 171, 174,
184, 195, 197–8, 202–3, 211–12, 219, 226,
229, 241, 245, 249, 252, 261–3, 263n, 267,
276, 290–1, 293–4, 298, 303, 331
Cirecire xii, xv, xviii, 13, 51, 53, 58, 62, 73–4,
78–9, 82, 88–9, 99–101, 107–8, 110, 125,
130–1, 138, 172, 196, 215, 218, 226–7, 240,

Subject index

Lightning Source UK Ltd.
Milton Keynes UK
UKOW04f0357011216
288973UK00010B/723/P